AF707066

CRITICAL AND COMPARATIVE RHETORIC

Unmasking Privilege and Power in Law and Legal Advocacy to Achieve Truth, Justice, and Equity

Elizabeth Berenguer, Lucy Jewel, and
Teri A. McMurtry-Chubb

BRISTOL
UNIVERSITY
PRESS

First published in Great Britain in 2023 by

Bristol University Press
University of Bristol
1–9 Old Park Hill
Bristol
BS2 8BB
UK
t: +44 (0)117 374 6645
e: bup-info@bristol.ac.uk

Details of international sales and distribution partners are available at bristoluniversitypress.co.uk

© Bristol University Press 2023

British Library Cataloguing in Publication Data
A catalogue record for this book is available from the British Library

ISBN 978-1-5292-2601-0 hardcover
ISBN 978-1-5292-2602-7 ePub
ISBN 978-1-5292-2603-4 ePdf

The right of Elizabeth Berenguer, Lucy Jewel, and Teri A. McMurtry-Chubb to be identified as authors of this work has been asserted by them in accordance with the Copyright, Designs and Patents Act 1988.

All rights reserved: no part of this publication may be reproduced, stored in a retrieval system, or transmitted in any form or by any means, electronic, mechanical, photocopying, recording, or otherwise without the prior permission of Bristol University Press.

Every reasonable effort has been made to obtain permission to reproduce copyrighted material. If, however, anyone knows of an oversight, please contact the publisher.

The statements and opinions contained within this publication are solely those of the authors and not of the University of Bristol or Bristol University Press. The University of Bristol and Bristol University Press disclaim responsibility for any injury to persons or property resulting from any material published in this publication.

Bristol University Press works to counter discrimination on grounds of gender, race, disability, age and sexuality.

Cover design: Nicky Borowiec
Front cover image: iStock/GeorgePeters
Bristol University Press use environmentally responsible print partners.
Printed and bound in Great Britain by CPI Group (UK) Ltd, Croydon, CR0 4YY

FSC
www.fsc.org
MIX
Paper | Supporting responsible forestry
FSC® C013604

Contents

Detailed Contents

List of Figures and Tables

Figures

Tables

About the Authors

Elizabeth Berenguer is Associate Professor of Law, Co-Director of the Institute for the Advancement of Legal Communication, and Director of Online Legal Education Strategies at Stetson University College of Law, Gulfport, Florida.

Lucy Jewel is Professor of Law and Director of Legal Writing at University of Tennessee Knoxville.

Teri A. McMurtry-Chubb is Professor of Law, Director of the Critical Race & Gender Studies JD Concentration at the University of Illinois Chicago School of Law, and the Inaugural Affiliate in Inclusive Pedagogy at the UIC Center for the Advancement of Teaching Excellence.

Introduction

Through the lenses of comparative rhetoric and critical rhetoric, this book theorizes how alternative approaches to communication can transform legal meanings and legal outcomes, infusing them with more inclusive participation, more equity, and more justice. This book views legal language through a radical lens, setting aside long-standing norms that derive from White and Eurocentric approaches to argument and resituating legal methods as products of different rhetorical models that come from diasporic and non-Western cultures. From the outset, this book urges readers to rethink how they think about logic and rhetoric and to consider other ways of building knowledge that can heal the law's ailing thought structures that often perpetuate and reinforce systems of privilege and power.

This book challenges some deeply entrenched foundations relating to logic and rhetoric. In doing so, we recognize that some of the material we present requires introspection and a patient mind. For instance, Western rhetoric and logic rely on a speaker orientation, the view that the speaker is held accountable for making meanings clear. This is, however, a relatively arbitrary construct; many other cultures, especially Eastern cultures, preserve a listener orientation, where it is up to the listener to work to understand the nuances and subtleties of the message. In engaging with this book, we ask readers to adopt a listener orientation when working to understand this challenging new discipline.

The three authors of this volume are all veteran teachers, scholars, and practicing attorneys (we all have active law licenses). Our deep familiarity with theory, pedagogy, and law practice uniquely situates us to discuss the *Five Ws and How* of critical and comparative rhetoric. *Who*—this book will discuss who has historically been imbued with the power to engage in lawmaking speech and who has historically constructed the rules of the game. *Where*—we will center geopolitical issues by explaining that, in a number of ways, White European settlers created modern legal processes to support colonial and capitalistic systems built upon enslavement, oppression of indigenous peoples, and imperial domination. In answering the *Who* and *Where* questions, we center the historical facts that Western law is a product of a White, European male tradition, but the answer to the Who question also includes a liberating salvo that envisions critical and comparative rhetors as inclusive, diverse, and representative of previously marginalized cultures and underserved communities. *Why*—this book will answer why traditional rhetoric needs to be reformed. We do this by offering a concise critique of the Western rhetorical canon, building upon the previous work of other scholars who have mounted the same critique.

What—what is comparative and critical rhetoric? In the legal context, *comparative rhetoric* studies non-Western reasoning forms that offer new, alternative, and more inclusive approaches to legal argumentation. *Critical rhetoric* views rhetoric from the perspective of structure and power asking how traditional and dominant rhetoric forms tend to reproduce and reinforce pre-existing inequality and inequity, particularly in the context of marginalized and minoritized peoples. This volume will provide readers with a deeply interactive introduction to critical and comparative rhetoric, explaining the underlying disciplines (legal rhetoric, diasporic rhetoric, comparative rhetoric, critical theory) that give rise to the practice of comparative rhetoric. *When*—this book will look to the past, studying legal opinions that have produced injustice along the lines of race, gender, class, and other subordinated statuses. But this book also looks to the future, asking readers to reconsider and rewrite past legal opinions using new frameworks and tools. We challenge readers to incorporate these frameworks and tools in the traditional law-school classroom to cultivate legal advocates who are fluent not only in traditional rhetoric, but also in critical and comparative rhetoric. By developing knowledge and expertise around critical and comparative rhetoric, advocates become equipped to challenge the systems that replicate and perpetuate bias, injustice, and inequity.

How—this book will guide readers in how to apply alternative rhetorical strategies to build analytic frameworks that can be used to persuade. We will convey these lessons through case studies that rely on judicial opinions as well as fact-based hypotheticals. We aim to guide readers through legal case decisions to consider how the judicial authors used traditional rhetoric to reach problematic outcomes, have readers read paradigm-shifting briefs to consider how lawyers changed the world by rethinking traditional categories, and also have readers consider how legal advocates might dispense with the traditional reasoning forms altogether and create alternative frameworks built from non-Western and Diasporic rhetoric approaches.

Finally, we note that this volume exists in spaces where law can change. Recognizing that, in a common law system, legal advocates are bound by case-law precedent but also by path-dependence (traditional reasoning is how it has always been done), this book locates areas where new voices and new approaches might change the law. The law can change in cases of first impression, on the appellate level at a court of last resort, but also as previously 'unsayable'[1] concepts become more common in the legal culture.

As teachers and practitioners, the authors challenge readers to seize moments, whether those instances occur in an appellate argument or in a more informal setting like a mediation hearing, to use alternative legal processes to make new arguments and, eventually, new law. In addition to using these methods in law practice, doing this work within legal education and in legal scholarship sets the law up to change—in its procedures, argument forms, and doctrine. Across the board, applying new approaches that draw upon non-Western frameworks will begin to populate our legal culture with new reasoning forms that can demolish the old, toxic ways and make room for liberating transformation.

Comparative and critical legal rhetoric present a novel area of inquiry. While the law has been studied from a rhetorical standpoint, legal rhetoric has not been approached from either a comparative or a critical angle. This book will do both. In a nutshell, this book will introduce critical and comparative rhetoric from a theoretical standpoint; it will contrast critical and comparative rhetoric with traditional common-law reasoning; and it will offer specific examples of how to disrupt traditional legal rhetoric with alternative, more inclusive forms of reasoning and knowledge-building.

Critical rhetoric analyzes existing canons of rhetoric, reviewing canonical texts to view how interlocking systems of oppression—imperialism, capitalism, White supremacy, and patriarchy—contribute to rhetorical meanings. Critical rhetoric examines how Eurocentric epistemologies (ways of knowing, sources for knowledge) and ontologies (ways of being, how we are who we are) have been used to perpetuate outcomes that advance racism, sexism, heteronormativity, and classism. On the other hand, traditional rhetoric involves the study of thought patterns that persuade. For instance, throughout U.S. legal history, the deductive reasoning form (that is, the syllogism) was deployed to justify enslavement based on racial color-lines, to deny human rights to members of marginalized communities, and to take land held by Indigenous peoples. Critical rhetoric gets underneath well-worn rhetorical substrates to uncover hidden biases and toxic dichotomies. Critical rhetoric engages with how we think about knowledge and knowing, which has important ramifications for how we, as a society understand (or misunderstand) truth, justice, and equity.

Comparative rhetoric also sits in the field of communication studies. Comparative rhetoric focuses on the differences and similarities between different rhetoric cultures with an aim to increase cross-cultural understanding and identify potential universal practices. The act of comparison, however, can bring in one's own biases and predispositions as to how meanings should be made. Often, comparative scholars unconsciously place their own culture above the culture that they are comparing. There is always a need for self-awareness and criticality when scholars undertake to compare cultures. Critical rhetoric provides that criticality.

The study of law desperately needs critical and comparative approaches to rhetoric because legal rhetoric carries such immense power to shape individual and societal outcomes. For instance, in a common law legal system, when a judge utters the words "guilty" or "not guilty" those words immediately shape the material reality of the person being adjudged. Legal rhetoric is imbued with the power of the state, which gives it tremendous force. In a common law system, legal rhetoric is powerful in another way. In the form of a case opinion, legal rhetoric becomes binding precedent that then gets repeated over and over as the rule or holding of the case. In this way, the meanings shaped by the rhetoric become entrenched not only within the law, but also in the minds of those affected by the law.

Until now, legal rhetoric has been predominantly shaped by a limited range of forms such as the syllogism, the reasonableness standard, and inferences based on linear causality. However, communities outside of the White European-American tradition who reside in the U.S. do not always use the same epistemological tools. Accordingly, rhetoric communities situated outside the dominant culture can be silenced by the dominant culture's rhetorical practices. Silence can be oppression. Comparative and critical rhetoric illustrate that there are alternative ways of coming to a sense of truth, equity, and justice, ways that depart from the traditional tools we see in most legal rhetoric. Further, these alternative ways of knowing are produced by individuals living in diverse, often marginalized communities. In this work, comparative, critical, multicultural rhetorics are rooted in a critique of multiple interlocking oppressions and the cultural imperatives of non-Western peoples as they have adapted to and navigated the ravages of the West in the United States. We introduce and apply the foundational tenets of Indigenous, African Diasporic, Asian Diasporic, and Latine Rhetoric as a challenge to Western rhetoric and contemplate how each works in the service of justice. True democracy requires that alternative voices from marginalized communities have a voice in legal rhetoric, a rhetoric with a most powerful form. In this book, we argue that the law can and should adopt alternative reasoning forms, which would expand legal analysis process beyond its current, overly rigid boundaries.

Traditional legal rhetoric, in its narrow form, also reproduces the legal culture as a whole. Within this issue, there is an international or imperial angle because common law legal education has been exported across the globe (in its U.K. or U.S. form) into the Global South, Middle East, and Far East. We see the common law being taught not only in LL.M. programs across the world, but also within programs in the United States and U.K., which draw non-Western students into the study. While traditional common law legal reasoning is effective for solving many legal problems, it has also produced a host of tragically unjust outcomes. If law schools are going to export traditional common law reasoning around the world, they should do so in a more critical and culturally sensitive form. They should not, as they often do, elevate logic over democratic principles.

Finally, educating future attorneys on a wider variety of rhetoric approaches will help attorneys become better client advocates. Attorneys always strive to translate their client's narrative into a form that the law recognizes. Legal education, however, limits the set of tools available for this vital translation work. As we will show in this book, legal education is highly constrained in its efforts to teach students to think like a (White, European-American, wealthy) lawyer. In law practice, sometimes a more intercultural approach is necessary for attorneys to fully translate their client's narrative so that core meanings are not lost in translation. And sometimes, new forms will need to be constructed in order to bridge knowledge gaps that obstruct the law's path toward justice and equity.

This book will reference and build upon critical legal work that has previously been completed by scholars such as Duncan Kennedy, Morton Horwitz, and others affiliated with the critical legal studies movement[2] and the work of critical race scholars.[3] Critical race theory has become highly politicized recently, with conservative attacks aimed toward educational institutions that teach it. At this point, almost any kind of teaching related to honest U.S. history that refuses to whitewash the baldly violent, discriminatory, and terroristic acts leveled against enslaved, Indigenous, and other marginalized people, has been classified as "critical race theory." This is a tremendous misunderstanding. People seem to be most upset that U.S. history is being taught in an honest manner, and political actors are using critical race theory as a dog whistle to censor any discussion of the ugly ways that the U.S. government has terrorized and dispossessed people. In actuality, critical race theory originated in U.S. law schools in the late 1980s challenging the theory that the law is neutral or colorblind. Critical race theory engages with history, but in a way that reveals how law and legal institutions have enforced and perpetuated racialized hierarchies and hegemonies. This volume builds upon one of the central tenets of critical race theory, which is that the law, "as part of the social fabric and the larger hegemonic order, constitutes, constructs and produces race and race relations in a way that supports [W]hite supremacy."[4]

We also draw upon the work of Thomas Ross[5] and Lolita Buckner-Innis,[6] both of whom have written from a critical rhetoric perspective that addresses race and the law. We are also influenced by feminist critiques of the law, particularly the approaches found in the Feminist Judgments Project, which aims, in having feminist scholars rewrite precedential judicial decisions, to proffer an alternative jurisprudence that decenters patriarchal White European and formalistic reasoning norms.[7] These aforementioned scholars have established a valuable foundation that critically analyzes law's fundamental architecture to surface bias and oppression. These projects are predominantly jurisprudential and theoretical, however, and do not often venture into the trenches of law practice.

Further, the historical division, in U.S. legal education, between theoretical/doctrinal professors and legal skills professors, has created a blind spot. However, much of what exists within critical studies and critical race theory is not deeply connected to the practice of law. This book connects critical theory to the practice of law. In this way, the volume advances and builds upon the work of legal scholars like Kathryn Stanchi,[8] who argued that critical theory should be integrated into the teaching of legal writing, and Elizabeth Mertz and Lani Guinier,[9] who have both written compellingly of how law schools and legal education reproduce a mindset of hierarchy and inequality.

Our book also departs from the classical canon. So, while we will explain why and how classical rhetoric tends to reinforce pre-existing racial, gender, and economic inequality in the law, this book is primarily focused on new, innovative approaches to rhetoric that exist outside of elite White spaces. The work we propose here is not meant to be a justification for the departure from the classical canon. The purpose of this book is not to engage in a lengthy critique of the canon, but rather to develop a discipline for legal analysis that can achieve justice, equity, and inclusion in ways that the traditional canon cannot. Non-Western, Indigenous, and diasporic rhetorics predate and exist contemporaneously with the classical rhetorical canon. Thus far, the academy, rooted in capitalism, imperialism/settler colonialism, White supremacy, and patriarchy, has refused to engage with the rhetorical theory from these cultures. Until recently, scholars trained in the classical rhetorical canon, but writing outside of it to engage with non-Western cultures, have been excluded and/or marginalized in the academy. The social media hashtag #RhetoricSoWhite and the articles it has produced[10] are an introduction to this controversy.

Indeed, even critical critiques of Western thought structures (post-structuralism, postmodernism, and so on) are a part of a White Western tradition. On the point of decolonizing classical rhetoric and supplanting it with something new, this book is most concerned with scholars such as Dexter B. Gordon,[11] Molefi Asante,[12] Mark Lawrence McPhail,[13] Aaron David Gresson III,[14] Teun A. van Dijk,[15] Edward T. Hall,[16] Celeste Michelle Condit and John Lois Lucaites,[17] Michael Calvin McGee,[18] W.E.B. Du Bois,[19] Robert L. Scott,[20] Pat J. Gehrke,[21] Scott F. Aikin,[22] bell hooks,[23] Edward, Said,[24] Ngũgĩ wa Thiong'o,[25] Daniel Cole,[26] Mary Lynch Kennedy,[27] Scott Richard Lyons,[28] Adisa A. Alkebulan,[29] Maulana Karenga,[30] Ronald L. Jackson II,[31] LuMing Mao,[32] Guo-Ming Chen,[33] Bo Wang,[34] Georgette Wang,[35] Barbara Alice Mann,[36] Ryuiko Kubota,[37] Audra Simpson,[38] Michel-Rolph Trouillot,[39] Linda Alcoff,[40] Gayatri Chakravorty Spivak,[41] Min-Zhan Lu and Bruce Horner,[42] Andy Kirkpatrick and Zhichang Xu,[43] Victor

Villanueva,[44] Walter D. Mignolo,[45] Damian Baca,[46] Ayde Enríquez-Loya and Kendall Leon,[47] Barbara Couture and Patti Wojahn,[48] David Cisneros,[49] Iris Ruiz,[50] Raúl Sánchez,[51] Gloria Anzaldúa,[52] and so many more who write critical approaches to language and communication and about Indigenous, Asian and African Diasporic, and Latine rhetoric. This book centers these scholars and their work on non-Western rhetorical traditions—their promise for the practice of law in the service of justice.

Notes

1 Balkin, 2011.
2 Unger, 1974; Auerbach, 1976; Horwitz, 1992; Kennedy, 2004.
3 Williams, 1991; Bell, 1993, 1994; Delgado, 1995; Delgado and Stefancic, 2007.
4 Mutua, 2006, pp 333–4.
5 Ross, 1996.
6 Innis, 2010.
7 Stanchi et al, 2016.
8 Stanchi, 1998.
9 Guinier et al, 1997; Mertz, 2007.
10 Asante, 2019; Na'puti, 2019; Pham, 2019; Sowards, 2019; Wanzer-Serrano, 2019.
11 Gordon, 2006.
12 Asante, 1998, 2003.
13 McPhail, 1993, 2002.
14 Gresson, 1995.
15 Van Dijk, 1987.
16 Hall, 1977.
17 Condit and Lucaites, 1993.
18 McGee, 1980.
19 Du Bois, 1903.
20 Scott, 1999.
21 Gehrke, 1998.
22 Aikin, 2008.
23 Hooks, 2004.
24 Said, 1978.
25 Ngũgĩ wa Thiong'o, 1986.
26 Cole, 2011.
27 Kennedy, 1998.
28 Lyons, 2000.
29 Alkebulan, 2003, pp 23–4.
30 Karenga, 2003.
31 Jackson, 2003.
32 Mao, 2006, 2014; Mao and Young, 2008; Mao et al, 2015.
33 Chen, 2011.
34 Wang, 2014.
35 Wang, 2011.
36 Mann, 2016.
37 Kubota, 1997.
38 Simpson, 2014.
39 Trouillot, 2003.
40 Alcoff, 1991.

[41] Spivak, 1988.
[42] Lu and Horner, 2008.
[43] Kirkpatrick and Zu, 2012.
[44] Villanueva, 2016; Baca and Villanueva, 2010.
[45] Mignolo, 2005.
[46] Baca, 2008; Baca and Villanueva, 2010.
[47] Enríquez-Loya and Leon, 2017.
[48] Couture and Wojahn, 2016.
[49] Cisneros, 2014.
[50] Ruiz, 2016.
[51] Ruiz and Sánchez, 2016.
[52] Anzaldúa, 1987.

1

What's Wrong with Aristotle?

The power of legal rhetoric

Let's begin with some threshold definitions. What is legal rhetoric? Legal rhetoric is legal language that contributes in some way to the formation of legal meanings or lawmaking. In this view, legal rhetoric includes legal language that is found in primary legal documents such as cases and statutes. It also includes the language that lawyers use when they create legal documents, whether that language appears in advocacy documents like a brief or a motion, or a transactional document like a will or contract. In all of these settings, a lawyer's words have the power to create legal meanings. Helpful here is James Boyd White's expansive view of legal rhetoric as a dynamic "activity of mind and language: a kind of translation, a way of claiming meaning for experience and making that meaning real."[1] This project builds on this view but adds the critical dimension of exploring the voices and meanings that have been excluded from the process. Historically, not all legal actors have had the power or opportunity to participate in legal meaning making; many have been forcibly excluded from the process.

In both common law and civil law jurisdictions, the ability to create legal meanings carries enormous power. First, legal meanings create the material and social reality for individuals affected by the language. When a lawyer argues that her client is "not guilty," the jury agrees with the conclusion represented by those words, and the judge then pronounces the client "not guilty," the client's reality becomes that—they are not guilty. Second, the language is imbued with the power of the state. If a person is pronounced "guilty" of a felony, the power of the state removes their liberty, and they are imprisoned as a result of their guilty status. Or, if a person engages in conduct that a contract's language prohibits, a party can bring the power of the state to bear down on the person, to compel her/him to fulfill the terms of the contract through specific performance or to pay damages for their breach.[2]

A third power within the law comes from the fact that there is collective buy-in for the power of the words. The people in a civil society generally believe in the power of legal language and collectively accept the consequences of the various statuses created by legal words. The wide acceptance for the law's authority (and concomitant state power) enables it to compel, coerce, and persuade people to behave in ways that are legal, rather than illegal.[3]

The collective buy-in for the power of legal language gives rise to a fourth type of power, reinforcement of the concepts through reiteration. Legal rhetoric tends to grow in power because, in a common law system, the words are reiterated. Legal words that form the basis of a precedential court decision are repeated—repeated by lawyers using the court's language in their briefs and repeated again by later court decisions that are quoting earlier, binding precedent as authority for their current decision. Cognitive science explains why iteration and reiteration create additional power for legal rhetoric. When words and phrases are repeated, they become entrenched in individual minds as well as the collective mindset, further cementing the collective buy-in for the state power that enforces the meanings and consequences for the legal words.[4]

The troubling roots of traditional legal rhetoric

Critical and comparative legal rhetoric offers alternatives to traditional forms of legal rhetoric. In order to develop alternative ways of knowing and "doing" legal rhetoric, advocates must first study legal rhetoric in its traditional form. Traditional legal rhetoric refers to the accepted form of legal language. This accepted form has its roots in classical rhetoric and, as will be shown, originated in a process of severe exclusion. As it evolved in the U.S., traditional legal rhetoric grew within a root system that embraced White supremacy and trampled over the rights of the Indigenous people who lived on the soil before the European settlers arrived and forcibly colonized the land. The roots within traditional legal rhetoric are rhizomatic—deep, interlocking, but often invisible from the surface. Traditional legal rhetoric cannot be separated from its forms. Our proposed method is radical: legal advocates should tear out these infected thought forms and create new ones that originate from more inclusive ways of building knowledge.

To be accepted as valid, legal rhetoric must comply with a set of norms for how arguments are formulated. In this way, legal rhetoric operates in a universe of accepted norms, or *nomos*.[5] The kind of reasoning accepted in the legal *nomos* includes rule-based appeals (*logos*), emotion or value-based appeals (*pathos*), and speaker/author-based appeals (*ethos*). The legal *nomos* is stitched together with past court decisions and past reasoning forms, which together create boundaries for what is permissible and possible to argue. Working within the *nomos* to produce new arguments and new legal meanings usually reinforces the pre-existing concepts within the universe. Legal meanings are produced through a narrow process that allows certain forms of knowing (epistemology) and being (ontology) but excludes other methods. Linear causation, skepticism for collective forms of knowledge, and complete denial of experiential truths that lack the "right" kind of evidence are all norms that define the *nomos* of the legal system. Other forms of knowing, which exist outside of Western thought, present alternative ways to understand the world and solve social problems. It is time for lawyers to start considering these alternative modes of understanding.

Further, within the *nomos*, certain key legal terms operate as *ideographs*, abstract concepts that tend to communicate ideologies in an implicit way by drawing upon majoritarian-held norms. Concepts like causation and standing are binding legal principles, but they also reinforce a powerful ideology relating to fault, blame, and innocence. In the context of social justice issues, such as reparative remedies for past acts of violence, the *nomos* and its ideographs deny the possibility of even arguing that there could be collective responsibility for collective harms committed in the past.[6]

The accepted process of creating legal meanings dates back to ancient, classical times. Existing rhetorical forms reinforce Western ideologies. Specifically, traditional legal reasoning emphasizes a dichotomous type of categorizing that tends to reproduce and reinforce difference and hierarchy. The tendency to obstruct social justice and equity is especially discernible in the law's approach to racial differences. As Professor Kevin McPhail has written, Western rhetoric tends to enshrine knowledge structures (Black and White) in such a way that makes it difficult to find points of commonality between the two constructed poles.[7]

Inequality is a cornerstone within the law's *nomos*. Traditional legal rhetoric does not center equality or equity as a goal, rather, throughout much of history, legal process was deployed to maintain a strict, racially based hierarchy, where inequality was the norm. Traditional rhetoric's analytic templates (such as the deductive syllogism) are not just neutral tools; rather, these thought structures built and now maintain a system where power and resources remain in the hands of a few elites, to the exclusion of everyone else.

Classical thought patterns: Aristotle and Plato

Let's begin in ancient times with Aristotle and Plato, both of whom accepted human hierarchy and inequality in a society rife with male domination, ethnic prejudice, enslavement, and elitism. These ideas from ancient Greece and Rome were resurrected during the Enlightenment, which heavily influenced the development of early American thought and law. Classically based hierarchy can be summed up as "it is the nature of things that the few must lead and the many follow."[8]

Aristotle's and Plato's theory of essences lays the groundwork for understanding how human hierarchy has become so entrenched in Western thought. Both Plato and Aristotle subscribed to a theory of "essences" as a way of making sense of the world. Plato believed that once a thing is identified as an essence, it shares attributes with all other essences of that form. For Plato, the philosopher's task was to discern the essences that underlie all forms of things in the world. Aristotle also believed that essences were fixed things existing in the material world. Where the two men departed was in how essences were constructed. Whereas Aristotle believed that essences were pre-existing and fixed, Plato believed that essences were ideas constructed in the mind (one observes shadows as if one is inside a cave looking out, but one can never know whether the things seen are fully accurate).[9] During the Enlightenment, Aristotle's conception of fixed essences existing in the material world dominated Western thought, although Plato's cave allegory is often used to remind us of our biases as human observers of the world.

For Aristotle, creating knowledge required one to identify and categorize the essences existing in the world and then put these categories into the structure of a syllogism: All men are mortal, Socrates is a man, Socrates is mortal. For Aristotle, the syllogism is the structure that produces new knowledge.[10] In law, the syllogism is the "*sine qua non* of legal analysis."[11] The principles of bivalence, transitivity, and disembodied rational thought are all integral to how this type of reasoning works.

Bivalence is the concept that any one thing must belong inside or outside a single category. In Aristotle's view, it is not possible for the same thing to both belong and not belong in the same category. A fact must be either true or false. It is not possible for Socrates to be both a man and a god, to be both mortal and immortal. One can trace a host of thinking patterns to the concept of bivalence. First, in modern thought, the bivalence principle is responsible for mutual exclusivity and strict either/or dichotomies.[12] Second, in the law, bivalence is responsible for a winner takes all type of thinking—for instance, one is either guilty or not guilty. Western norms of competition, which are intensely embedded in the common law's adversarial system, deeply entrench these either/or thought patterns. And third, bivalence emphasizes a oneness of thinking, a monistic style of thinking, that has been reinforced by Judeo-Christian monotheism, where causal agents are identified as single things that necessarily exclude all other things.[13] Here, bivalence helps define linear thought, for instance, that there is usually only *one* primary reason or cause for any given event.

Similarly, in Aristotle's deductive reasoning paradigm, transitivity is the rule that mandates that if two things are identical to a third, then they must be identical to each other. Implicit in this concept is that if two things both fit inside a single categorical box, then they must be identical to each other. All men are the same in that they are all mortal. Transitivity fuels stereotypes, the idea that everyone situated in the same category has exactly the same attributes. This type of thinking tends to gloss over and even ignore complexity, in order to create "long and elaborate chains of arguments that move incessantly toward a logical conclusion about the essential properties of subjects, objects, and beings."[14] The problem is that this type of thinking rigidly excludes other, alternative forms of knowing that are equally valuable for understanding the world.

The theory of essences, thus far, seems relatively neutral. What is wrong with syllogistic reasoning, especially when it can be put to useful ends? Here, this chapter delves into the deep connections between classical approaches to reason (such as the syllogism) and beliefs about human hierarchy and democracy. Aristotle and his teacher Plato applied their methods of rational thinking to justify slavery and domination, based on gender, economic wealth, ethnicity, and class. Classical analytic methods cannot be separated from classical political science theories which are disturbingly steeped in inequality.

What's wrong with Aristotle?

Both Plato and his pupil Aristotle believed that social hierarchy was both natural and good. They used categorical thinking to devise types of people and to sort these people into their theorized political systems. Plato believed that only "guardians" had the wisdom and knowledge to govern, rule, and solve society's problems. In Plato's conception, guardians were elite individuals, well-born and well-educated, who possessed wisdom and virtue.[15] Most women, children, servants, and working-class individuals were not fit to rule as guardians; they were too emotional and lacked the capacity to engage in high-quality thought. Plato's guardians (or philosopher kings) should be individuals with pre-existing wealth, few material needs, and the leisure time to comfortably live a life of the mind. To his credit, Plato was skeptical of aristocracies and willing to let women serve as guardians. Finally, Plato believed that society would work best in a structured hierarchy where everyone stayed in their place without complaint.[16]

Aristotle further developed classical themes of categorical hierarchy, specifically lauding the virtues of a socially rigid society. Aristotle believed that a top-down order was *natural*, simply the way things are: "[A]lmost all things rule and are ruled according to nature. But the kind of rule differs[.] The freeman rules over the slave after another manner from that in which the male rules over the female, or the man over the child."[17]

Aristotle's hierarchy extended beyond the body politic and into the domestic sphere, with strict categorical divisions between master/slave, husband/wife, father/children. Aristotle is famous for linking virtue with a positive valence, but virtue was (and is) highly gendered. Aristotle wrote that in the family, the male is naturally superior and expressed virtue by "commanding." The female is naturally inferior and can only express virtue by "obeying."[18] Aristotle's categorical thinking undergirded his "natural" theory of social categorization, where "from the hour of their birth, some are marked out for subjection, others for rule."[19] Finally, Aristotle applied his social categorization theory to justify enslavement based on ethnic status, believing it proper for the victorious Greeks to enslave any non-Greek "barbarian" conquered[20] in war. Aristotle's categorical dichotomy between non-barbarians and barbarians and free persons and enslaved persons would have deleterious consequences as time progressed; similar dichotomies would later be used to justify the genocidal effects of slavery and colonization.[21]

These hierarchical and categorical beliefs about people connect to political science (who should rule), but they are also intertwined with Aristotle's ideas about persuasion and rhetoric. For Aristotle, only elite males could perform logocentric argumentation. Aristotle dismissed women from practicing the art of rhetoric as "all classes must be deemed to have their special attributes [in their mode of speaking]," but "[s]ilence is a woman's glory."[22] Further, Aristotle believed that lower class people had a base nature, beholden to physical and emotional yearnings whereas higher-class individuals enjoyed a powerful intellect and virtuous discipline.[23] Finally, Aristotle did not believe that low status persons even had the capacity to engage in rational thought.[24] The enslaved person, he wrote, "has no deliberative faculty at all."[25] Applying his rigid categorical thinking to the issue, Aristotle wrote that enslaved persons had a fixed essence that made it impossible for them to overcome their passionate thoughts and engage in rational analysis. On this point, Aristotle was wrong about the possibility of separating the rational mind with passionate body. Cognitive science tells us that human thinking, especially when engaging in the process of categorization, is a deeply embodied process that draws upon our brains and bodies together.[26] Aristotle's categorical thinking would reappear in the Enlightenment, as Anglo and U.S. thinkers theorized equality for all men, except for enslaved persons beyond the color line. Part of the rationalization was that low-status non-European persons did not even have the capacity to engage in deliberative reason.

The father of Western rhetoric was an intractable classist who wholly rejected democracy and equality. Aristotle, unlike Plato, extolled aristocracy as a model form of government, the rule of the many by the best, those individual citizens fit to rule because of their virtue. Only distinguished elite men possessed the virtue entitling them to be citizens with the right to participate in governance. Ordinary workers, women, seniors, resident aliens, and enslaved persons were excluded from citizenship. Aristotle firmly believed that working people should not and could not be citizens because having to work was "ignoble" and "inimical to virtue."[27] For Aristotle, wealth and privilege were required conditions for the emergence of the kind of virtue necessary for good thinking and good governance.

Classical thought, rational thought, and White supremacy

Aristotle's categorical thinking would have an outsized influence on Enlightenment thinkers, who would in turn influence how the law unforgivingly categorized and violently subjugated people on racial lines, Indigenous and enslaved, as the European colonizing project commenced. The Enlightenment, after the Middle Ages, extolled reason and science as the way to move society forward. But the Enlightenment also planted the seeds of a particularly violent form of racialism and settler colonialism, seeds that are still rooted in our jurisprudence today.

As historian Ibram X. Kendi has compellingly shown, two Enlightenment genres, natural science and political science, best illustrate classical thought's influence on White supremacist thought. The Enlightenment unleashed a vogue for natural science that had men formulating "rational" and "scientific" theories that sought to trace the contours of colonized subjects with elaborately theorized taxonomies. Visual categorization dominated these endeavors. In 1664, British Royal Society member Robert Boyle, considered the father of English chemistry, categorized White skin as normal and Black skin as an "ugly" deformity.[28] During this time, other eminent thinkers such as William Petty and François Bernier sketched out elaborate grids for humanity, placing White Europeans at the top, well above every other group.[29] John Locke, the father of Anglo-American property rights theory, hypothesized that African women had conceived infants with apes.[30]

Channeling Aristotle, these thinkers then merged their natural science hobbies with theories that justified violence and enslavement. Bernier wrote that "[t]hose who excel in the powers of the mind … [should] command those who only excel in brute force." And Bernier's friend, John Locke, justified the enslavement of violently kidnapped Africans because "slaves, who being captives taken in a just war, are by the right of nature subjected to the absolute dominion and arbitrary power of their masters."[31]

In the realm of political science, Enlightenment thinkers started to question and critique Aristotle's theory of natural human hierarchy, putting forth natural law theories that centered on equality. Nonetheless, these Enlightenment thinkers, almost all of whom are lauded as founders of modern democratic theory, planted viral White supremacist memes into the law's *nomos*. Indigenous persons and persons of African descent, caught up in the murderous colonial dragnet, were not included in the calculations for liberty

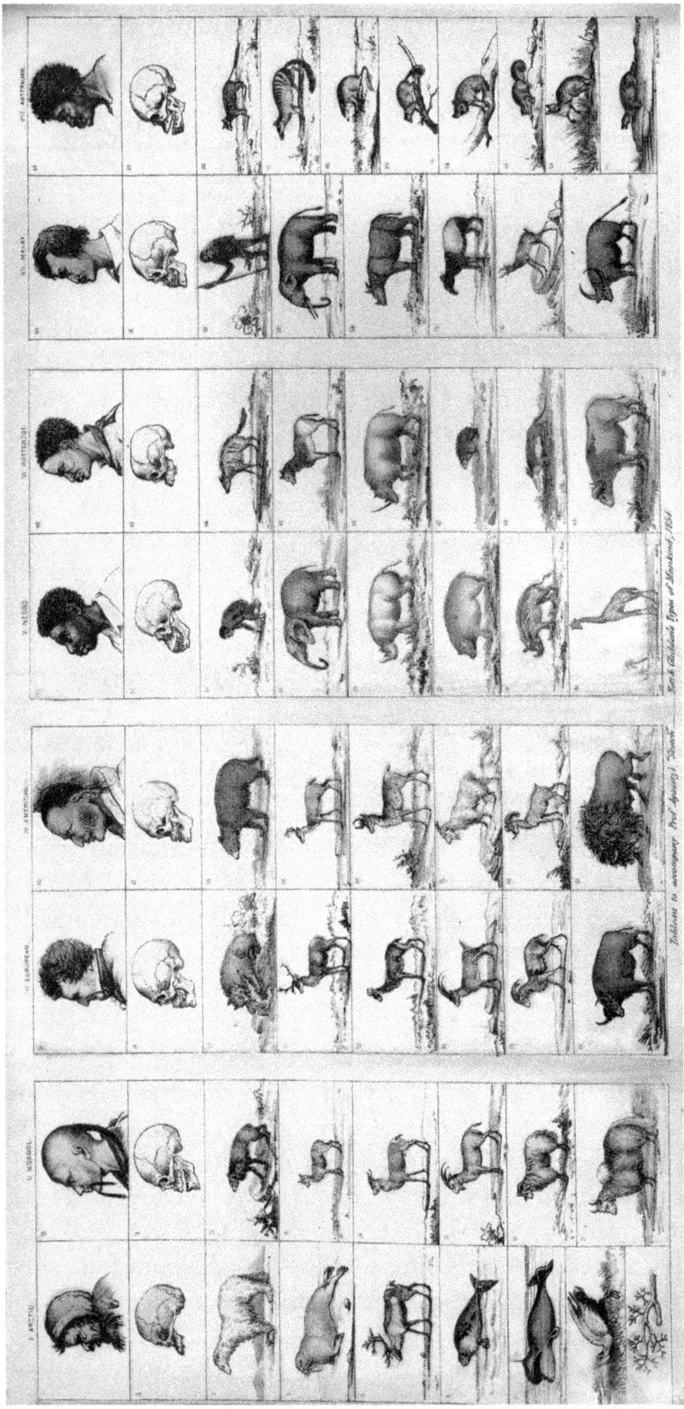

Figure 1.1: Louis Agassiz, "Tableau to accompany Prof. Agassiz's Sketch" in Nott and Gliddon's *Types of Mankind*, 1854

and equal rights. In *The Racial Contract*, Charles Mills devastatingly takes down Enlightenment thought as hopelessly hypocritical, elitist, and racist:

> In [Enlightenment] philosophy, one [can] trace this common [racial] thread through Locke's speculations on the incapacities of primitive minds, David Hume's denial that any other race but [W]hites had created worthwhile civilizations, Kant's thoughts on the rationality differentials between blacks and [W]hites, Voltaire's poly-genetic conclusion that [B]lacks were a distinct and less able species, John Stuart Mill's judgment that those races "in their nonage" were fit only for "despotism." The assumption of non[W]hite intellectual inferiority was widespread, even if not always tricked out in the pseudoscientific apparatus that Darwinism would later make possible.[32]

Although they were radical in postulating theories of natural law, Enlightenment thinkers clung to Aristotle's circular belief that out-group individuals must be ruled and subjugated because they did not have the capacity for deliberative reason.[33] In other words, at the same time that Enlightenment thinkers were formulating grand theories of natural rights, they were justifying the wholesale theft of land from Indigenous peoples and violent race-based enslavement for colonial exploitation.

In part because the founding fathers held these Enlightenment ideas in such high esteem, these ideas became embedded in the foundation of U.S. law. Equality, property rights, and liberty became buzzwords although "liberty" and "property" were much more prevalent than equality in the minds of the founders.[34] And, ironically, liberty was a profoundly inegalitarian (and Aristotelian) concept. As Virginia colonizer and enslaver John Randolph famously declared: "I am aristocrat. I love liberty; I hate equality."[35]

Classical thought and White supremacy in U.S. law

Aristotle's approach to categorization has influenced and continues to influence legal reasoning. Relative to this project, there are two jurisprudence styles that should be surfaced. The first is an explanation of how classical and ancient thought bolstered the promulgation of antebellum slave law, which subjugated the enslaved through codified codes of corporal violence, forced imprisonment, and armed surveillance. The second is an explanation of legal formalism, which operated on a less overt plane of violence, but nonetheless used classical theories of essences and categories to produce deeply unequal outcomes.

In antebellum times, Southern writers were busy concocting all manner of arguments in favor of slavery and against abolition. "The ancient societies of Greece and Rome emerged as an essential support base for the development of pro-slavery arguments."[36] Southern slaveholders frequently referenced Greek, Roman, and Christian (the Bible) texts to support their arguments that slavery was morally right. These depraved thinkers, including John Henry Hammond, Louisa McCord, George Fitzhugh, and Thomas R.R. Cobb, constantly cited ancient authors to support their theses that White supremacy, might is right, and violent enslavement were above-board, moral, and virtuous. They would argue that the South's version of racialized slavery was better than ancient Rome's version because the Romans enslaved White people, an anathema. Others, like George Fitzhugh, would take the then novel ideas of Marx and Engels and argue that enslavement was a better system because it did not require White men to be subject to the vagaries of industrialized wage labor. After the Civil War, the classics would play a vital role in the resurrection of White supremacist tropes in lost cause narratives.[37]

Some Southern intellectuals were writing pro-slavery texts, but some were lawyers who were actively involved in developing jurisprudence of enslavement. Of these thinkers, Thomas R.R. Cobb, of Georgia, was highly prolific.[38] Cobb was a legal educator, legal scholar, and central figure in writing and compiling the antebellum Slave Statutes as well as the Confederate Constitution. He heavily cited sources from ancient Greece and Rome to favorably compare the South to these classical societies.[39] As a legal scholar, he also founded the Lumpkin Law School, which would become the University of Georgia School of Law. In its promotional materials, the new law school pronounced that an education in law would provide great value to the "large number of young men who intend to devote themselves to the honorable employment of cultivating the [slave plantations] they inherit from their fathers."[40] This quote illustrates the classical ideal of a "gentleman" farmer, enslaver, and lawyer; the Aristotelian ideal of honor or "virtue" in practicing law and violent enslavement; and the elite status that would attach to one with legal credentials. For enslavers attending law school, the practice of law embodied the ideals of White supremacy, virtue, and aristocracy.

In 1861, on the eve of the Civil War, Cobb authored an extensive treatise on the law of slavery.[41] Also in 1861, he co-authored a compilation of Georgia's statutes, which was the last set of statutes compiled before the Civil War.[42] In introducing his treatise on the Law of Slavery, Cobb drew heavily upon classical Roman writers like Gaius, Justinian, and Virgil to give Southern violence the aura of ancient wisdom. In addition to Roman writers and poets who wrote about enslavement, Cobb also cited Greek notions of slavery (Aristotle's view that slavery was "natural"). To construct his narrative of slavery as a positive good, Cobb ceaselessly adulated the Classics and classical authors.[43]

The Georgia statutes Cobb synthesized and compiled are a monument to violent categorization and racial domination. For instance, in a section as mundane as setting out court costs payable to the sheriff for carrying out various legal duties, the law provides that the sheriff is entitled to 50 cents a day for the costs of feeding an imprisoned White person but only 30 cents for feeding an imprisoned criminal of color. Sheriffs were entitled to one dollar for whipping an enslaved person with the consent of their owner (but not more than 39 lashes).[44] For criminal acts, "killing [an enslaved person] in the act of revolt, or when the said [person] forcibly resists a legal arrest, shall be justifiable homicide."[45] This is a categorical defense to murder. These White supremacist, antebellum laws continue to haunt the United States. We can see these ghosts in the continuous violence leveraged against Black people as aggressive police officers and White citizens alike cut down the lives of people like Ahmaud Arbery, Trayvon Martin, George Floyd, Breonna Taylor, Tamir Rice, and so many others.

When the slave codes are read together with Cobb's treatise on slave law, one sees that enslavement jurisprudence was deeply inspired by the ancient Greco-Roman world. Cobb's thoughts were written to justify slavery but his work as a statutory compiler is closer to 'doing' slavery. He succeeded in making the social and material world real, by inscribing the legal categories that would fuel blood, pain, and suffering for generations to come.[46] Culturally, Cobb presented antebellum violence as virtue. Violence as virtue would then become a trope after the Civil War and the Reconstruction, as the Ku Klux Klan began menacing non-White people across the country and as Jim Crow laws were enacted to bolster this terror. Classical sources helped Cobb and his fellow White supremacist thinkers to successfully propel this most mendacious form of rhetoric.

Bivalent categories were the analytic engine that underlaid the Southern common law. Scholars of antebellum common law decisions have documented how Southern legal opinions "bracketed slave law off from other areas of the law," a practice that allowed judges "to confine the influence of market notions that were giving shape to the law of contracts and of accidents."[47] Mark Tushnet has written that antebellum Southern law was at odds with the "bourgeoise" law of the non-slave states, laws that were evolving to support an industrialized, capitalistic, market economy where notions of market concepts were influencing contract law and tort law.[48] The way that Southern jurists managed this tension-filled legal landscape was to increasingly rely on a categorical approach, one that cordoned the law for enslaved people outside and apart of the law of White people.[49] During Jim Crow, the categorization process stayed rigid with "one-drop" rules determining whether people belonged to the majority White population or not. In the case of apartheid, whether in the U.S. South or in South Africa, the use of categories to define social and material realities causes bias to become deeply embedded in both our culture and our collective mental infrastructures.[50]

Aristocratic and Aristotelian legal methods: categorizing from Olympus

As detailed, the Western classical tradition, which condoned slavery as natural and just, rationalized the violent subjugation of people of African descent as well as the Indigenous peoples of the U.S. Now, this chapter pivots to a different angle. The classical and Enlightenment approach to categorization, wherein people were rigidly divided into legal categories, created a legal system in which this racial order was codified, generating a loop where social categories were constructed and then reinforced by the law. Mirroring Aristotle's approach to both political science and rhetoric, only the most elite individuals in U.S. society had the power to make the kind of categorical pronouncements that would become binding law.

Hudgins v. Wright is an early example of how this style of categorization worked. In this case, the plaintiff sued claiming that she was entitled to her freedom because she descended, via her mother's ancestry, from a free Indian woman and not an African person. Virginia Supreme Court Judge St. George Tucker viewed the evidence and fixated on the plaintiff's hair and nose. Because the plaintiff did not have "wooly hair" or a "flat nose" (presumed to be African), the plaintiff should be deemed White and thus entitled to her freedom.[51] This decision nicely illustrates the Enlightenment practice of "natural science" principles being used to categorize and subdivide people, but it also shows just who is entitled to make these sweeping categorizations. Judge Tucker opined that in adjudicating these cases, the judge "must judge from his own view [of the supposed physical characteristics]."[52] Tucker represented the best of Virginia's landed gentry, hailing from a well-to-do merchant family in Bermuda. As a child, he read the Enlightenment's best writers, imbibing their values. He traveled from Bermuda to Virginia to attend the College of William and Mary and studied law privately. After passing the bar, he became both a law professor (at the College of William and Mary), a judge, and a slave owner.[53] Judges like Tucker, like Aristotle's guardian rulers, were in the best position to make these categorical pronouncements that carried such sweeping material consequences (free or not free). And, solving legal problems by having the judge "judge from his own view," necessarily implies a comfortable and privileged place from which to do this judging and viewing.

This aristocratic legal method, where elite White male judges rigidly categorized with impunity, combined with Enlightenment thought, has dominated, and indeed continues to dominate, U.S. jurisprudence. The method presumes that the judge is a good avatar for reason and objectivity that operates separately and apart from a person's baser processes, like emotion. Based on their ways of thinking and being, judges would put people and things into dichotomous categories, either/or, which would have intense effects. The method is discernible starting with *Johnson v. M'Intosh*, where Chief Justice John Marshall, citing John Locke, decided that White European Christians, by virtue of their "discovery" of the land, held the exclusive title to the land. Indigenous persons, though they might have some right of occupancy, could never hold free and clear title to the land and could therefore never sell that land with clear title to another.[54] Justice Marshall categorized the indigenous people as "heathens" and "savages" who lived off the land but who did not cultivate the land, thus justifying their inferior property rights with respect to the agriculturist Europeans.[55] Chapter 3 will further address *Johnson v. M'Intosh* in the context of the development of Indigenous rhetoric.

Similarly, in the *Dred Scott* decision, Justice Roger Taney used bivalence to forever categorize people of African descent as non-citizens, with no constitutional rights.[56] This style of reasoning is also discernible in the *Plessy v. Ferguson* decision, where Justice Henry Billings Brown opined that legal segregation did not offend the Constitution, which only prohibited the category of political distinctions.[57] Channeling both Enlightenment and classical thinking about natural categories, Justice Brown stated that legal categories "must always exist so long as White men are distinguished from the other race by color."[58]

Outside of these cases, which most consider to be embarrassing and unfortunate examples within U.S. jurisprudence, the categorical legal method nonetheless appears again and again. Sometimes the method seems harmless, such as when Justice Potter Stewart declared that he could not define obscene, illegal pornography other than to say "I know it when I see it."[59] However, a closer look at this style of legal analysis stems from a straight male view of what obscene pornography is and is not; it does not consider other viewpoints. It also may have been innocuous when Justice Oliver Wendell Holmes declared that a vehicle is not an airplane because, in his mental interior, an airplane does not "call … up the picture of a thing moving on land."[60] While Justice Holmes did little harm in categorizing the airplane as not a vehicle, the results were far worse when he categorized Carrie Buck as an imbecile, based on sparse and tenuous testimony advocating that she was the daughter of a "feeble-minded" woman who had given birth to a "feeble-minded" child.[61] By virtue of what he saw in "his own view,"[62] Justice Holmes condoned Ms. Buck's eugenic sterilization, unable to resist another categorical pronouncement, that "[t]hree generations of imbeciles are enough."[63]

Legal formalism: a classical style of legal reasoning

After the Civil War, a new, more abstract style of legal reasoning became popular, a style known as legal formalism. Before this point, legal analysis was something that one just did. With legal formalism, scholars attempted to articulate the contours of how legal thinking should work.

Legal formalism has been defined as the process of using categories to impose an order and structure onto the law and using those categories to reason analytically about the law, usually in a syllogistic form.[64] The project to organize the law hierarchically progressed in the same way and at the same time as Enlightenment thinkers were creating plant, animal, and human taxonomies. In the 1870s, Harvard Law Professor Christopher Columbus Langdell conjoined the law with the Enlightenment's emphasis on scientific reason when he declared that the law should be treated as a science.[65] In Langdell's view, students would immerse themselves in a laboratory of legal materials consisting of appellate court decisions, and, with proper thinking (deductive reasoning, rule-based reasoning, and analogical reasoning, for example), a law student could learn and know the law. Embracing the classical theme, Langdell pioneered the Socratic method in legal education, wherein a law professor would query students individually and prod them to use their analytic and reasoning skills, so that they could practice their skills.

Within U.S. jurisprudence, legal formalism was ascendent in the 19th century. It has been described as "classical" and as "overwhelmingly dominated by clear, distinct, bright-line classification of legal phenomena."[66] In a powerful way, legal formalism operated in tandem with the hierarchically minded power elites who created and controlled legal meanings in the United States. The decisions described earlier, *M'Intosh*, *Scott*, and *Plessy*, could all be characterized as legal formalist decisions, heavily dependent on syllogistic logic and reason.[67] But legal formalism lived beyond these "bad" decisions. In the beginning of the 20th century, some jurists and scholars challenged legal formalism and argued that it should be replaced with more realistic forms of analysis. Many, many thinkers have thrown shade on the view that the law could be reduced to a science. Other scholars have roundly criticized legal formalism because it avoids and ignores important contextual details that are often left out of appellate opinions.[68] Challenges to legal formalism led to the adoption of other methods, including legal realism, the legal process school, law and economics, and critical legal studies. Instead of strict bright-line element-based rules, things like balancing tests and factor tests were introduced as common law rules.[69] Despite these tweaks to legal formalism, though, legal formalism is not dead. It lives on with the IRAC acronym (Issue, Rule, Analysis, Conclusion), which instantiates legal formalism as the default or starting point for solving any legal problem. Legal formalism lives on in the pronouncements of how law should be done—it should just be neutral umpires calling "balls and strikes" and should not involve the emotions or passions of the jurist.[70]

Problematizing the classical roots of traditional legal rhetoric

To synthesize what has been explained thus far, most, if not all, of legally cognizable methods encompass an Aristotelian approach to reasoning and ruling. This approach reifies an elite, White, straight, Christian male perspective, reinforces social, racial, and ethnic hierarchies, and silences outsider voices. The classical Western approach to legal rhetoric and legal reasoning includes the following attributes:

1. traditional legal reasoning is based on aristocratic and patriarchal norms;
2. traditional legal reasoning ruthlessly divides things, oftentimes unfairly; and
3. traditional legal reasoning incorrectly and unjustly occupies a privileged epistemological space.

These syllogistic, categorical, and aristocratic norms for solving legal problems are, collectively, *traditional legal rhetoric.* Let's break down each of these concepts, one by one, and show how classically influenced legal methods do harm.

Traditional legal rhetoric is based on aristocratic and patriarchal norms

Traditional legal rhetoric assumes that both the jurist and the advocate come from a position of elite privilege in terms of sex, gender, economic wealth, race, ethnic identity, and religion. Aristotle theorized that ruling guardians should come from a life of property and leisure, with the means to think comfortably without having to perform physical or manual labor. In practice, in ancient Greece, a rhetor's credibility derived from the adoption of an upper-class demeanor that was restrained and confident at the same time. These upper-class mannerisms, drawn from the physical habits of wealthy male soldiers, soon became linked with "rationality and truth."[71] These ancient mannerisms became embedded in the United States's legal culture, where lawyers have long been associated with the class-privileged, White, straight, aristocratic man who practices law with little material concern.[72] This ideal of upper-class masculinity came to be intertwined with notion of legal professionalism, virtue, and ethics. It was considered unvirtuous and unethical for U.S. lawyers to actively seek out clients. Instead, a lawyer should await paying clients "[l]ike young maidens awaiting suitors."[73]

Historically, the vast majority of U.S. judges and lawyers have also been Christian. The type of Christian theology ascendant in U.S. history emphasized that good things come from order, even at the expense of equality.[74] There was a religious belief in the natural order of people and beings that was deeply unequal. For instance, the Puritans, studying Aristotle alongside the Bible, believed that they were superior to Indigenous people, African people, and other non-Puritans.[75] Similarly, the colonial Anglicans treasured order and rigid social categories, believing that God "has created and appointed all things in heaven, earth, and water, in a most excellent and perfect order … [s]ome are in high degree; some in low."[76] Traditional Christianity, as it was practiced for hundreds of years in the United States, was deeply patriarchal. Most Christians believed that God ordained the rule that the male husband is the head of the female wife, who must submit to him.[77]

As recently as the 1960s, courts were citing to biblical precepts in an effort to preserve slavery's gender and racial order. For instance, in *Loving v. Virginia*, before the United States Supreme Court intervened to hold that people have a constitutional right to marry a person of a different race, the trial court upheld Virginia's miscegenation law as a sacred, divine concept:

> Almighty God created the races white, black, yellow, malay, and red, and he placed them on separate continents. And but for the interference with this arrangement there would be no cause for such marriages. The fact that he separated the races shows that he did not intend for the races to mix.[78]

In striking down Virginia's miscegenation statute, the United States Supreme Court disapprovingly quoted the trial court's decision. However, the trial judge's reasoning was not out-of-step with other state trial court judges throughout the U.S. South. This hierarchical, and patriarchal style of Christianity was rarely questioned as an acceptable form of legal process.[79]

The assumption that a lawyer will be a White, straight male mirrors the sociodemographic makeup of the legal profession (judges and lawyers) which has, until recently, been overwhelmingly White and male. As Chapter 2 explains in more depth, while diversity is improving, the profession, in many ways, still lags behind demographic representation in the general population. For instance, as of 2020, the vast majority of U.S. lawyers (86 percent) were White,[80] despite the fact that Whites only comprise 57.8 percent of the total population.[81] As of 2020, 37 percent of lawyers were female[82] despite constituting 50.5 percent of the general population.[83] A 2022 survey of law firms found that only 4.17% percent of lawyers at law firms identified as LGBTQ[84] despite the fact that LGBTQ identification in the U.S. has been measured at 7.1%.[85]

Even with improved diversity within the legal profession, this does not change the fact that legal precedents and lawyering norms, forming the *nomos* of law, have long been forged by White males. As Chapter 2 will show in more depth, in their work product, the men doing law as lawyers and judges mirror and repeat their perspective *a priori*. This perspective includes the implicit concepts that inequality and patriarchy are good and virtuous.

Further, U.S. legal culture requires lawyers to adopt the mannerisms and culture of those who came before him/her—upper-class, White, straight, and Christian. Drawing upon classical, ancient norms, U.S. legal culture ties up class, race, and sex with the perceived quality of the author's legal rhetoric. The rhetor is envisioned as a man, sitting in a mansion on a hill where he can freely pontificate, analyze, and categorize. It is from this comfortable position that our concept of virtuous, neutral "reason" emerges.

Traditional legal reasoning ruthlessly divides things, oftentimes unfairly

Traditional legal reasoning is ruthlessly dichotomous and monistic. This aspect of legal reasoning reinforces hierarchy and patriarchy. In a dichotomy, one either wins or loses, is guilty or not guilty, is liable or not liable. *Stare decisis* and *res judicata*, the respect that must be afforded to previous decisions, entrenches the winners and losers. With monistic thinking, there is usually only one explanation for a set of facts, or, there can only be one individual who can hold a certain status. Aristotle popularized monistic thinking, but it was heavily reinforced in European Christianity, where there is only one God and one method for salvation.[86] The common law's adversarial system pits the different sides against each other, and the arbiter determines who wins and who loses. *Michael H. v. Gerald D.*,[87] illustrates both of these concepts. In this case, Michael H. fathered a child with a woman who was married to another man at the time. The Supreme Court decided that the law did not provide Michael H. with an avenue for establishing a relationship with his child. There could be only *one* father and that father was presumed to be the person legally married to the mother.[88] In writing about this case, Bruner and Amsterdam (2000) remarked that the decision "perpetuate[d] a basic symbol of established hegemonies—political as well as religious, as well as social and sexual—by consecrating a patriarchal notion of the family that simultaneously exclude[d] outsiders."[89] Because there could only be one father in this constellation, Michael H., the biological father, lost out on having a relationship with his child.

The *Michael H.* case illustrates the classical concept bivalence, discussed earlier as the idea that something is either A or not A. This case also shows how, in Western reasoning, there is great difficulty with the concept that two things might be true at the same time. But this difficulty is not present as much in Eastern thought, which thrives on multiple definitions and holding contradictory ideas in the mind at the same time.[90] Finally, the competitive winner takes all approach dominates Western problem-solving methods, but it is not the only method. There are other ways. Consensus, which is followed by Quakers and Anarchists, allows for a decision that nonetheless recognizes significant disagreement. While the consensus carries the day, the understanding is that the decision can be revisited, later, if the "sense of the meeting" starts to differ.[91] Later chapters of this book will explore ways of thinking that depart from these competitive, winner-takes-all approaches.

Traditional legal reasoning incorrectly occupies a privileged epistemological space

U.S. legal doctrines are replete with references to reason and reasonableness. There is the reasonable person (né Man), the reasonable police officer (in Fourth Amendment jurisprudence), the "rule of reason" (from antitrust law) and so on. Reasonableness, objectivity, and neutrality are held up as the gold standards that all lawyers and jurists should aspire to. Supreme Court Justice Antonin Scalia famously quipped that "[g]ood judges pride themselves on the rationality of their rulings and the suppression of their personal proclivities, including most especially their emotions."[92] Objective neutrality relates back to belief, first voiced in classical times and amplified during the Enlightenment, that human beings could use their higher, rational forms of reason to make sense of the world and solve its most enduring problems. Here, there are several grounds for skepticism about Western reason.

First, liberal discourse on reason was markedly non-inclusive. The undercurrent, running through classical and Enlightenment thought, is that only certain people have the capacity for reason. Aristotle believed that baser peoples—enslaved persons or conquered non-Greek "barbarians"—were incapable of engaging in reason.[93] Enlightenment acolyte Thomas Jefferson further cemented this toxic trope, applying it to the swath of people caught up in the transatlantic slave trade's bondage dragnet, arguing that persons of African descent could not reason and had no aptitude for poetry.[94]

Second, because Western reason does not reflect how people really think, it should not be considered the only knowledge-building method for law. It is now generally accepted that reason is not disembodied, it is not neutral, and it is not free from emotion or bias. The idea that facts or perceptions are socially constructed, or least socially mediated, has also become more mainstream. Cognitive science has roundly challenged the old Cartesian idea that the rational mind can be separated from the emotional body.[95] Since the 1990s, research on the embodied mind,[96] cognitive bias and heuristic thinking,[97] behavioral economics,[98] implicit bias,[99] racialized biases in witness identification,[100] the fallibility of human memory,[101] and psychological and neuroscientific approaches to persuasion[102] all point to the reality that the mind cannot be fully separated from the body. Most social scientists would agree that it is not possible to exercise rational thought patterns entirely free from cognitive, racial, or emotional influence. And, other theories have posited that "objective" or "reasonable" modes of thought are also riddled with emotional undercurrents, like fear.[103] Nonetheless, reason was and still is extolled as the only way to approach knowledge. Critics consistently dismiss other forms of generating knowledge, such as critical race theory's use of narrative, as "extreme," lacking in "common sense," and too "emotional."[104] This critique, however, does not comport with how human reasoning actually works.

Third, Western reasoning has a credibility problem. As White founding fathers chained up enslaved Black people and forced them into back-breaking labor (physical and sexual), they celebrated the links between reason and individual rights. This chasm—between the way these "great men" theorized in the abstract and how they treated other human beings—has produced immense distrust and cynicism about their analytic methods. For those who can see and feel history, bald, non-critical appeals to reason carry absolutely no credibility or, in the framework of Aristotle, *ethos*. To paraphrase James Baldwin, any evidence that the White approach is good or virtuous would be thrown out of court as irrelevant to the main body of the case.[105]

Legal advocates *must* confront this contradiction. Ignorance or glossing over strategies will not repair or heal. The long U.S. history of inhumane enslavement and dispossession—accomplished with the aid of elite men deploying reason—poisons reason as something that everyone can and should aspire to. It is not possible separate reason as an epistemology (way of knowing) with its use as a rhetorical tool for advocating good outcomes. Reason has not been a neutral tool. Reason rooted in a framework of patriarchal elitism easily promotes and reproduces White supremacism. The inherent moral contradictions contained in appeals to reason (and virtue) provides a strong argument for why legal advocates can and should look beyond "reason" and *logos* for alternative persuasive frameworks.

Fourth, Western rational reason presents us with a too myopic approach to knowledge, which is highly dependent on linear connections, empirical standards, and rigid categorization. The general idea is that if you cannot prove atomistic causation (that A caused B to suffer individualized harm), then the law does not allow one to recover. And more so than that, the reality of that harm is written out of existence.[106] This line of thinking underlies all sorts of legal doctrines including tort and civil rights causes of action. The hard limits of linear reasoning become clear in arguments about reparations for slavery. Arguments in favor of reparations are based on a theory of collective remedies for collective harms. In the *nomos* of the lived experiences of Black persons in the United States, "reparations are logical because the collective, lived, and remembered experiences of people of African descent are themselves evidence of harm that requires redress."[107] Because the law does not recognize this non-atomistic framework, however, evidence of continuing intergenerational trauma[108] is written off as non-cognizable, written out of reality.

Fifth and finally, Western reasoning norms have always been used to cement power, reinforce human hierarchy, and silence the voices of others.

Comparative literature scholar Edward Wadie Said[109] referred to this practice as inflicting epistemological pain. European writers traveled East and described what they saw, reifying their view as the only accepted version of reality while also silencing the voices of their subjects. Writing about Gustav Flaubert's description of a Near Eastern woman, Said noted that the woman "never spoke of herself, she never represented her emotions, presence, or history. *He* spoke for and represented her."[110] Said cogently indicted Western reasoning, which he also referred to as "liberal humanism" because it unfairly limited the processes by which "true understanding can be attained."[111]

In the hands of the law, the use of language to corral humans into rigid categories is even more disturbing. Settler colonial judges used words to create the social and material reality for those that came into their purview. In *Hudgins v. Wright*, discussed earlier, Judge Tucker, wrote his judicial opinion to categorize the plaintiff as likely Indigenous or non-Black, anointing her with citizenship rights so strongly withheld from others. In his opinion, the reader learns quite a bit about what Judge Tucker thought he knew about natural science and the hierarchy that places Black persons below Indigenous persons. The reader learns almost nothing, however, about Plaintiff Hudgins as a human being.[112]

Continuing along this theme, Derrida and Moore labeled Western reasoning in explicitly racial terms, referring to reason as a "White mythology," where White Europeans framed "reason" as the "universal form." Except that reason is decidedly not universal.[113] There are many other methods for generating knowledge about the world. The later chapters of this book will explore ways of building knowledge that exist separately from Western conceptions of reason. For instance, instead of starting with an IRAC framework focused on the individual and the rule of law, advocates could surface the collective *ethos* of care that exists in a community, which is a knowledge building method seen in both Indigenous and Diasporic approaches to rhetoric.[114] There is space to consider the Black rhetorical concept (descended from ancient Egyptian rhetoric) of *nommo*, the idea that verbal incantation is there not to summarily categorize and argue but to generate "life-giving power" over "life, death, disease, health, and … liberation."[115] Studying these other rhetorical forms will prepare legal advocates to make legal meanings in ways that counter pre-existing pools of power and centers social justice and equity.

Future directions: "the last shall be first, and the first last" (Matthew 20:16)

Classical rhetoric has historically promoted White supremacy, patriarchy, and inequality. Classical thinkers pioneered a way of thinking that created clean, box-like categories for people and things. Enlightenment thinkers delighted in arranging people on elaborate ladders and grids. Clean and linear, this uniquely Western style of thinking has appreciably impacted legal argument norms.[116] Within U.S. law, objective reason became the universal standard for maintaining power, law, and order, by keeping people confined to their allotted rung. Until recently, however, only elites had the ability to use these rhetorical tools. In most Western jurisdictions, the practice of law was only open to White upper-class men. And even with the diversification of the legal profession and judiciary, the tools are still infected with bias. Chapter 2 will take up this theme and explore it in more detail.

These elitist and aristocratic reasoning forms, however, are not the only rhetorical tools that are available. As later chapters will illustrate, there are other, alternative legal process methods that offer better approaches to solve legal problems in a way that facilitates greater diversity, inclusion, and equity. At this point, this chapter engages with two counterarguments likely to be levied against the book and its approach.

Why we need to get rid of traditional rhetoric even though it has produced some good legal outcomes

One of the strongest counterarguments to a study of critical and comparative legal rhetoric runs as follows: Why must advocates throw out the traditional forms of doing things when some of these forms work to promote social justice and radical restructurings of the law? After all, some hallmark legal decisions relied on syllogistic arguments infused with *pathos*-based social science to reach conclusions that shifted society toward equality and equity. For instance, *Brown v. Board of Education*,[117] used a syllogistic structure to frame and propel the argument. Using Brown and other cases as examples, Chapter 2 will explore how advocates might work within traditional legal structures to bend the arc of justice toward equality and equity. Sometimes, the strategy requires the advocate to disguise alternative rhetoric as traditional rhetoric. Knowledge of alternative frameworks is necessary so that the advocate can effectively revamp and remix the traditional framework or jettison the old forms and move in with new approaches.

Another response to the "why throw out the baby with the bath water" counterargument relates to how law should be taught. To fully prepare students to transform the law, law teachers should not teach using stagnant methods that perpetuate the status quo. Instead, law teachers must guide students beyond the classical and traditional; we must move our students beyond the syllogism and IRAC. How did Thurgood Marshall, who successfully litigated the *Brown* decision (and eventually became the first Black Justice on the United States Supreme Court) learn the law? Justice Marshall's teacher was Charles Hamilton Houston of Howard Law School. In speaking about the *Brown* case, Justice Marshall noted that Dean Houston had molded most of the lawyers who litigated the case.[118]

At Howard Law School, Houston trained his students to center racial equality in their legal process and to think about the law with a group focus and with an intense political engagement, certainly not the individualistic, atomistic, and apolitical way of thinking that predominated legal education at the time (and still does). Houston famously said that a "lawyer is either a social engineer or a parasite on society."[119] In Houston's view, a social engineer must have exceptional rhetorical prowess in order to be "the mouthpiece of the weak and a sentinel guarding against wrong."[120]

Dean Houston encouraged his students, many of whom became major players in the Civil Rights movement, to look explicitly beyond the law's classical roots in Greece and consider how the law had and could progress to protect "wider and less favored classes."[121] Houston embraced a holistic, interdisciplinary approach to learning the law. Howard law students were assigned to visit the FBI and local penitentiaries to observe how ground-level legal machinations impacted race and justice.[122] Houston also exposed his students to the various philosophical and theoretical approaches to law, asking his students to consider how these theories might justify legal change. His written exams reflected his holistic approach:

> Compare the doctrine held and set forth by the nineteenth century historical school with those held by the nineteenth century analytical school.
>
> Sketch the philosophy of Kant.
>
> Which nineteenth century school of jurisprudence emphatically denied the power of conscious effort to change or modify the course of law, and why?
>
> Contrast the principles common to the various schools of sociological jurisprudence of the twentieth century with the principles common to the various schools of jurisprudence of the nineteenth century.
>
> Write a short discussion of the sociological aspect of capital punishment as applied under our present form of the administration of justice in criminal cases.[123]

Houston refused to shield his students from rigorous intellectual inquiry even though the traditional view was (and still is) that non-elite students (such as those at historically Black law schools) should focus exclusively on practical skills while students at elite, Ivy League schools can focus on more theoretical and interdisciplinary approaches to law. A deeply troubling idea resides under the surface of this two-tiered approach to legal education, which is that students at elite law schools are more likely to become powerful judges, statesmen, and high-level corporate attorneys, and therefore need exposure to theoretical and interdisciplinary knowledge. Students at the less elite law schools can do without exposure to legal theory because they will mostly be representing individual clients, which does not require complex thought or knowledge.[124] Howard students were exposed to sociological and theoretical knowledge, but they also received intense education in law practice.[125] Houston soundly rejected the elitist tiered approach to legal education, expecting his students to become fluent in both legal theory and law practice. And he exhibited high expectations for this students in critically learning the law, famously quipping, that there is "[n]o tea for the feeble, no crepe for the dead."[126]

Houston's law graduates, though hailing from a non-elite institution, were armed with the right tools to change the world, which they did. In a truly radical approach to legal education, Houston's vision of law teaching merged theory and practice to forge nonpareil advocates who overturned Jim Crow's binding precedents and ushered in a more egalitarian approach to jurisprudence. Houston's prescient vision for Howard Law School should serve as a beacon for the many contemporary law schools that struggle to merge theory (typically a bastion at the elite schools) with practice (typically associated with less selective, less elite law schools).

Why we need to get rid of traditional rhetoric even though the classical norms relate more to the political than the rhetorical

Another point of critique is the point that classical norms relate to political science, not rhetoric and argument. Perhaps Aristotle's work on persuasion and rhetoric should be evaluated separately from his political science views, which are concededly misogynistic, elitist, and proto-racist. Aristotle's work on rhetoric might be less problematic examined in a vacuum. Classical thought structures, however, cannot be wholly separated from the legal substance of what is being argued for at least two reasons.

First, these tools have been used to inflict harm in our jurisprudence, harm that remains in the infrastructure of the law. As described in depth earlier, classical rhetoric tools have been used to sanction the kidnapping and enslaving of people from Africa,[127] the dispossession of Indigenous peoples from their land,[128] and preventing outsiders from achieving the full protection of the law.[129] Although *de jure* discrimination has been formally outlawed, classical rhetorical tools such as abstract thinking, syllogistic reasoning, and narrow constructions support legal outcomes that perpetuate *de facto* inequality and oppression.

The second reason relates to practical advocacy. Classical rhetoric, by its very nature, perpetuates a narrow, closed way of thinking—categories, syllogisms, precedent, linear causation—that forecloses alternative visions of what the law can be. As Delgado and Stefancic have written, these old ways of doing law "function like eyeglasses that we have worn for a long time. They enable us to see better, but conceal the possibility that we might be able to see even better with a different pair."[130] In order to inspire new, redemptive visions of what the law can be, advocates must allow other tools to occupy the top shelf. Legal visionaries like Thurgood Marshall envisioned a different legal landscape than the one that then existed.[131] But that vision came from somewhere beyond the classical legal world that gave birth to the precedent cases like *Plessy v. Ferguson*. The alternative legal methods presented in subsequent chapters are designed to inspire competing visions of what the law can be and can do. As Robbins, Johansen, and Chestek have written—all effective legal advocates craft a *shadow story*, which is the story they wish they could tell without any procedural or legal strictures. In a way, critical and comparative rhetoric allows advocacy students to construct their own shadow stories, using new sets of tools. The shadow story can then be infused into more formal legal documents. Or, the shadow story can stand on its own as an alternative piece of advocacy that operates outside of the formal legal system.[132]

In today's parlance, Aristotle, the syllogism, or IRAC should not be "canceled." But law advocates should learn to identify the biases and limitations within the law's knowledge infrastructure, including these reasoning forms. And advocates should learn about and deploy the different tools and frameworks discussed in subsequent chapters. We can retain some of the old forms for our arsenal, as these tools can be effective for certain purposes, but the *process* of doing law has to change. These old forms should never be considered the default or exclusive forms of legal reasoning.

Notes

1 White, 2011, p 382.
2 Bourdieu, 1987.
3 Bourdieu, 1987.
4 Jewel, 2017.
5 Cover, 1983.
6 McMurtry-Chubb, 2018, pp 911–12.
7 McPhail, 1993.
8 Kirk, 1957 [2002], pp 49, 53, 55.
9 Lakoff and Johnson, 1999.
10 Aristotle (n.d.) Posterior Analytics.
11 Robbins-Tiscione, 2009, p 150.
12 Lakoff and Johnson, 1999.
13 Mann, 2016.
14 McPhail, 1993, p 24.
15 Plato (n.d.), Politics, Bk. V.
16 Plato (n.d.), Politics, Bks. IV, V, VII.
17 Aristotle (n.d.), Politics, Bk. I, Pt. XIII.
18 Aristotle (n.d.), Politics, Bk. I, Pts. III, IV, V, XII.
19 Aristotle (n.d.), Politics, Bk. I, Pt. XIII.
20 Aristotle (n.d.), Politics, Bk. I, Pt. II; Popper, 2002, p 76; Isaac, 2004, p 3.
21 Isaac, 2004.

[22] Aristotle (n.d.), Bk. I, Pt. XIII.
[23] Aristotle (n.d.), Bk. I, Pt. V.
[24] Aristotle (n.d.), Bk. I, Pt. XIII.
[25] Aristotle (n.d.), Bk. I, Pt. XIII.
[26] Lakoff and Johnson, 1999.
[27] Aristotle (n.d.), Politics, Bk. VII, pt. IX.
[28] Kendi, 2017, p 54.
[29] Kendi, 2017, pp 65–6.
[30] Kendi, 2017, p 60.
[31] Kendi, 2017, pp 67, 69–70.
[32] Mills, 1999, pp 59–60.
[33] Mills, 1999.
[34] Condit and Lucaites, 2003.
[35] Bruce, 1922, p 203.
[36] Jodoin, 2019, p 186.
[37] Jodoin, 2019.
[38] Jodoin, 2019.
[39] Finkelman, 1999.
[40] Stevens, 1983, p 21.
[41] Cobb, 1858.
[42] Clark et al, 1861.
[43] Finkelman, 1999.
[44] Clark et al, 1861, p 686.
[45] Clark et al, 1861, p 822.
[46] Jodoin, 2019.
[47] Tushnet, 1981, p 7.
[48] Tushnet, 1981, p 8.
[49] Tushnet, 1981, p 10.
[50] Bowker and Star, 2000.
[51] *Hudgins v. Wright*, 11 Va. 134, 138–40 (1806).
[52] *Hudgins*, 11 Va. at 140.
[53] Douglas, 2021.
[54] *Johnson v. M'Intosh*, 21 U.S. 543, 571–9 (1823).
[55] *M'Intosh*, 21 U.S. 543 at 576–91.
[56] *Dred Scott v. Sandford*, 60 U.S. 393, 404, 408 (1856).
[57] *Plessy v. Ferguson*, 163 U.S. 537, 545–8 (1896).
[58] *Plessy*, 163 U.S. at 543.
[59] *Jacobellis v. State of Ohio*, 378 U.S. 184, 197 (1964) (Stewart, J., concurring).
[60] *McBoyle v. U.S.*, 283 U.S. 25, 26 (1931).
[61] *Buck v. Bell*, 274 U.S. 200 (1927).
[62] *Hudgins*, 11 Va. at 140.
[63] *Buck*, 274 U.S. at 207.
[64] Jewel, 2016.
[65] Jewel, 2016.
[66] Horwitz, 1992, p 17.
[67] Jewel, 2016.
[68] Jewel, 2016.
[69] Jewel, 2016, p 18.
[70] Terrell, 2012, p 37.
[71] O'Regan, 2017, p 387.
[72] Berenguer et al, 2020b, p 213.

[73] Auerbach, 1976, p 41.
[74] Jewel, 2019.
[75] Kendi, 2017, p 339.
[76] Fischer, 1989, p 398, quoting "An Exhortation to Obedience," *The Anglican Book of Homilies*.
[77] Fischer, 1989, p 84.
[78] *Loving v. Virginia*, 388 U.S. 1, 3 (1967).
[79] *Forbes v. Warren*, 184 Miss. 526, 186 So. 325, 330 (1939) ("The power that a parent has over his/her child is an emanation from God, and every attempt to infringe upon it, except from dire necessity, should be resisted in all well-governed states"); *Carden v. Bland*, 199 Tenn. 665, 681 (1956) ("[T]he highest duty of those who are charged with the responsibility of training the young people of this State in the public schools is in teaching both by precept and example that in the conflicts of life they should not forget God").
[80] American Bar Association, 2020.
[81] Wikipedia, nd.
[82] American Bar Association, 2021.
[83] Statista, 2021.
[84] National Association of Law Placement, 2023, p 39.
[85] Gallup, 2022.
[86] Jewel, 2022, p 135.
[87] *Michael H. v. Gerald D.*, 491 U.S. 110 (1989).
[88] *Michael H. v. Gerald D.* 491 U.S. 110.
[89] Amsterdam and Bruner, 2002, p 105.
[90] Jewel, 2022, p 132.
[91] Jewel, 2022, p 162.
[92] Scalia and Garner, 2008, p 32.
[93] Aristotle (n.d.), Bk. I, Pt. XIII.
[94] Kendi, 2017, p 109.
[95] Lakoff and Johnson, 1999; Lloyd, 2016; Jewel, 2017.
[96] Lakoff and Johnson, 1999.
[97] Kahneman et al, 1982; Kahneman, 2013.
[98] Jolls et al, 1988; Thaler and Sunstein, 2009; Samson, 2017.
[99] Greenwald and Krieger, 2006; Kang and Lane, 2010; Project Implicit (n.d.).
[100] Johnson, 1984.
[101] Loftus and Pickrell, 1995.
[102] Westen, 2007.
[103] Jewel, 2019.
[104] Farber and Sherry,1997, pp 3, 5–6.
[105] Baldwin, 1963 [1993], p 72.
[106] McMurtry-Chubb, 2018, pp 915–38.
[107] McMurtry-Chubb, 2018, p 956. See also Innis, 2010.
[108] Jewel, 2018.
[109] Said, 1979.
[110] Said, 1979, p 6.
[111] Said, 1979, p 254.
[112] *Hudgins v. Wright*, 11 Va. 134, 138–40 (1806).
[113] Derrida and Moore, 1974, pp 5, 11.
[114] McMurtry-Chubb, 2019; Jewel, 2022.
[115] Jewel, 2017, p 694; McMurtry-Chubb, 2018, p 910, n 10.
[116] Robbins-Tiscione, 2009.

[117] *Brown v. Board of Education*, 347 U.S. 483 (1954).
[118] McNeil, 1983.
[119] Scott, 2020.
[120] McNeil, 1983, p 85.
[121] McNeil, 1983, pp 67.
[122] McNeil, 1983, p 84.
[123] McNeil, 1983, pp 66–7.
[124] Jewel, 2013.
[125] McNeil, 1983, p 71.
[126] McNeil, 1983, p 82.
[127] *Dred Scott v. Sandford*, 60 U.S. 393, 404, 408 (1856).
[128] *Johnson v. M'Intosh*, 21 U.S. 543 (1823) at 576–91.
[129] *Michael H. v. Gerald D.*, 491 U.S. 110 (1989).
[130] Delgado and Stefancic, 2007, p 308.
[131] Ross, 1996, p 17.
[132] Robbins et al, 2012.

2

Problematizing Aristotle: Renovating and Remodeling Traditional Legal Rhetoric

Introduction: legal education's role in maintaining oppressive feedback loops

As explained in Chapter 1, traditional legal rhetoric, based on classical thought structures, silences outsiders, limits the story that can be told, and produces unjust outcomes. Chapter 1 explored the ancient and historic foundations sustaining the oppressive nature of traditional legal rhetoric, providing some examples from U.S. case law. This chapter looks at the same phenomenon, but from the vantage point of contemporary legal education, and in particular how legal education operates as an agent of oppression through its reinforcement and propagation of traditional legal rhetoric.

Within legal education, traditional legal rhetoric creates feedback loops that perpetuate and exacerbate White privilege and patriarchal hierarchy and authority. A feedback loop is a self-reinforcing and cumulative system that locks in inequity and unfair advantage.[1] Within this feedback loop, the tools of *stare decisis*, originalism, and the legal syllogism are just a few of the legal "institutional feedback loops [that] parlay earlier advantage into continuing advantage."[2]

Law schools, particularly in the South, were created for the purpose of teaching young men how to preserve and "cultivat[e] the estates they inherited from their fathers."[3] Legal education acted not only as a barrier to entry to minorities and women, but it also locked in the monopoly on political power that Whites had already enjoyed for decades.[4] It did so by securing "self-reinforcing structural processes like social networks and family wealth distribution,"[5] a phenomenon known as the "lock-in model." Locked-in systems are unlikely to change without intervention.

The lock-in model has two salient features: (1) "unfairness of early anticompetitive conduct"; and (2) "the need for significant ... 'antitrust' intervention to dismantle White monopoly on advantage."[6] By focusing exclusively on traditional legal rhetoric as the only acceptable mode of reasoning, legal education reinforces the unfairness of early anticompetitive conduct and can never dismantle the White monopoly on advantage.

A "system switch," which is an intentional action that dismantles an existing system that has locked in inequality and disparity over time, offers an intervention that can change or replace an inequitable system with another more equitable system or systems. Alternatives to traditional legal rhetoric operate as a system switch capable of dismantling this inequality and the locked-in White monopoly on advantage. System switches are difficult, though, because frequently "the cost of switching to a system that reduces racial disparity—in technical parlance, the 'switching costs'—may be too high for people to pay voluntarily,"[7] and the results even when buy-in is achieved are often imperfect. For example, in the context of racial segregation, "the cost … to bring [W]hites back to a hyperghetto … may be prohibitive … [and] were such a move to be successful, it would inevitably cause the neighborhood to tip toward gentrification and displace low-income residents of color."[8] In this way, getting buy-in for a system switch and ensuring it achieves the desired equitable result can be challenging.

The greatest cost to achieving the system switch in law schools is institutional buy-in, but the profession is already demanding that this very type of system switch occur. The American Bar Association recently adopted new Standard 303(c), and law schools across the nation are seeking guidance on how to develop training programs in response to the American Bar Association's newly adopted Standard 303(c). This Standard requires law schools to "provide education to law students on bias, cross-cultural competency, and racism: (1) at the start of the program of legal education, and (2) at least once again before graduation."[9] It also requires that "the second educational occasion … take place before, concurrently with, or as part of their enrollment in clinical or field placement courses."[10] Standard 303(c) does not require, however, that law schools add additional courses so long as law schools can "demonstrate that all law students are required to participate in a substantial activity designed to reinforce the skill of cultural competency and their obligation as future lawyers to work to eliminate racism in the legal profession."[11]

Through the Interpretations, the American Bar Association has tacitly recognized that, on the whole, law school curricula have historically not offered "an intentional exploration of the values, guiding principles, and well-being practices" essential to lawyering, and that, moving forward, such exploration should be a standard part of the curriculum, providing students with "frequent opportunities for such development during each year of law school and in a variety of courses and co-curricular and professional development activities."[12] It also recognizes "the importance of cross-cultural competency to professionally responsible representation and the obligation of lawyers to promote a justice system that provides equal access and eliminates bias, discrimination, and racism in the law."[13] It is axiomatic that teaching students alternative rhetorics is likely to create legendary advocates capable of confronting the deep-seated biases and injustices locked into the legal U.S. system, just like Charles Hamilton Houston (discussed in Chapter 1) of Howard Law School did when he taught students to center racial equality in their legal problem-solving and to engage *en masse* in politics and other aspects of society.

Since the ratification of new Standard 303(c), law schools across the nation have been actively exploring ways in which to meet its mandate, as evidenced by the number of conferences that have recently addressed the issue. The University of Buffalo School of Law formed a national, ad hoc committee to explore ways to comply with the new Standard,[14] and four separate sessions addressed the topic at the 2023 Annual Meeting of The Association of American Law Schools.[15]

Although new Standard 303(c) does not go far enough, because it "lacks any acknowledgement of the institutional bias at the center of the epidemic of injustice and over-incarceration,"[16] incorporating the teaching of critical and comparative rhetoric across the law school curriculum is one way to meet the new Standard. The obvious challenge to achieving the system switch is that the system functions as it was created to function, as explained in Chapter 1, and the powerful individuals who enjoy the benefits of the natural function are unlikely to welcome the change; they may even struggle to imagine any other way the system could work. Much like "[m]any religious people find it hard to imagine how, without religion, one can be good, or would even want to be good,"[17] legally trained minds have difficulty understanding how to make arguments and reach legal conclusions without traditional legal rhetoric. The legal field has deified traditional legal rhetoric, presuming it to be neutral and infallible so long as the information plugged into the formula is correct. But, just like humans can be good without God,[18] sound legal reasoning can occur using tools other than traditional legal rhetoric. Once students are trained in these other modes of reasoning, they will inevitably use them in practice to promote justice and eliminate bias and discrimination. Judges who were trained as students in these other modes of rhetoric will inevitably be more receptive to arguments that spring from other rhetorical forms and do not adhere strictly to the Western Aristotelian model, just as the late Justice Thurgood Marshall did when he served as an associate Justice on the Supreme Court, where he was known for his liberal voice and judicial activism in "upholding individual rights, expanding civil rights, and limiting the scope of criminal punishment."[19]

Over time, the system can switch from one that exclusively privileges traditional legal rhetoric to one that recognizes the limitations of traditional legal rhetoric and acknowledges it as merely one tool out of many available to the advocate.

Legal education's preservation of White patriarchy is a feature, not a bug

Racial bias in the U.S. is well-documented,[20] and the very structure of legal education is designed to replicate toxic White patriarchal hierarchies. The Implicit Association Test (IAT) developed by Mahzarin Banaji and her colleagues at Harvard revealed that "[a] significant percentage of subjects tend to respond more quickly on the task that associates race with stereotypically pleasant or unpleasant associations—White with nonviolence, [B]lack with violence, for example."[21] The differences in response time indicated that "[e]ven [B]lack test takers typically demonstrate an unconscious bias in favor of [W]hites."[22] Legal education perpetuates this unconscious bias in favor of Whites by privileging laws and legal systems created by powerful White men for the purpose of preserving their power.

All systems eventually lock in when "[t]he group that is first to occupy an institution gets to make up the rules of the game to structure future competition."[23] These groups essentially operate as a cartel "focuse[d] on the material benefits to collective action that monopolize benefits for one group at the expense of another."[24] As Chapter 1 established, in the U.S., White, wealthy, straight Christian men were the cartel that first made up the rules of the game—they drafted the Declaration of Independence and the Constitution, they created the laws that determined who was allowed to vote and hold office, they drafted every single law on the books for well over a century until minoritized people and women were allowed to hold office. By the time minoritized people and women gained a voice, the system was already locked in; in fact, many modern laws are traceable to predecessor laws enacted when legislatures were comprised exclusively of powerful White men.

For example, Georgia's modern citizen's arrest law[25] is directly traceable to Georgia's Slave Patrol Act of 1865. As the Confederacy's power waned, the Slave Patrol Act was changed to a seemingly neutral citizen's arrest law so that White people could continue to control the movement of Black people.[26] But, as Chapter 1 points out, these antebellum laws established violence as a virtue, justifying more than a century of White terrorism against Black people and other minoritized groups.

As recently as 2020, Travis McMichael, Gregory McMichael, and William "Roddie" Bryan used the law to justify their actions in stalking and murdering Ahmaud Arbery, a Black man who was unarmed and out for a jog. They decided he was in a place where he did not belong, and when he would not submit to their commands and efforts to control his movement, they killed him and felt justified in doing so. They evaded arrest until May of 2020 while three different prosecutors were protecting these murderers and rationalizing their refusal to arrest or indict them. All the judges in that jurisdiction recused themselves,[27] and ultimately a special prosecutor[28] and a judge had to be brought in from other areas of Georgia to hold the trial.[29] Georgia's Attorney General also requested the federal Department of Justice investigate the case to determine how the case was handled from the outset.[30] The grip of traditional rhetoric justified the deep-seated conviction that Georgia's citizen's arrest law permitted these men to murder Ahmaud Arbery, and without the public outcry, may have permitted these men to evade prosecution forever.[31]

The antebellum legacy of violence as virtue endures because it locked in as a natural result of existing first. Chapter 1 laid out that elite, White, straight Christian men were responsible for establishing laws and legal systems at the nation's founding. Theirs were the first and only voices in the legal system for more than a century. In *Reproducing Racism*, Roithmayr explains how primacy locks in systemic advantage using the Polya urn model experiment:

> In a Polya urn model experiment, researchers fill an urn with two balls, one red and one white. The experimenter draws a single ball from the urn, and then replaces it together with an additional ball of the same color as the ball that she originally drew. If the draw produces a red ball, that ball goes back into the urn, together with another red ball. Same goes for white. The experimenter continues drawing and replacing for an infinite number of times. In a typical set of draws, the percentage of red and white balls will fluctuate wildly in the first few draws. But at some key threshold point in the drawing process, as the urn continues to fill, the percentage of reds and whites settles at a particular proportion, and remains very stable for all later draws. Amazingly, later events don't change the final percentages in any appreciable way.[32]

Importantly, the proportion never settles at 50/50. The final proportion could settle at any ratio, but the salient features are that "early draws determine the composition of the urn," "[t]he very earliest draws will tip the urn toward some equilibrium mix, and this mix will persist from then on."[33] Once the ratio locks in, the repetitive, seemingly neutral process of drawing balls does not change the proportion. An entire system change is necessary to change the ratio. In this way, once inequality is locked in, later events (such as facially neutral statutes) are unlikely to change the circumstances unless the system itself is disrupted, changed, or switched.

In the U.S., legal systems were locked in for decades before minoritized people and women had an opportunity to participate in legislatures or courts. Even considering just a narrow slice of U.S. history, that of Black U.S. Senators, the figures are startling. Hiram Revels, the first Black U.S. Senator, was not elected until 1870, nearly a century after Congress was initially formed, and he only served a one-year term. Thereafter, Blanche K. Bruce was elected to the United States Senate where he served from 1875 to 1881. Then, nearly 90 years passed before the next Black senator, Edward Brook, was elected in 1967. As of the publication of this book, only 11 Black individuals have ever served as U.S. Senators, and they have served for a combined total of 49.5 years. During the years 1789–1870, 1881–1967, 1979–93, and 1999–2005, there were no Black Senators serving in the United States Senate, and it was not until February 1, 2013, that two Black Senators served simultaneously.[34]

Other minoritized people and women are also noticeably unrepresented, historically speaking. The first woman, Rebecca L. Felton, served one year in 1922, and the Senate did not see another woman in its ranks until 1931.[35] There have only been three Native American Senators, Robert L. Owens, Charles Curtis, and Ben N. Campbell, to ever serve; no Native American woman has ever served, and there has not been a Native American U.S. Senator since 2005.[36] Historically, there have only been two senators who openly identify as LGTBQ+—Kyrsten Sinema and Tammy Baldwin—both of whom were elected in 2018 and serve in the Senate as of the time of this writing.[37] In 2021, a Pew Research Center Study found that "[n]early nine-in-ten members of Congress identify as Christian (88%), compared with two-thirds of the general public (65%). Congress is both more heavily Protestant (55% vs. 43%) and more heavily Catholic (30% vs. 20%) than the U.S. adult population overall."[38] Of the 531 members of Congress, only two identified as Buddhist, three as Muslim, two as Hindu, and three as Unitarian Universalist.[39]

Even after minoritized people and women were permitted to participate, the system demanded that they engage in the existing system without disrupting it.[40] Evidence of these demands can be readily adduced from the late Justice Ruth Bader Ginsburg's legacy. By way of background, the late Justice reported that, while attending Harvard Law School, "the highest authorities there … chastised her for taking a man's spot at Harvard Law."[41] Even so, she repeatedly proved herself worthy by rising to the top of her class, becoming the first woman member of the Harvard Law Review, and ultimately graduating first in her class at Columbia Law School, where she transferred after her husband graduated and moved to New York. Those academic achievements were not enough to secure for her reliable employment, however, or to shield her from the pervasive discrimination rampant during that time. In the 1970s, she began to take on gender discrimination cases, and she notably had the greatest success when she argued on behalf of men, not women, who were suffering some form of discrimination. After her appointment to the United States Supreme Court, she was known not for "creating sweeping limitations on gender discrimination, [but rather for attacking] specific areas of discrimination and violations of women's rights one at a time."[42] She believed that "major social change should not come from the courts, but from Congress and other legislatures,"[43] even though the United States Supreme Court is a co-equal branch of the government, courts are permitted and even encouraged to create law (otherwise, why would *stare decisis* exist), and the United States Supreme Court has been known to lead social change when necessary (such as during the Civil Rights movement).

When even one of the brightest and most progressive United States Supreme Court Justices believes that she must continue to operate within the long-established legal system rather than challenge the very system itself, it reveals that the system demands such compliance. The late Justice Ruth Bader Ginsburg is an inspiring example of a woman who, despite all odds, achieved great successes in a system that was not designed to permit such success. Yet, her work also illustrates just how little power and influence minoritized voices have once a system is locked in. The same can be seen in the late Justice Marshall's legacy, too—his influence and voice diminished dramatically as the Court became more conservative.[44] The incremental changes they achieved during their tenures on the Court are all too narrow to prevent injustice and discrimination on a large scale. Additionally, as the 2022 United States Supreme Court decision in *Dobbs v. Jackson Women's Health Organization*[45] demonstrated, incremental change can be rapidly dismantled using the very tools of traditional legal rhetoric. The majority in *Dobbs* held that *stare decisis* did not demand continued adherence to *Roe v. Wade*,[46] characterizing it as an "abuse of judicial authority" that "was egregiously wrong from the start."[47] The majority dove into a constitutional analysis guided by originalism to ultimately hold that women do not enjoy any constitutional liberty interest that would guarantee them the right to an abortion.[48]

Under this rationale, the majority would have the Constitution serve to protect only those rights that were recognized when it was first ratified, but the analysis did not account for the fact that women had no voice in politics at the time of the country's founding. Women and other minoritized persons undoubtedly had no political power at the time the United States Constitution was ratified. In a letter to her husband dated March 31–April 5, 1776, Abigail Adams implored:

> and by the way in the new Code of Laws which I suppose it will be necessary for you to make I desire you would Remember the Ladies,

> and be more genererous and favourable to them than your ancestors. Do not put such unlimited power into the hands of the Husbands. Remember all Men would be tyrants if they could. If perticuliar care and attention is not paid to the Laidies we are determined to foment a Rebelion, and will not hold ourselves bound by any Laws in which we have no voice, or Representation.[49]

Even if the majority opinion could be read to permit interpretation of the Fourteenth Amendment at the time that it was framed, as Justice Thomas reasoned in his concurring opinion,[50] the rationale still suffers from the same defect as if it were interpreted under 1776 standards. In 1868, when the Fourteenth Amendment was ratified, women still did not have the right to vote or participate in the legal system. Thus, even though the Fourteenth Amendment "granted citizenship to those born or naturalized in the United States and guaranteed freedom, due process, and equal protection under the law to all Americans,"[51] it still did not recognize that women enjoyed all freedom, due process, or equal protection as men. What *Roe* did for women was protect their liberty and equality, as Justices Breyer, Sotomayor, and Kagan reasoned in their dissenting opinion. The weakness of *Roe* was that it attempted to protect women's liberty and equality through traditional legal rhetoric in a system that never recognized women's liberty and equality. For that reason, as a precedent, it eroded over time and was vulnerable to being overruled, just as it was in *Dobbs*.

Because traditional legal rhetoric justifies originalism as the most correct reasoning possible, it perpetuates a locked-in system that privileges the elite White men who originally created the system. Even later constitutional Amendments have been unable to reset the system to achieve greater equity for minoritized persons and women. To solve the pervasive and systemic injustice that has resulted from blind adherence to traditional legal rhetoric, advocates must be empowered with many tools of persuasion, not the single tool of traditional legal rhetoric, and courts must be empowered to achieve justice through other rhetorics when traditional rhetoric is incapable of doing so.

As more fully explained in the section "Interrupting traditional legal rhetoric" later in this chapter, law schools are a training ground for learning and operating within the system—an indoctrination, if you will—and new Standard 303(c) is likely inadequate to ensure that law schools teach students to question, dismantle, and replace the system. Traditional law schools punish efforts to disrupt and failures to learn the system by creating barriers to entry or outright excluding students from the field through racially biased tests like the LSAT (Law School Admission Test)[52] and bar exams,[53] and even the accreditation process itself.[54] Notwithstanding the barriers traditional law schools create to entry into the field, history informs us that a holistic approach to legal education cultivates brilliant advocates who are capable of generating change, which should be a goal of law schools, especially after adoption of Standard 303(c). Like Chapter 1 detailed, at Howard Law School, Charles Hamilton Houston created social engineers with exceptional rhetorical prowess so that they could be "the mouthpiece of the weak and a sentinel guarding against wrong,"[55] and law schools today can continue this legacy by explicitly teaching critical and comparative rhetoric.

Expanding on the themes addressed in Chapter 1, here, we reflect on the traditional principles that every student of the common law learns in an uncritical fashion. *Stare decisis* is one such principle that works to preserve White male power by affirming that the law is a self-validating universal truth. This is so even when a law is racist or has a racist effect. Consider *Hansberry v. Lee* by way of example. In that case, a restrictive covenant was the subject of the litigation, providing that "for a specified period no part of the land should be 'sold, leased to, or permitted to be occupied by any person of the colored race.'"[56] The Hansberrys claimed "that the [covenant] had never become effective because owners of 95 per cent of the frontage had not signed it."[57] In response, the "respondents pleaded that that issue was *res judicata* [or already settled] by the decree in the earlier suit,"[58] a case known as *Burke v. Kleiman*.[59] In *Burke*, the parties had stipulated that 95 percent of the owners had indeed signed the agreement, but at the trial in *Hansberry*, the evidence showed that only 54 percent of the owners had in fact signed.[60] Even so, the trial court held that the issue as to the percentage of owners who had signed was *res judicata*, despite the actual evidence to the contrary as presented in *Hansberry*.[61] The trial court blindly relied on the self-validating "truth" of the holding in *Burke*, despite actual evidence to the contrary, to permit the enforcement of an objectively racist restrictive covenant.

In the appeal to the Supreme Court, the Hansberrys claimed:

> that they were not parties to that suit or bound by its decree, and that denial of their right to litigate, in the present suit, the issue of performance of the condition precedent to the validity of the agreement would be a denial of due process of law guaranteed by the Fourteenth Amendment.[62]

Ultimately, the Supreme Court agreed with the procedural argument, but it declined to address the enforceability of the covenant itself, implicitly ratifying *Burke*'s holding that, if there had been evidence of a sufficient number of landowners signing onto the covenant, it would have been enforceable despite the fact that it was substantively racist.

Notwithstanding the overtly racist language of the covenant, the United States Supreme Court completely side-stepped the question of validity and instead focused on a procedural question as to whether the Respondents were members of a class that had already litigated the enforceability of the covenant.[63] Although the Opinion ultimately "paved the way for a dramatic change in the neighborhood's racial composition,"[64] it stands as a stark example of the self-validating effect of law, and indeed quasi-laws in the form of private agreements and covenants.

The law is replete with similar examples of courts ignoring reality in favor of some procedure, even to the point that innocent people remain incarcerated despite unequivocal evidence of actual innocence:[65]

> consensus among scholars, advocates, and inquiry commissions about the primary causes of wrongful convictions, including official misconduct by police and prosecutors, ineffective assistance of counsel ("IAC") who have heavy caseloads and inadequate preparatory resources, junk science, faulty eyewitness identifications and suggestive identification procedures, coercive interrogations and false confessions, and incentivized informants ("snitches").[66]

Nevertheless, overturning a wrongful conviction is nearly impossible.

This blind acceptance of the law as self-validating is exactly how traditional law schools train students to think and present arguments. In this way, the law and legal systems reproduce the feedback loops that perpetuate and lock in inequality. By introducing other forms of reasoning through multicultural rhetorical traditions, a low-cost system switch can be deployed to dismantle inequality and take steps toward achieving true justice and equity.

Indoctrination versus education in teaching law students legal reasoning and analysis

From the first day of law school, students are encouraged to leave behind their personal experiences so they can learn how to think like lawyers, as if the legal world is some form of alternate reality.[67] During 1999 and 2000, the Carnegie Foundation for the Advancement of Teaching conducted a study of law schools and later produced a report entitled *Educating Lawyers: Preparation for the Practice of Law*.[68] Described in the Carnegie Report as the "[r]apid [s]ocialization into the [s]tandards of [l]egal [t]hinking,"[69] law school in effect indoctrinates students to "to set aside their desire for justice"[70] in order to replicate the toxic hierarchies that traditional legal rhetoric was created to preserve. The Report criticized legal education for oversimplifying "thinking like a lawyer" to mean reducing complex circumstances to disconnected, legally relevant facts for the purpose of solving a legal problem without "connecting [them] with the rich complexity of actual situations that involve full-dimensional people, [or] thinking through the social consequences or ethical aspects of the conclusions."[71]

In law school, the core subjects are referred to as "doctrine." In a "doctrinal" classroom, the primary teaching method has historically been the Socratic method.[72] Under the Socratic method the teacher inquires of the students, who have presumably read materials, to explain the doctrine. In a purely Socratic classroom, the teacher is more of a guide as students teach themselves; the professors are not necessarily teaching in the traditional sense of the word.[73] Even for casebook professors who have adopted better pedagogical approaches, such as group work, formative assessment, peer review, and other methods, most professors continue to operate exclusively within the boundaries defined by traditional legal rhetoric which emphasizes the syllogism and the reduction of complex circumstances to the legally relevant facts. There is little room within traditional legal rhetoric to account for "the rich complexity of actual situations that involve full-dimensional people, [or] thinking through the social consequences or ethical aspects of the conclusions."[74]

By comparison, in a clinic, writing, or other skills classroom, the pedagogical treasure chest tends to be richer than in a "doctrinal" classroom. This phenomenon occurs in part due to the size of the classes—clinic, writing, and other skills classrooms tend to be smaller, so it is easier to engage in more personalized educational methods. It also occurs due to the nature of what is being taught. It is impossible to run a clinic without clients, for example, and clients are complex human beings with complex problems that cannot be reduced to merely the legally relevant facts. Similarly, in the legal writing classroom, professors rely on hypothetical fact patterns to provide students with a universe within which, over time, the students research and draft arguments aimed at resolving the problem posed in the hypothetical. These fact patterns are generally more complex than a typical exam question in a "doctrinal" classroom because students have more time to research and draft their final papers, and writing professors often want to create realistic scenarios for the students.

Skills professors generally combine lecture, demonstration, and practice to teach, and they often encourage students to explore the malleability of rule structure, question and redefine the legal question, or otherwise think creatively to find solutions to more complex legal problems. Yet, even within the experiential classroom, most professors continue to operate exclusively within the boundaries defined by traditional legal rhetoric. The legal syllogism, *stare decisis*, and the other tools of traditional legal rhetoric are ill-equipped to account for the complexities of the human condition, especially those complexities not commonly experienced by straight, White, elite, Christian men. Traditional legal rhetoric is also not concerned about the social consequences or the ethical implications of a given decision so long as the legal standard is articulated correctly in the form of the major premise and the legally relevant facts are identified as the minor premise.

Even as many law professors have embraced formative assessment and pedagogies other than the Socratic method, many law schools continue to privilege the indoctrination of students in traditional legal rhetoric over their practical education.[75] Of course, education in legal doctrines is necessary; it is simply not sensible to send graduates out into practice without a basic understanding of legal doctrine, traditional legal rhetoric, and the tools of traditional legal rhetoric like the legal syllogism and *stare decisis*.[76] Just because the law's reality has been constructed does not mean that it is not real. That said, traditional legal rhetoric is not the only way to reason. It is not the only way to solve legal problems. It is not the best way to account for the complexities of the human condition, social consequences, or ethical implications of any given resolution. Traditional legal rhetoric is the best tool for replicating and perpetuating the existing legal system, but that it can never be adequately leveraged to dismantle the systemic injustice and inequity that it has locked in for over a century.

As explained in the section "Legal education's preservation of White patriarchy is a feature, not a bug" earlier in this chapter, the U.S. legal system is a locked-in system that is designed to exclude players who are not conversant in its language and systems. It would therefore be incredibly irresponsible for law schools to graduate students who do not understand the basic doctrine of contracts or torts, for example, as constructed by traditional legal reasoning and analytic paradigms, because that is their entry ticket into the profession.

Not only must graduates have a working understanding of existing legal principles, but they must be fluent in legal methods of argumentation, namely traditional legal rhetoric, so that they can effectively engage in the practice. In fact, most legal thinkers believe that the legal syllogism is not only the bedrock of logical, rational legal thought, but it is the only legitimate form of reasoning. It has historically been and remains the lawyer's principal tool of persuasion.[77] So, in addition to knowing the doctrine itself, graduates must understand how to advance an argument rooted in *logos* because, for most legal decisionmakers, it is the essential foundation for any sound legal argument.[78]

One of the reasons that traditional legal rhetoric gained a foothold and became the predominant mode of legal reasoning is that it is portrayed as a neutral process, disembodied and free from emotion. Chapter 1 laid out how the U.S. legal system was created by elite, White, straight, Christian men who were deeply inspired by the ancient Greco-Roman world. The illusion that traditional legal rhetoric was disembodied created a façade of objectivity while simultaneously concealing their prejudices and biases against anyone who was not just like them in the trappings of aristocratic ideals.

The legal mind continues to believe that *logos* legitimizes an argument, and judges pride themselves on deciding cases based purely on the rules, as opposed to their own individual preferences or political proclivities.[79] But this belief in the self-proving, automatic legitimacy of *logos* is an exercise in self-deception. *Logos* obscures the biases underlying the creation of the laws that govern the ultimate outcome by pretending to exist beyond human emotion and bias; it claims universal infallibility unmarred by the deficiencies of the human spirit. This idea that judges are removed from their experiences is utter fiction, of course, but the façade of traditional legal rhetoric, and especially the legal syllogism, permits even judges to buy in to the delusion.[80] Knowing how to effectively create a syllogism can even facilitate the reverse engineering of any judicial opinion to justify whatever outcome a judge might desire, whether those desires are conscious or not.

The syllogism makes legal argumentation seem deceptively simple because, "[w]hen presented with the properly framed major and minor premises of a syllogism, the human mind seems to produce the conclusion without any additional prompting. Moreover, the mind recognizes the conclusion to be of such compelling force that the conclusion simply cannot be denied."[81] In other words, *logos* arguments "carve a path through the law's complexity that is straight, simple, and quick."[82] Most lawyers and judges believe that they make legal arguments and decisions based purely on *logos*, and for this reason "[t]he … legal syllogism is the *sine qua non* of legal analysis."[83]

The syllogism makes quick work of reasoning in two ways: chunking and fluency. The syllogism acts like a legal phone number, providing information in chunks that are easy to remember. When giving someone a phone number, we chunk the digits 3-3-4, at least in the U.S. That is how the listener expects to hear the phone number, and any deviation from that pattern will likely cause confusion. The legal syllogism works in a similar way. The chunks are familiar and seem true, so the listener or reader can easily agree with each, remember each chunk of information, and ultimately agree with the inevitable conclusion. The syllogism is the chunking formula: Chunk 1—Major Premise; Chunk 2—Minor Premise; and Chunk 3—Conclusion. Because legal readers expect the information to be delivered in the form of the syllogism, deviations from the syllogism disrupt the chunking and can cause confusion.

Turning to fluency, studies show that people understand information more easily when it is presented clearly and coherently because humans respond well to information that is presented in a clean and easy way. Once the legal mind has learned the syllogistic formula, or gained fluency in traditional legal rhetoric, it will be a familiar pattern, and any argument presented in this form will naturally seem correct. When material is presented in the form of the syllogism, the reader is more likely to understand, retain, and agree with the argument.

The legal syllogism is a mathematically precise formula that employs the theory of transitivity, as Chapter 1 explained. There are three parts to the syllogism—the major premise, the minor premise, and the conclusion. The major premise states some universal truth, the minor premise states a more specific fact, and the conclusion naturally flows from the major and minor premise. Because the syllogism "is a reflection of what we take to be a basic fact about the universe that we inhabit[,] [t]o deny the syllogism's conclusion is to deny the world itself as we know it."[84] A common example is:

> Major Premise: All men are mortal.
> Minor Premise: Socrates is a man.
> Conclusion: Socrates is mortal.

This example demonstrates how the theory of transitivity governs the ultimate conclusion because it asserts that two things, men and Socrates, are both equal to mortal. The repetition of key words between the major premise, minor premise, and conclusion is essential to establishing the validity of the syllogism. Of course, if the universal truth upon which the syllogism depends is disproven, the syllogism obviously fails. The universal truth of the syllogism generally derives from statutes and precedent, which is why *stare decisis* is such a powerful tool of traditional legal rhetoric. If the law is self-proving because of *stare decisis*, then the universal truth of the syllogism is nearly impossible to dismantle using the tools of traditional legal rhetoric.

Defining the universal truth is perhaps the most critical part of crafting the legal syllogism, and container theory offers a useful lens in this regard. In container theory, each universal truth nestles neatly into another, similar to a Russian nesting doll. In our Socrates example, the category of "mortal" is broader than "men," but men fits neatly within the category because all men are indeed mortal. Similarly, Socrates is only one man, not all men, but he fits neatly within the category of "men." "In an ideal world, categories are clearly demarcated bins, into which any object addressed by the system will neatly and uniquely fit."[85]

In their book, *Minding the Law*, Harvard professors Anthony G. Amsterdam and Jerome Bruner explain that crafting the legal syllogism requires the creation of categories, not identification of a fixed essence as Aristotle claimed. They identify seven principles that govern categories:

1. categories are made, not found;
2. categorizing is an act of meaning making;
3. categories imply a world that contains them;
4. categories are not always clean-cut;
5. categories serve a particular function;
6. categories become entrenched in practice; and
7. categories are never final.[86]

Categories do not exist independently of human creation; they are not discovered, they are made by humans. Amsterdam and Bruner note that once "you inquire where categories come from, you quickly recognize that they are almost never constructed arbitrarily. Typically, they are extracted from some larger-scale, more encompassing way of looking at things—either from some theory about the world or from a narrative about the human condition and its vicissitudes."[87] In the U.S. legal system, categories were historically created nearly exclusively by powerful, elite White men during a time when people of color were considered property, not people, and women had little agency, voice, or power within society. In fact, Chief Justice Taney used categorization to justify the decision in *Dred Scott v. Sandford*, a case holding that a Black person could not be a citizen of the United States.[88] In denying that Dred Scott was a citizen of the United States, Chief Justice Taney wrote:

> The words "people of the United States" and "citizens" are synonymous terms, and mean the same thing. They both describe the political body who, according to our republican institutions, form the sovereignty, and who hold the power and conduct the Government through their representatives. They are what we familiarly call the "sovereign people," and every citizen is one of this people, and a constituent member of this sovereignty. The question before us is, whether the class of persons described in the plea in abatement [a Black man] compose a portion of this people, and are constituent members of this sovereignty? We think they are not, and that they are not included, and were not intended to be included, under the word "citizens" in the Constitution, and can therefore claim none of the rights and privileges which that instrument provides for and secures to citizens of the United States. On the contrary, they were at that time considered as a subordinate and inferior class of beings, who had been subjugated by the dominant race, and, whether emancipated or not, yet remained subject to their authority, and had no rights or privileges but such as those who held the power and the Government might choose to grant them.
>
> It is not the province of the court to decide upon the justice or injustice, the policy or impolicy, of these laws. The decision of that question belonged to the political or law-making power; to those who formed the sovereignty and framed the Constitution. The duty of the court is, to interpret the instrument they have framed, with the best lights we can obtain on the subject, and to administer it as we find it, according to its true intent and meaning when it was adopted.[89]

As Chapter 1 details, these elite, White, straight, Christian men created meaning based on their understanding of the world within the categories and was necessarily influenced by their personal experiences, which were decidedly not Black, female, or minoritized. To pretend that their personal experiences are somehow not infused in the law is to reject entirely the nature of the human condition.

> Once we put a creature, thing, or situation in a category, we will attribute to it the features of that category and fail to see the features of it that don't fit. We will miss the opportunities that might have existed in all the alternative categories we did *not* use. We will see distinctions where there may be no differences and ignore differences because we fail to see distinctions.[90]

The categories created by elite, White, straight Christian men served the purpose of preserving their positions of power and supremacy, as Chief Justice Taney demonstrated in *Dred Scott*. In other words, they locked-in a legal system that, without a system switch, will continue to operate in a self-perpetuating way to preserve that power, much like the Polya urn maintains its proportionate distribution after reaching the key threshold of draws. Regrettably, this "culture … ha[s] been and continue[s] to be enormously tenacious in holding onto and passing on their traditional theories, narratives forms, and normative system."[91]

In modern times, these legacies of power and supremacy are perpetuated through legal syllogisms that persistently seek to categorize new situations within existing precedent and legal standards. In an interview in 2009, Chief Justice Roberts remarked that:

> Everybody tells a lawyer [arguing before the Supreme Court] that you have to answer the questions. Don't try to avoid the question or distinguish your case in any way. I hope I did that when I was a lawyer. But the importance of that is very accentuated. You have to appreciate that the justices are engaged in a process of trying to help themselves decide the case correctly. So, they are going to ask hard questions. It is good to establish some dispassion. When they ask you a question about a difficult case, it is better to sometimes say I appreciate that that case doesn't support my side. I appreciate that that causes us some difficulty. They like you to be part of the process that is helping them come to the right result.[92]

His comments acknowledge that sometimes new cases do not fit neatly into the categories created by precedent, and he admits that working within the confines of legal rhetoric is challenging to both lawyers and judges as they attempt to "come to the right result."[93] Yet, he continues to accept that traditional legal rhetoric is the only acceptable tool for legal argumentation, despite its obvious flaws and shortcomings. In this view, the "right result" is figuring out how traditional legal rhetoric ratifies the conclusion; "right result" does not necessarily mean justice and equity. Much like the trial court in *Hansberry* pledged blind allegiance to the holding in *Burke*, the legal field maintains blind allegiance to traditional legal rhetoric, even when it cannot produce the "correct" or "right" result. Instead, finding a way to deploy traditional legal rhetoric is seen as the "correct" or "right" outcome, regardless of any absurdity or injustice that might result in reality.

The Order Granting Qualified Immunity authored by Judge Carlton Reeves in *Jamison v. McClendon*[94] provides a relevant case study. Chapter 3 of this book studies this Opinion as an example of "[a] compelling but unsuccessful challenge to the racialized *nomos*." In this chapter, the purpose of the examination is to identify deviations from, or interruptions to, traditional rhetoric.

Clarence Jamison is a Black man who was traveling through Mississippi driving a 2001 Mercedes-Benz CLK-Class on July 29, 2013. Officer McClendon pulled him over, purportedly because he could not see the temporary tag which he claimed was folded. During the stop, Officer McClendon repeatedly pressured Mr. Jamison to consent to a search of his vehicle. Officer McClendon eventually convinced Mr. Jamison to allow the search. In the aftermath of this ordeal, Mr. Jamison suffered not only damage to his car, but severe emotional and psychological trauma. He described being unable to sleep, feeling angry, and having flashbacks every time he saw a news report of Black people being killed by law enforcement.[95] He was traumatized.

Mr. Jamison eventually filed a lawsuit against Officer McClendon and the City of Pelahatchie alleging in several counts that they had violated his constitutional and civil rights. The City and Officer McClendon moved for summary judgment claiming they were entitled to sovereign immunity. The doctrine of sovereign immunity protects the government and government actors from being sued for actions occurring while they are executing their duties.[96]

Ultimately, Judge Reeves found that Officer McClendon was protected by the doctrine of sovereign immunity, and he dismissed the suit. The first three and a half pages of the Opinion are composed of short, one-sentence stories that recount the numerous killings by police officers of ordinary Black people doing ordinary things. (The specific text of this part of the Order is reproduced in Chapter 3.) In the footnotes accompanying each one-sentence story, Judge Reeves names each Black person who has been killed by a police officer while they were doing ordinary things like "playing with a toy gun," "walking home from an after school job," or "hanging out on a college campus."[97] Despite his barely controlled rage at the wrongness of the outcome, Judge Reeves concludes that he is "required to apply the law as stated by the Supreme Court … [and find] the officer who transformed a short traffic stop into an almost two-hour, life-altering ordeal is entitled to qualified immunity."[98] Judge Reeves knows that this outcome is not "right," as he acknowledges by saying "let us not be fooled by legal jargon. Immunity is not exoneration. And the harm in this case to one man sheds light on the harm done to the nation by this manufactured doctrine."[99]

This raises the question: was Judge Reeves bound to dismiss the case? Under a strict application of traditional legal rhetoric, yes. *Stare decisis* operated to create the universal truths demanded by the syllogism, and lower courts are bound to follow precedent set forth by the Supreme Court which does provide immunity from suit to law enforcement for actions occurring during the execution of their duties. That said, even operating within the confines of *stare decisis*, the syllogism, and traditional legal rhetoric, judges frequently distinguish precedent or more broadly or narrowly interpret legal standards to justify the conclusions they wish to reach. Additionally, some judges are not frightened by the potential of being reversed on appeal, so they are less hesitant to depart from *stare decisis* when justice demands they do so. Had Judge Reeves denied the motion to dismiss, he would have teed up a juicy question for the appellate courts to consider. Because he submitted to *stare decisis*, however, the issue on appeal is rather mundane and the case is likely to be affirmed.

Here, Justice Reeves expressed frustration with the limits of the form, noting with apparent exasperation, "[t]his has to stop."[100] But it is not only the substantive doctrine of sovereign immunity that must stop; rather, it is also the unflappable adherence to traditional legal rhetoric, the syllogism, and *stare decisis* that must stop. Even judges who are protected by lifetime appointments and have the power to create law feel hamstrung by legal discourse's dominant methods and are forced to adopt rulings that privilege form over substance and eschew justice in favor of rote protocol. For however progressive his judicial opinion is, Judge Reeves's moment of resistance ultimately fell flat when he succumbed to the power of *stare decisis* and traditional legal rhetoric.

Using critical and comparative rhetoric, however, Judge Reeves would not have been bound to follow *stare decisis* when *stare decisis* resulted in an unjust or harmful decision. Traditional legal rhetoric and its tools would have been just one of many ways of solving the problem, and he would not have been strictly bound to follow *stare decisis* assuming another tool would have reached a more just result. This is not to say that *stare decisis* has no value whatsoever. Certainly, knowing how courts have answered specific legal questions in the past or responded to discrete issues is helpful to practicing lawyers who must advise their clients in myriad ways. *Stare decisis* influences decisions on whether to file a complaint, what to allege, how to respond, whether to settle, how to prepare for trial, and how to best exercise Constitutional rights. But blind adherence to *stare decisis* creates harm when it is used to avoid making decisions that promote justice and equity.

While it is true that courts from time to time overrule precedent, that usually occurs only when they can "reinterpret" the scope of the

Constitution, which is wholly dependent upon the composition of the court in terms of conversative versus liberal voices. As seen in *Dobbs*, originalism generally demands that the right protected by the Constitution have been recognized by the Framers.[101] As Chapter 1 explained, the Framers were unabashedly elitist and racist and even revered these qualities as virtuous. So, it is not possible to reliably achieve justice and equity for all by looking back to the time when the nation was founded. Even when precedent has been overruled by a more liberal court, those decisions are vulnerable to erosion, over time and even overruling, precisely because the social science data that generally supports these opinions is not law or otherwise firmly rooted in the values held by the Framers.[102]

As Chapter 1 details, the U.S. legal system is an alternate reality that was constructed by an exclusive subsection of society consisting of predominantly elite, White, straight, Christian men, and law schools perpetuate these systems by indoctrinating students. Students who quickly learn to identify the relevant rule of law and the legally relevant facts are rewarded with high grades because they have learned to identify the "universal truths" that have been historically acceptable in law by clearly articulating holdings and applying them to new hypothetical circumstances with slightly different facts. Those who cannot identify or understand these universal truths are publicly shamed and humiliated—no law student or graduate can deny the public shame and humiliation felt when facing a barrage of questions that they cannot answer or arriving to class underprepared to be "on call." A culture of cut-throat competition and isolation among students is created by grading them comparatively and eschewing independent identity in favor of relational status and hierarchical positioning. These practices discourage students from questioning the correctness of the rule of law and reinforce that lawyers are constrained by status and place as dictated by the realities of rigid rules of law, despite absurd outcomes.[103]

It follows that as students are indoctrinated into the practice of law, they are expected to replicate these very same systems of power; "most law professors favor their own experiences as students: the best way to teach is the way they were taught."[104] Through *logos*, traditional legal rhetoric deploys the syllogism to ratify laws historically created by elite, White, straight, Christian men to reach conclusions that are embedded in their narrow, non-Black, non-minoritized world view and privilege them.[105] As explained in the section "Legal education's preservation of White patriarchy is a feature, not a bug" earlier in this chapter, the law is self-proving and treated as an unquestionable universal truth. Through *pathos*, the appeal to emotions/values, and *ethos*, the advocate's reputation/ethics, those laws and rules are interpreted through a lens that inevitably results in an outcome beneficial to the elite, White, straight, Christian men who wrote the law to begin with.[106]

The glimmer of hope in legal rhetoric is that, although categories may become entrenched over time, they are never final. This "never final" principle is where teaching, rather than indoctrination, occurs. The paradox is that students who were once reticent to learn how to "think like a lawyer" have quickly become so conditioned to identify and apply the law that they are terribly uncomfortable questioning its "universal truths." The very thought that the legal world's boundaries are malleable creates discomfort and anxiety. They do not know how to responsibly or ethically raise questions about boundaries and systems. The notion that the law *can* be questioned seems radical, foreign, and wrong.

As demonstrated by the *Jamison v. McClendon* example, operating outside traditional legal rhetoric is not widely acceptable in the U.S. legal system. Nevertheless, historically, there have been times when justice has been achieved—*Brown v. Board of Education*,[107] *Loving v. Virginia*,[108] and *Gideon v. Wainwright*,[109] to name a just few examples. But all these cases had to shroud their radical arguments in the trappings of traditional legal rhetoric. In *Brown v. Board of Education*, for example, classical, syllogistic reasoning is discernible in the way the advocates crafted the Question Presented:

> Whether the finding of the court below—that racial segregation in public elementary schools has the detrimental effect of retarding the mental and educational development of [children of color] and connotes governmental acceptance of the conception of racial inferiority—compels the conclusion that appellants here are deprived of their rights to share equally in educational opportunities in violation of the equal protection clause of the Fourteenth Amendment.[110]

Aristotle's syllogism is visible here as:

> State-sanctioned racial segregation palpably harms children of color by retarding their mental and educational development.
>
> Public educational facilities, such as those maintained by appellee, are state actors who maintain racial segregation in public schools.
>
> Racial segregation in public educational facilities palpably harms children of color by retarding their mental and educational development.

Although *Brown* successfully used traditional legal rhetoric to dismantle the separate but equal doctrine, *Brown* did not rely exclusively on traditional legal rhetoric. It was just one tool of many that bent the law away from Jim Crow and toward equality. The overall brief was radical in its form, using the so-called Brandeis method (thus named because former Supreme Court Justice Louis Brandeis, while in practice, pioneered this type of brief) to heavily center social science within the argument. In the *Brown* Petitioner brief's appendix, the future Justice Thurgood Marshall and his colleagues cited social science studies, detailing the emotional and psychological harm that segregation caused not only Black students, but also their white counterparts in the majority. The brief, as a whole, strayed from norms of pure reason (which promotes quantitative, empirical analysis over qualitative analysis) in that the cited social science studies were *qualitative* in nature, detailing the destructive impact that segregation had on the minds of Black schoolchildren as well as White schoolchildren. The key to getting a foot in the door at all was centering the Court's White, privileged experience and revealing the damage segregation had caused to White people. Until that time, the damage caused by segregation to Black persons had not mattered.[111] The actual legal argument section consisted of 13 pithy pages, a tremendously skeletal argument in logocentric terms. Such a concise argument section would be considered a tremendous risk in today's appellate world, where dense appellate briefs are the norm and thought to signal intellectual rigor. The Appendix, by comparison, consisted of 24 pages, including five pages of references to social science studies and other non-legal sources of data regarding the impact of racism and segregation on both minoritized people and those in the majority.

A system switch requires traditional legal argument forms be modified, melted down, recast, and subjected to radically different legal processes. A critical legal process centers justice, equality, and equity, as opposed to the archaic, narrow legal categories established by a subset of elite, White, straight, Christian men. Their narrow way of applying facts to binding precedents does not inherently provide the best solution to complex legal problems. To be sure, *stare decisis* has some positive attributes, namely its predictability. But predictability of unjust outcomes surely cannot be the goal of the U.S. legal system.

The next section of this chapter acknowledges that change has been achieved by advocates trapped operating within traditional legal rhetoric. Their tactics are described as interrupters. Interrupters have historically been deployed to advance the cause of justice. The section is not an exhaustive index of every possible interrupter that has ever been used. Rather, it provides exemplars of interrupters and, perhaps more importantly, explains the drawbacks. Of course, the main drawback is that interrupters continue to operate within the problematic framework of traditional legal rhetoric, which will ultimately continue to reinforce the systems locked in centuries ago to preserve the power of the elite, White, straight, Christian men who created the U.S. legal system.

Interrupting traditional legal rhetoric

An interrupter is a tool for pausing the inertia of traditional legal rhetoric to create space to redefine one of the premises. It does not replace traditional legal rhetoric; rather, it operates within it to demonstrate that some input into the formula is flawed and must be changed. This section explores boldness, empathy, shame, invisibilization, exasperation, and flattery as examples.

Boldness

Boldness alerts the audience that something is amiss with the law and urges the audience to change the law. It questions the major premise of the syllogism and replaces it with a stronger, more correct universal truth. Boldness confronts the major premise by declaring some idea that has long been accepted as a universal truth is actually untrue. Because law is self-realizing, boldly declaring that a major premise has always been wrong can be dangerous. It accuses past decisionmakers of making a mistake, of being wrong, of lacking intelligence.

When used correctly, boldness forces a pause that allows the advocate time to deconstruct what is wrong with the existing major premise and to also propose a new input for the syllogism to replace the former standard. Boldness shocks the audience and makes it question its own assumptions about the correctness of a legal standard. But it can be risky to deploy boldness. Judges who are deeply entrenched in the status quo may not be willing to think that they and their predecessors have been wrong about long-standing legal premises. They may also view the advocate as biased without taking seriously the question of whether the major premise is truly flawed.

In the *Jamison v. McClendon* example, introduced earlier, boldness is one of the tactics deployed by Judge Reeves, but he does not deploy it to escape the natural consequences of applying the syllogism. Rather, he frames it as a plea to a higher court, one with more authority to make law and not just follow it, to abolish the doctrine of sovereign immunity. He is using boldness to create an interruption, a pause. This interruption, however, did not offer an escape from the trappings of traditional legal rhetoric. At best, his Opinion may provide an opportunity for a higher court to reconsider sovereign immunity, whether that be by adopting a new legal doctrine to replace it, widening the lens of what is relevant in considering whether sovereign immunity is appropriate, or abolishing the doctrine altogether. Chapter 6 of this book explores boldness as an interrupter in the context of *Gideon v. Wainwright*.

Empathy

In June 2009, Chief Justice Roberts, as well as other justices, agreed to be interviewed as part of C-SPAN's Supreme Court Week. In his interview, the Chief Justice "talked about a wide variety of topics, including the history of the court, its role in society, the role of the Chief Justice, and the process that unfolds at the Supreme Court—from how the court decides which cases to hear [to] how they ultimately decide these cases."[112] He commented that the justices of the Supreme Court want to see a level of dispassion to demonstrate to the Court that the advocate is working together with the Court to achieve the best result. In other words, the Court wants to see the advocates express some empathy for the Court as it faces the difficult task of deciding the case.

But advocates also hope to persuade courts to feel empathy toward their clients. Consider the example of the now infamous oral argument from the Seventh Circuit, *United States v. Johnson*.[113] In that case, Robert Johnson was charged with possession with intent to distribute in excess of 500 grams of cocaine in violation of 21 U.S.C. § 841(a)(1), (b)(1)(B)(ii)(II). Before trial, Mr. Johnson's attorney filed a motion to suppress evidence obtained during a traffic stop where a dog alerted to the presence of drugs. The motion argued that Mr. Johnson did not voluntarily consent to the canine search of his vehicle. The motion to suppress was denied, and Mr. Johnson was ultimately convicted by a jury and sentenced to 130 months in prison followed by four years of supervised release.[114] His attorney then appealed his conviction to the Seventh Circuit Court of Appeals.

Between the filing of the appellate brief and the oral argument, the Supreme Court issued an opinion in *Illinois v. Caballes*[115] that was arguably dispositive of the issue in *Johnson*. In *Caballes*, the Court held that "official conduct that does not 'compromise any legitimate interest in privacy' is not a search subject to the Fourth Amendment," thus, "the use of a well-trained narcotics-detection dog—one that 'does not expose noncontraband items that otherwise would remain hidden from public view,'" cannot be an unlawful search under the Fourth Amendment.[116]

The *Caballes* decision left Mr. Johnson's attorney in a tough position as he struggled to distinguish the two cases. During the oral argument, he expressed great empathy for his client who he characterized as the victim of a pretextual stop, but he ultimately failed to meaningfully distinguish *Caballes*, even going so far as to say that he hoped the court of appeals would help him distinguish it.[117] In that case, pure empathy failed to achieve the desired outcome because the Court felt compelled to follow *Caballes*. From their perspective, there was no obvious reason why the holding in *Caballes* would not control the outcome in *Johnson*, given how similar the fact patterns were.

When deployed effectively, however, empathy can create an interruption sufficient to capture the audience's attention and affect the ultimate outcome. Empathy works as an interrupter because it lowers the defenses of the audience. Once their defenses are lowered, the decisionmakers can think more rationally about the problem they are tasked with solving. Empathy makes it safe to admit a past decision was mistaken, and it paves a path toward a better future. In other words, it gives the decisionmaker an out that is palatable and nonjudgmental.

A main reason empathy failed in *Johnson* is that the judges likely did not relate or feel empathy for the client in the way the attorney did. Erwin Chemerinsky has hypothesized that, in the area of Fourth Amendment jurisprudence, empathy determines the outcome because the justices are likely to find unreasonable those stops and searches that the justices could see happening to them while finding reasonable those stops and searches that are unlikely to happen to them.[118] Considering the Supreme Court has historically been dominated by elite, White, straight, Christian men, it is no wonder that this narrow worldview is infused throughout its jurisprudence.

In her dissent in *Utah v. Strieff*, Justice Sotomayor demonstrated what it means to expand the worldview of the judiciary. At Section IV of her dissent, she says,

> Writing only for myself, and drawing on my professional experiences, I would add that unlawful "stops" have severe consequences much greater than the inconvenience suggested by the name.
>
> …
>
> Although many Americans have been stopped for speeding or jaywalking, few may realize how degrading a stop can be when the officer is looking for more.
>
> …
>
> The indignity of the stop is not limited to an officer telling you that you look like a criminal. The officer may next ask for your "consent" to inspect your bag or purse without telling you that you can decline.
>
> …
>
> The officer's control over you does not end with the stop. If the officer chooses, he may handcuff you and take you to jail for doing nothing more than speeding, jaywalking …
>
> For generations, [B]lack and [B]rown parents have given their children "the talk"—instructing them never to run down the street; always keep your hands where they can be seen; do not even think of talking back to a stranger—all out of fear of how an officer with a gun will react to them.[119]

Justice Sotomayor could write this dissent because she herself is a Brown woman, someone who has experienced firsthand through her community the ways in which law enforcement controls their movement in ways that elite, White, straight, Christian men could never imagine. Traditional legal rhetoric will never demand the legal system to reckon with its locked-in biases because its purpose is to perpetuate those biases. For this reason, courts remain disturbingly homogenous and continue to operate strictly within the confines of traditional legal rhetoric. In this system, the court can never conjure enough empathy toward an individual or circumstance because the universal truths tell them that the elite, White, straight, Christian is correct. No amount of empathy can truly control the outcome. At most, empathy can create the opportunity for identifying alternate major or minor premises to those that have historically governed outcomes in similar cases. Chapter 6 of this book explores empathy as an interrupter in the context of *Gideon v. Wainwright*.

Shame

Similar to empathy, shame works as an interrupter because it provokes a strong negative emotion in the decisionmaker causing the decisionmaker to pivot or adjust course. Like with other interrupters, shame operates within traditional legal rhetoric to question a universal truth as adopted in either a major or minor premise of the syllogism.

Shame has historically made an appearance in cases involving race and the United States's deplorable legacy in that regard. A notable example is *Brown v. Board of Education*[120] (establishing that separate can never be equal) which overruled *Plessy v. Ferguson*[121] (creating the separate but equal doctrine). The shame of the 1857 *Dred Scott*[122] decision (holding that a Black person could not be a U.S. citizen under the Constitution) was dismantled by Constitutional amendment in 1868, but during those 11 years, the holding was a powerful, self-evidencing major premise that controlled the outcome of numerous cases.

Another shameful decision, *Korematsu v. United States*[123] (permitting the internment of Japanese Americans in World War II) was not abrogated until 2018 when the United States Supreme Court finally acknowledged in *Trump v. Hawaii*, that "[t]he forcible relocation of U.S. citizens to concentration camps, solely and explicitly on the basis of race, is objectively unlawful and outside the scope of Presidential authority."[124] Interestingly, the majority in *Trump* rejected the dissent's efforts at deploying shame by stating that "it is wholly inapt to liken that morally repugnant order [in *Korematsu*] to a facially neutral policy denying certain foreign nationals the privilege of admission."[125] In other words, it rejected the dissent's accusation that the majority's syllogism relied on *Korematsu*, and thereby shrugged off the cloak of shame the dissent sought to assign.

Like empathy, shame is limited in its effectiveness because it must continue to operate within traditional legal rhetoric. At most, shame can create the opportunity for identifying alternate major or minor premises to those that have historically governed outcomes in similar cases. But that depends on the elite, White, straight, Christian patriarchy to self-reflect and admit that a prior decision was shameful. As the majority demonstrated in *Trump v. Hawaii*, claiming responsibility for past shames is something judges are reticent to do. Chapter 6 of this book explores shame as an interrupter in the context of *Loving v. Virginia*.

Invisibilization

Invisibilization works as an interrupter to prevent inherent biases from triggering prejudiced responses. Typically, invisibilization occurs when the advocate replaces an unlikable client with a reified idea. A reified idea works as a character, usually the protagonist, and it personifies a generally accepted principle such as justice or equality.

In the law school setting, students are often taught to personalize their clients, but this advice can cut against the client when the client is not easily redeemable or is downright unlikable. Sometimes it is not possible to create empathy for the client, like the advocate in *Johnson* experienced at the oral argument. In this circumstance, invisibilization is a technique that takes the attention away from a single individual or act and refocuses the court's attention on some idea that is arguably more important.

Invisibilization operates within traditional legal rhetoric by deconstructing the minor premise and replacing it with a more palatable idea. By making the case about a universal principle the justices would want to support, like fairness or justice, the advocate interrupts the inherent biases that can be triggered by a particularly unlikable client or heinous act and replaces them with positive principles fundamental to American identity.

Chapter 6 of this book explores invisibilization as an interrupter in the context of *Gideon v. Wainwright*.

Exasperation

Exasperation works as an interrupter because it provokes an emotional response that demands the decisionmaker change the status quo. It operates within the traditional legal rhetorical universe by questioning the moral correctness of the legal conclusion. Frequently, exasperation is triggered because the major premise is "correct" from a rhetorical standpoint, meaning that it is *stare decisis*, or stated correctly and derived from existing law, whether statutory or through precedent. Generally, the minor premise is also correct. The advocate becomes exasperated by being stuck in a rhetorical universe that commands an absurd or unfair outcome. In other words, there may be no legitimate way to question or deconstruct either the major or minor premise, and the advocate is left to plead to a higher power to correct the problem by departing from *stare decisis* and changing the law that governs the major premise.

The Order by Judge Reeves in *Jamison v. McClendon* is a good example of exasperation. In the penultimate paragraph of the introduction, Judge Reeves refers to the "legal jargon" of sovereign immunity as a jester by whom he will not be fooled. He continues to condemn the actions of the officer, despite being powerless to punish him. And he demands that "someone" put a "stop" to the nonsense. Throughout the Order, Judge Reeves eloquently explains the major and minor premises that support the absurd result, yet he does not dismantle the premises. The fact that a federal judge with a lifetime appointment cannot administer justice because of the doctrines established by the elite, White, straight, Christian patriarchy proves that traditional legal rhetoric is fatally flawed as an exclusive tool of legal argumentation.

Chapter 6 of this book explores exasperation as an interrupter in the context of *Loving v. Virginia.*

Flattery

Flattery works as an interrupter because it makes the decisionmaker the center of attention and demonstrates how a favorable decision would preserve or promote the decisionmaker's position. Human beings tend to act in ways that protect and preserve their own self-interests, and judges are no different. Even Judge Reeves, who clearly disagreed with the result of applying the sovereign immunity doctrine, still explained it and applied it in a way that resulted in dismissal. Failure to observe the sovereign immunity doctrine would certainly interfere with his future career goals, and despite his lifetime appointment, the threat of impeachment exists. When he entered an order that he obviously disagreed with, he put some personal value or goal at the forefront, refusing to take any risks in meaningfully challenging the sovereign immunity doctrine.

Like invisibilization, flattery takes the attention off the client and the situation, so it is effectively deployed in cases where the client is particularly unlikable, or the fact pattern is particularly heinous. It operates within the traditional rhetorical universe to create an alternate syllogism that seemingly governs the outcome. It tends to redefine the question that the court must answer and recenter the court's focus on values that it holds dear, thereby creating possibilities for redefining the major and minor premises, which obviously impact the ultimate conclusion.

Chapter 6 of this book explores flattery as an interrupter in the context of *Gideon v. Wainwright.*

Conclusion

While interrupters are sometimes effective tools for advocating a change in the legal standard, for the most part they still presume the correctness of the universal truths created by elite, White, straight Christian men and espoused by traditional legal rhetoric. An interrupter may cause the audience to question the correctness of a premise or conclusion, for example, but it still seeks to identify a just or fair legal standard to apply in the classic syllogistic form.

Traditional legal rhetoric has a powerful hold on the way legal advocates and decisionmakers understand fundamental justice and fairness. It demands that legal analysis and solutions conform to its structure regardless of whether the outcome makes sense. This rigidity is necessary to ensure that the boundaries remain impenetrable by outsiders, ensuring that the vise-grip elite, White, straight, Christian men locked in centuries ago cannot be weakened. True justice and equality cannot be consistently achieved if its appeals must always conform to traditional rhetoric because traditional rhetoric is designed to exclude those values except as they pertain to the wealthy, powerful elite. Thus, the legal canon requires renovation and remodeling through critical comparative legal rhetoric to unmask the shortcomings of traditional rhetoric and infuse it with alternative modes of generating legal meanings.

Notes

1 Roithmayr, 2014.
2 Roithmayr, 2014, p 6.
3 Stevens, 1983, p 21, quoting *Lumpkin Law School Announcement*, 1859.
4 Roithmayr, 2014, p 8.
5 Roithmayr, 2014, p 9.
6 Roithmayr, 2014, p 9.
7 Roithmayr, 2014, p 9.
8 Roithmayr, 2014, p 9.
9 American Bar Association (2022–23).
10 American Bar Association (2022–23).
11 American Bar Association (2022–23), Interpretation 303-7.
12 American Bar Association (2022–23), Interpretation 303-5.
13 American Bar Association (2022–23), Interpretation 303-6.
14 University of Buffalo School of Law, nd.
15 AALS 2023 Annual Meeting Program.
16 Fehrman, 2022.
17 Dawkins, 2016, p 241
18 Dawkins, 2016, pp 259–67.
19 Oyez, ndb.
20 Glesner Fines, 1997, pp 902–5; Mutua, 1999, 2010; Jewel, 2013, 2018; Megale, 2014; Chamboupin, 2015; Keene, 2015, 2017; Kendi, 2017; McMurtry-Chubb, 2017, 2019; *State v. Sum*, 199 Wash. 2d 627 (2022); *Utah v. Strieff*, 579 U.S. 232, 252–4 (2016) (Sotomayor, J., dissenting); *Brown v. Board of Education of Topeka, Shawnee County, Kan.*, 347 U.S. 483 (1954), Appendix to Appellants' Brief, 1952 WL 47265, 13 (U.S.); and countless other scholars and courts.
21 Roithmayr, 2014, p 20.
22 Roithmayr, 2014, p 20.
23 Roithmayr, 2014, p 71.
24 Roithmayr, 2014, pp 27–8.
25 Ga. Code Ann. § 17-4-60 (2018), *repealed by* HB 0479 (2021).
26 GA 1867 Penal Code § 4627 (2011); Berenguer et al, 2020a.
27 Stevens, 2020.
28 Wiley, 2020.
29 Stevens, 2020.
30 Stevens, 2022.
31 Berenguer et al, 2020a.
32 Roithmayr, 2014, p 28.

33 Roithmayr, 2014, p 28.
34 United States Senate, nda.
35 United States Senate, ndc.
36 United States Senate, ndb.
37 Reynolds, 2019.
38 Pew Research Center, 2021.
39 Pew Research Center, 2021.
40 Guinier et al, 1997, pp 85–9.
41 Oyez, nda.
42 Oyez, nda.
43 Oyez, nda.
44 Oyez, ndb.
45 142 S. Ct. 2228 (2022).
46 410 U.S. 113 (1973).
47 *Dobbs*, 142 S. Ct. at 2243.
48 *Dobbs*, 142 S. Ct. at 2244–61.
49 Adams, 1776.
50 *Dobbs*, 142 S. Ct. at 2300.
51 Jack Miller Center, nd.
52 Abrahamson, 1984; Amabebe, 2020; Woodson, 2021.
53 Curcio, 2002; Weatherspoon, 2010; Quintanilla et al, 2020; Chang, 2021.
54 Shepherd, 2003.
55 McNeil, 1983, p 85.
56 *Hansberry*, 311 U.S. at 37.
57 *Hansberry v. Lee*, 311 U.S. 32 (1940).
58 *Hansberry*, 311 U.S. at 38.
59 277 Ill. App. 519.
60 *Hansberry*, 311 U.S. at 38.
61 *Hansberry*, 311 U.S. at 38.
62 *Hansberry*, 311 U.S. at 37.
63 *Hansberry*, 311 U.S. at 44–6.
64 Roithmayr, 2014, p 40.
65 Leonetti, 2021, pp 97, 102–3.
66 Leonetti, 2021, pp 100–1.
67 Sullivan et al, 2007, p 6.
68 Sullivan et al, 2007.
69 Sullivan et al, 2007, p 5.
70 Sullivan et al, 2007, p 6.
71 Sullivan et al, 2007, p 6.
72 Sullivan et al, 2007, p 5.
73 Sullivan et al, 2007, p 4.
74 Sullivan et al, 2007, p 6.
75 Sullivan et al, 2007, *supra* note 78, at 8–11.
76 Robbins-Tiscione, 2009, pp 117–20.
77 Smith, 2002.
78 Schlag and Skover, 1986.
79 Scalia and Garner, 2008, pp 32, 41.
80 DeRuy, 2016; Eren and Mocan, 2018.
81 Gardner, 2007, pp 5–6.
82 Armstrong and Terrell, 2009, p 4.
83 Robbins-Tiscione, 2009, p 150.

[84] Gardner, 2007.
[85] Bowker and Star, 2000, p 10.
[86] Amsterdam and Bruner, 2000.
[87] Amsterdam and Bruner, 2000, pp 11–12.
[88] 60 U.S. 393 (1857), superseded (1868).
[89] 60 U.S. 393, 404–5 15 L. Ed. 691 (1857), superseded (1868).
[90] Amsterdam and Bruner, 2000, pp 40, 49.
[91] Amsterdam and Bruner, 2000, pp 40, 49.
[92] Swain, 2009.
[93] Swain, 2009.
[94] *Jamison v. McClendon*, No. Order Granting Qualified Immunity, 3:16-CV-595-CWR-LRA, 2020 WL 4497723 (S.D. Miss. Aug. 4, 2020).
[95] *Jamison v. McClendon*.
[96] *Jamison v. McClendon*.
[97] *Jamison v. McClendon*, pp 1, 3.
[98] *Jamison v. McClendon*, p 6.
[99] *Jamison v. McClendon*, p 6.
[100] *Jamison v. McClendon* opinion, p 6.
[101] *Dobbs v. Jackson Women's Health Org.*, 142 S. Ct. 2228, 2237–38 (2022).
[102] See *Roe v. Wade*, 410 U.S. 113 (1973); *Gideon v. Wainwright*, 372 U.S. 335 (1963); *Brown v. Bd. of Ed. of Topeka, Shawnee County, Kan.*, 347 U.S. 483 (1954); *Miranda v. Arizona*, 384 U.S. 436 (1966); *Terry v. Ohio*, 392 U.S. 1 (1968); and countless others.
[103] Glesner Fines, 1997, pp 883–8, 895–908.
[104] Glesner Fines, 1997, p 879.
[105] See McMurtry-Chubb, 2018, pp 889, 895, 910–12 (arguing that *logos* cannot be understood apart from the epistemological foundation upon which it operates).
[106] McMurtry-Chubb, 2018, pp 938–9 (explaining the racialized roots of *pathos* and *ethos*).
[107] 347 U.S. 483 (1954).
[108] 388 U.S. 1 (1967).
[109] 372 U.S. 335 (1963).
[110] 347 U.S. 483 (1954), Appendix to Appellants' Brief, 1952 WL 47265, 13 (U.S.)
[111] See *Plessy v. Ferguson*, 163 U.S. 537 (1896); *McCabe v. Atchison, T. & S.F. Ry. Co.*, 186 F. 966 (8th Cir. 1911), aff'd sub nom. *McCabe v. Atchison, T. & S.F. R. Co.*, 235 U.S. 151 (1914); *Tyler v. Harmon*, 158 La. 439 (1925); *Boyer v. Garrett*, 88 F. Supp. 353 (D. Md. 1949), aff'd, 183 F.2d 582 (4th Cir. 1950); and more than 100 other cases.
[112] Swain, 2009.
[113] 123 Fed. Appx. 240 (2005), Oral Argument.
[114] 123 Fed. Appx. 240 (2005).
[115] 543 U.S. 405 (2005).
[116] 543 U.S. 405, 409 (2005).
[117] 123 Fed. Appx. 240 (2005), Oral Argument.
[118] Chemerinsky, 2012.
[119] Utah v. Strieff, 579 U.S. 232, 252–4 (2016) (Sotomayor, J., dissenting).
[120] 347 U.S. 483 (1954).
[121] 163 U.S. 537 (1896).
[122] 60 U.S. 393 (1857).
[123] 323 U.S. 214 (1944).
[124] 138 S. Ct. 2392 (2018).
[125] 138 S. Ct. 2392 (2018).

3

Shifting the Focus from the West

Contested terrain: challenging foundational narratives

The idea of the West, in theory and in practice, has shaped the way American law is practiced and judicial opinions are written. As discussed in Chapter 1, the context for American law and jurisprudence is the *nomos*, or the universe in which law functions. The *nomos* operates invisibly to deploy Western European ways of knowing (epistemology) and ways of being (ontology) through the reasoning and analytic processes that create and recreate the body of law.[1] As an import to the United States, Western European epistemologies and ontologies manifest as the imperialist, capitalist, White supremacist blueprint for the U.S. and its legal system. The collective, social memory of the U.S., the active past that forms our identities and projects our group identity to the world,[2] is a narrative of a country that begins with the arrival of White European immigrants seeking refuge from religious persecution. As expressed in the report commissioned by the 45th presidential administration (2016–20) about the nation's political founding in 1776:

> [B]y the time of the American founding, political life in the West had undergone two momentous changes. The first was the sundering of civil from religious law with the advent and widespread adoption of Christianity. The second momentous change was the emergence of multiple denominations within Christianity that undid Christian unity and in turn greatly undermined political unity. Religious differences became sources of political conflict and war [and] it was in response to these fundamentally new circumstances that the American founders developed the principle of religious liberty.
>
> While the founders' principles are both true and eternal, they cannot be understood without also understanding that they were formulated by practical men to solve real-world problems. For the founders' solution to these problems we must turn to the Constitution [of the United States of America].[3]

The preamble to the Constitution establishes it as a document written by "we the people, in order to form a more perfect union, establish justice, insure domestic tranquility, provide for the common defense, promote the general welfare, and secure the blessings of liberty to ourselves and our posterity."[4] The first ten amendments to the Constitution, the Bill of Rights, protect the inhabitants of the republic from the overreach of its representatives by bestowing upon them the right to religious liberty, free speech, trial by jury and speedy trials, the due process of the law, the right to bear arms, to be secure in their homes and persons from unwarranted governmental intrusion without their consent, protections against criminal prosecution, excessive bail, and cruel and unusual punishments.[5] It also reserves rights not expressly enumerated in it to the people and to the governments of the individual states.

The 1776 report goes on to establish the United States Constitution as the lodestar for American politics and jurisprudence. In the authors' words,

> The bedrock upon which the American political system is built is the rule of law. The vast difference between tyranny and the rule of law is a central theme of political thinkers back to classical antiquity. The idea that the law is superior to rulers is the cornerstone of English constitutional thought as it developed over the centuries. The concept was transferred to the American colonies, and can be seen expressed throughout colonial pamphlets and political writings.[6]

One such colonial political writer, Alexander Hamilton, is quoted in the report for his words:

> The safety of a republic depends essentially on the energy of a common national sentiment; on a uniformity of principles and habits; on the exemption of the citizens from foreign bias, and prejudice; and on that love of country which will almost invariably be found to be closely connected with birth, education and family.[7]

Narratives of the country's founding that challenge its Constitutional ideals and rights have long threatened this concept of safety. Historians such as Howard Zinn (*The People's History of the United States*), Ronald Takaki (*Through A Different Mirror, Strangers From A Different Shore*), James Loewen (*Lies My Teacher Told Me*), Linda Kerber and Jane DeHart (*Women's America*), Darlene Clark Hine (*Black Women in America*), Roxanne Dunbar-Ortiz (*An Indigenous Peoples' History of the United States*), and Christopher Clark, Nancy Hewitt, Roy Rosenzweig, Nelson Lichtenstein, Joshua Brown, and David Jaffee (*Who Built America*), to name a few, have worked to create a fuller narrative of the American story that reflects the experiences of the racially, ethnically, and socioeconomically diverse inhabitants of the country before, during, and beyond the country's political founding in 1776. These authors' interventions have landed their books on banned book lists and outside of the normative narratives of America found in textbooks routinely utilized in K–12 public education. However, this threat crystallized in 2019 with the *New York Times*'s publication of "The 1619 Project," which placed the ideological founding of the U.S. at the arrival of its first indentured Africans in 1619 at Point Comfort, Virginia—the descendants of whom would become enslaved and remain so by provisions in the Constitution ratified some 170 years later.[8] In response to this threat, no less than 17 states—Alabama,[9] Florida,[10] Georgia,[11] Idaho,[12] Iowa,[13] Kentucky,[14] Mississippi,[15] Montana,[16] New Hampshire,[17] North Dakota,[18] Oklahoma,[19] South Carolina,[20] South Dakota,[21] Tennessee,[22] Texas,[23] Utah,[24] and Virginia[25]—passed legislation in 2021 and 2022 prohibiting public school teachers in the U.S. from deviating too sharply from a whitewashed and Eurocentric story of the country's political founding.[26] For example, the Georgia General Assembly stated in its legislation that:

> (1) Slavery, racial discrimination under the law, and racism in general are so inconsistent with the founding principles of the United States that Americans fought a civil war to eliminate the first, waged long-standing political campaigns to eradicate the second, and rendered the third unacceptable in the court of public opinion, all of which dispels the idea that the United States and its institutions are systemically racist and confutes the notion that slavery, racial discrimination under the law, and racism should be at the center of public elementary, secondary, and post-secondary educational institutions;
> (2) Democratic societies built on the ideals of individual freedom and the self-driven pursuit of prosperity with a dedication to equal opportunity for all will thrive in perpetuity, while societies built on the false promises of equity and equal outcomes for all have consistently ended in failed states; and
> (3) Americans should be allowed, in the words of civil rights activist Robert Woodson, "an aspirational and inspirational take on America's history, debunking the misguided argument that the present-day problems of black Americans are caused by injustices of past failures, such as slavery."[27]

A key feature of all of the legislation is that it frames naming oppressive structures and their actors in the telling of the United States story as a discriminatory, unlawful act against the oppressors. Four states—Mississippi, Iowa, Oklahoma, and Tennessee—have passed "divisive concepts" provisions in their legislation that prohibit not only public school teachers, but professors at state colleges and universities from teaching concepts that include, but are not limited to:

a. One race or sex is inherently superior to another race or sex;
b. An individual, by virtue of the individual's race or sex, is inherently privileged, racist, sexist, or oppressive, whether consciously or subconsciously;
c. An individual should be discriminated against or receive adverse treatment because of an individual's race or sex;
d. An individual's moral character is determined by the individual's race or sex;
e. An individual, by virtue of the individual's race or sex, bears responsibility for actions committed in the past by other members of the same race or sex;
f. An individual should feel discomfort, guilt, anguish, or another form of psychological distress solely because of the individual's race or sex;
g. A meritocracy is inherently racist or sexist, or designed by a particular race or sex to oppress members of another race or sex;
h. This state [state in which the legislation is passed] or the United States is fundamentally or irredeemably racist or sexist;
i. Promoting or advocating the overthrow of the United States government;
j. Promoting division between, or resentment of, a race, sex, religion, creed, nonviolent political affiliation, social class, or class of people;
k. Ascribing character traits, moral or ethical codes, privileges or beliefs to a race or sex, or to an individual because of the individual's race or sex;
l. The rule of law does not exist, but instead is a series of power relationships and struggles among racial or other groups;
m. All Americans are not created equal and are not endowed by their Creator with certain unalienable rights, including life, liberty, and the pursuit of happiness; or
n. Governments should deny to any person within the government's jurisdiction the equal protection of the law.[28]

A federal judge, Judge Mark E. Walker, struck down legislation with similar language in Florida with respect to its application to state colleges and universities.[29] In his opinion, Judge Walker likened the legislation to the use of double-speak in George Orwell's novel *1984*, and declared "[The legislation] is positively dystopian. It should go without saying that [if] liberty means anything at all it means the right to tell people what they do not want to hear."[30] Florida's legislation remains in effect in its primary and secondary schools.[31]

Moreover, organizations such as Citizens for Renewing America,[32] Manhattan Institute,[33] and PragerU[34] have created "Anti-CRT" toolkits made available online to parents in school districts where teachers have introduced "divisive concepts" into the curriculum. These toolkits provide strategies and resources for parents and community members to identify where the concepts are being taught, build a grassroots network of support to stop them from proliferating the curriculum, and mobilize their networks for political action such as influencing school board elections.

In this context, the 1619 Project emerges as a piece of cultural memory, "a memory that is shared outside of the avenues of formal historical discourse yet is entangled with cultural products and imbued with cultural meaning."[35] The U.S. is a country of varied cultural memories, not only those of its early Western European immigrants fleeing religious persecution, but of the Indigenous inhabitants of the country who predated them, the kidnapped and imprisoned African migrants who were subsequently enslaved, and the Latine and Asian peoples who immigrated in great part because of the United States's imperialist and capitalist designs abroad.

The existence of these groups in the United States and their experiences in the country pose a challenge to the idea of America, Hamilton's vision of a democratic republic dependent upon a commonality, uniformity, and a love of country connected to birth, education, and family.[36] Their varied cultural epistemologies and ontologies, their ways of knowing and being in the world they forged in the United States, have been and continue to be met with resistance to the extent they cannot be assimilated into those of the West, into "the American melting pot." Moreover, their existence also challenges the rule of law as a protector of rights and as a tool to maintain American Constitutional ideals. On the contrary, the rule of law has established and maintained the inequitable treatment of Indigenous, Black, Latine, and Asian people in significant ways that directly undermine collective buy-in for the idea that the United States Constitution and the Bill of Rights protect the liberty and promote the happiness of all people.

Building the legal framework for White cultural hegemony

U.S. law and policy with respect to Indigenous peoples, African people and their descendants caught up in the transatlantic human trafficking dragnet, Latine peoples living in land once belonging to Mexico, and immigration policies directed toward Korean, Indian, Chinese, and Japanese people is instructive in this regard. Of the plight of Indigenous peoples, President James Monroe declared to the nation in his 1818 State of the Union Address that

> Experience has clearly demonstrated that independent savage communities cannot long exist within the limits of a civilized population. The progress of the latter has almost invariably terminated

> in the extinction of the former, especially of the tribes belonging to our portion of this hemisphere, among whom loftiness of sentiment and gallantry in action have been conspicuous. **To civilize them, and even to prevent their extinction, it seems to be indispensable that their independence as communities should cease, and that the control of the United States over them should be complete and undisputed.** The hunter state will then be more easily abandoned, and recourse will be had to the acquisition and culture of land and to other pursuits tending to dissolve the ties which connect them together as a savage community and to give a new character to every individual. I present this subject to the consideration of Congress on the presumption that it may be found expedient and practicable to adopt some benevolent provisions, having these objects in view, relative to the tribes within our settlements.[37] (Emphasis added)

Congress passed the first "benevolent provision" on March 3, 1819, the Indian Civilization Fund Act.[38] The purpose of the Act was to fund Indian assimilation into Western ideals, allegedly for their benefit—to prevent their "further decline and final extinction"—both precipitated by the U.S. government's forcible removal of the people from their lands.[39] Another benevolent provision came 11 years later as the Indian Removal Act of 1830, which authorized the President, then President Andrew Jackson, to relocate Indigenous peoples west of the Mississippi River and reallocate their lands.[40] This Act resulted, in part, in the forced march of the Cherokee Indians from their tribal home in Georgia during which approximately 10,000 died.[41] Their removal yielded an "interesting tract of country [that] contains four millions three hundred & sixty six thousand five hundred & fifty four acres, many rich gold mines & many delightful situations & though in some parts mountainous, some of the richest land belonging to the state [of Georgia]."[42] U.S. and state courts enforced the Act, through facilitating and legitimating land sales of newly divided Cherokee lands to White men, women, and children through the Georgia Land Lotteries.[43]

Contemporaneous to Congressional action and military might, Chief Justice John Marshall would author three United States Supreme Court opinions from 1823 to 1832—*Johnson v. M'Intosh* (1823),[44] *Cherokee Nation v. Georgia* (1831),[45] and *Worcester v. Georgia* (1832)[46]—that would subvert indigenous sovereignty and problematize indigenous self-determination in American jurisprudence.

On this Trail of Tears rode in the plantation economy, the seeds of which had been nurtured in the Fugitive Slave Clause of the United States Constitution.[47] Present in the Constitution's ratification, the Fugitive Slave Clause protected enslavers' property interest in their enslaved by requiring their swift return if discovered upon escape. Congress passed two additional

Fugitive Slave Acts in 1793 and 1850, the latter of which increased the role of the federal government in procuring and returning the enslaved thus buttressing the institution of chattel slavery.[48] Under the 1850 Act, federal judges appointed commissioners and each had the authority to issue warrants to U.S. marshals, slave catchers, and plantation owners/enslavers for enslaved persons suspected of escaping their enslavers, although warrants were not required for the execution of the law.[49] The Act also commanded citizens to aid in the capture of suspected escapees, and penalized their inaction, rescue, or attempts to hide them with a fine of up to $1,000 and imprisonment of up to six months.[50] If successfully captured, the enslaved was hauled before a commissioner to determine proof of their identity. During these "hearings" they were prohibited from giving testimony or evidence in their defense.[51]

In the context of more draconian laws enforcing enslavement was the Mexican American War. As it ended in 1848 with the signing of the Treaty of Guadalupe Hidalgo, President James Polk continued Presidents James Monroe's and Andrew Jackson's expansionist dreams through the United States's acquisition of Mexican lands—present day New Mexico, Arizona, Utah, Nevada, Colorado, Texas, and California.[52] Mexicans, now Americans, lost their lands immediately through treaty provisions or through the execution of the California Land Act of 1851.[53]

In between the Treaty of Guadalupe Hidalgo and the California Land Act, Chinese laborers were pushed out of China and into the U.S. labor market as a result of the British Opium Wars.[54] These immigrants built the railroads that mapped United States westward expansion, but were excluded from the benefits of citizenship by the 1790 Nationality Act, which limited that privilege to free White persons who had been residents of the United States for two years and their children under the age of 21.[55] Their exclusion, as well as that of their Japanese, Korean, and Indian counterparts, would be further precipitated by the Page Act of 1875, the Chinese Exclusion Act of 1882, and the Japanese Exclusion Act of 1907—all culminating in the Immigration Act of 1924, which set quotas for Asian immigrants and the context for the creation of the U.S. Border Patrol.[56] Approximately one month after the passage of the Act, the *New York Times* would declare "America of the Melting Pot Comes to End; Effects of New Immigration Legislation Described by Senate Sponsor of Bill—Chief Aim, He States, Is to Preserve Racial Type as It Exists Here Today."[57] The preservation of which "racial type" was rigorously discussed on the floor of the House of Representatives where the bill that became the Immigration Act was introduced. After being granted permission by the chair to offer extended remarks on the bill, Michigan Congressman Grant M. Hudson proceeded as follows:

> Now today we are thinking of the new problem that confronts us, not so much a problem of the past as of the future. The old theory of

> "no bars" [to immigration] was that in the atmosphere of America we could make full-fledged Americans out of any and all racial groups. All we needed to do was to let them see the flag, put their children in public school, teach them to speak English, and the miracle was performed. We have become sadly disillusioned. The "melting pot" has proved to be a myth. We are slowly awakening to consciousness that education and environment do not fundamentally alter racial values. Today we face the serious problem of the maintenance of our historic republican institutions. … George Washington in his Farewell Address said: **"Citizens by birth or choice, of common country, that country has a right to concentrate your affection … with slight shades of difference, you have the same religion, manners, habits, and political principals."** Washington observed—"slight shades of difference." But today we see huge masses of non-American-minded individuals, living in colonies or ghettoes, or even cities and counties of their own. Here they perpetuate their racial mindedness, their racial character, and their racial habits. Here they speak their own tongue, read their own newspapers, maintain their separate educational system.[58] (Emphasis added)

Quoting a newspaper story on the immigration issue, Congressman Hudson continued,

> And we must recognize the danger in the fact that we have armed these heterogenous American stocks with a political weapon which many of them are congenitally unfit to use [arguably a reference to the Constitution], and clothed legions of them by legislative fiat with an "equality" which flies in the face of nature and their history.[59]

A similar rationale was applied to those who were already within U.S. borders, though not originally of their own volition. About one month prior to Congressman Hudson's remarks, Virginia had passed its 1924 Act to Preserve Racial Integrity. Influenced by the eugenics movement, the law's purpose was to preserve the integrity of the White race by discouraging mixing it with "lesser" racial stock. Its chief administrator, Dr. W.A. Plecker, State Registrar of Vital Statistics would explain:

> The [law] aims at correcting a condition which only the more thoughtful people of Virginia know the existence of. It is estimated that there are in the State from 10,000 to 20,000 possibly more near [W]hite people, who are known to possess an intermixture of colored blood, in some cases to a slight extent it is true, but **still enough to prevent them from being [W]hite.** In the past, it has been possible

> for these people to declare themselves as [W]hite, or even to have a court declare them. Then they have demanded the admittance of their children into [W]hite schools, and in not a few cases have intermarried with [W]hite people. In many counties they exist as distinct colonies holding themselves aloof from negroes, but not being admitted by the [W]hite people as of their race. In any large gathering or school of colored people, especially in the cities, many will be observed who are scarcely distinguishable as colored. These persons, however, are not [W]hite in reality, nor by the new definition of this law, that a [W]hite person is one with no trace of the blood of another race, except that person with one-sixteenth of the American Indian, if there is no other race mixture, may be classed as [W]hite. Their children are likely to revert to the distinctly negro type even when all apparent evidence of mixture has disappeared … Unless radical measures are used to prevent it, Virginia and other parts of the Nation must surely in time go the way of all other countries in which people of two or more races have lived in close contact. With the exception of the Hebrew race, complete intermixture or amalgamation has been the inevitable result. To succeed, **the intermarriage of the [W]hite race with mixed stock must be made impossible. But that is not sufficient, public sentiment must be so aroused that intermixture out of wedlock will cease. The public must be led to look with scorn and contempt upon the man who will degrade himself and do harm to society with such abhorrent deeds.**[60] (Emphasis added)

This law was the basis for criminalizing the marriage between Mildred Jeter, a Black woman, and Richard Loving, a White man, who were the litigants in the landmark Supreme Court case *Loving v. Virginia* (1967).[61] Chapter 6 discusses this case as well as the exemplary brief that the petitioner filed, which resulted in the Supreme Court striking down Virginia's miscegenation law.

While these are but a few of the experiences of Indigenous, African, Latine, and Asian people as they built lives in and built the U.S., these lived experiences, in tandem with the Western thought structures detailed in Chapter 1, underscore how the rule of law operates to maintain White supremacy and enshrine each group's difference as legally binding inequity. The Western *nomos* is not capacious enough to hold their stories and experiences. Rather, its cohesion depends on silencing them to the extent that they reveal existing inequalities and demand justice. For our legal system to acknowledge these varied experiences and its practitioners to deem them relevant would run counter to the fundamental belief that Lady Justice is blind, and her blindness allows her to dispense justice to all groups equally. If lawyers and jurists desire to act in the service of justice, then they must jettison systems of reasoning and analysis that work against it and are dependent on our ignorance of and blindness to the human condition.

These examples make it readily apparent that the Western *nomos*, the legal universe in which American law is made and practiced, is a racialized one. The reasoning and analytic processes that occur there establish White cultural hegemony and reify it through the doctrine of *stare decisis* or the precedential value of legal opinions. The common reasoning paradigm used in legal writing—issue, rule, analysis, conclusion (IRAC)—serves as a form of discourse bounded by the imperatives of the racialized *nomos*. Issues are framed using information relevant to resolve a legal problem or acceptable sources for legal arguments. Among these sources, cases and statutes take primacy. Rules are culled from and explained through the language of those opinions, which serve as either binding or persuasive precedent. The framework built from these "rules," the analytic framework, is then "applied" to the relevant facts of the case or the law that is the subject of the analysis. Again, the relevance of the facts and scope of the law to be analyzed are determined by the acceptable sources for legal arguments, the precedential authority. The process of analysis requires the writer to determine how the fact or law meets or does not meet the requirements as detailed in the analytic framework. The conclusion is a resolution of the legal problem within the parameters set by the framework. In sum, this form of reasoning used to arrive at a viable legal conclusion cannot deviate from the racialized norms of the *nomos*. This is true even in those legal memos, briefs, and judicial opinions that are universally considered progressive.

A compelling but unsuccessful challenge to the racialized nomos*:* Jamison v. McClendon

---

Judge Carlton Reeves's opinion in *Jamison v. McClendon* (2020) is widely regarded as one of the most progressive judicial opinions ever written by a federal judge.[62] In the opinion, Judge Reeves was called upon to determine whether Richland, Mississippi Police Officer Nick McClendon, a White man, was entitled to qualified immunity from a lawsuit involving his stop and detention of Clarence Jamison, a Black man, on July 29, 2013. On this question, Judge Reeves answered "yes."[63] Officer McClendon stopped Mr. Jamison while he was driving through Pelahatchie, Mississippi, as he continued his cross-country trip from Phoenix, Arizona, to his home in Neeses, South Carolina.[64] Mr. Jamison purchased the car he used for his journey, a 2001 Mercedes-Benz CLK-Class convertible, estimated retail price $10,000, 13 days prior to his trip, which meant that the car had a temporary paper license plate or temporary tag. Officer McClendon gave as his reason for the stop that he could not see the tag because it was folded.[65]

Upon stopping Mr. Jamison by flashing his blue lights and pulling him over to the shoulder of Interstate 20, Officer McClendon exited his police car and moved to the passenger side of Mr. Jamison's car. Jamison rolled down the window, and after remarking that he "noticed that Jamison had recently purchased his car in Pennsylvania," McClendon asked Jamison for "his license, insurance, [and] the paperwork" on the car because it only had a temporary tag. Jamison told the officer where he was traveling from and complied with the request by giving McClendon the bill of sale for the car, proof of insurance, and his driver's license from his home state of South Carolina.[66] McClendon then entered this information into the El Paso Intelligence Center (EPIC) database to conduct a criminal background check on McClendon. McClendon was not in the database—an indication that he had not been involved in any criminal activity. McClendon subsequently contacted the National Criminal Information Center (NCIC) to request a criminal background check on Jamison, as well as on the Vehicle Identification Number (VIN) on his car. McClendon walked back to Jamison's car, returned his documents through the passenger side of the car, and proceeded to have a conversation with Jamison without telling him that the EPIC search was clear. Because McClendon returned the documentation for Jamison's car and his driver's license, Jamison believed that he was free to leave. Officer McClendon's expectation was that Jamison would allow him to search the car.[67]

McClendon asked Jamison if he could search the car, to which Jamison replied "For what?" McClendon allegedly responded with questions about Jamison's profession—Jamison is a welder—and explained that he wanted "to search for illegal narcotics, weapons, large amounts of money, anything illegal." McClendon asserts that Jamison then gave him permission to search the car. Jamison disputes this account and alleges that first McClendon placed his hand "over the passenger door threshold" of Jamison's car, which effectively prevented Jamison from leaving, and asked to search his car for the first time. Jamison refused.[68] McClendon then asked to search the car four additional times; at each request Jamison refused. During the second request, Officer McClendon allegedly communicated that he had information that there were 10 kilos of cocaine in Jamison's car, which was not true. During McClendon's third request, Jamison and McClendon discussed how police officers sometimes plant evidence in suspects' cars. McClendon allegedly began patting the inside of the car through the passenger's side window during his fourth request.[69] The fifth request was an echo of the second, with McClendon emphasizing a phone call he had received about there being cocaine in Jamison's car. After Jamison's repeated refusals for the search and his denial that anything illegal was in the car, he tired of the colloquy between him and McClendon and allowed the officer to search the car, provided Jamison could see McClendon's actions.[70]

When Jamison exited the car, McClendon conducted a pat down search of his body and told him to stand in front of McClendon's patrol car where he could see the search. The search spanned "from the engine compartment to the trunk to the undercarriage to underneath the engine to the back seat to anywhere to account for all the voids inside the vehicle."[71] As the search proceeded, McClendon received a call from the NCIC dispatcher about a possible flag on Jamison's license that would suggest it was suspended. McClendon instructed the dispatcher to search Jamison's driving history, which also came back clear, although the timing of when McClendon received this information is unknown.[72] McClendon continued the search, allegedly all the while telling Jamison about the call concerning the cocaine and "[asserting] that the car was stolen, [asking] Jamison how many vehicles he owned, and [claiming] that Jamison did not have insurance on the car." McClendon did grant Jamison's requests to use the bathroom during the search but instructed him to stay in front of the patrol car when Jamison attempted to check on the car after hearing a loud sound. The search concluded with a check of the car by McClendon's police dog, who failed to uncover any hidden contraband. After Jamison searched the car for damage at McClendon's urging, the search concluded. It had taken 1 hour and 50 minutes.[73]

Mr. Jamison subsequently, in 2016, sued Officer McClendon and the City of Pelahatchie pursuant to title 42 of the United States Code, section 1983 on the following claims:

> [Claim 1:] Jamison alleged that the defendants violated his Fourth Amendment rights by "falsely stopping him, searching his car, and detaining him."
>
> [Claim 2:] Brought under the Fourteenth Amendment to the [U.S. Constitution] stated that the defendants should be held liable for using "race [as] a motivating factor in the decision to stop him, search his car, and detain him."
>
> [Claim 3:] Alleged a violation of the Fourth Amendment [to the U.S. Constitution] by Officer McClendon for "recklessly and deliberately causing significant damage to Mr. Jamison's car by conducting an unlawful search of the car in an objectively unreasonable manner amounting to an unlawful seizure of his property."[74]

Additionally, Jamison requested actual, compensatory, and punitive damages against McClendon for damage to his car, approximately $4,000, and for psychological harm he sustained as a result of the stop.[75] In Jamison's words:

> 'When I first got home, I couldn't sleep. So I was up for like—I didn't even sleep when I got home. I think I got some rest the next day because I was still mad just thinking about it and then when all this killing and stuff come on TV, that's like a flashback. I said, man, this could have went this way. It had me thinking all kind of stuff because it was not even called for ... Then I seen a story about the guy in South Carolina [Walter Scott], in Charleston, a busted taillight. They [police officers from the North Charleston Police Department] stopped him for that and shot him in the back, and that just went through my mind ... I don't even watch the news no more. I stopped watching the news because every time you turn it on something's bad.'[76]

On December 1, 2017, the City of Pelahatchie and Officer McClendon filed a motion for summary judgment, pursuant to Federal Rule of Civil Procedure 56, on grounds that no genuine issue of material fact existed to support Jamison's first two claims, and therefore judgment was required in their favor as a matter of law. During the time when the parties were briefing the issues to support the motion for summary judgment, they agreed to dismiss the City of Pelahatchie as a party to the lawsuit.[77]

The federal district court, a trial court, ruled on the motion on September 26, 2018, granting Officer McClendon summary judgment on Claim 2, the "racially motivated stop." Although the court found that Officer McClendon was protected by qualified immunity against Jamison's allegations in Claim 1, that he had no reasonable suspicion for the stop, it requested additional briefing on whether qualified immunity extended to protect McClendon against Jamison's allegations that he did not consent to the search and its length. Judge Reeves entered his opinion upon the completion of the briefing.[78]

The genre of a judicial opinion issued by a trial court is generally structured with the following parts:

Summary of the Case and Ruling: a summary of the case before the court, what the court is being asked to decide, and a brief statement of and explanation for its ruling on the matter.

Factual Background: the facts of the case as summarized, paraphrased, and quoted from pleadings, answers to interrogatories, depositions, and other documents in the record. This section contains background facts, as well as legally relevant facts.

Procedural History: the legal path the case took to arrive in the present court.

Legal Standard/Motion Standard of Review: the legal criteria by which a court can grant or deny various types of motions brought before or during a trial (*motion for summary judgment, motion to suppress, motion to dismiss, motion* in limine, *and so on*).

Issue: the question or questions that the court is tasked with resolving. In distilling the question for its review, the court is free to take the question as presented by the parties in their briefs or otherwise, or create a question or questions based on the same.

Analysis: the court builds an analytic framework from the appropriate and available sources for arguments, primarily case law as precedent, that articulates the legal criteria for resolving each issue before it. It then applies that framework to the relevant facts as stated in the **Factual Background** for each legal issue to arrive at conclusions for each.

Conclusion: An overall conclusion to the Issue before the court.

This structure is contextualized in the Western/Aristotelian analytic paradigm of IRAC (Issue, Rule, Analysis, Conclusion).

Judge Reeves's opinion proceeds along this structure with three main interventions, which interrupt the *nomos*, but, because of *stare decisis* surrounding the controlling rule, fail to capsize it in its entirety. The first intervention is beginning the case with a poem of his own creation, which places Mr. Jamison's experiences within the context of other Black children, women, and men who were stopped and killed by the police. His poem:

Clarence Jamison wasn't jaywalking [like Michael Brown].
He wasn't outside playing with a toy gun [like Tamir Rice].

He didn't look like a "suspicious person" [like Elijah McClain].
He wasn't suspected of "selling loose, untaxed cigarettes" [like Eric Garner].
He wasn't suspected of passing a counterfeit $20 bill [like George Floyd].
He didn't look like anyone suspected of a crime [like Philando Castile and Tony McDade].
He wasn't mentally ill and in need of help [like Jason Harrison].
He wasn't assisting an autistic patient who had wandered way from a group home [like Charles Kinsey].
He wasn't walking home from an after-school job [like James Earl Green].
He wasn't walking back from a restaurant [like Ben Brown].
He wasn't hanging out on a college campus [like Phillip Gibbs].
He wasn't standing outside of his apartment [like Amadou Diallo].
He wasn't inside of his apartment eating ice cream [like Botham Jean].
He wasn't sleeping in his bed [like Breonna Taylor].
He wasn't sleeping in his car [like Rayshard Brooks].
He didn't make an "improper lane change" [like Sandra Bland].
He didn't have a broken tail light [like Walter Scott].
He wasn't driving over the speed limit [like Hannah Fizer].
He wasn't driving under the speed limit [like Ace Perry].
No, Clarence Jamison was a Black man driving a Mercedes convertible.[79]

Judge Reeves's second intervention is to include the section "Historical Context," in which he traces the historical origins of Title 42 of the United States Code section 1983 in "A. Section 1983: A New Hope,"[80] and the court's backlash to that code provision through the creation of qualified immunity in "B. The Empire Strikes Back."[81] Both headings "A New Hope" and "The Empire Strikes Back" are a nod to the original *Star Wars* franchise, in which the resistance to the oppressive regime known as the Galactic Empire sees its hope in the newly identified but yet untrained Jedi knight Luke Skywalker (*A New Hope*), who the Empire, under the leadership of the draconian Darth Vader, swiftly seeks to destroy (*The Empire Strikes Back*). In Reeves's opinion, Section 1983 was the new hope for recently freed Black children, women, and men who in emancipation from enslavement faced the Ku Klux Klan, a White, domestic terrorist organization formed in 1866 for the sole purpose of destroying their forward progress. In Reeves's telling,

> The Ku Klux Klan, formed in 1866 by six [W]hite men in a Pulaski, Tennessee law office, "engaged in extreme violence against [the formerly enslaved] and Republicans [at this time the party of Abraham Lincoln, recently deceased]," assaulting and murdering its victims and destroying their property. The Klan "spread rapidly across the South" in 1868, orchestrating a "huge wave of murder and arson" to discourage [Black people] from voting. "[B]lack schools and churches were burned with impunity in North Carolina, Mississippi, and Alabama." The terrorism in Mississippi was unparalleled. During the first three months of 1870, 63 Black Mississippians "were murdered … And nobody served a day for these crimes." In 1872, the U.S. Attorney for Mississippi wrote that Klan violence was

ubiquitous and that "only the presence of the army kept the Klan from overrunning north Mississippi completely."[82]

Many of the perpetrators of the racial terror were members of law enforcement. It was a twisted law enforcement, though, as it prevented the laws of the era from being enforced. When the Klan murdered five witnesses in a pending case, one of Mississippi's District Attorneys complained, "I cannot get witnesses as all feel it is sure death to testify." White supremacists and the Klan "threatened to unravel everything ... Union soldiers had accomplished at great cost in blood and treasure."

***

Congress sought to respond to "the reign of terror imposed by the Klan upon black citizens and the sympathizers in the Southern States." It passed the Ku Klux Klan Act of 1871, which "targeted the racial violence in the South undertaken by the Klan, and the failure of the states to cope with that violence."[83]

The Act's mandate was expansive, Section 2 of the Act provided for civil and criminal sanctions against those who conspired to deprive people of the "equal protection of the laws. Sections 3 and 4 authorized the use of federal force to redress a state's inability or unwillingness to deal with Klan or other violence. The Act was strong medicine."[84]

Section 1 of the Ku Klux Klan Act, now codified as 42 U.S.C. [section] 1983, uniquely targeted state officials who "deprived persons of their constitutional rights." While the Act as a whole "had the Klan particularly in mind, Section 1 recognized the local officials who created 'the lawless conditions' that plagued 'the South in 1871.' Thus, the doors to the courthouse were opened to "any person who ha[d] been deprived of her federally protected rights by a defendant acting under color of state law." The Act reflected Congress's recognition that—to borrow the words of today's abolitionists—"the whole damn system [was] guilty as hell."[85]

In "Part B. The Empire Strikes Back," Reeves tells a parallel tale of how courts in the 20th century promptly set to undermining the aims of Section 1983 by constructing the doctrine of qualified immunity to shield law enforcement from its reach.[86]

Reeves's third intervention is his section "VI. The Return of Section 1983,"[87] again an allusion to the third installment of the *Star Wars* franchise "The Return of the Jedi," in which Luke Skywalker heads the resistance as a Jedi Knight against the Empire. Here, Reeves appeals to the Supreme Court's ability to abolish qualified immunity in the interests of justice, by hearkening back to its ruling in *Brown v. Board of Education* and offering it the precedential authority to do so with the case *Dulin v. Board of Commissioners of Greenwood Leflore Hospital*.[88] He explains:

Our nation has always struggled to realize the Founders' vision of "a more perfect Union." From the beginning, "the Blessings of Liberty" were not equally bestowed

> upon all Americans. Yet, as people marching in the streets remind us today, some have always stood up to face our nation's failings and remind us that "we cannot be patient." Through their efforts we become more perfect.
>
> The U.S. Congress of the Reconstruction era stood up to the [W]hite supremacists of its time when it passed Section 1983. The late Congressman John Lewis stared down the racists of his era when he marched over the Edmund Pettus Bridge. The Supreme Court has answered the call of history as well, most famously when it issued its decision in *Brown v. Board of Education* and resigned the "separate but equal" doctrine to the dustbin of history. The question of today is whether the Supreme Court will rise to the occasion and do the same with qualified immunity.[89]

What is striking in Reeves's "historical context" is that his narrative—detailing the conflict between the hope of Section 1983 and the judges who thwarted that promise by developing the qualified immunity doctrine—is fashioned separately from the legal analysis that ultimately resolves the case in McClendon's favor. In the section that follows "IV. Qualified Immunity Analysis,"[90] Judge Reeves comports with the Western/Aristotelian paradigm IRAC to build an analytical framework from the case precedent that upholds the qualified immunity doctrine to Mr. Jamison's detriment. Judge Reeves considers each issue relevant to the qualified immunity doctrine in turn—whether Deputy McClendon violated a statutory or constitutional right, and whether that violation was of a clearly established law about which McClendon would have known. Judge Reeves pauses briefly when dealing with the issues of whether McClendon's search of Jamison's car was unreasonably intrusive in violation of Fourth Amendment constitutional protections against unreasonable searches and seizures, and whether in this context Jamison's consent of the search was voluntary.[91] The legal standard to resolve the physical intrusion issue is "whether the officer's actions were no more intrusive than necessary to accomplish his objective."[92] In applying this standard to the facts of the case, Judge Reeves deemed McClendon's search unreasonable in violation of the Fourth Amendment. Given that McClendon's objective was to obtain Jamison's permission to search Jamison's car, it was not necessary for him to place his arm in the car and prevent Jamison's departure to accomplish this objective.[93]

Moving to the issue of consent, Judge Reeves articulates the following legal standard to determine the voluntariness of Jamison's consent: "(1) the voluntariness of the suspect's custodial status; (2) the presence of coercive police procedures; (3) the nature and extent of the suspect's cooperation; (4) the suspect's awareness of his right to refuse consent; (5) the suspect's education and intelligence; and (6) the suspect's belief that no incriminating evidence will be found." In this analysis, no single factor is determinative and courts consider other factors relevant to this inquiry.[94]

Finding three factors weighing in favor of Jamison (1, 2, and 3) and three in favor of McClendon (4, 5, and 6), Judge Reeves reasons that there exists an issue of material fact as to whether the search was voluntary.[95] However, after he makes this determination and concludes his reasoning on this issue, he turns to the "other factors relevant to the inquiry." Now in direct conversation with the reader of the opinion, Reeves opines:

> A reader would be forgiven for pausing here and wondering whether we forgot to mention something. When in this analysis will the Court look at the elephant in the room—how race may have played a role in whether Officer McClendon's actions were coercive?
>
> Jamison was a Black man driving through Mississippi, a state known for the violent deaths of Black people and others who fought for their freedom. Pelahatchie is an hour south of Philadelphia, a town made infamous after a different kind of traffic stop that resulted in the brutal lynching of James Chaney, Michael Schwerner, and Andrew Goodman [the three Civil Rights activists who were in Mississippi to register Black people to vote]. Pelahatchie is less than 30 minutes east of Jackson, where on June 26, 2011, a handful of young [W]hite men and women engaged in some old-fashioned Redemption and murdered James Craig Anderson, a 47-year-old Black, gay man. Pelahatchie is also in Rankin County, the same county the young people called home. Only a few miles separate the two communities.
>
> For Black people, this isn't merely history. It's the present.[96]
>
> By the time Jamison was pulled over, more than 600 people had been killed by police officers in 2013 alone. Jamison was stopped just 16 days after the man who killed Trayvon Martin was acquitted. On that day, Alicia Garza [a co-founder of Black Lives Matter] wrote a Facebook post that said, "Black people. I love you. I love us. We matter. Our lives matter. Black lives matter." And that week, "thousands of demonstrators gathered in dozens of cities" to commemorate Martin "and to add their voices to a debate on race that his death ... set off." A movement was in its early stages that would shine a light on killings by police and police brutality writ large—a problem Black people have endured since "states replaced slave patrols with police officers who enforced Black Codes."
>
> Jamison's traffic stop cannot be separated from this context. Black people in this country are acutely aware of the danger traffic stops pose to Black lives. Police encounters happen regardless of station in life or standing in the community; to Black doctors, judges, and legislators alike. United States Senator Tim Scott was pulled over seven times in one year—and has even been stopped while a member of what many refer to as "the world's greatest deliberative body." The "vast majority" of the stops were the result of "nothing more than driving a new car in the wrong neighborhood or some other reason just as trivial."[97]
>
> The situation is not getting better. The number of people killed by police each year has stayed relatively constant, and Black people remain at disproportionate risk of dying in an encounter with police. It was all the way

> back in 1968 when Nina Simone famously said that freedom meant "no fear! I mean really, no fear!" Yet decades later, Black male teens still report "a fear of police and a serious concern for their personal safety and mortality in the presence of police officers."
>
> In an America where Black people "are considered dangerous even when they are in their living rooms eating ice cream [Botham Jean], asleep in their beds [Breonna Taylor], playing in the park [Tamir Rice], standing in the pulpit of a church [Clementa C. Pinckney], birdwatching [Christian Cooper], exercising in public [Ahmaud Arbery], or walking home from a trip to the store to purchase a bag of Skittles [Trayvon Martin]," who can say that Jamison felt free that night on the side of Interstate 20? Who can say that he felt free to say no to an armed Officer McClendon?
>
> It was in this context that Officer McClendon repeatedly lied to Jamison. It was in this moment that Officer McClendon intruded into Jamison's car. It was upon this history that Jamison said he was tired. These circumstances point to Jamison's consent being involuntary, a situation where he felt he had "no alternative to compliance" and merely mouthed "pro forma words of consent."[98]

Although compelling, this reasoning takes place outside of the analytic framework concerning the voluntariness of Jamison's consent. While Judge McClendon ends his reasoning in this section with the statement "Accordingly, Officer McClendon's search of Clarence Jamison's vehicle violated the Fourth Amendment,"[99] he had already stated the same prior to his analysis on the issue of consent in the subsection preceding it titled "Physical Intrusion." By offering this commentary after his formal reasoning in the Western/Aristotelian paradigm had taken place for the issue of consent, Judge Reeves failed to make race key in the Fourth Amendment jurisprudence for whether a person's consent to a search of their vehicle is voluntary.

Ultimately Judge Reeves rules for McClendon by answering no to the issue as he frames it: "whether it was clearly established that an officer who has made five sequential requests for consent to search a car, lied, promised leniency, and placed his arm inside of a person's car during a traffic stop while awaiting background check results has violated the Fourth Amendment."[100] He arrives at a legal conclusion determined by the racialized *nomos*—even as he rails against the injustices of the qualified immunity doctrine, he renders himself unable to change it despite identifying and giving time to effort to explaining the context and tools for doing so. In his words,

> That the Justices [of the United States Supreme Court] haven't acted so far is perhaps understandable. Not only would they likely prefer that Congress fixes the problem, they also value *stare decisis*, the legal principle that means "fidelity to precedent." *Stare decisis*, however, "isn't supposed to be the art of methodically ignoring what everyone knows to be true." From TikTok to the chambers of the

> Supreme Court, there is increasing consensus that qualified immunity poses a major problem to our system of justice.[101]

Judge Reeves concludes:

> Earlier this year, the [Supreme] Court explained something true about wearing the robe: "Every judge must learn to live with the fact that he or she will make some mistakes; it comes with the territory. But it is something else entirely to perpetuate something we all know to be wrong only because we fear the consequences of being right." Let us waste no time righting this wrong.[102]

In this context, the robe is the court, and its authority to act to uphold the rule of law is to be disjointed from justice.

Discussion questions

1. Judge Reeves frames the issue in this case as "whether it was clearly established that an officer who has made five sequential requests for consent to search a car, lied, promised leniency, and placed his arm inside of a person's car during a traffic stop while awaiting background check results has violated the Fourth Amendment." Does this framing, particularly with respect to the legally significant facts listed, signal to the reader a departure from or adherence to the racialized *nomos*? Please explain your answer.
2. In what ways does Judge Reeves supplement the factual account of Mr. Jamison's interactions with Officer McClendon?
3. Does the additional factual context that Judge Reeves offers alter which facts he deems relevant for the purposes of legal analysis? Please explain your answer.
4. From which legal authority does Judge Reeves draw the concepts with which he builds the legal framework or rules by which he analyzes the relevant facts of Mr. Jamison's case?
5. Judge Reeves introduces the reader to legal authority that he ultimately does not use in his analytic framework for Mr. Jamison's case. How are his choices not to use the authority guided and constrained by the racialized *nomos*?
6. Is the authority that Judge Reeves declines to use relevant given how he frames the issue in Mr. Jamison's case? Please explain your answer.
7. Is the authority that Judge Reeves declines use relevant to resolve Mr. Jamison's case? If it is relevant, is it useful to resolve Mr. Jamison's case? Please explain your answer.

Crafting justice based on the lived legal experiences of people of color: Washington v. San Kim Sum

The chasm between the rule of law and justice, visible in *Jamison v. McClendon*, need not exist. This was recently demonstrated by the Washington State Supreme Court in its ruling in *Washington v. San Kim Sum* on whether a person has been seized unlawfully by the police in violation of the Washington State Constitution for the purposes of adjudicating a motion to suppress. Mr. Sum, an Asian/Pacific Islander, came under the scrutiny of Officer Mark Rickerson, a Pierce County Sheriff's Deputy, while Rickerson was on patrol in an unmarked police car. It was Rickerson's practice to patrol in a place where there were "some problem houses" that he wanted to "keep an eye on."[103] At the time of his encounter with the Sheriff, Mr. Sum was in a Honda Civic and parked legally, in close proximity to an entrance gate of a church parking lot.[104] Rickerson's interest in this location was piqued, because one of his co-workers had made an arrest of a person in a stolen vehicle in the same location approximately four months prior.[105] Also during this time, a person from the community had approached Rickerson in a grocery store parking lot near the church to inform him of cars in the lot that were not from the neighborhood.[106]

When Rickerson came upon Sum, he was sitting in the driver's seat with another male passenger in the car. Rickerson parked his car in a manner that "[left] enough room so as not to block the Honda Civic or prevent it from leaving."[107] According to Rickerson, both Sum and his passenger "appeared to be unconscious and did not notice [him] approach."[108] Before engaging either man, Rickerson first conducted a check on the Honda's license plates, which revealed that the car had not been reported stolen and that the Honda had been sold.[109] The name of the new owner was not available. Rickerson also checked the VIN number to see if it matched the license plates and found no discrepancy. He then walked toward the car on the driver's side and knocked on the window.[110]

When Mr. Sum awoke, he saw a police officer in full uniform through the window and rolled down his window a crack. Rickerson asked Sum what the two were doing parked in the current location, to which Sum replied "we were waiting for a friend." Rickerson asked Sum who owned the car, and Sum responded that he was not the owner.[111] However, he did give Rickerson the first name of the owner, after which Rickerson asked for identification from both men. Sum inquired why Rickerson wanted their identification, and Rickerson replied "that [they] were sitting in an area known for stolen vehicles and that [Sum] did not appear to know to whom the vehicle he was sitting in belonged." Sum and his passenger provided Rickerson with their names and dates of birth—Sum's information was false; his passenger's was true.[112]

While Rickerson was in his car checking each man's identification, Sum sped away from the scene.[113] Thus began a high-speed car chase complete with flashing police lights, which ended when Sum crashed into a neighborhood yard. At the conclusion of the chase, Rickerson arrested Sum, informed him of his *Miranda* rights, and searched

Sum and his car, the latter of which revealed the title and registration documents. The car was registered to Sum, and the title indicated that he had purchased the car two weeks prior. During a pat down search of Sum's person, Rickerson discovered an empty gun holster in his pants. When the officer obtained a warrant to search the car, the search yielded a pistol.[114]

Sum was subsequently charged with "unlawful possession of a firearm in the first degree, attempting to elude a pursuing police vehicle, and making a false or misleading statement to a public servant."[115] Sum answered these charges with a motion to suppress all evidence against him following his seizure by Officer Rickerson. In support of its proposition that Sum's seizure was lawful, the State argued:

> [T]hat Sum was not seized until Rickerson illuminated his emergency lights[;] [and] that by that time, Rickerson had a reasonable suspicion sufficient to justify detaining Sum because (1) Sum was parked in a high-crime area, (2) stolen cars had been recovered from the same location in the past, (3) Sum told Rickerson that the vehicle he was sitting in did not belong to him, (4) when asked who the car belonged to, Sum provided only a first name, and (5) after Rickerson returned to his car to run Sum's identification information, Sum drove off at a high rate of speed.[116]

After a hearing, the trial court denied Sum's motion and stated its legal conclusions in relevant part:

> The facts that Defendant then told Rickerson that the vehicle in which he was sitting did not belong to him, that he could not fully identify the owner of that vehicle, and, to a lesser extent, the fact that the location in which Defendant had parked was a high-crime area from which stolen vehicles had been recovered, were specific and articulable facts which would lead one to believe that there was a substantial possibility that criminal conduct had occurred, and hence, justified a [police stop in accordance with *Terry v. Ohio*] of [Mr. Sum] which rendered Rickerson's request for Defendant and his passenger to identify themselves lawful and reasonable.
>
> Because Rickerson did not retain [Mr. Sum's] physical identification to conduct his records check, Defendant was not seized when Rickerson asked him to identify himself, and Defendant's present motion to suppress evidence obtained thereafter as a product of unlawful seizure is therefore denied, and such evidence is admissible.[117]

Sum's case proceeded to trial, where he was found guilty on all the charges in the indictment. The guilty verdict was due primarily to the State's argument that he made "a false or misleading statement to a public servant based on the false identity information he provided to Rickerson."[118] Sum then appealed the trial court's denial of his motion to suppress, specifically as to whether the trial court's admission of his false statement to

Rickerson about his identity was improper, given that the reason Rickerson requested the information was that he suspected Sum of car theft. Sum argued that given Rickerson's actions it was reasonable for him to believe that he was suspected of criminal activity, and therefore "believe that ignoring the officer's requests, terminating the encounter, or leaving the scene were not viable options."[119]

The Washington State Court of Appeals upheld the trial court opinion. It found that under the totality of the circumstances, Sum's seizure did not occur when Rickerson asked for his identification on the suspicion that Rickerson had committed car theft. Rather it deemed Officer Rickerson's engagement with Sum a "social contact," or activity that "exists someplace between an officer's saying 'hello' to a stranger on the street and, at the other end of the spectrum, an investigative detention."[120] In the court's judgment, Rickerson purposely did not block Sum's car from leaving the scene, did not persist in questioning him about the car's ownership, and initially was drawn to check on Sun out of concern for his welfare.[121] Drawing on the precedential authority of Washington State courts to determine the scope of activity considered a seizure, the Court of Appeals reasoned that:

> the threatening presence of several officers, the display of a weapon by an officer, some physical touching of the person of the citizen, or the use of language or tone of voice indicating that compliance with the officer's request might be compelled. Without evidence of this nature, "otherwise inoffensive contact between a member of the public and the police cannot, as a matter of law, amount to a seizure of that person." Not every interaction between a police officer and an individual rises to the level of a seizure such that the individual's rights under article I, section 7 [of the Washington State Constitution] become implicated.[122]

Notably, the Court of Appeals declined to publish its opinion pursuant to the Revised Code of Washington section 2.06.040, which provides that a judicial panel hearing a case may decline to publish its opinion if it lacks precedential value.[123]

Mr. Sum appealed the Court Appeals decision to the Washington State Supreme Court. Like the opinion in *McClendon*, the genre for its decision is a judicial opinion that follows the same general structure outlined for the same. It is also contextualized in the Western/Aristotelian analytic paradigm of IRAC. However, the signature intervention of this opinion is that it expands the analytic framework in the *Sum* case to make Mr. Sum's race and ethnicity part and parcel of the applicable legal standard required to resolve the issue before it: "When did Sum's interaction with Deputy Rickerson rise to the level of a warrantless seizure."[124] As the court explained:

> Today, we are asked whether "all the circumstances" of the encounter includes the race and ethnicity of the allegedly seized person. As the parties correctly agree, the answer is yes. Our precedent has always required that the seizure inquiry be made in light of the totality of the circumstances, and we have never stated that race and ethnicity cannot be relevant circumstances. However, we have

> not explicitly held that in interactions with law enforcement, race and ethnicity matter. We do so today. Furthermore, to ensure that all of the circumstances of a law enforcement encounter are properly considered, including race and ethnicity, we take this opportunity to clarify the seizure inquiry as a matter of **independent state law**, taking guidance from [Washington State Court Rules General Rule 37, concerning peremptory strikes exercised on the basis of a juror's race or ethnicity].
>
> As set forth in this court's precedent, the seizure inquiry is an objective test in which the allegedly seized person has the burden to show that a seizure occurred. To aid courts in the application of this test, we now clarify that a person is seized for the purposes of article I, section 7 [of the Washington State Constitution] if, based on the totality of the circumstances, an objective observer could conclude that the person was not free to leave, to refuse a request, or to otherwise terminate the encounter due to law enforcement's display of authority or use of physical force. **For the purposes of this analysis, an objective observer is aware that implicit, institutional, and unconscious biases, in addition to purposeful discrimination, have resulted in disproportionate police contacts, investigative seizures, and uses of force against Black, Indigenous, and other People of Color (BIPOC) in Washington.** Finally, in accordance with our precedent, if the person shows there was a seizure, then the burden shifts to the State to prove that seizure was lawfully justified by a warrant or an applicable exception to the warrant requirement.
>
> Based on the totality of the circumstances presented in this case, we hold that petitioner [Sum] was seized when a sheriff's deputy requested Sum's identification while implying that Sum was under investigation for car theft. As the State properly concedes, at that time, the deputy did not have a warrant, reasonable suspicion, or any other lawful authority to seize Sum. As a result, Sum was unlawfully seized, and the false name and birthdate he gave to the deputy must be suppressed.[125] (Emphasis added)

In building its analytic framework to support this ruling, the court looked to its legal requirements for conducting an independent state law analysis based on its state constitutional provisions. The guiding standard is "whether the unique characteristics of the state constitutional provision and its prior interpretations actually compel a particular result."[126] The factors the court considers when conducting such an inquiry are (1) the text of the constitutional provision at issue, (2) the relevant common law and statutory treatment of the constitutional interest at issue historically; and (3) the consequences for failing to recognize or recognizing the interest.[127] With respect to article I, section 7 of the Washington State Constitution, the court found that its guarantee of privacy rights to Washingtonians had "no express limitations."[128] Although the court did find Washington's historical record lacking in protecting the civil rights of BIPOC "deplorable," it also found that history to be evolving.[129] In its words "history is not a static factor in our analysis. Every decision of this court makes new history, in which we are 'constantly striving for better.' "[130]

With this declaration, the court recognized the epistemic, meaning-making nature of its decision, specifically its obligation to include the experiences of people of color as it evaluates and refines legal standards. As to the last factor, the court declared race and ethnicity relevant to "how the person was brought into the criminal justice system in the first place."[131] Key in this determination is that in Washington State, the question of whether a seizure occurred is an objective consideration "looking to the actions of the law enforcement officer."[132] In Washington State, an objective observer "is aware that implicit, institutional, and unconscious biases, in additional to purposeful discrimination," have resulted in "many injustices against BIPOC, particularly in the criminal justice system."[133] The court's reasoning is significant here, because congruent with the guidance of its general court rule for peremptory challenges (GR 37), allegations of discriminatory conduct are not required to be proven through statistical or other evidence of racial discrimination.[134] On the contrary, weaving together Supreme Court Justice Sonya Sotomayor's dissenting opinion in *Utah v. Streiff* with its own, the court stated that:

> when it comes to police encounters without reasonable suspicion, "it is no secret that people of color are disproportionate victims of this type of scrutiny." Indeed our own GR 37 recognizes the disproportionate police contacts experienced by BIPOC and provides that factors such as "having prior contact with law enforcement officers"; "expressing a distrust of law enforcement or a belief that law enforcement officers engage in racial profiling"; "having a close relationship with people who have been stopped, arrested, or convicted of a crime"; and "living in a high-crime neighborhood" are all "presumptively invalid reasons for a peremptory challenge." All such factors have historically "been associated with improper discrimination in jury selection."[135]
>
> As a result, the relevance of race and ethnicity in the seizure inquiry cannot turn on whether there has been recent, well-publicized discrimination and violence by law enforcement directed at individuals of the same race or ethnicity as the allegedly seized person. Instead, we must be cognizant that "[f]or generations, [B]lack and [B]rown parents have given their children 'the talk'—instructing them never to run down the street; always keep your hands where they can be seen; do not even think of talking back to a stranger—all out of fear for how an officer with a gun will react to them." Simply put, a person's race or ethnicity does not become relevant with media reports of targeted police discrimination or violence, nor does it become irrelevant in the temporary absence of such reports.[136]
>
> Similarly, requiring an allegedly seized person to produce statistics showing precisely how their race and ethnicity should be factored into the seizure analysis would artificially raise their burden, while unjustly ignoring the "pain, suffering, and distrust that statistics fail to capture." Statistics, like media reports, may add weight to the impact of race or ethnicity in particular cases. However, a lack of statistics cannot totally negate the relevance of a person's race or ethnicity

> because statistical data are limited by the manner and means in which they are collected.[137]
>
> Some statistical limitations are particularly relevant to Sum's case. For instance, "[a]t times, 'Asian' is used by reporting agencies or groups as an umbrella designation that includes Native Hawaiians and other Pacific Islanders." Therefore, while some aggregated data show that "Asians" are less likely to be subjected to police force, "individuals who are Native Hawaiians and Other Pacific Islanders are 3.3 times more likely than a White person to be killed by police. Statistics also may fail to include non-English speakers, resulting in data that 'may not be representative of the overall U.S. Asian population.' "
>
> Thus holding that a person's race and ethnicity are irrelevant unless the person produces statistics showing a pattern of targeted police discrimination or violence would reinforce the same systemic inequalities that prevent such statistics from being reliably compiled in the first instance. **History has shown that when courts create "crippling" legal burdens to recognizing the constitutional rights of BIPOC, their lived experiences are unjustly disregarded, and their rights go unprotected. We decline the invitation to impose such burdens here.**[138] (Emphasis added)

The court reiterated that its reasoning framework was not a repudiation of its existing precedent, but a clarification of what is to be considered within it—namely the lived experiences of people of color and their interactions with law enforcement.[139] In the court's analysis, a reasonable person includes the lived experiences of people of color. To further emphasize this point, the court proceeded to recount the facts of the case from Mr. Sum's perspective,[140] and apply its expanded analytic framework to those facts to resolve the issue in Mr. Sum's favor.[141] This part of the Court's opinion is discussed in detail in Chapter 4.

Discussion questions

1. Whose experiences does the trial court center in the factual account of Mr. Sum's interactions with Deputy Rickerson?
2. How does the trial court's choice of who to center shape the outcome of Mr. Sum's case?
3. How are both the trial and appellate court's decisions about which facts are and are not legally relevant in determining when and whether Mr. Sum was seized guided by the racialized *nomos*?
4. What is the implied meaning of the Court of Appeals' choice not to publish its decision in the *Sum* case on grounds that it lacked precedential value?

5. The Washington Supreme Court frames the issue in the case as "when did Sum's interaction with Deputy Rickerson rise to the level of a warrantless seizure." Does this framing signal to the reader a departure from or adherence to the racialized *nomos*? Please explain your answer.
6. From which authority does the Washington Supreme Court draw the concepts with which it builds the legal framework or rules by which it analyzes the relevant facts of Mr. Sum's case?
7. Does the authority that it uses differ from or remain the same as the authority used by the trial and appellate courts? In what ways?
8. Whose experiences does the Washington Supreme Court choose to center in the factual account of Mr. Sum's interactions with Deputy Rickerson?
9. How does the Washington Supreme Court's choice of who to center shape the outcome of Mr. Sum's case?

Conclusion: the need to critically engage with legal genres and analytic paradigms and to infuse legal reasoning with inclusive frameworks

The Washington State Supreme Court's ruling in *Sum* is distinguishable in several key ways from Judge Reeves's decision in *McClendon*. At issue in *Sum* was the prohibition against unlawful seizures under the Washington State Constitution, which gives more protections to Washingtonians than the United States Constitution gives to U.S. residents and citizens. In *McClendon*, the court considered the legal interpretations, both by the federal circuit courts and the United States Supreme Court, of 42 U.S.C. 1983, a legislative intervention to protect recently freed people of African descent from the terrorism of the Ku Klux Klan. It also considered the constitutionality, under the United States Constitution, of McClendon's stop of Jamison and search of his car under the Fourth Amendment's protections against unreasonable searches and seizures. The Washington State opinion was issued by a state Supreme Court, the greatest charge to which is to interpret the constitution of its state. In Washington State, Supreme Court Judges are elected for six-year terms and must retire at the age of 75. Judge Reeves is a judge in a U.S. District Court, a trial court, charged with "resolving disputes by determining the facts and applying legal principles to decide who is right."[142] U.S. District Court judges are appointed by the President of the United States, confirmed by the Senate, and then enjoy a lifetime appointment unless impeached.

What is problematic about these opinions is the inconsistency in their evaluation of the relevance of people of color's lived experiences. Black people are Black in states other than Mississippi and Asian people are Asian outside of Washington State. However, in Washington State, McClendon's actions as a White police officer toward Jamison, a Black man, would have been judged by a standard that respected the historical struggles between law enforcement and Black communities, and regarded Jamison's stop in light of them. The dispensation of justice cannot depend on the will of a judge or panel of judges to utilize the Western/Aristotelian analytic paradigm in a manner that serves justice—Judge Reeves's opinion demonstrates the inability of the paradigm to do so.

The one constant for jurists and lawyers is how they learn to draft legal genres and engage in legal reasoning and analysis throughout their legal education. The structure and function of state and federal court systems is not within the authority of legal educators, but we can formalize instruction on (1) how analytical paradigms shift given the historical and cultural imperatives of the groups impacted by the decisionmaking; and (2) how to use the formal strategies offered to us by non-White racial groups to build, expand, and remake analytic frameworks that serve the interests of justice to benefit us all. The formal strategies, multicultural rhetorics, are the focus of Chapter 4.

Notes

1 McMurtry-Chubb, 2018, pp 889, 895.
2 McMurtry-Chubb, 2018, pp 889, 895.
3 President's Advisory 1776 Commission, 2021, p 6.
4 U.S. Const. pmbl., www.archives.gov/founding-docs/constitution-transcript.
5 U.S. Const. amend. I–X, www.archives.gov/founding-docs/bill-of-rights-transcript.
6 President's Advisory 1776 Commission, 2021, p 6.
7 President's Advisory 1776 Commission, 2021, p 6.
8 Silverstein and Hannah-Jones, 2019.
9 Divisive Concepts Act HB 312 2022 (Alabama).
10 Stop W.O.K.E. Act HB 7 2022 (Florida).
11 Divisive Concepts Act HB 888 2022 (Georgia).
12 Dignity and Nondiscrimination in Public Education Act HB 377 2021 (Idaho).
13 Act Providing for Requirements Related to Racism or Sexism Trainings at, and Diversity and Inclusion Efforts by, Governmental Agencies and Entities, School Districts, and Public Postsecondary Educational Institutions HB 802 2021 (Iowa).
14 Act Relating to Public Education and Declaring an Emergency HB 18 2021 (Kentucky).
15 Prohibited Funding for Divisive Concepts Act SB 2113 2022 (Mississippi).
16 Prohibition on Critical Race Theory and Antiracism Atty. Gen. Op. 1 2021 (Montana).
17 Divisive Concepts Act HB 544 2021 (New Hampshire).
18 Bill for an Act Prohibiting the Teaching of Critical Race Theory in Public Schools HB 1508 2021 (North Dakota).
19 Divisive Concepts Act HB 1775 2021 (Oklahoma).
20 Bill to Amend the Laws of South Carolina to Prohibit Instruction in Critical Race Theory and Related Instruction HB 4325 2021 (South Carolina).
21 An Act to Protect Students from Critical Race Theory HB 1012 2022 (South Dakota).
22 Divisive Concepts Act HB 580 2021 (Tennessee).
23 An Act Relating to the Social Studies Curriculum in Public Schools HB 3979 2021 (Texas).
24 Senate Resolution on Critical Race Theory in Public Education S.R. 901 2021 (Utah).

25 Prohibition on Teaching Declared Unlawful and Discriminatory HB 787 2022 (Virginia).
26 Stout and Wilburn, nd.
27 Divisive Concepts Act HB 888 2022 (Georgia), pp 2.
28 Divisive Concepts Act HB 580 2021 (Tennessee), pp 6–7.
29 *Pernell v. Florida Board of Governors of the State University System*, No. Order Granting in Part and Denying in Part Motions for Preliminary Injunction, 4:22cv304-MW/MAF (N.D. Fla. November 17, 2022).
30 *Pernell v. Florida Board of Governors of the State University System*, No. Order Granting in Part and Denying in Part Motions for Preliminary Injunction, 4:22cv304 MW/MAF (N.D. Fla. November 17, 2022), pp 2–3.
31 Stop W.O.K.E. Act HB 7 2022 (Florida).
32 Citizens for Renewing America, 2021.
33 Manhattan Institute, 2021.
34 PREP, 2022.
35 McMurtry-Chubb, 2018, p 895.
36 President's Advisory 1776 Commission, 2021, p 6.
37 Monroe, 1818.
38 Indian Civilization Fund Act 1819.
39 Indian Civilization Fund Act 1819.
40 Indian Removal Act 1830.
41 Thornton, 1984, pp 293, 296–8.
42 Bethune, 1831.
43 See generally Williams, 1989.
44 21 U.S. 543 (1823).
45 30 U.S. 1 (1831).
46 31 U.S. 515 (1832).
47 U.S. Const. amend. art. IV, § 2, cl. 3, www.senate.gov/civics/constitution_item/constitution.htm#a4_sec2.
48 Fugitive Slave Act 1850.
49 Fugitive Slave Act 1850.
50 Fugitive Slave Act 1850; see generally, Eggert, 1985.
51 Eggert, 1985; Horton and Horton, 1993.
52 Klein, 1996, p 201.
53 California Land Act of 1851.
54 Takaki, 2008, pp 192–3.
55 Nationality Act 1790.
56 Diamond, 2020.
57 Reed, 1924.
58 Hudson 1924.
59 Hudson, 1924.
60 Racial Integrity Act 1924 (Virginia).
61 388 U.S. 1 (1967).
62 2020 WL 4497723.
63 *Jamison*, 2020 WL 4497723 at *2.
64 *Jamison*, 2020 WL 4497723 at *2.
65 *Jamison*, 2020 WL 4497723 at *2.
66 *Jamison*, 2020 WL 4497723 at *2–3.
67 *Jamison*, 2020 WL 4497723 at *3.
68 *Jamison*, 2020 WL 4497723 at *3.
69 *Jamison*, 2020 WL 4497723 at *3.
70 *Jamison*, 2020 WL 4497723 at *3.

[71] *Jamison*, 2020 WL 4497723 at *3–4.
[72] *Jamison*, 2020 WL 4497723 at *4.
[73] *Jamison*, 2020 WL 4497723 at *4.
[74] *Jamison*, 2020 WL 4497723 at *4.
[75] *Jamison*, 2020 WL 4497723 at *4.
[76] *Jamison*, 2020 WL 4497723 at *5.
[77] *Jamison*, 2020 WL 4497723 at *5.
[78] *Jamison*, 2020 WL 4497723 at *5.
[79] *Jamison*, 2020 WL 4497723 at *1–.
[80] *Jamison*, 2020 WL 4497723 at *5–.
[81] *Jamison*, 2020 WL 4497723 at *8–.
[82] *Jamison*, 2020 WL 4497723 at *6.
[83] *Jamison*, 2020 WL 4497723 at *7.
[84] *Jamison*, 2020 WL 4497723 at *7.
[85] *Jamison*, 2020 WL 4497723 at *7.
[86] *Jamison*, 2020 WL 4497723 at *8–.
[87] *Jamison*, 2020 WL 4497723 at *18.
[88] *Jamison*, 2020 WL 4497723 at *18–.
[89] *Jamison*, 2020 WL 4497723 at *18.
[90] *Jamison*, 2020 WL 4497723 at *12–.
[91] *Jamison*, 2020 WL 4497723 at *13.
[92] *Jamison*, 2020 WL 4497723 at *13.
[93] *Jamison*, 2020 WL 4497723 at *13.
[94] *Jamison*, 2020 WL 4497723 at *14–.
[95] *Jamison*, 2020 WL 4497723 at *14–.
[96] *Jamison*, 2020 WL 4497723 at *15.
[97] *Jamison*, 2020 WL 4497723 at *15–.
[98] *Jamison*, 2020 WL 4497723 at *16.
[99] *Jamison*, 2020 WL 4497723 at *16.
[100] *Jamison*, 2020 WL 4497723 at *16.
[101] *Jamison*, 2020 WL 4497723 at *18.
[102] *Jamison*, 2020 WL 4497723 at *21.
[103] 2022 WL 2071560, at *3 (Wash. June 9, 2022).
[104] *Sum*, 2022 WL 2071560 at *3.
[105] *Sum*, 2022 WL 2071560 at *4.
[106] *Sum*, 2022 WL 2071560 at *4.
[107] *Sum*, 2022 WL 2071560 at *4.
[108] *Sum*, 2022 WL 2071560 at *5.
[109] *Sum*, 2022 WL 2071560 at *4,* 6.
[110] *Sum*, 2022 WL 2071560 at *4.
[111] *Sum*, 2022 WL 2071560 at *5.
[112] *Sum*, 2022 WL 2071560 at *5.
[113] *Sum*, 2022 WL 2071560 at *5–6.
[114] *Sum*, 2022 WL 2071560 at * 6.
[115] *Sum*, 2022 WL 2071560 at *6.
[116] *Sum*, 2021 WL 1382608.
[117] *Sum*, 2021 WL 1382608.
[118] *Sum*, 2021 WL 1382608.
[119] *Sum*, 2021 WL 1382608.
[120] *Sum*, 2021 WL 1382608.
[121] *Sum*, 2021 WL 1382608.

[122] *Sum*, 2021 WL 1382608.
[123] *Sum*, 2021 WL 1382608 at *7.
[124] *Sum*, 2021 WL 1382608 at *8.
[125] *Sum*, 2022 WL 2071560 at *2–3.
[126] *Sum*, 2022 WL 2071560 at *13.
[127] *Sum*, 2022 WL 2071560 at *13.
[128] *Sum*, 2022 WL 2071560 at *13.
[129] *Sum*, 2022 WL 2071560 at *14.
[130] *Sum*, 2022 WL 2071560 at *14.
[131] *Sum*, 2022 WL 2071560 at *16.
[132] *Sum*, 2022 WL 2071560 at *18.
[133] *Sum*, 2022 WL 2071560 at *18.
[134] *Sum*, 2022 WL 2071560 at *18.
[135] *Sum*, 2022 WL 2071560 at *19–20.
[136] *Sum*, 2022 WL 2071560 at *20–1.
[137] *Sum*, 2022 WL 2071560 at *21.
[138] *Sum*, 2022 WL 2071560 at *22.
[139] *Sum*, 2022 WL 2071560 at *24–5; *28–9; *32–3.
[140] *Sum*, 2022 WL 2071560 at *33–4.
[141] *Sum*, 2022 WL 2071560 at *35–6.
[142] United States Courts, nd.

4

Multicultural Rhetorics

The making of multicultural legal reasoning and analytic paradigms

As discussed in the previous chapters, legal rhetoric operates to inculcate White cultural hegemony into our reasoning and analytic processes for resolving legal problems—how we "do" law. It makes its racialized tools normative and renders them neutral through its failure to acknowledge their origins in Western epistemologies and ontologies that idolize and protect imperialism, capitalism, White supremacy, and patriarchy. The lens through which legal rhetoric views the landscape of legal conflict is focused on White racial and cultural experiences. These experiences are rendered monolithic in the machinations of legal reasoning and analysis insomuch as they become synonymous with the maintenance of power in White supremacist terms—White cultural hegemony. This singular focus renders historic and contemporaneous cultural experiences blurry and unformed, when in fact, Indigenous, Black, Latine, and Asian communities have forged formal rhetorical traditions imbued with their culture and experiences in the United States that are more than adequate to widen that lens. These rhetorical traditions can be contained under the banner of what critical rhetorician Aaron David Gresson III describes as "recovery rhetorics."[1] Recovery rhetorics are marked by

> (4) (1) a motive to recover something perceived as lost through violation, failure, or betrayal; (2) the use of narrative to describe a discovery with inferred relevance for both one's own and the Other's ability to deal better with duplicity and uncertainty; and (3) an implicit invitation to identify with and accept the liberative powers of that discovery.[2]

In the law, the liberative powers of that discovery lead us to utilize multicultural reasoning and analytic paradigms as tools in the service of justice outside of norms calibrated to White cultural hegemony. These paradigms can help us to build a legal system, the goal of which is not to preserve unequal power relationships, but to facilitate an interracial code of conduct guided by respect, acknowledgment, and a commitment to make right historic and ongoing wrongs.

However, in learning these paradigms and their possibilities, we would be remiss to stop at their integration into existing inequitable paradigms; the Reeves Opinion, discussed in Chapters 2 and 3, makes the folly of that exercise evident. Rather, our charge is to use them to change the way we "do" law to create equitable problem-solving frameworks that work for us all. Each of the rhetorical traditions discussed in the sections that follow lead us toward what rhetorician Mark Lawrence McPhail describes as the rhetoric of coherence, in that they

> (1) [offer] an alternative epistemology to the foundationalism and externalism of Western thought, one that acknowledges the role of subjective conviction; (2) [affirm] concrete personal experience or personal acceptance as the final arbiter justifying true belief; and (3) [call] for the minimizing of inconsistencies as necessary to achieve an accurate connection between mind and material experience.[3]

The different rhetorical strategies offered by these traditions aid us in creating oppositional discourse—"discourse that engages 'the dominant culture's language, idiom, and rhetoric' while advancing the writer's cultural concerns."[4]

Formal instruction in the reasoning and analytic tools that these traditions give to us is important. Without it, law students who become lawyers and jurists write in a manner akin to a person who plays the piano by ear without understanding how to read music, and with no knowledge of music theory. As they write, they engage in complex, nuanced, rhetorical moves attributable to diverse rhetorical traditions, but they lack the language to describe those tools or wield them consistently in the service of justice as they practice law and engage in legal decisionmaking. Likewise, students who come from these rhetorical traditions may operate in them, but like a native speaker of a language without formal instruction in it, they might be unfamiliar with key tenets and how they function in shaping legal practice and decisionmaking. It is significant to recognize that Indigenous, African and Asian Diasporic, and Latine peoples have "made space" for their experiences with their rhetorical traditions as they have navigated imperialism, capitalism, White supremacy, and patriarchy, and that these rhetorical traditions are the subject of serious scholarly study.[5]

Furthermore, these traditions predate or arose contemporaneously with their Western counterparts and evolved alongside them. To perpetuate the mythic idea of "West as first and best" is an exercise in White cultural hegemony that renders all other groups and traditions subservient and inferior. By teaching various cultural rhetorical traditions in concert, we increase the capacity of law students to critically evaluate the tools of legal practice and jurisprudence, and actively work to change them to create an equitable legal system. They move us all toward a rhetoric of coherence necessary for the dispensation of justice.

What follows is an explanation of Indigenous, African Diasporic, Asian Diasporic, and Latine rhetorics, the strategies we can learn from them to inform how we practice law and critically examine legal decisionmaking, and how they can be used to create oppositional discourse.

Types of multicultural rhetoric

Indigenous rhetorics

Background

Indigenous histories of invasion, decimation, resistance, and survival have forged Indigenous rhetorics on the contested terrain of the colonizer and colonized. In the settler colonialist imagination, America was an uninhabited place of endless possibilities, available to White settlers for their wealth, freedom, and infinite opportunities for land acquisition.[6] The problem was that the land was already occupied by Indigenous peoples, roughly seven million[7] of them by the time the French and English had "America" in their sights. These peoples, among them the Mohawk, Oneida, Onondaga, Cayuga, Seneca, Abenakis, Shawnees, Delawares, Micmacs, Mahicans, Pequots, Powhatans, Catawbas, Cherokees, Creeks, Natchez, Choctaws, Chickasaws, Pueblos, Zunis, Navajos, Hopis, Ojibwe, Ottawa, and Potawatomi, were flattened to the descriptor "Indian" to serve the purposes of colonization. Literary scholar Roy Harvey Pearce explains in his work *Savagism and Civilization: A Study of the Indian and the American Mind*,

> The Renaissance Englishmen who became Americans were sustained by an idea of order. They were sure, above all, of the existence of an eternal and immutable principle which guaranteed the intelligibility of their relations to each other and to their world and thus made possible their life in society. It was a principle to be expressed in the progress of elevation of civilized men, who striving to imitate their God, would bring order to chaos. America was such a chaos, a newfound chaos. Her natural wealth was there for the ordering. So were her natural men.
>
> Thus colonial Americans were from the very beginning beset by an Indian problem at once practical and theoretical. Practically, they had to overcome this man and to live with him; theoretically, they had to understand him. And they brought with them a pattern of culture, an

> idea of order, in which theory and practice were taken to be identical. They were certain that man could realize his highest potentialities in only that sort of society which they had left behind them in England. Here in America it would be possible to realize such a society at its purest and most abundant. Aware to the point of self-consciousness of their specifically civilized heritage, they found in America not only an uncivilized environment, by uncivilized men—natural men, as it was said, living in a natural world. And they knew that the way to civilize a world was to civilize the men in it. Theoretically, savages, as men, were capable of being civilized; practically were bound to be. But practice did not support theory. **Indians were not civilized, but destroyed.**
>
> Such, in general was the colonial experience with the Indian; such had been the experience of revolutionary Americans when, in the 1770's, they set out to establish their glorious new-world civilization. The colonial concern with the savage Indian was a product of the tradition of Anglo-French primitivistic thinking—an attempt to see the savage, the ignoble savage, as a European manqué [an unfulfilled European, a failed attempt at a European]. **When by the 1770's, the attempt had obviously failed, Americans were coming to understand the Indian as one radically different from their proper selves; they knew he was bound inextricably in a primitive past, a primitive society and a primitive environment, to be destroyed by God, Nature, and Progress to make way for Civilized Man. Americans after the 1770's worked out a theory of the savage which depended on an idea of a new order in which the Indian could have no part.**[8] (Emphasis added)

Simply put by Native American rhetorician Malea Powell, "the Indian (whatever that may be) must disappear so that 'America' can live."[9]

Indigenous rhetorics are acts of resistance against erasure and cultural identity as imagined by those outside of it. They are characterized by the need for Indigenous peoples to have sovereignty and agency, in representations of themselves and their stories. Rhetoric and communication scholar Scott Richard Lyons calls for the same in his foundational article, *Rhetorical Sovereignty: What Do American Indians Want from Writing?*[10] Using the boarding school experience, in which Native American children were taken from their homes and violently socialized to be "civilized" and "American," as an ideological site for the convergence of cultural violence, Lyons argues,

> [T]he duplicitous interrelationships between writing, violence, and colonization developed during the nineteenth-century—not only in the boarding schools but at the signings of hundreds of treaties, most of which were dishonored by [W]hites—would set into motion a

> persistent distrust of the written word in English, one that resonates in homes and schools and courts of law still today. If our respect for the Word remains resolute, our faith in the written word is compromised at best.[11]

In response, Lyons offers rhetorical sovereignty as a set of rhetorical practices based on Indigenous peoples' requirements for communication that preserve cultural dignity and autonomy.[12]

Rhetorical sovereignty is an oppositional discourse to rhetorical imperialism, which is defined as "the ability of dominant powers to assert control of others by setting the terms of debate."[13] These terms are descriptions of the parties that have legal meanings and consequences detrimental to those that did not choose them.[14] With respect to Indigenous peoples, descriptors that increasingly cast them as beneficiaries of their colonizer's paternalism have led to legal divestments of their sovereignty, while simultaneously shifting the site of resistance to how those divestments would be remembered.[15] This narrative of imperialistic remembrance, rhetorical imperialism, is prevalent throughout the Marshall Trilogy, the foundational set of legal opinions—Johnson v. M'Intosh (1823), Cherokee Nation v. Georgia (1831), and Worcester v. Georgia (1832)—that legally established Native American dependence, and the relationship of Indigenous tribes to U.S. state and federal governments. *Johnson v. M'Intosh* begins the narrative with a tale of discovery and conquest, thus solidifying the myth of land empty and ripe for the taking by European settlers.[16] Chapter 1 briefly explained how *Johnson v. M'Intosh* deployed a racialized type of Enlightenment philosophy to summarily dispossess Indigenous people of their land. Here, we discuss *M'Intosh* as a legal decision that is foundational to the emergence of an Indigenous rhetoric centered on resistance and sovereignty. In *M'Intosh*, Justice Marshall asserted,

> **On the discovery of this immense continent, the great nations of Europe were eager to appropriate to themselves so much of it as they could respectively acquire. Its vast extent offered an ample field to the ambition and enterprise of all, and the character and religion of its inhabitants afforded an apology for considering them as people over whom the superior genius of Europe might claim ascendency.** The potentates of the old world found no difficulty in convincing themselves that they made ample compensation to the inhabitants of the new by bestowing on them civilization and Christianity in exchange for unlimited independence. But as they were all in pursuit of the same object, it was necessary, in order to avoid conflicting settlements and consequent war with each other, to establish a principle which all should acknowledge as the law

> by which the right of acquisition, which they all asserted should be regulated as between themselves. **This principle was that discovery gave title to the government by whose subjects or by whose authority it was made against all other European governments, which title might be consummated by possession.**
>
> The exclusion of all other Europeans gave the nation making the discovery the sole right of acquiring the soil from the natives and establishing settlements upon it. It was a right with which no Europeans could interfere. It was a right which all asserted for themselves. The right thus acquired being exclusive, no other power could interpose between them.[17] (Emphasis added)

Marshall follows with the narrative of benevolent paternalism in *Cherokee Nation v. Georgia*, which casts Indigenous peoples as dependents of the United States government,

> The Indians are acknowledged to have an unquestionable, and heretofore an unquestioned, right to the lands they occupy until that right shall be extinguished by a voluntary cession to our Government. It may well be doubted whether those tribes which reside within the acknowledged boundaries of the United States can, with strict accuracy, be denominated foreign nations. They may more correctly, perhaps, be denominated domestic dependent nations. They occupy a territory to which we assert title independent of their will, which must take effect in point of possession when their right of possession ceases; meanwhile, they are in a state of pupilage. Their relations to the United States resemble that of a ward to his guardian. They look to our Government for protection, rely upon its kindness and its power, appeal to it for relief to their wants, and address the President as their Great Father.[18]

Marshall concludes this narrative of rhetorical imperialism in *Worcester v. Georgia*, by bestowing upon the federal government the sole authority to deal with the Cherokee Nation and, through the operation of precedent, all other Indigenous peoples within the United States "for the benefit and comfort of the Indians, and for the prevention of injuries or oppressions on the part of the citizens or Indians … managing all of their affairs as they think proper," authority previously granted to the same by treaty.[19]

In contrast, rhetorical sovereignty rests in how Indigenous peoples chronicle their own culture and history, story and representation, which throws dominant accounts of their realities into discord.[20] This is especially true when dominant stories of Indigenous/colonizer conflict are mined as acceptable sources for argument and frame interpretation.[21] Sovereignty, given Indigenous peoples' particular experience with colonization, is a place-centric principle of wholeness, one that aims to preserve and continue community and culture.[22] It can be demonstrated in how Indigenous peoples invert imperialist representations of their cultures and personhood to assert agency. For example, in an 1851 meeting between the Arapaho, Cheyenne, and Lakota Sioux and President Abraham Lincoln over rights granted to the tribes under the Treaty of Fort Laramie, namely the U.S. obligation to protect the tribes against White settlers, tribal leaders referred to the settlers as Lincoln's "White children."[23] If the President had positioned himself as the tribes' Great Father, then tribal leaders treated him as one responsible for his own children's armed incursions into their tribal spaces and for disturbing the peace the Treaty had put in place.

The Washington Supreme Court's retelling of the facts in the *Sum* case, detailed in Chapter 3, offers an example of how rhetorical sovereignty operates as a place-centric principle of wholeness that aims to preserve and continue community and culture. The court took into account Asian/Pacific Islanders' history with law enforcement to craft Mr. Sum's encounter with Deputy Rickerson from Mr. Sum's perspective. In the court's words,

> [A]lthough Sum's race is relevant to the seizure inquiry, it certainly is not dispositive. We must instead consider all of the circumstances to determine whether an objective observer could conclude that Sum was not free to refuse Deputy Rickerson's request for identification based on the deputy's display of authority. The answer is yes.
>
> The circumstances as found by the trial court were as follows. Sum, a person of color, was asleep in his car, which was parked on a public street in a "high crime area." At 9:15 in the morning, Sum was awoken by a sheriff's deputy in full uniform knocking on the car window next to where Sum was sleeping. Deputy Rickerson did not ask about Sum's health or safety and he did not ask if Sum and his passenger required assistance. Instead, the deputy asked what Sum and his passenger were doing, clearly implying that they did not belong there.
>
> Sum answered that "they were visiting a friend across the street." This answer proved insufficient to satisfy the deputy's interest in Sum and his passenger because Deputy Rickerson next asked "to whom the Honda Civic belonged." Sum provided a name, but this also failed to satisfy the deputy because he then requested Sum's identification. When Sum "asked him why he wanted" identification, the deputy "explained that the two men were sitting in an area known for stolen vehicles and that [Sum] did not appear to know to whom the vehicle he was sitting in belonged."
>
> Assuming, without deciding, that Sum was not already seized, then Deputy Rickerson's explanation was certainly "the tipping point at

> which the weight of the circumstances transformed a simple encounter into a seizure."[24]

Compare the Washington State Supreme Court's factual account with a part of the account written by the Washington State Court of Appeals,

> Pierce County Sheriff's Deputy Mark Rickerson was on patrol at 9:15 in the morning when he noticed a car that was parked in front of a church. Stolen vehicles had previously been recovered from that location, which was considered a "high crime" area. And about four or five months prior, a resident of a house across the street from the church had informed Rickerson that he had noticed suspicious vehicles parking in the same location.
>
> Rickerson parked to the east of the car, careful to leave substantial room between them. Rickerson then ran the car's license plate through a database to see who the registration belonged to and to check whether it had been reported stolen. The bill of sale was filed in Oregon, matching the Oregon license plate.
>
> Rickerson ran a check on the license plate on the car and identified the vehicle identification number (VIN) to confirm that his records matched the number displayed on the dash. It was at that moment that Rickerson saw that both Sum, who was in the driver's seat, and Sum's passenger, were "slumped over" and appeared unconscious. Rickerson knocked on the driver's side window until Sum roused several seconds later.[25]

By its account, the Washington State Supreme Court wrote Mr. Sum back into the story, both in the facts and the analysis, from which he had been erased by the Washington State Court of Appeals' statement of the facts relevant to the case. The Court of Appeals' account centers Deputy Rickerson's perspective of the encounter without challenging his neutrality as an "objective" observer. However, the Washington State Supreme Court underscores that in Washington State "an objective observer 'is aware that implicit, institutional, and unconscious biases, in addition to purposeful discrimination, have resulted in' many injustices against BIPOC [Black, Indigenous and other People of Color], particularly in the criminal justice system."[26] The court's expansion of the analytic framework for seizures to include a person's race and history of racism made the totality of Mr. Sum's experiences relevant. Thus, its opinion is an exercise of rhetorical sovereignty as a response to the Court of Appeals' exercise of rhetorical imperialism in shaping its analytical framework and determining the facts relevant to resolving Mr. Sum's dispute. It is important to recognize that although the Washington Supreme Court's work is an example of rhetorical sovereignty, it was likely playing by ear due to American law schools' lack of "sheet music" sufficient to train law students (future jurists) on how to use Indigenous rhetorical strategies.

Also key to Indigenous rhetorical practice is survivance (survival + resistance).[27] Coined by writer and scholar Gerald Vizenor, "Native survivance stories are renunciations of dominance, tragedy, and victimry. Survivance is resisting those marginalizing, colonial narratives and policies so Indigenous knowledge and lifeways may come into the present with new life and new commitment to that survival."[28] Survivance is expressed through recognizing the existence of Indigenous rhetorics, identifying Indigenous peoples' strategic use of Western rhetorical forms, and the epistemic nature of Indigenous communication.[29]

Ulali, a First Nation A Capello Trio consisting of all women members of the Tuscarora, Taino, Mayan, Apache, and Yaqui tribes, demonstrates the concept of survivance in their song "All My Relations."[30] The melody of the song is taken from the Garry Owen March, a song routinely played by Lieutenant Colonel George Armstrong Custer, as he led the 7th Calvary into war with Indigenous peoples. The March is a bombastic military tune performed with pomp and circumstance, which was routinely played by the 7th Calvary band.[31] Its celebratory and triumphant nature is a stark juxtaposition against the decimation for which it provided a soundtrack. Ulali reimagines the march in the singing style of their tribal traditions and with the sole accompaniment of the drum. The lyrics, delivered as spoken word over the melody played in a constant loop, are as follows:

> To our elders who teach us of our creation and of our past so
> that we may preserve it for ancestors yet to come.
>
> We are the land.
>
> This is dedicated to our relatives before us, thousands of years ago
> And to the 150 million who were exterminated across the
> Western Hemisphere in the first four hundred years' time,
> starting in 1492
>
> To those who have kept their homelands
> And to the nations extinct due to mass slaughter, slavery,
> deportation and disease unknown to them
> And to the ones who are subjected to the same treatment today
>
> To those who survived the relocations
> And to those who died along the way
>
> To those who carry on traditions and live strong
> among their people

To those who left their communities by force or by choice and
through generations no longer know who they are

To those who search and never find
To those who turn away the so-called 'non-accepted'
To those who bring us together
And to those living outside, keeping touch, the voice for many

To those that make it back to live and fight the struggles of
their people
To those that give up
And those who do not care

To those who abuse themselves and others
And those who revive again

To those who are physically, mentally, or spiritually incapable,
by accident or by birth

To those who seek strength in our spirituality and way of life
To those who exploit it
even our own

To those who fall for the lies and join the dividing lines that
keep us fighting amongst each other

To the outsiders who step in
—good or bad
And those of us who don't know better

To the leaders and prisoners of war, politics, crime, race and religion
—innocent or guilty

To the young
The old
The living
And the dead

To our brothers and sisters in all living things across Mother
Earth and her beauty we've destroyed and denied the honour
that the Creator has given each individual:
The truth that lies in our hearts
All my relations[32]

These verses strategically remake the song of the colonizer into a medium by which meaning is made with the listener, descendants of the colonizer and colonized, through their cultural, historical, and present experiences of colonization. Ulali's use of survivance demonstrates how we can remake the law to change how and what we know. With this knowledge we can reshape our practice of it to redress systems of oppression.

Indigenous rhetorical strategies

See Tables 4.1 and 4.2.

Table 4.1: Rhetorical sovereignty (agency)

Cultural dignity	Cultural autonomy	Culturally informed issue-framing	Remembrance
Respect for the histories of Indigenous communities	Respect for Indigenous community-led determination (charting a course forward through culturally derived solutions to community-based problems)	Centering Indigenous experiences in decisions about the relevant sources for arguments	Understanding various Indigenous identities as constituted by their respective communities
Acknowledgment of Indigenous histories and traditions	Acknowledgment of Indigenous communities' right to community-led determination	Centering Indigenous experiences in evaluating the relevance and significance of accounts of wrongdoing	Resisting the erasure of Indigenous peoples in narratives of American social, political, military, and legal history
Communication of Indigenous histories and traditions	Active support of Indigenous communities in their exercise of community-led determination	Acknowledgment of Indigenous uses of language to expose Western biases about their history and culture and to persuade	Centering Indigenous actors in narratives involving their experiences

Table 4.2: Survivance (survival + resistance)

Renouncing U.S. dominance	Renouncing Indigenous tragedy	Renouncing Indigenous victimry	Resisting marginalization
Exposing the function of imperialism, capitalism, White supremacy (as White cultural identity) in assertions of U.S. dominance over Indigenous communities	Naming the actors that crafted the political, military, social, and legal policies that led to the decimation of Indigenous communities and their impact in the present day	Naming the actors and actions (historical, legal, political, and social) that facilitated the decimation of Indigenous communities and their impact in the present day	Rejecting colonial narratives of Indigenous personhood and community decimation

African Diasporic rhetoric

Background

The African holocaust forced Black bodies from the continent of Africa and scattered them throughout the world through the vehicle of human trafficking. Africans endured, and their encounters with non-Africans throughout the Diaspora forced cultural syncretism from shared history. In their path-forging work, *Understanding African American Rhetoric: Classical Origins to Contemporary Innovations*, rhetoric scholars Ronald L. Jackson II and Elaine B. Richardson position African American rhetoric as a valid subject of study in the academy worthy of scholarly inquiry.[33] The foreword by activist and critical rhetorician Orlando L. Taylor notes that this work is important because scholars of African Diasporic rhetoric who are African Diasporic people are its contributors, engaged in the enterprise of decolonizing the knowledge of the discipline and their place in it.[34] He writes, "Volumes such as these interrogate the flawed singularity of truth telling in rhetorical studies not only by exposing the limitations of the European-centered literature's hegemonic intent, but also by centralizing and celebrating the uniqueness of another rhetorical tradition, that of African Americans."[35]

Understanding African American Rhetoric moves us beyond an understanding of African American rhetoric as oratory to an introduction of its African Diasporic rhetorical practices and traditions.[36] African Diasporic rhetoric challenges Western "classical" rhetorical frameworks as "culturally generic [normative/neutral] paradigms" inadequate to examine the cultural specificity of rhetorical strategies.[37] Accordingly, Africology (the study of the histories and cultures of African peoples on the African continent) and Afrocentricity (an African centered worldview) are foundational to building the culturally specific paradigms and methods by which to study African Diasporic rhetorical practices.[38]

African Diasporic rhetoric marks the Kemetic texts of ancient Egypt as a starting point.[39] These texts are a conceptual departure from Greco-Roman rhetorical texts, in that the latter are connected to the marketplace while the former are not.[40] Rather, the Kemetic texts are an expression of community, an exercise in community building, and a practice of safeguarding community well-being.[41]

Additionally, African Diasporic rhetoric originates in an oral tradition, rather than a written one. Scholar Maulana Karenga grounds the African oral tradition in the Black nationalist[42] Kawaida philosophy, described as "a cultural core that forms the central locus of our self-understanding and self-assertion in the world and which is mediated by constantly changing historical circumstances and an ongoing internal dialog of reassessment and continuous development."[43] Karenga defines Kawaida as:

> [t]he ideological and practical struggle to: (1) transform the cultural context in which people live; (2) transform them in the process, making them self-conscious agents of their own liberation; and (3) build the institutional base to sustain and constantly expand that transformation. It implies and necessitates revitalizing, creating and recreating culture.[44]

An example of Kawaida in practice is illustrated by Africana and American Studies scholar Tricia Rose in her analysis of the African Diasporic cultural form hip hop. She argues that hip hop arose as a cultural form in response to the postindustrial realties of 1980s New York City.[45] This period was marked by unprecedented poverty and unemployment, a housing crisis, and limited opportunities that disproportionately affected Black and Latine communities.[46] Hip hop emerged here, its birth tied to the South Bronx but a gift to all New Yorkers, as a youth culture forged by "the tools of obsolete industrial technology to traverse contemporary crossroads of lack and desire in urban Afrodiasporic communities."[47] Hip hop is composed of the art forms of break dancing, graffiti, and rapping—all "shared approaches to sound and motion found in the Afrodiaspora."[48] Stylistically, these approaches are characterized by "flow, layering, and ruptures inline," a phenomenon in which the "visual, physical, musical, and lyrical lines are set in motion, broken abruptly with sharp angular breaks, yet sustain motion and energy through fluidity and flow."[49] Far from limited to artistic/cultural expression, flow, layering, and rupture form a theoretical framework by which to understand and grapple with African Diasporic community phenomena, in this case postindustrial New York. Rose explains,

> What is the significance of flow, layering, and rupture as demonstrated on the body and in hip hop's lyrical, musical, and visual works? Interpreting these concepts theoretically, one can argue that they create and sustain rhythmic motion, continuity, and circularity via flow; accumulate, reinforce, and embellish this continuity through layering; and manage threats to these narratives by building in ruptures that highlight the continuity as it momentarily challenges it. These effects at the level of style and aesthetics suggest affirmative ways in which profound social dislocation and rupture can be managed and perhaps contested in the cultural arena. Let us imagine these hip hop principles as a blueprint for social resistance and affirmation: create sustaining narratives, accumulate them, layer, embellish, and transform them. However, also be prepared for rupture, find pleasure in it, in fact plan on social rupture. When these ruptures occur, use them in creative ways that will prepare you for a future in which survival will demand a sudden shift in ground tactics.[50]

In this context, hip hop operates (1) to transform the cultural context in which people live through its physical, musical, and lyrical expression; (2) transform its practitioners in the process by making them agents of their liberation, both experientially, through the art form and the stories it tells about minoritized communities, and materially, through commercial transactions involving the art form; and (3) by setting the foundation for community transformation both in and outside of African Diasporic communities—hip hop is a global phenomenon that resonates with minoritized people around the world.

Kawaida also serves as a guide for the scholarly interpretation of ancient African rhetorical texts.[51] The Book of Ptahhotep, an Egyptian text and the oldest rhetorical text in existence,[52] has two basic tenets: "rhetoric as eloquent and effective speech itself *(mdt nfrt—medet neferet)* and rhetoric as the rules or principles for eloquent and effective speech *(tp-hsb n mdt nfrt—tep-heseb en medet neferet)*."[53] This idea of eloquence as unity is reflective of ethical speech as a tool for community building, an expression of the ancient Egyptian moral tenet of Maat.[54]

Maat, or "rightness in the world" has seven principles: "truth, justice, propriety, harmony, balance, reciprocity, and order," truth being the most important.[55] Maat also affirms the value of all people, regardless of race, class, gender, or sexuality and stresses the partnership between rhetor and audience in community building.[56] Instructions for the practice of African rhetoric are found in the Book of Khunanup, which considers the rhetor's use of Maat to argue for justice.[57] Maat's loose parallels in the Western world are Aristotle's persuasive appeals (*logos*, *pathos*, and *ethos*).[58]

Judge Carleton Reeves's opinion in *Jamison v. McClendon*, discussed in Chapters 2 and 3, calls upon several of the principles of Maat through his introductory poem, and his "Historical Context" and "Supreme Court" sections. Judge Reeves points out the discordant, inharmonious history of qualified immunity as a challenge to its efficacy as a legal doctrine. He seeks to expose the truth of 42 U.S.C. section 1983 by telling us its origin story in the post–Civil War South. Judge Reeves also calls for justice from the Supreme Court, by demonstrating how the qualified immunity doctrine undermines the propriety of section 1983. Lastly, through his invocation of *Star Wars* he advocates for the Court to bring balance to the force, in this case balance between the intent and application of section 1983.

The African *nommo* or *nummo* is the universe in which invocations for justice function. In the Malian creation story "the Creator, Amma, sends *nommo*, the word, in the collective sense of speech, to complete the spiritual and material reorganization of the world and to assist humans in the forward movement in history and society."[59] The word, *nommo*, makes community building, safeguarding, and well-being possible; it is the space that gives Maat meaning and form to achieve good in the world.[60]

As expressed in African American rhetoric, *nommo*, literally "the word," is resistance to oppressive regimes that made it illegal for enslaved persons to read and write.[61] As an import to the United States through the bodies of trafficked Africans, *nommo* persists as a weapon of cultural resistance and a testament to cultural retention.[62] It embodies the ethics of speech found in the Book of Ptahhotep that unify African American rhetoric:

> [1] the dignity and rights of the human person; [2] the well-being and flourishing of community; [3] the integrity and value of the environment [to repair ecological, social, and ontological damage in the world resulting from acts of commission and omission]; and [4] the reciprocal solidarity and cooperation for mutual benefit of humanity ["speak truth, do justice"].[63]

These tenets provide the source for petitions to justice, and guide their arrangement and the medium through which they are presented.[64] The media for petitions to justice, the manner in which they are presented, are fluid—there is no distinction between intellectual and artistic expression.[65] In the words of philosopher and African American Studies scholar Molefi Kete Asante, "[what constitutes a functional medium or object, which includes] sculpture, music, [poetry], dance, [or] speech [is] that [which] possesses a meaning within the communicator's and audience's worldview, a meaning that is constructed from the social, political, and religious moments in society's history."[66]

Judge Reeves's opinion is an example of the limited impact of the Western/Aristotelian reasoning paradigm as it operates in the *nomos*, the universe in which law functions, even as he draws upon poetry and history as the media through which to make petitions to justice. Because of Western distinctions between artistic/literary expression and (appropriate) intellectual expression in the genre of the judicial opinion, his opening poem about Black death by law enforcement is of little impact. It does not propel Judge Reeves toward a deviation from the Western/Aristotelian reasoning paradigm or an equitable reconstitution of his analytic framework for qualified immunity. Moreover, because of the racialized boundaries of the *nomos*, Judge Reeves's petitions to justice are not given meaning by the sources for petitions to justice in the *nommo*—the dignity and rights of all people; community well-being; the integrity and value of the environment to repair ecological, social, and ontological damage in the world resulting from acts of commission and omission; and our obligations to community to speak truth and do justice. These requirements would have supported Judge Reeves in creating a framework of analysis that respected Mr. Jamison's dignity; protected Black life and allowed Black communities to flourish in safety; acknowledged and facilitated repairing the damage and demoralization of human trafficking, enslavement, Jim Crow, and criminalization; and encouraged jurists to speak truth and do justice.

African Diasporic rhetorical strategies

See Tables 4.3 and 4.4.

Guidance for Maat as it functions in the nommo

See Tables 4.5 through 4.11.

Table 4.3: Kawaida

Cultural context	Agency and liberation	Expansive transformation
Envisions the transformation of the cultural contexts in which people live in the absence of boundaries between artistic and intellectual expression	Envisions the myriad ways in which people can be transformed through a reimagining of their cultural contexts to became agents of their own liberation	Envisions a capacious structure by which cultural and material transformation can be sustained and expanded to include minoritized communities
Takes steps to transform the cultural contexts in which people live by eliminating the boundaries between artistic and intellectual expression	Facilitates such transformation by articulating and carrying out viable action steps	Builds that structure through various media (poetry, prose, case law, statutes, and so on)

Table 4.4: Guidance for textual interpretation and ethical speech from the Book of Ptahhotep

Rhetoric as eloquent and effective communication	**Rhetoric as the rules or principles for eloquent and effective communication**
Does the communication respect the rights of minoritized persons?	Do the rules for communication, the expectations for the media (the type), and the manner in which the communication will proceed (structure) consider and respect the rights of minoritized persons?
Does the communication preserve the well-being and flourishing of the affected community or communities?	Do the rules for communication, the expectations for the media (the type), and the manner in which the communication will proceed (structure) preserve the well-being and flourishing of the affected community or communities?
Does the communication consider the integrity and value of the environment to repair ecological, social, and ontological damage in the world resulting from acts of commission and omission?	Do the rules for communication, the expectations for the media (the type), and the manner in which the communication will proceed (structure) consider the integrity and value of the environment to repair ecological, social, and ontological damage in the world resulting from acts of commission and omission?
Does the communication facilitate the reciprocal solidarity and cooperation for the mutual benefit of humanity? Does it allow community members to speak truth, and do justice?	Do the rules for communication, the expectation for the media (the type), and the manner in which the communication will proceed (structure) facilitate reciprocal solidarity and cooperation for the mutual benefit of humanity? Do they allow community members to speak truth, and do justice?

Table 4.5: Truth

Are truths (historical, legal, social, experiential) communicated in a manner that respects the dignity and rights of all people regardless of race, class, gender, and sexuality, and engages community members in their construction?
Are truths (historical, legal, social, experiential) communicated in a manner that preserves the well-being and flourishing of the affected community or communities?
Are truths (historical, legal, social, experiential) communicated in a manner that considers the integrity and value of the environment to repair ecological, social, and ontological damage in the world resulting from acts of commission and omission?
Are truths (historical, legal, social, experiential) communicated in a manner that facilitates the reciprocal solidarity and cooperation for the mutual benefit of humanity? Does the communication allow community members to speak truth, and do justice?

Table 4.6: Justice

Is justice communicated through a given communication in a manner that respects the dignity and rights of all people regardless of race, class, gender, and sexuality, and engages community members in its construction?
Is justice communicated through a given communication in a manner that preserves the well-being and flourishing of the affected community or communities?
Is justice communicated through a given communication in a manner that considers the integrity and value of the environment to repair ecological, social, and ontological damage in the world resulting from acts of commission and omission?
Is justice communicated through a given communication in a manner that facilitates reciprocal solidarity and cooperation for the mutual benefit of humanity? Does the communication allow community members to speak truth, and do justice?

Table 4.7: Propriety

Does the communication conform to the requirements for ethical speech that guide the *nommo* to protect the dignity and rights of all people regardless of race, class, gender, and sexuality, and engage community members in its construction?
Does the communication conform to the requirements for ethical speech that guide the *nommo* to preserve the well-being and flourishing of the affected community or communities?
Does the communication conform to the requirements for ethical speech that guide the *nommo* to consider the integrity and value of the environment to repair ecological, social, and ontological damage in the world resulting from acts of commission and omission?
Does the communication conform to the requirements for ethical speech that guide the *nommo* to facilitate reciprocal solidarity and cooperation for the mutual benefit of humanity? Does the communication allow community members to speak truth, and do justice?

Table 4.8: Harmony

Does the communication achieve harmony among community members through its respect of the dignity and rights of all people regardless of race, class, gender, and sexuality, and engage community members in its creation?
Does the communication achieve harmony among community members by preserving the well-being and flourishing of the affected community or communities?
Does the communication achieve harmony among community members by considering the integrity and value of the environment to repair ecological, social, and ontological damage in the world resulting from acts of commission and omission?
Does the communication achieve harmony among community members in a manner that facilitates reciprocal solidarity and cooperation for the mutual benefit of humanity? Does the communication allow community members to speak truth, and do justice?

Table 4.9: Balance

Does the communication achieve balance among community members through its respect of the dignity and rights of all people regardless of race, class, gender, and sexuality, and engage community members in their construction?

Does the communication achieve balance among community members by preserving the well-being and flourishing of the affected community or communities?

Does the communication achieve balance among community members by considering the integrity and value of the environment to repair ecological, social, and ontological damage in the world resulting from acts of commission and omission?

Does the communication achieve balance among community members in a manner that facilitates reciprocal solidarity and cooperation for the mutual benefit of humanity? Does the communication allow community members to speak truth, and do justice?

Table 4.10: Reciprocity

Does the communication involve reciprocity (mutual exchange and cooperation) among community members in its demonstration of respect for the dignity and rights of all people regardless of race, class, gender, and sexuality?

Does the communication involve reciprocity (mutual exchange and cooperation) among community members by demonstrating how it preserves the well-being and flourishing of the affected community or communities?

Does the communication involve reciprocity (mutual exchange and cooperation) among community members in its demonstration of the integrity and value of the environment to repair ecological, social, and ontological damage in the world resulting from acts of commission and omission?

Does the communication involve reciprocity (mutual exchange and cooperation) among community members in its demonstration of reciprocal solidarity and cooperation for the mutual benefit of humanity? Does the communication allow community members to speak truth, and do justice?

Table 4.11: Order

Does the communication achieve order among community members through its respect of the dignity and rights of all people regardless of race, class, gender, and sexuality, and engage community members in its construction?

Does the communication achieve order among community members by preserving the well-being and flourishing of the affected community or communities?

Does the communication achieve order among community members by considering the integrity and value of the environment to repair ecological, social, and ontological damage in the world resulting from acts of commission and omission?

Does the communication achieve order among community members in a manner that facilitates reciprocal solidarity and cooperation for the mutual benefit of humanity? Does the communication allow community members to speak truth, and do justice?

Asian Diasporic rhetoric

Background: Chinese and South Asian rhetorics

The study of Chinese rhetoric dominates intellectual inquiry into Asian rhetoric.[67] Scholars of Asian rhetoric look to China for its origins and influence.[68] Arguably, rhetoric as a discipline did not emerge in China until the early 1900s.[69] However, rhetoric existed in China from ancient times, and its use in creating a discourse of persuasion was expressed as the following six types: *yan*, *ci*, *jian*, *shui*, *ming*, and *bian*.[70] *Yan* is the use of language to influence political leaders and outcomes, and to demonstrate political ambition.[71] *Ci* is closely related to *yan*, but refers to the artistry of language as a persuasion strategy, and also as a cover for lack of substance in a stated position or argument.[72] Its counterpart in Aristotelian rhetoric is *ethos*, or the rhetor's reputation as a factor that can weigh in favor of persuasion or against it. For example, a rhetor who speaks well to advance substantive arguments will have a better reputation than one who speaks well to advance spurious ones.[73] *Jian* are persuasion strategies directed toward an authority figure.[74] In U.S. political culture, lobbyists and elected officials engage in *jian* in their attempts to persuade someone with greater authority to make changes for the benefit of the people, special interests, for which they are employed.[75] The greater consensus among *jian* practitioners, the more persuasive they appear to the authority figure who they wish to influence.[76] *Shui* refers to persuasion strategies used between people from the same peer group to a person of greater authority on political and military matters. *Shui* is primarily exercised by those who are learned and respected for their wisdom. During the SARS-CoV-2 (COVID-19) pandemic, Dr. Anthony Fauci, Chief Medical Advisor to the President of the United States and Director of the National Institute of Allergy and Infectious Disease at the National Institutes of Health routinely employed *shui* to two presidential administrations.

Ming is a judgment about the proper manner of persuasion. It is guided by cultural notions of morality, which is more important than emotion or emotional appeals—*pathos* in the Aristotelian tradition.[77] However, emotions are the source of moral appeals, as transmitted through the virtues of "'*ren*—kindness, *yi*—righteousness, *zhong*—loyalty, *xin*—faith, [and] *cheng*—sincerity.'"[78] Lastly *bian*, translated literally as "debate," is a type of analogical reasoning process through which differences are illustrated by description, with each distinction lending weight to the wisdom or folly of a particular decision in any given matter. In the political arena it can take the form of a pros and cons list of sorts, akin to narrative reasoning; in academia and scholarly work it involves well-stated definitions, and comparison and contrast between like concepts and ideas. All of these strategies are context-dependent and gain meaning from their use in concert.[79]

Chinese rhetorical strategies reflected the ideals of varied dynasties and philosophers in articulating the uses and purposes of language. For example, rulers of the Ming Dynasty and followers of Confucius viewed rhetoric as an ethical means to build knowledge in the service of social justice.[80] In contrast, the Mohists, Ancient Chinese philosophers, focused on rhetoric as a means of "rational" argument, or argument that draws on "metaphorical, anecdotal, analogical, paradoxical, chain reasoning, classification, and inference."[81] Different still was the Daoist (Taoist) regime, which was most concerned with rhetoric as a tool of transcendental philosophy.[82] Lastly, the concept of legalism emerged to conceptualize language as a means to support the existing ruling power.[83]

Li Ji or *The Book of Rites* espoused the unifying principle for Chinese rhetoric as the preservation of relationships.[84] *Li Ji* underscored the most important of these relationships, Confucian in origin, as relationships between "prince and minister; father and son; husband and wife; elder and younger; [and] friends."[85] To preserve these relationships, the rhetor had to be cognizant of audience and the epistemic function of argument as it supported *yian*, *ci*, *jian*, *shui*, *ming*, and *bian*.[86] The arrangement of language into arguments followed the "because therefore" or "frame-main" sequence, an indirect style of argumentation where reasons, presented as stories, histories, and symbols, precede main assertions.[87] History and its lessons were a significant and weighty source for persuasion through analogy because "events from the past could not be changed, neither could they be erased."[88] The "because therefore" or "frame-main" arrangement style was part and parcel of a joint knowledge-making exercise that required the rhetor and audience to explore the relationship between "reasons."[89]

Similar to the "because therefore" or "frame-main" argument arrangement is the problem-solution argumentation structure.[90] Like its counterpart, it also contextualizes problem solving in historical, cultural, social, and experiential narratives to arrive at a set of solutions.[91] This structure is based in Indian epistemology, and in Indian and Hindi language traditions. A guiding tenet of Indian epistemology is that higher knowledge is obtained by discussion (*Samvāda*), through which many viewpoints are collected and assessed—the Indian textbook of philosophical systems (*Sarva-darśana-samgraha*) literally translates to "a compilation of viewpoints."[92] In the problem-solution structure, the narratives presented are in conversation with each other, spurring the reader and listener on to the higher knowledge necessary to resolve the problem.[93] Both styles of argument arrangement, "because therefore" or "frame-main" and problem-solution, would gain increased significance as those native to Asia and India left for Europe and the Americas to begin new lives abroad.

Asian Diasporic rhetorics

In his *Strangers from a Different Shore: A History of Asian Americans*, historian Ronald Takaki acquaints us with the Asian Diaspora through the encounters of diverse Asian peoples as they entered and settled beyond U.S. shores.[94] Asian American Studies professor Elaine H. Kim, in her review of Takaki's text, positions the historian's study as the manifestation of "Asian American historian Yuji Ichioka['s] [call to center] Asian Americans as 'subjects' instead of as 'objects' of history."[95] Ichioka is credited with originating the term "Asian Americans" as a unifier for Asian Diasporic peoples living in the United States.[96] His descriptive term for inhabitants of the Asian Diaspora as they reside in the United States is a political, social, cultural, and rhetorical space. As if answering Ichioka's call, Asian Diasporic rhetoricians identify a need for those involved in scholarly rhetorical inquiry to "treat the Others of transcultural communication as agents of knowledge making rather than the objects of 'study' and domination."[97]

Because Asian Diasporic history is an immigrant one, real and mythologized, Asian American rhetoric studies are rooted in the study of language, specifically the fluidity of English as adapted by Asian native English and multiple language speakers for use in a variety of spoken and written contexts.[98] Scholars of Asian American rhetoric study, in part, how choices of words, idioms, and argument strategies reflect Asian worldviews and philosophies, just as a resistance to those choices result in oppressive structures that limit their expression.[99] For example, the ubiquitous sign found on lawns throughout the United States, "Keep Off the Grass," is translated into Chinese as "Little Grass Has Life." Far from a humorous blunder, this "translation" reflects a philosophy of a person and/or animal's legal and societal relationship to the environment.[100] In this sense, "Asian Americans' use the symbolic resources of language in social, cultural, and political arenas to disrupt and transform dominant European American discourse and its representations of Asians and Asian Americans, thus re-presenting and reclaiming their identity and agency."[101] Similar examples are found in the protests to stop AAPI hate, violence against Asian Americans and Pacific Islanders, where protestors held signs that read "Love Our People Like You Love Our Food" and "My Race Is Not A Virus. Racism Is."

When framed in this manner, language itself, its use and arrangement, becomes the source of argument. Language also becomes epistemic, as it seeks to recreate Asian Diasporic knowledge as Western knowledge by decentering Western knowledge as its source.[102] Lastly, the fluidity of language rejects canonization, and moves beyond categorization as a means of persuasion.[103] In this context, the "because therefore" or "frame-main" reasoning style can be employed to resituate Asian American experiences with imperialism, capitalism, White supremacy, and patriarchy in the United

States as sources of authority to resolve legal problems. An example of this reasoning style in action follows:

Reason (history): Japanese internment was marked by the divestment of Japanese Americans of their land and personal property, and the criminalization of their race and national origin. This practice was "legal," because at the time the U.S. was fighting in World War II and the country of Japan was seen as a threat. Thus, legal and political officials saw Japanese Americans as loyal to Japan rather than America, because of their shared ancestry with Japan. This perceived disloyalty informed U.S. domestic policy toward Japanese citizens.

Assertion 1: The children of immigrants, primarily from Mexico and Central America are being separated from their parents and held in U.S. detention centers. [The listener/reader understands that Assertion 1 is an analogy to what happened with Japanese internment.]

Assertion 2: Immigrant women held in U.S. detention centers have suffered invasive gynecological procedures, namely hysterectomies, to which they have not consented and that have left them infertile. [The listener/reader understands that Assertion 2 is an analogy to what happened with Japanese internment.]

Legal Issue for Resolution #1: In what ways does U.S. law and domestic policy reflect assumptions about immigrant loyalty and their contributions to U.S. society?

Legal Issue for Resolution #2: How can U.S. law and domestic policy directed at immigrant groups balance concerns about scarce resources with maintaining the humanity of all people and keeping families together?

This structure is echoed in the problem-solution method of argument arrangement, which showcases how argumentative texts are arranged within the Indian epistemological frame. It begins with an initiation component, in which a statement or set of statements broadly define the problem to be solved in the context of the society in which it occurs.[104] Next is the initiation act, where the problem is explained using historical, social, cultural, and experiential narratives.[105] What follows the initiation act is an articulation of the current problem, or a distillation of the initiation component to continue the historical, social, cultural, and experiential narratives.[106] In this section, the writer often describes present day events or experiences that are analogous to the narratives presented. The reasoning ends in a set of proposed solutions to the problem that take in account the historical, social, cultural, and experiential context of it.[107] Consider the same "because therefore" "frame-main" examples reconstituted in the problem-solution structure:

Initiation Component: In the U.S., misinformation about immigration and assumptions about immigrant loyalty to "American" ideals have led to flawed immigration policies.

Initiation Act 1: For example, Japanese internment was marked by the divestment of Japanese Americans of their land and personal property, and the criminalization of their race and national origin. This practice was "legal," because at the time the U.S. was fighting in World War II and the country of Japan was seen as a threat. Thus, legal and political officials saw Japanese Americans as loyal to Japan rather than America, because of their shared ancestry with Japan. This perceived disloyalty informed U.S. domestic policy toward Japanese citizens.

Initiation Act 2: In the present day, children of immigrants, primarily from Mexico and Central America, are being separated from their parents and held in U.S. detention centers. [The listener/reader understands that Initiation Act 2 is an analogy to what happened with Japanese internment.]

Initiation Act 3: Immigrant women held in U.S. detention centers have suffered invasive gynecological procedures, namely hysterectomies, to which they have not consented and that have left them infertile. [The listener/reader understands that Initiation Act 3 is an analogy to what happened with Japanese internment.]

Solution #1: Treat immigrant groups the dignity and respect.

Solution #2: Look at their actions and do not make assumptions about how they will act based on racial stereotypes and fear.

As employed, "because therefore" or "frame-main" and problem-solution reasoning stand in stark contrast to the linearity of the syllogism by their contextualization in community, societal, and historical imperatives. In sum, Asian Diasporic rhetorical strategies can produce powerful analytic frameworks that can be used to build persuasive arguments in the law. They are comprehensive in scope and preserve vital relationships between communities and among their members.

Asian Diasporic rhetorical strategies

See Tables 4.12 through 4.15.

Table 4.12: Discourse of persuasion/persuasion strategies

Yan	Use of language to influence political leaders and outcomes, and to demonstrate political ambition.
Ci	Refers to the artistry of language as a persuasion strategy, and also as a cover for lack of substance in a stated position or argument.
Jian	Directed toward an authority figure; attempts to persuade someone with greater authority to make changes for the benefit of the people; consensus among the rhetors has the greatest persuasive weight.
Shui	Primarily utilized by the learned and wise; used between people from the same peer group to a person of greater authority on political and military matters.
Ming	A judgment about the proper manner of persuasion; guided by cultural notions of morality; emotions are the source of moral appeals, as transmitted through the virtues of *ren*—kindness, *yi*—righteousness, *zhong*—loyalty, *xin*—faith, and *cheng*—sincerity.
Bian	Literally "debate"; a type of analogical reasoning process through which differences are illustrated by description; each distinction lends weight to advantages or disadvantages of a decision; can take the shape of narrative reasoning in the political arena and analogical reasoning in scholarly arguments.

Note: These concepts operate in concert and are foremost utilized to preserve relationships.

Table 4.13: Language as a symbolic resource

Identifies the issue, stereotype, or negative characterization for the communication to address (for example, AAPI hate);

Reframes it in the context of a community's culture as generated from within or as viewed by outsiders (for example, "Asian" culture is usually viewed as monolithic and related to experiences with "Asian" cuisine);

Translates these concepts through language that reflects a world view informed by a community's experience navigating capitalism, imperialism, White supremacy (White cultural hegemony), and patriarchy (for example, "Love Our People Like You Love Our Food").

Table 4.14: "Because therefore" "frame-main" reasoning

Reasons	Assertions	Legal question(s)/problem at issue
Presented as stories, histories, and symbols that precede assertions; histories are the most persuasive reasons.	Articulation of a problem/situation/issue analogous to the stories, histories, and symbols presented as reasons; the assertions guide the selection of stories, histories, and reasons.	Facilitate resolution of the issues raised by the assertions; problem solving occurs between and among the community members in which the problem(s) arise or with those who are cognizant of the cultural traditions and histories of the impacted community.

Table 4.15: Problem-solution structure

Initiation component (definition of the broad problem)	Initiation act (background information on the problem from cultural, historical, experiential, and social sources)	Articulation of the current problem (a distillation of the initiation component)	Proposed set of solutions
A statement or set of statements that broadly define the problem in the context of the society in which it occurs.	An explanation of the problem using historical, social, cultural, and/or experiential narratives.	A continuation of the historical, social, cultural, and/or experiential narrative, which includes a comparison to analogous situations in the present day.	A set of solutions based on the historical, social, cultural, and/or experiential context for the problem.

Latine rhetoric

Background

The study of Latine rhetorics includes the rhetorical strategies of people within the idea and reality of Latin America.[108] Because Latine histories encompass colonization and immigration, Latine rhetorical strategies are similar to those of Indigenous and Asian Diasporic peoples. This is especially true as Latine rhetoric includes Chicanx/Mestix@s[109] rhetoric; this group remains the largest Latine group residing in the United States.[110]

Latine rhetorics are an engagement with the borderlands, in language, place, and space.[111] As imagined by Gloria Anzaldúa in *Borderlands/La Frontera: The New Mestiza*:

> The U.S. Mexican border *es una herida abierta* where the Third World grates against the first and bleeds. And before a scab forms it hemorrhages again, the lifeblood of two worlds merging to form a third country—a border culture. Borders are set up to define the places that are safe and unsafe, to distinguish *us* from *them*. A border is a dividing line, a narrow strip along a steep edge. A borderland is a vague and undetermined place created by the emotional residue of an unnatural boundary. It is in a constant state of transition. The prohibited and forbidden are its inhabitants. *Los atrevesados* live here: the squint-eyed, the perverse, the queer, the troublesome, the mongrel, the mulato, the half-breed, the half dead; in short, those who cross over, pass over, or go through the confines of the "normal." Gringos in the U.S. Southwest consider the inhabitants of the borderlands transgressors, aliens—whether they possess documents or not, whether they're Chicanos, Indians or Blacks. Do not enter, trespassers will be raped, maimed, strangled, gassed, shot. The only "legitimate" inhabitants are those in power, the [W]hites and those who align themselves with [W]hites. Tension grips the inhabitants of the borderlands like a virus. Ambivalence and unrest reside there and death is no stranger.[112]

The colonized academy hosts its assault at the border, as it contends with Latine students in its physical and intellectual spaces occupied by the Western rhetorical canon.[113] The Western/Aristotelian paradigm is the dividing line in the legal academy and law practice, filled with culturally constructed categories that exclude more than they include. Ideas like freedom, justice, rights, privileges, and obligations live at the border, and the minoritized people who live in its borderlands are its constant trespassers as they try, through the machinations of the law available to them, to cross over, pass over, or go through its confines of the neutral and normative. The 1776 Report introduced in Chapter 3 establishes the strength of that border and the inhabitants of either side.[114]

The guiding methodology of Latine rhetorics is the disruption of the boundaries, "border insurrections."[115] Articulated in Anzaldúa's work on the concept of *conocimiento* or knowledge, centering Latine rhetorics requires "developing a critical and decolonized consciousness that moves from rupturing, to fragmentation, to connecting, to assembling and rebuilding."[116] The absence of borders, cultural, physical, and spiritual, is the beginning of knowledge. There must be a critical rupture of our invisible ("neutral") epistemologies, the fragmentation and uncertainty that comes with such a rupture, connections made between the fragmented pieces, and a reassembling of them to build something new and better.

This is the Latine rhetoric of coherence. It requires us to jettison oppressive analytic frames as sites for the operation of justice—aspirationally, theoretically, and actually. It forces us to first recognize, then to cross the borders of race, culture, gender, class, and sexuality—real and imagined—to capture something new beyond. Latine rhetoric is a challenge to the law to recognize itself as a series of borders that restrict how we can proceed to resolve disputes equitably. For example, in *McClendon v. Jamison*, Judge Reeves sets up the Ku Klux Klan Act (and later 42 U.S.C. section 1983) as a border to the tolerable amount of violence the state will allow against newly freed Black children, women, and men. Qualified immunity crossed that border, by allowing the police, who were complicit with the Ku Klux Klan, cover and protection for their brutal treatment of Black people. It is against this border that Black people grate and bleed. Their myriad deaths are no strangers here. A border insurrection involving qualified immunity, in Judge Reeves's analysis, would require decisive action by the United States Supreme Court. However, the possibility of an insurrection within the Western/Aristotelian paradigm is limited because as an oppressive analytic frame it can be no site for justice.

Inherent in Latine rhetorics is the idea of "epistemic delinking" or exposing the role of Western epistemology in Western rhetorical traditions, and in othering non-Westerners and non-Western rhetorics.[117] In Anzaldúa's words, "[c]ulture forms our beliefs. We perceive the version of our reality that it communicates. Dominant paradigms, predefined concepts that exist as unquestionable, unchallengeable, are transmitted to us through the culture. Culture is made by those in power—men."[118] Advancing our understanding of equity and law requires us to grapple with White cultural and patriarchal hegemony in our legislatures, classrooms, and courtrooms. The rupture occurs when we engage in epistemic delinking, by exposing the cultural underpinnings of what we call "neutral" and "normative" and giving Lady Justice sight. Anzaldúa admonishes us to "stop importing Greek myths and the Western Cartesian split [mind/body split] point of view and root ourselves in the mythological soil of this continent."[119] Hers is an invitation to grapple with what really is, instead of what we believe or want reality to be.

Latine rhetorics are also a disruption of the binary; the terms Latinx/Chicanx/Mestiz@ eschew gendered language and invite previously excluded Latine, like Afro Latine, into the community.[120] This disruption extends into written and performed symbols (such as painting, writing, movement/dance, religious symbols and texts) as rhetoric, and their role in creating new sources of knowledge in and about colonized spaces and the borderlands.[121] In this context, critical examination of a piece of art or music, like the piece "All My Relations" by Ulali, can be used as or to create a framework for analysis.

"All My Relations," described earlier as an example of Indigenous rhetoric, does both. As a framework for analysis, the song forces a comparison of settler colonialist and Indigenous experiences through its melody, recognizable but remade from Indigenous artistic traditions, and the spoken word, which details Indigenous peoples' experiences with imperialism, capitalism, White supremacy, White cultural hegemony, and patriarchy. As a source of knowledge for the creation of an analytic framework, it forces us to shift our world view to encompass Indigenous epistemologies and to accept artistic production as knowledge creation relevant in legal and academic contexts. In doing so, Latine rhetorical strategies not only reinscribe our own histories; they also assert that the "dominant narratives of Western rhetoric and writing must also be retold and revised."[122]

Latine rhetorical strategies

See Tables 4.16 through 4.18.

Together, these multicultural rhetorical strategies provide powerful tools to reshape how we read, analyze, and practice law, and resolve legal disputes. They hold the promise of justice and the power to remake those who use them in the process. Chapter 7 provides the opportunity to practice these strategies through exercises involving the most commonly utilized legal genres: pleadings, memos, trial and appellate briefs, and judicial opinions.

Table 4.16: *Conocimiento*/knowledge and developing a decolonized consciousness

Rupture	Expose hidden epistemologies (how we know what we know) through epistemic-delinking.
Fragmentation	Identify and critically examine the component parts of those epistemologies. What aspects of the epistemologies reflect imperialist, capitalist, White supremacist, and patriarchal imperatives? Out of which cultural traditions do they arise?
Connection	Which pieces of the fragmented epistemologies can be retained? Which of the pieces must be jettisoned?
Assembly	In what new ways can the fragmented epistemologies be assembled to create a decolonized consciousness? (That is, a consciousness that is free of biases against minoritized populations informed by White supremacy/White cultural hegemony.)
Rebuilding	In what ways can the epistemology be rebuilt and communicated in a manner that does not replicate imperialist, capitalist, White supremacist, and patriarchal imperatives?

Table 4.17: Epistemic delinking

Exposes the role of Western epistemology in Western rhetorical traditions;
Exposes the role of Western epistemology in othering non-Westerners (minoritized peoples);
Exposes the role of Western epistemology in othering multicultural reasoning and analytical paradigms/practices.

Table 4.18: Binary disruption

Categories	Performed symbols
In what way do the categories I employ reinforce borders between the West (ideologically and practically) and minoritized communities, and cultures?	In what ways can cultural symbols relevant to a given moment serve as rhetorical strategies in their own right, as well as sources of knowledge in and about colonized spaces and the borderlands?

Acknowledgments

Portions of the section "Types of Multicultural Rhetoric" in this chapter were originally published in a slightly different form in McMurtry-Chubb, 2019. Reprint permission has been acquired from the originating journal, *The Scholar: St. Mary's Law Review on Race and Social Justice.*

Notes

1 Gresson, 1995, pp 4–5.

2 Gresson, 1995, p 5.

3 Gordon, 2006, pp 17–18 (citing McPhail, 1993, pp 129–30, 132).

4 Cole, 2011, pp 122, 136; see also Kennedy, 1998 p 50.

5 Du Bois, 1903 [1987]; Hall, 1978; Said, 1979; McGee, 1980, reprinted in Lucaites et al, 1999, pp 427–9; Ngũgĩ wa Thiong'o, 1986; van Dijk, 1987; Spivak, 1988; Alcoff, 1991; Condit and Lucaites, 1993; McPhail, 1993, 2002; Gresson, 1995; Kubota, 1997; Asante, 1998, 2003; Gehrke, 1998; Kennedy, 1998; Scott, 1999; Lyons, 2000; Alkebulan, 2003; Jackson and Richardson, 2003; Karenga, 2003, pp 3–12; Trouillot, 2003; hooks, 2004; Mignolo, 2005; Gordon, 2006; Mao, 2006, 2014; Aikin, 2008; Baca, 2008; Lu and Horner, 2008; Mao and Young, 2008; Baca and Villanueva, 2010; Chen, 2011, pp 157–67; Cole, 2011; Wang 2011, pp 58–64; Kirkpatrick and Xu, 2012; Cisneros, 2014; Simpson, 2014; Wang, 2014; Mao et al, 2015; Couture and Wojahn, 2016; Mann, 2016; Ruiz, 2016; Ruiz and Sanchez, 2016; Villanueva, 2016; Enríquez-Loya and Leon, 2017; Arroyo, 2018; Asante, 2019; Na'puti, 2019; Pham, 2019; Sowards, 2019; Wanzer-Serrano, 2019.

6 Powell, 2002, pp 401–2.

7 Schulten, 2018, p 10.

8 Pearce, 1988, pp 3–4.

9 Powell, 2002, p 402.

10 Lyons, 2000.

11 Lyons, 2000, p 449.

12 Lyons, 2000, p 449–50.
13 Lyons, 2000, p 452.
14 Lyons, 2000, p 452–3.
15 Lyons, 2000, p 453; see also King et al, 2015, pp 6–7.
16 *Johnson v. M'Intosh*, 21 U.S. 543, 543–60 (1823).
17 *Johnson*, 21 U.S. at 573.
18 *Cherokee Nation v. Georgia*, 30 U.S. 1, 2 (1831).
19 *Worcester v. Georgia*, 31 U.S. 515, 518 (1832); author's emphasis.
20 Lyons, 2000, pp 458–9; see also King et al, 2015, pp 8–9.
21 Lyons, 2000, pp 459–62.
22 Lyons, 2000, pp 456–7.
23 Fowler, 2015, p 376.
24 *Washington v. Sum*, No. 99730-6, 2022 WL 2071560, at *12 (Wash. June 9, 2022).
25 *State v. Sum*, 17 Wash. App. 2d 1009, review granted, 198 Wash. 2d 1025, 497 P.3d 395 (2021), and rev'd, No. 99730-6, 2022 WL 2071560 (Wash. June 9, 2022).
26 *Sum*, 2022 WL 2071560, at *1.
27 Cole, 2011, p 125; see also Kennedy, 1998, p 50.
28 King et al, 2015, p 7 (internal citation omitted).
29 King et al, 2015, p 7.
30 Ulali, 2005.
31 Gleason, 2009, p 69.
32 Printed by permission from Corn, Beans & Squash (ASCAP), by exclusive arrangement with Heyday Media Group. Written by Pure Fe Antonia Crescioni (ASCAP), Carmen Caballero (ASCAP) and Jennifer Elizabeth Kreisberg (ASCAP). "All My Relations" as performed by Ulali was originally released by Corn, Beans & Squash Music in 1997 on the album *Mahk Jchi*.
33 Jackson and Richardson, 2003.
34 Jackson and Richardson, 2003, pp ix–x.
35 Jackson and Richardson, 2003, p x.
36 Jackson and Richardson, 2003, p xiii.
37 Jackson and Richardson, 2003, p xiii.
38 Jackson and Richardson, 2003, p xvi; see also Alkebulan, 2003, pp 23–4; Hine, 1992; but see Wallace, 1978 (critiquing, in part, Afrocentricity as practiced in the Black Power Movement).
39 Karenga, 2003, p 3.
40 Karenga, 2003, p 3.
41 Karenga, 2003, pp 3, 5.
42 See Jackson, 2003, p 124 (describing Maulana Karenga's Kawaida theory as "[a] Black nationalist theory, not a metatheory, nor is it a conceptual rubric of the Afrocentric paradigm").
43 Jackson, 2003, p 5.
44 Kalonji, 2014, p 197.
45 Rose, 1994, pp 28–9.
46 Rose, 1994, pp 28–9.
47 Rose, 1994, p 35.
48 Rose, 1994, p 38.
49 Rose, 1994, p 38.
50 Rose, 1994, p 39.
51 Karenga, 2003, p 10.
52 Karenga, 2003, p 14.
53 Jackson, 2003, p 11.

54 Jackson, 2003, p 11.
55 Jackson, 2003, p 11; see also Alkebulan, 2003, pp 23–5.
56 Karenga, 2003, pp 15–17.
57 Karenga, 2003, pp 11–12.
58 Karenga, 2003, p 11.
59 Karenga, 2003, p 8; Alkebulan, 2003, pp 28–9.
60 Karenga, 2003, p 8.
61 Karenga, 2003, p 8.
62 Karenga, 2003, p 9.
63 Karenga, 2003, pp 14–19.
64 Karenga, 2003, pp 10, 14; see also Alkebulan, 2003, p 33.
65 Alkebulan, 2003, p 33.
66 Karenga, 2003, p 10.
67 See, for example, Tomasi, 2004 (setting the introduction of Western rhetoric as the beginning of Japanese rhetoric and discussing its waxing and waning relevance); but see Sung-Gi, 2010 (arguing for a general rhetoric inclusive of the East and West, while referencing a Korean rhetorical tradition); and compare Muller, 2015 (citing the Chinese influence on the development of Korean rhetoric); Oliver, 1959.
68 See generally Lu and Horner, 2008; Mao and Young, 2008, pp 1–21.
69 Kirkpatrick and Xu, 2012, p 13.
70 Kirkpatrick and Xu, 2012, p 14.
71 Chen, 2005, p 29.
72 Chen, 2005, p 29.
73 Chen, 2005, p 29.
74 Chen, 2005, p 29.
75 Chen, 2005, p 29.
76 Chen, 2005, p 29.
77 Chen, 2005, pp 32–3.
78 Chen, 2005, pp 32–3.
79 Chen, 2005, p 29.
80 Kirkpatrick and Xu, 2012, p 14.
81 Kirkpatrick and Xu, 2012, pp 14–15.
82 Kirkpatrick and Xu, 2012, pp 14–15.
83 Kirkpatrick and Xu, 2012, pp 14–15.
84 Kirkpatrick and Xu, 2012, pp 20–4.
85 Kirkpatrick and Xu, 2012, pp 20–4.
86 Kirkpatrick and Xu, 2012, pp 20–4.
87 Kirkpatrick and Xu, 2012, pp 18, 25–9, 42–5, 126–8; Mao, 2006, pp 70–1.
88 Chen, 2005, p 29.
89 Mao, 2006, pp 74–5.
90 Tirkkonen-Condit, 1985, pp 21–41; Kachru, 1997, p 341 (quoting Betty Heimann, 1964, pp 170–1).
91 Kachru, 1997, p 342.
92 Kachru, 1997, p 341 (quoting Heimann, 1964, pp 170–1).
93 Kachru, 1997, p 342.
94 Takaki, 1989.
95 Kim, 1990, p 101.
96 Arroyo, 2018.
97 Lu and Horner, 2008, pp vii–viii.
98 Lu and Horner, 2008, pp x–xi.
99 Lu and Horner, 2008, pp xi–xii.

[100] Lu and Horner, 2008, pp xi–xii.

[101] Mao and Young, 2008, p 2.

[102] Mao and Young, 2008, pp 2–3.

[103] Mao and Young, 2008, p 4.

[104] Kachru, 1997, p 342.

[105] Kachru, 1997, p 342.

[106] Kachru, 1997, p 342.

[107] Kachru, 1997, p 342.

[108] See generally Alonso, 1998; Mignolo, 2005; Baca and Villanueva, 2010.

[109] Baca, 2008, pp xvi, 2. Baca (p. 2) describes the term "Mestiz@" as: "a dynamic spectrum of shifting and contested subjectivity. At one extreme of this continuum are people who understand their individual and communal identity as primarily indigenous. At the other extreme are those who deny indigenous affiliation as part of their lineage and instead see themselves within a largely isolated Spanish Iberian inheritance of the past 400–500 years in America."

[110] Baca, 2008, pp xvi, 2, 13–14.

[111] Enríquez-Loya and Leon, 2017, pp 212–13; see also Villanueva, 2016, pp 34–5, 4 (arguing that the border is a fiction within the idea of nation as fiction). See generally Anzaldúa, 1987; DeChaine, 2012; Cisneros, 2014.

[112] Anzaldúa, 1987, pp 3–4.

[113] Enríquez-Loya and Leon, 2017, pp 212–13; see also Baca, 2008, p 1. The author also utilizes Anzaldúa's "la conciencia de la mestizo" or "new mestizo consciousness." Anzaldúa's consciousness is a call to resist the subject–other binary in characterizing Mexican/Chicanx colonial and border encounters. Anzaldúa, 1987, pp 77–91.

[114] President's Advisory 1776 Commission, 2021.

[115] Baca, 2008, p 5.

[116] Enríquez-Loya and Leon, 2017, pp 212–13; see generally Ruiz, 2016, pp 1–16.

[117] Ruiz and Sánchez, 2016, pp xiv–xv.

[118] Anzaldúa, 1987, p 16.

[119] Anzaldúa, 1987, p 68.

[120] Garcia, 2017, p 210; Baca, 2008, p 2 (arguing that '[t]he reinvention of the typographic logogram '@' is primarily for purposes of gender inclusivity').

[121] Baca, 2008, pp 2–5.

[122] Baca, 2008, p 14 (quoting E.A. Mares).

5

Reproducing the Canon, Reproducing Inequity (Traditional Rhetoric)

United States v. Bhagat Singh Thind, 43 S. Ct. 338 (United States Supreme Court 1923)

This case is about an immigration statute enacted in 1870, just after the Civil War. As you read this case, think about how the court constructed the framework of knowledge and history that supports its holding.

(All footnotes have been omitted.)

Opinion

Mr. Justice SUTHERLAND delivered the opinion of the Court.

This cause is here upon a certificate from the Circuit Court of appeals requesting the instruction of this Court in respect of the following questions:

"1 Is a high-caste Hindu, of full Indian blood, born at Amritsar, Punjab, India, a white person within the meaning of section 2169, Revised Statutes?"

"2 Does the Act of February 5, 1917 (39 Stat. 875, § 3), disqualify from naturalization as citizens those Hindus now barred by that act, who had lawfully entered the United States prior to the passage of said act?"

The appellee was granted a certificate of citizenship by the District Court of the United States for the District of Oregon, over the objection of the Naturalization Examiner for the United States. A bill in equity was then filed by the United States, seeking a cancellation of the certificate on the ground that the appellee was not a white person and therefore not lawfully entitled to naturalization. The District Court, on motion, dismissed the bill (*In re Bhagat Singh Thind*, 268 Fed. 683), and an appeal was taken to the

Circuit Court of Appeals. No question is made in respect of the individual qualifications of the appellee. The sole question is whether he falls within the class designated by Congress as eligible.

Section 2169, Revised Statutes (Comp. St. § 4358), provides that the provisions of the Naturalization Act "shall apply to aliens being free white persons and to aliens of African nativity and to persons of African descent." If the applicant is a white person, within the meaning of this section, he is entitled to naturalization; otherwise not. In *Ozawa v. United States*, 260 U.S. 178, 43 Sup. Ct. 65, 67 L. Ed. 199, decided November 13, 1922, we had occasion to consider the application of these words to the case of a cultivated Japanese and were constrained to hold that he was not within their meaning. As there pointed out, the provision is not that any particular class of persons shall be excluded, but it is, in effect, that only white persons shall be included within the privilege of the statute. "The intention was to confer the privilege of citizenship upon that class of persons whom the fathers knew as white, and to deny it to all who could not be so classified. It is not enough to say that the framers did not have in mind the brown or yellow races of Asia. It is necessary to go farther and be able to say that had these particular races been suggested the language of the act would have been so varied as to include them within its privileges"—citing *Dartmouth College v. Woodward*, 4 Wheat. 518, 644, 4 L. Ed. 629. Following a long line of decisions of the lower Federal courts, we held that the words imported a racial and not an individual test and were meant to indicate only persons of what is popularly known as the Caucasian race. But, as there pointed out, the conclusion that the phrase "white persons" and the word "Caucasian" are synonymous does not end the matter. It enabled us to dispose of the problem as it was there presented, since the applicant for citizenship clearly fell outside the zone of debatable ground on the negative side; but the decision still left the question to be dealt with, in doubtful and different cases, by the "process of judicial inclusion and exclusion." Mere ability on the part of an applicant for naturalization to establish a line of descent from a Caucasian ancestor will not *ipso facto* to and necessarily conclude the inquiry. "Caucasian" is a conventional word of much flexibility, as a study of the literature dealing with racial questions will disclose, and while it and the words "white persons" are treated as synonymous for the purposes of that case, they are not of identical meaning—*idem per idem*.

In the endeavor to ascertain the meaning of the statute we must not fail to keep in mind that it does not employ the word "Caucasian," but the words "white persons," and these are words of common speech and not of scientific origin. The word "Caucasian," not only was not employed in the law, but was probably wholly unfamiliar to the original framers of the statute in 1790. When we employ it, we do so as an aid to the ascertainment of the legislative intent and not as an invariable substitute for the statutory words. Indeed, as used in the science of ethnology, the connotation of the word is by no means clear, and the use of it in its scientific sense as an equivalent for the words of the statute, other considerations aside, would simply mean the substitution of one perplexity for another. But in this country, during the last half century especially, the word by common usage has acquired a popular meaning, not clearly defined to be sure, but sufficiently so to enable us to say that its popular as distinguished from its scientific application is of appreciably narrower scope. It is in the popular sense of the word, therefore, that we employ it as an aid to the construction of the statute, for it would be obviously illogical to convert words of common speech used in a statute into words of scientific terminology when neither the latter nor the science for whose purposes they were coined was within the contemplation of the framers of the statute or of the people for whom it was framed. The words of the statute are to be interpreted in accordance with the understanding of the common man from whose vocabulary they were taken. See *Maillard v. Lawrence*, 16 How. 251, 261, 14 L. Ed. 925.

They imply, as we have said, a racial test; but the term "race" is one which, for the practical purposes of the statute, must be applied to a group of living persons now possessing in common the requisite characteristics, not to groups of persons who are supposed to be or really are descended from some remote, common ancestor, but who, whether they both resemble him to a greater or less extent, have, at any rate, ceased altogether to resemble one another. It may be true that the blond Scandinavian and the brown Hindu have a common ancestor in the dim reaches of antiquity, but the average man knows perfectly well that there are unmistakable and profound differences between them to-day; and it is not impossible, if that common ancestor could be materialized in the flesh, we should discover that he was himself sufficiently differentiated from both of his descendants to preclude his racial classification with either. The question for determination is not, therefore, whether by the speculative processes of ethnological reasoning we may present a probability to the scientific mind that they have the same origin, but whether we can satisfy the common understanding that they are now the same or sufficiently the same to justify the interpreters of a statute—written in the words of common speech, for common understanding, by unscientific men—in classifying them together in the statutory category as white persons. In 1790 the Adamite theory of creation—which gave a common ancestor to all mankind—was generally accepted, and it is not at all probable that it was intended by the legislators of that day to submit the question of the application of the words "white persons" to the mere test of an indefinitely remote common ancestry, without regard to the extent of the subsequent divergence of the various branches from such common ancestry or from one another.

The eligibility of this applicant for citizenship is based on the sole fact that he is of high-caste Hindu stock, born in Punjab, one of the extreme northwestern districts of India, and classified by certain scientific authorities as of the Caucasian or Aryan race. The Aryan theory as a racial basis seems to be discredited by most, if not all, modern writers on the subject of ethnology. A review of their contentions would serve no useful purpose. It is enough to refer to the works of Deniker (*Races of Man*, 317), Keane (*Man, Past and Present*, 445, 446), and Huxley (*Man's Place in Nature*, 278) and to the Dictionary of Races, Senate Document 662, 61st Congress, 3d Sess. 1910–1911, p 17.

The term "Aryan" has to do with linguistic, and not at all with physical, characteristics, and it would seem reasonably clear that mere resemblance in language, indicating a common linguistic root buried in remotely ancient soil, is altogether inadequate to prove common racial origin. There is, and can be, no assurance that the so-called Aryan language was not spoken by a variety of races living in proximity to one another. Our own history has witnessed the adoption of the English tongue by millions of negroes, whose descendants can never be classified racially with the descendants of white persons, notwithstanding both may speak a common root language.

The word "Caucasian" is in scarcely better repute. It is at best a conventional term, with an altogether fortuitous origin, which under scientific manipulation, has come to include far more than the unscientific mind suspects. According to Keane, for example (*The World's Peoples*, 24, 28, 307, et seq.), it includes not only the Hindu, but some of the Polynesians (that is, the Maori, Tahitians, Samoans, Hawaiians, and others), the Hamites of Africa, upon the ground of the Caucasic cast of their features, though in color they range from brown to black. We venture to think that the average well informed white American would learn with some degree of astonishment that the race to which he belongs is made up of such heterogeneous elements.

The various authorities are in irreconcilable disagreement as to what constitutes a proper racial division. For instance, Blumenbach has 5 races; Keane following Linnaeus, 4; Deniker, 29. The explanation probably is that "the innumerable varieties of mankind run into one another by insensible degrees," and to arrange them in sharply bounded divisions is an undertaking of such uncertainty that common agreement is practically impossible.

It may be, therefore, that a given group cannot be properly assigned to any of the enumerated grand racial divisions. The type may have been so changed by intermixture of blood as to justify an intermediate classification. Something very like this has actually taken place in India. Thus, in Hindustan and Berar there was such an intermixture of the "Aryan" invader with the dark-skinned Dravidian.

In the Punjab and Rajputana, while the invaders seem to have met with more success in the effort to preserve their racial purity, intermarriages did occur producing an intermingling of the two and destroying to a greater or less degree the purity of the "Aryan" blood. The rules of caste, while calculated to prevent this intermixture, seem not to have been entirely successful.

It does not seem necessary to pursue the matter of scientific classification further. We are unable to agree with the District Court, or with other lower federal courts, in the conclusion that a native Hindu is eligible for naturalization under section 2169. The words of familiar speech, which were used by the original framers of the law, were intended to include only the type of man whom they knew as white. The immigration of that day was almost exclusively from the British Isles and Northwestern Europe, whence they and their forebears had come. When they extended the privilege of American citizenship to "any alien being a free white person" it was these immigrants—bone of their bone and flesh of their flesh—and their kind whom they must have had affirmatively in mind. The succeeding years brought immigrants from Eastern, Southern and Middle Europe, among them the Slavs and the dark-eyed, swarthy people of Alpine and Mediterranean stock, and these were received as unquestionably akin to those already here and readily amalgamated with them. It was the descendants of these, and other immigrants of like origin, who constituted the white population of the country when section 2169, re-enacting the naturalization test of 1790, was adopted, and, there is no reason to doubt, with like intent and meaning.

What, if any, people of primarily Asiatic stock come within the words of the section we do not deem it necessary now to decide. There is much in the origin and historic development of the statute to suggest that no Asiatic whatever was included. The debates in Congress, during the consideration of the subject in 1870 and 1875, are persuasively of this character. In 1873, for example, the words "free white persons" were unintentionally omitted from the compilation of the Revised Statutes. This omission was supplied in 1875 by the act to correct errors and supply omissions. 18 Stat. c. 80, p 318. When this act was under consideration by Congress efforts were made to strike out the words quoted, and it was insisted upon the one hand and conceded upon the other, that the effect of their retention was to exclude Asiatics generally from citizenship. While what was said upon that occasion, to be sure, furnishes no basis for judicial construction of the statute, it is, nevertheless, an important historic incident, which may not be altogether ignored in the search for the true meaning of words which are themselves historic. That question, however, may well be left for final determination until the details have been more completely disclosed by the consideration of particular cases, as they from time to time arise. The words of the statute, it must be conceded, do not readily yield to exact interpretation, and it is probably better to leave them as they are than to risk undue extension or undue limitation of their meaning by any general paraphrase at this time.

What we now hold is that the words "free white persons" are words of common speech, to be interpreted in accordance with the understanding of the common man, synonymous with the word "Caucasian" only as that word is popularly understood. As so understood and used, whatever may be the speculations of the ethnologist, it does not include the body of people to whom the appellee belongs. It is a matter of familiar observation and knowledge that the physical group characteristics of the Hindus render them readily distinguishable from the various groups of persons in this country commonly recognized as white. The children of English, French, German, Italian, Scandinavian, and other European parentage, quickly merge into the mass of our population and lose the distinctive hallmarks of their European origin. On the other hand, it cannot be doubted that the children born in this country of Hindu parents would retain indefinitely the clear evidence of their ancestry. It is very far from our thought to suggest the slightest question of racial superiority or inferiority. What we suggest is merely racial difference, and it is of such character and extent that the great body of our people instinctively recognize it and reject the thought of assimilation.

It is not without significance in this connection that Congress, by the Act of February 5, 1917, 39 Stat. 874, c. 29, § 3 (Comp. St. 1918, Comp. St. Ann. Supp. 1919, § 4289 1/4b), has now excluded from admission into this country all natives of Asia within designated limits of latitude and longitude, including the whole of India. This not only constitutes conclusive evidence of the congressional attitude of opposition to Asiatic immigration generally, but is persuasive of a similar attitude toward Asiatic naturalization as well, since it is not likely that Congress would be willing to accept as citizens a class of persons whom it rejects as immigrants.

It follows that a negative answer must be given to the first question, which disposes of the case and renders an answer to the second question unnecessary, and it will be so certified.

Answer to question No. 1, No.

Discussion questions

1. Within the questions presented, what rhetorical choices did Justice Sutherland make as a framing method, to foreshadow the reasoning?
2. What was the historical context behind the 1875 immigration statute?
3. What right was at the heart of this case?
4. What party initiated the legal action that brought the case to the Supreme Court?
5. What category was the court defining and what is the source of the category?
6. Map out Mr. Thind's syllogistic argument for why he was entitled to citizenship.
7. How did Mr. Thind's argument, even though he was ostensibly a member of a minoritized community, nonetheless reinforce the racialized and racist reasoning norms that pervaded U.S. law at the time?
8. What choices did the court make in selecting the type of knowledge (relating to race and ethnicity) that would control the outcome of the case?
9. How does the court deploy the concepts of "popular" and beliefs of the "average man" to reach its holding?
10. What legal authority did the Supreme Court cite to bolster its conclusion toward the end of its opinion?

Haynes v. Alfred A. Knopf, Inc., 8 F.3d 1222 (7th Cir. 1993)

This is a privacy rights case that raises the issue of who has the right to tell one's story. This case illustrates the concerns that Edward Said raised about when powerful voices write and describe "the other." As you read this case, think about (1) which authorial voices held the most power to speak and (2) which voices were involuntarily spoken for.

Opinion

POSNER, Chief Judge.

Luther Haynes and his wife, Dorothy Haynes née Johnson, appeal from the dismissal on the defendants' motion for summary judgment of their suit against Nicholas Lemann, the author of a highly praised, best-selling book of social and political history called *The Promised Land: The Great Black Migration and How It Changed America* (1991), and Alfred A. Knopf, Inc., the book's publisher. The plaintiffs claim that the book libels Luther Haynes and invades both plaintiffs' right of privacy. Federal jurisdiction is based on diversity, and the common law of Illinois is agreed to govern the substantive issues. The appeal presents difficult issues at the intersection of tort law and freedom of the press.

Between 1940 and 1970, five million [Black people] moved from impoverished rural areas in the South to the cities of the North in search of a better life. Some found it, and after sojourns of shorter or greater length in the poor black districts of the cities moved to middle-class areas. Others, despite the ballyhooed efforts of the federal government, particularly between 1964 and 1972, to erase poverty and racial discrimination, remained mired in what has come to be called the "urban ghetto." *The Promised Land* is a history of the migration. It is not history as a professional historian, a demographer, or a social scientist would write it. Lemann is none of these. He is a journalist and has written a journalistic history, in which the focus is on individuals whether powerful or representative. In the former group are the politicians who invented, executed, or exploited the "Great Society" programs. In the latter are a handful of the actual migrants. Foremost among these is Ruby Lee Daniels. Her story is the spine of the book. We are introduced to her on page 7; we take leave of her on page 346, within a few pages of the end of the text of the book.

When we meet her, it is the early 1940s and she is a young woman picking cotton on a plantation in Clarksdale, Mississippi. "[B]lack sharecropper society on the eve of the introduction [in the 1940s] of the mechanical cotton picker [a major spur to the migration] was the equivalent of big-city ghetto society today in many ways. It was the national center of illegitimate childbearing and of the female-headed family." Ruby had married young, but after her husband had been inducted into the army on the eve of World War II she had fallen in love with a married man, by whom she had had a child. The man's wife died and Ruby married him, but they broke up after a month. Glowing reports from an aunt who had moved to Chicago persuaded Ruby Daniels to move there in 1946. She found a job doing janitorial work, but eventually lost the job and went on public aid. She was unmarried, and had several children, when in 1953 she met "the most important man in her life." Luther Haynes, born in 1924 or 1925, a sharecropper from Mississippi, had moved to Chicago in an effort to effect a reconciliation with his wife. The effort had failed. When he met Ruby Daniels he had a well-paying job in an awning factory. They lived together, and had children. But then "Luther began to drink too much. When he drank he got mean, and he and Ruby would get into ferocious quarrels. He was still working, but he wasn't always bringing his paycheck home." Ruby got work as a maid. They moved to a poorer part of the city. The relationship went downhill. "It got to the point where [Luther] would go out on Friday evenings after picking up his paycheck, and Ruby would hope he wouldn't come home, because she knew he would be drunk. On the Friday evenings when he did come home—over the years Ruby developed a devastating imitation of Luther, and could re-create the scene quite vividly—he would walk into the apartment, put on a record and turn up the volume, and saunter into their bedroom, a bottle in one hand and a cigarette in the other, in the mood for love. On one such night, Ruby's last child, Kevin, was conceived. Kevin always had something wrong with him—he was very moody, he was scrawny, and he had a severe speech impediment. Ruby was never able to find out exactly what the problem was, but she blamed it on Luther; all that alcohol must have gotten into his sperm, she said."

Ruby was on public aid, but was cut off when social workers discovered she had a man in the house. She got a night job. Luther was supposed to stay with the children while she was at work, especially since they lived in a dangerous neighborhood; but often when she came home, at 3:00 a.m. or so, she would "find the older children awake, and when she would ask them if Luther had been there, the answer would be, 'No, ma'am'. " Ruby's last aid check, arriving providentially after she had been cut off, enabled the couple to buy a modest house on contract—it "was, by a wide margin, the best place she had ever lived." But "after only a few months, Luther ruined everything by going out and buying a brand-new 1961 Pontiac. It meant more to him than the house did, and when they couldn't make the house payment, he insisted on keeping the car" even though she hadn't enough money to buy shoes for the children. The family was kicked out of the house. They now moved frequently. They were reaching rock bottom. At this nadir, hope appeared in the ironic form of the Robert Taylor Homes, then a brand-new public housing project, now a notorious focus of drug addiction and gang violence. Ruby had had an application for public housing on file for many years, but the housing authority screened out unwed mothers. Told by a social worker that she could have an apartment in the Taylor Homes if she produced a marriage license, she and Luther (who was now divorced from his first wife) were married forthwith and promptly accepted as tenants. "The Haynes family chose to rejoice in their good fortune in becoming residents of the Robert Taylor Homes. As Ruby's son Larry, who was twelve years old at the time, says, 'I thought that was the beautifullest place in the world.' "

Even in the halcyon days of 1962, the Robert Taylor Homes were no paradise. There was considerable crime, and there were gangs, and Ruby's son Kermit joined one. Kermit was not Luther's son and did not recognize his authority. The two quarreled a lot. Meanwhile Luther had lost his job in the awning factory "that he had had for a decade, and then bounced around a little. He lost jobs because of transportation problems, because of layoffs, because of a bout of serious illness, because of his drinking, because he had a minor criminal record (having been in jail for disorderly conduct following a fight with Ruby), and because creditors were after him." He resumed "his old habit of not returning from work on Fridays after he got his paycheck." One weekend he didn't come home at all. In a search of his things Ruby discovered evidence that Luther was having an affair with Dorothy Johnson, a former neighbor. "Luther was not being particularly careful; he saw in Dorothy, who was younger than Ruby, who had three children compared to Ruby's eight, who had a job while Ruby was on public aid, the promise of an escape from the ghetto, and he was entranced." The children discovered the affair. Kermit tried to strangle Luther. In 1965 Luther moved out permanently, and eventually he and Ruby divorced.

Ruby remained in the Robert Taylor Homes until 1979, when she moved back to Clarksdale. She had become eligible for social security in 1978; and with her surviving children (one of her sons had died, either a suicide or murdered) now adults, though most of them deeply troubled adults and Kevin, whom Ruby in a custody proceeding described as retarded, still living at home, Ruby "is settling into old age with a sense of contentment about the circumstances she has found." But "there has always been that nagging sensation of incompleteness, which made itself felt most directly in her relationships with men."

After divorcing Ruby, Luther Haynes married Dorothy Johnson. He is still married to her, "owns a home on the far South Side of Chicago, and has worked for years as a parking-lot attendant; only recently have he and Ruby found that they can speak civilly to each other on the phone."

There is much more to the book than our paraphrase and excerpts—much about other migrants, about the travails of Ruby's children, about discrimination against [Black people] in both the North and the South, and about the politics of poverty programs in Washington and Chicago. But the excerpts we have quoted contain all the passages upon which the Hayneses' lawsuit is founded.

***

The major claim in the complaint, and the focus of the appeal, is not defamation, however; it is invasion of the right of privacy. In tort law the term "right of privacy" covers several distinct wrongs. [The court discusses different theories and identifies the one at issue], publicizing personal facts that while true and not misleading are so intimate that their disclosure to the public is deeply embarrassing to the person thus exposed and is perceived as gratuitous by the community. *Daily Times Democrat v. Graham*, 276 Ala. 380, 162 So.2d 474 (1964); *Barber v. Time, Inc.*, 348 Mo. 1199, 159 S.W.2d 291 (1942); *Diaz v. Oakland Tribune, Inc.*, 139 Cal.App.3d 118, 188 Cal.Rptr. 762, 767–78 (1983); *Banks v. King Features Syndicate, Inc.*, 30 F. Supp. 352 (S.D.N.Y.1939). The last, the publicizing of personal facts, is the aspect of invasion of privacy charged by the Hayneses.

Even people who have nothing rationally to be ashamed of can be mortified by the publication of intimate details of their life. Most people in no wise deformed or disfigured would nevertheless be deeply upset if nude photographs of themselves were published in a newspaper or a book. They feel the same way about photographs of their sexual activities, however "normal," or about a narrative of those activities, or about having their medical records publicized. Although it is well known that every human being defecates, no adult human being in our society wants a newspaper to show a picture of him defecating. The desire for privacy illustrated by these examples is a mysterious but deep fact about human personality. It deserves and in our society receives legal protection. The nature of the injury shows, by the way, that the defendants are wrong to argue that this branch of the right of privacy requires proof of special damages. *Manville v. Borg–Warner Corp.*, 418 F.2d 434, 436–37 (10th Cir.1969); *Vassiliades v. Garfinckel's*, 492 A.2d 580, 594 (D.C.App.1985).

But this is not the character of the depictions of the Hayneses in *The Promised Land*. Although the plaintiffs claim that the book depicts their "sex life" and "ridicules" Luther Haynes's lovemaking (the reference is to the passage we quoted in which the author refers to Ruby's "devastating imitation" of Luther's manner when he would come home Friday nights in an amorous mood), these characterizations are misleading. No sexual act is described in the book. No intimate details are revealed. Entering one's bedroom with a bottle in one hand and a cigarette in the other is not foreplay. Ruby's speculation that Kevin's problems may have been due to Luther's having been a heavy drinker is not the narration of a sexual act.

The revelations in the book are not about the intimate details of the Hayneses' life. They are about misconduct, in particular Luther's. (There is very little about Dorothy in the book, apart from the fact that she had had an affair with Luther while he was still married to Ruby and that they eventually became and have remained lawfully married.) The revelations are about his heavy drinking, his unstable employment, his adultery, his irresponsible and neglectful behavior toward his wife and children. So we must consider cases in which the right of privacy has been invoked as a shield against the revelation of previous misconduct.

Two early cases illustrate the range of judicial thinking. In *Melvin v. Reid*, 112 Cal. App. 285, 297 Pac. 91 (1931), the plaintiff was a former prostitute, who had been prosecuted but acquitted of murder. She later had married and (she alleged) for seven years had lived a blameless respectable life in a community in which her lurid past was unknown—when all was revealed in a movie about the murder case which used her maiden name. The court held that these allegations stated a claim for invasion of privacy. The Hayneses' claim is similar although less dramatic. They have been a respectable married couple for two decades. Luther's alcohol problem is behind him. He has steady employment as a doorman. His wife is a nurse, and in 1990 he told Lemann that the couple's combined income was $60,000 a year. He is not in trouble with the domestic relations court. He is a deacon of his church. He has come a long way from sharecropping in Mississippi and public housing in Chicago and he and his wife want to bury their past just as Mrs. Melvin wanted to do and in *Melvin v. Reid* was held entitled to do. Cf. *Briscoe v. Reader's Digest Ass'n*, 4 Cal.3d 529, 93 Cal.Rptr. 866, 483 P.2d 34, 43 (1971). In Luther Haynes's own words, from his deposition, "I know I haven't been no angel, but since almost 30 years ago I have turned my life completely around. I stopped the drinking and all this bad habits and stuff like that, which I deny, some of [it] I didn't deny, because I have changed my life. It take me almost 30 years to change it and I am deeply in my church. I look good in the eyes of my church members and my community. Now, what is going to happen now when this public reads this garbage which I didn't tell Mr. Lemann to write? Then all this is going to go down the drain. And I worked like a son of a gun to build myself up in a good reputation and he has torn it down."

But with *Melvin v. Reid* compare *Sidis v. F–R Publishing Corp.*, 113 F.2d 806 (2d Cir.1940), another old case but one more consonant with modern thinking about the proper balance between the right of privacy and the freedom of the press. A child prodigy had flamed out; he was now an eccentric recluse. The *New Yorker* ran a "where is he now" article about him. The article, entitled "April Fool," did not reveal any misconduct by Sidis but it depicted him in mocking tones as a comical failure, in much the same way that the report of Ruby's "devastating imitation" of the amorous Luther Haynes could be thought to have depicted him as a comical failure, albeit with sinister consequences absent from Sidis's case. The invasion of Sidis's privacy was palpable. But the publisher won. No intimate physical details of Sidis's life had been revealed; and on the other side was the undoubted newsworthiness of a child prodigy, as of a woman prosecuted for murder. Sidis, unlike Mrs. Melvin, was not permitted to bury his past.

[Discussion of other precedent cases omitted.]

[T]he implications of those [precedential First Amendment] decisions for the branch of the right of privacy that limits the publication of private facts are profound, even for a case such as this in which, unlike *Melvin v. Reid*, the primary source of the allegedly humiliating personal facts is not a public record. (The primary source is Ruby Daniels.) The Court must believe that the First Amendment greatly circumscribes the right even of a private figure to obtain damages for the publication of newsworthy facts about him, even when they are facts of a kind that people want very much to conceal. To be identified in the newspaper as a rape victim is intensely embarrassing. And it is not invited embarrassment. No one asks to be raped; the plaintiff in *Melvin v. Reid* did not ask to be prosecuted for murder (remember, she was acquitted, though whether she actually was innocent is unknown); Sidis did not decide to be a prodigy; and Luther Haynes did not aspire to be a representative figure in the great black migration from the South to the North. People who do not desire the limelight and do not deliberately choose a way of life or course of conduct calculated to thrust them into it nevertheless have no legal right to extinguish it if the experiences that have befallen them are newsworthy, even if they would prefer that those experiences be kept private. The possibility of an involuntary loss of privacy is recognized in the modern formulations of this branch of the privacy tort, which require not only that the private facts publicized be such as would make a reasonable person deeply offended by such publicity but also that they be facts in which the public has no legitimate interest.

The two criteria, offensiveness and newsworthiness, are related. An individual, and more pertinently perhaps the community, is most offended by the publication of intimate personal facts when the community has no interest in them beyond the voyeuristic thrill of penetrating the wall of privacy that surrounds a stranger. The reader of a book about the black migration to the North would have no legitimate interest in the details of Luther Haynes's sex life; but no such details are disclosed.

Such a reader does have a legitimate interest in the aspects of Luther's conduct that the book reveals. For one of Lemann's major themes is the transposition virtually intact of a sharecropper morality characterized by a family structure "matriarchal and elastic" and by an "extremely unstable" marriage bond to the slums of the northern cities, and the interaction, largely random and sometimes perverse, of that morality with governmental programs to alleviate poverty. Public aid policies discouraged Ruby and Luther from living together; public housing policies precipitated a marriage doomed to fail. No detail in the book claimed to invade the Hayneses' privacy is not germane to the story that the author wanted to tell, a story not only of legitimate but of transcendent public interest.

The Hayneses question whether the linkage between the author's theme and their private life really is organic. They point out that many social histories do not mention individuals at all, let alone by name. That is true. Much of social science, including social history, proceeds by abstraction, aggregation, and quantification rather than by case studies; the economist Robert Fogel has won a Nobel prize for his statistical studies of economic history, including, not wholly unrelated to the subject of Lemann's book, the history of Negro slavery in the United States. But it would be absurd to suggest that cliometric or other aggregative, impersonal methods of doing social history are the only proper way to go about it and presumptuous to claim even that they are the best way. Lemann's book has been praised to the skies by distinguished scholars, among them black scholars covering a large portion of the ideological spectrum—Henry Louis Gates Jr., William Julius Wilson, and Patricia Williams. Lemann's methodology places the individual case history at center stage. If he cannot tell the story of Ruby Daniels without waivers from every person who she thinks did her wrong, he cannot write this book.

Well, argue the Hayneses, at least Lemann could have changed their names. But the use of pseudonyms would not have gotten Lemann and Knopf off the legal hook. The details of the Hayneses' lives recounted in the book would identify them unmistakably to anyone who has known the Hayneses well for a long time (members of their families, for example), or who knew them before they got married; and no more is required for liability either in defamation law, *Rosenblatt v. Baer*, 383 U.S. 75, 79–87, 86 S. Ct. 669, 672–77, 15 L.Ed.2d 597 (1966); *Stevens v. Tillman*, 855 F.2d 394, 397 (7th Cir.1988); *Brown & Williamson Tobacco Corp. v. Jacobson*, 713 713 F.2d 262, 267 (7th Cir. 1983), or in privacy law. *Daily Times Democrat v. Graham*, *supra*, 162 So.2d at 476; *Vassiliades v. Garfinckel's*, *supra*, 492 A.2d at 588. Lemann would have had to change some, perhaps many, of the details. But then he would no longer have been writing history. He would have been writing fiction. The nonquantitative study of living persons would be abolished as a category of scholarship, to be replaced by the sociological novel. That is a genre with a distinguished history punctuated by famous names, such as Dickens, Zola, Stowe, Dreiser, Sinclair, Steinbeck, and Wolfe, but we do not think that the law of privacy makes it (or that the First Amendment would permit the law of privacy to make it) the exclusive format for a social history of living persons that tells their story rather than treating them as data points in a statistical study. Reporting the true facts about real people is necessary to "obviate any impression that the problems raised in the [book] are remote or hypothetical." *Gilbert v. Medical Economics Co.*, 665 F.2d 305, 308 (10th Cir. 1981). And surely a composite portrait of ghetto residents would be attacked as racial stereotyping.

The Promised Land does not afford the reader a titillating glimpse of tabooed activities. The tone is decorous and restrained. Painful though it is for the Hayneses to see a past they would rather forget brought into the public view, the public needs the information conveyed by the book, including the information about Luther and Dorothy Haynes, in order to evaluate the profound social and political questions that the book raises.

Ordinarily the evaluation and comparison of offensiveness and newsworthiness would be, like other questions of the application of a legal standard to the facts of a particular case, matters for a jury, not for a judge on a motion for summary judgment. But summary judgment is properly granted to a defendant when on the basis of the evidence obtained in pretrial discovery no reasonable jury could render a verdict for the plaintiff, *Anderson v. Liberty Lobby, Inc.*, 477 U.S. 242, 250–52, 106 S. Ct. 2505, 2511–12, 91 L.Ed.2d 202 (1986), and that is the situation here. No modern cases decided after *Cox*, and precious few before, go as far as the plaintiffs would have us go in this case. Almost all the recent cases on which they rely, such as *Capra v. Thoroughbred Racing Ass'n of North America, Inc.*, 787 F.2d 463 (9th Cir.1986) (*per curiam*); *Hawkins by Hawkins v. Multimedia, Inc.*, 288 S.C. 569, 344 S.E.2d 145 (1986), and *Times Mirror Co. v. Superior Court*, 198 Cal.App.3d 1420, 244 Cal.Rptr. 556, 564 (1988), involve the vindication of paramount social interests, such as the protection of children, patients, and witnesses—interests not involved in this case.

Does it follow, as the Hayneses' lawyer asked us rhetorically at oral argument, that a journalist who wanted to write a book about contemporary sexual practices could include the intimate details of named living persons' sexual acts without the persons' consent? Not necessarily, although the revelation of such details in the memoirs of former spouses and lovers is common enough and rarely provokes a lawsuit even when the former spouse or lover is still alive. The core of the branch of privacy law with which we have been dealing in this case is the protection of those intimate physical details the publicizing of which would be not merely embarrassing and painful but deeply shocking to the average person subjected to such exposure. The public has a legitimate interest in sexuality, but that interest may be outweighed in such a case by the injury to the sensibilities of the persons made use of by the author in such a way. Restatement (Second) of Torts, *supra*, § 652D, comment h. At least the balance would be sufficiently close to preclude summary judgment for the author and publisher. *Miller v. Motorola, Inc.*, 202 Ill.App.3d 976, 148 Ill.Dec. 303, 306, 560 N.E.2d 900, 903 (1990); *Garner v. Triangle Publications, Inc.*, 97 F. Supp. 546, 550 (S.D.N.Y.1951).

The judgment for the defendants is
Affirmed.

Discussion questions

1. What subject did the author, Nicholas Lemann, tackle in this case? What was the political subtext, referenced by Judge Posner, within the book? [You might need to do some outside research to answer this question.]
2. Do some brief outside research and identify the different authors and stories being told in this case. What were their identities?
3. Perform a bit of background research on the authors. Of the authors, who held the most social, cultural, and economic power?
4. Why did Mr. Haynes bring his suit?
5. What are the elements of the privacy cause of action for which Mr. Haynes sought relief?
6. What rigid categories and dichotomies did Judge Posner use to determine that Mr. Haynes did not have a cause of action for invasion of privacy? Were these particular rhetorical choices supported by authority or precedent? Or were they merely a matter of the Judge's personal view?
7. One of the elements of the privacy tort is that the publication of the facts must not be perceived "as gratuitous by the community." What community did Judge Posner use to determine that the deployment of the facts was not "gratuitous?"
8. What book reviewers did Judge Posner reference to establish credibility for Lemann's book, and how did Judge Posner leverage identity for this point?

Grand Upright Music Limited v. Warner Bros. Records, Inc., 780 F. Supp. 182 (S.D.N.Y. 1991)

This is a copyright law case about sampling. At the time, sampling was a novel technique being pioneered by hip-hop artists, who took older recordings and infused them into radically new contexts. As you read this case, consider the origins of two key concepts within copyright law: property ownership and theft. Before reading this case, look up and view (YouTube will work) the two songs at issue: Biz Markie's *Alone Again* and Gilbert O'Sullivan's *Alone Again Naturally*.

Kevin Thomas Duffy, District Judge:

"Thou shalt not steal" has been an admonition followed since the dawn of civilization. Unfortunately, in the modern world of business this admonition is not always followed. Indeed, the defendants in this action for copyright infringement would have this court believe that stealing is rampant in the music business and, for that reason, their conduct here should be excused. The conduct of the defendants herein, however, violates not only the Seventh Commandment, but also the copyright laws of this country.

This proceeding was instituted by Order To Show Cause to obtain a preliminary injunction against the defendants for the improper and unlicensed use of a composition "Alone Again (Naturally)" written and performed on records by Raymond "Gilbert" O'Sullivan. Defendants admit "that the Biz Markie album 'I Need A Haircut' embodies the rap recording 'Alone Again' which uses three words from 'Alone Again (Naturally)' composed by Gilbert O'Sullivan and a portion of the music taken from the O'Sullivan recording." Defendants' Post–Hearing Memorandum at 2. The only issue, therefore, seems to be who owns the copyright to the song "Alone Again (Naturally)" and the master recording thereof made by Gilbert O'Sullivan.

Three categories of proof lead me to the conclusion that the plaintiff is the true owner of these copyrights: (1) copies of the original copyrights made out to NAM Music, Inc., along with a deed vesting title to the copyrights in Gilbert O'Sullivan and another deed transferring the copyrights to the plaintiff corporation; and (2) the testimony of Gilbert O'Sullivan the acknowledged writer of the composition "Alone Again (Naturally)" and the performer who is featured on the master recording pirated by the defendants; and (3) the defendants' actions both before and after the issuance of the defendant album in contacting Gilbert O'Sullivan and his brother/agent in an attempt to obtain a license to use the copyrighted material.

Defense counsel objected to the admission of copies of the certificates of copyright because they were not "authenticated." It was apparent that defense counsel was not using this term "authenticated" in the sense that it is normally used in the law, particularly in the law of evidence. Since the original copyright was in the name of NAM Music, Inc., defense counsel seemed to argue that someone authorized by NAM Music, Inc. would have to identify the certificates in order to "authenticate" them.

Of course, the reader should be aware that NAM Music, Inc. had long been dissolved, as defense counsel knew. It was clear to me that the use of the word "authenticate" by defense counsel had nothing whatsoever to do with self-authentication of public records under Rule 902 of the Federal Rules of Evidence. Nor did counsel believe that the certificate was anything less than a true and complete copy of the public record.

Counsel for the defendants also attempted to keep out evidence of the transfer to the plaintiff of copyrights in the work at issue. Defense counsel did not conduct any discovery in the time between the institution of this lawsuit and the hearing on the preliminary injunction and claimed to be surprised when the plaintiff produced documentation of the transfer. However, that defense counsel did not adequately prepare for this hearing does not give the court cause to reject evidence of the transfer.

Defense counsel also objected to the admission of the transfer documents on the grounds that, since they had not been filed with the Registrar of Copyrights, they were without legal effect. This is not the law and the specific section upon which the defense counsel relied has long been repealed. These documents, taken together, prove valid copyrights vested in the plaintiff.

In addition to the documents offered into evidence by the plaintiff, Gilbert O'Sullivan—who the defendants acknowledge was the composer, lyricist and first performer of the piece at issue—testified that plaintiff is the owner of the copyright. There can be no one more interested in the question of valid copyright than a person in Gilbert O'Sullivan's position and he was a thoroughly credible and believable witness. Defense counsel did not effectively controvert O'Sullivan's testimony in any way. Indeed, the thrust of the cross-examination of O'Sullivan went to the artist's motive for refusing to give the defendants a license to use the song.

However, the most persuasive evidence that the copyrights are valid and owned by the plaintiff comes from the actions and admissions of the defendants. Prior to the time that Biz Markie's album was released, the various defendants apparently discussed among themselves the need to obtain a license. They decided to contact O'Sullivan and wrote to his brother/agent, enclosing a copy of the tape. In this letter, an attorney for the defendant states:

> This firm represents a recording artist professionally known as Biz Markie, who has recorded a composition for Cold Chillin' Records entitled "Alone Again" which incorporates portions of the composition entitled "Alone Again Naturally" originally recorded by Gilbert O'Sullivan (the "Original Composition").
>
> Biz Markie would like to obtain your consent to the use of the "Original Composition."

In writing this letter, counsel for Biz Markie admittedly was seeking "terms" for the use of the material. One would not agree to pay to use the material of another unless there was a valid copyright! What more persuasive evidence can there be!

Each defendant who testified knew that it is necessary to obtain a license—sometimes called a "clearance"—from the holder of a valid copyright before using the copyrighted work in another piece. Warner Bros. Records, Inc. had a department set up specifically to obtain such clearances. Brown Deposition of 11/19/91 at 30 et seq.; Tillman Deposition of 11/22/91 at 7. WEA International, Inc. knew it had to obtain "consents, permissions or clearances ..." Rossi Deposition of 11/22/91 at 10–11. Cold Chillin' Records, Inc. knew that such clearances were necessary. Fitchelberg Deposition of 11/21/91 at 34 et seq.

Clearly, the attorneys representing Biz Markie and acting on his behalf also knew of this obligation. Biz Markie's attorneys sent copies of an August 16 letter, addressed to counsel for Cold Chillin' Records, Inc., to the other defendants. That letter contains the following:

> In light of the fact that Cold Chillin' knew that other sample clearance requests were pending at that time, it follows that Cold Chillin' should have known that similar denials of permission by rightsholders of other samples used on the album and single might be forthcoming, for which similar action would have been appropriate. Nevertheless, instead of continuing to communicate with our client and us and otherwise cooperating to ensure that all rights were secured prior

> to release of the album and single, as it did in the situation involving the Eagles samples, Cold Chillin' unilaterally elected to release the album and single, perhaps with the thought that it would look to Biz for resolution of any problems relating to sampling rights, or the failure to secure such rights, that may arise in the future.
>
> Consequently, if any legal action arises in connection with the samples in question, such action will not arise due to the fact that Biz used the samples in his recorded compositions, but rather, due to the fact that Cold Chillin' released such material prior to the appropriate consents being secured in connection with such samples.

From all of the evidence produced in the hearing, it is clear that the defendants knew that they were violating the plaintiff's rights as well as the rights of others. Their only aim was to sell thousands upon thousands of records.[1]

This callous disregard for the law and for the rights of others requires not only the preliminary injunction sought by the plaintiff but also sterner measures.

The application for the preliminary injunction is granted. The plaintiff is to submit within five (5) days hereof an appropriate decree. This matter is respectfully referred to the United States Attorney for the Southern District of New York for consideration of prosecution of these defendants under 17 U.S.C. § 506(a) and 18 U.S.C. § 2319.[2]

SO ORDERED.

Footnotes:

[1] The argument suggested by the defendants that they should be excused because others in the "rap music" business are also engaged in illegal activity is totally specious. The mere statement of the argument is its own refutation.

[2] The resolution of any issue left open in this civil matter should have no bearing on the potential criminal liability in the unique circumstances presented here.

Discussion questions

1. Do some brief internet research on the biographical information for hip-hop artist Biz Markie and 1970s soft-rock musician Gilbert O'Sullivan. Describe (in your own words) the attributes of the two musicians and the two songs.
2. How does Judge Duffy deploy Judeo-Christian religion to frame his opinion?
3. One strategy that defense lawyers can always use is to hold the plaintiff or prosecutor to their proof and point out any evidentiary or procedural holes in the other side's case. How did Judge Duffy respond to Biz Markie's attorneys' attempts to hold the plaintiff to their proof?
4. What type of bias is discernible in footnote one of Judge Duffy's opinion?
5. What did Judge Duffy do at the end of his opinion, in terms of referring the copyright case?

6. In terms of hip hop and rap as artistic forms that make innovative use of recombinant culture (sampling), what did this opinion miss?
7. Did Judge Duffy properly categorize Biz Markie (and his record label) as copyright thieves?

Luke Records, Inc. v. Navarro, 960 F.2d 134 (11th Cir. 1992)

This is the one example case where the minoritized/marginalized party won on appeal. This case is about another hip-hop group (2 Live Crew) and whether their album was properly categorized as obscene. As you read this case, consider how the trial court judge (who was overruled) applied the concepts of "community value" and "literary, artistic, political, or scientific value."

Opinion

PER CURIAM:

In this appeal, appellants Luke Records, Inc., Luther Campbell, Mark Ross, David Hobbs, and Charles Wongwon seek reversal of the district court's declaratory judgment that the musical recording "As Nasty As They Wanna Be" is obscene under Fla. Stat. § 847.011 and the United States Constitution, contending that the district court misapplied the test for determining obscenity. We reverse.

Appellants Luther Campbell, David Hobbs, Mark Ross, and Charles Wongwon comprise the musical group "2 Live Crew," which recorded "As Nasty As They Wanna Be." In response to actions taken by the Broward County, Florida Sheriff's Office to discourage record stores from selling "As Nasty As They Wanna Be," appellants filed this action in federal district court to enjoin the Sheriff from interfering further with the sale of the recording. The district court granted the injunction, finding that the actions of the Sheriff's office were an unconstitutional prior restraint on free speech. The Sheriff does not appeal this determination.

In addition to injunctive relief, however, appellants sought a declaratory judgment pursuant to 28 U.S.C.A. § 2201 that the recording was not obscene. The district court found that "As Nasty As They Wanna Be" is obscene under *Miller v. California*.

This case is apparently the first time that a court of appeals has been asked to apply the Miller test to a musical composition, which contains both instrumental music and lyrics. Although we tend to agree with appellants' contention that because music possesses inherent artistic value, no work of music alone may be declared obscene, that issue is not presented in this case. The Sheriff's contention that the work is not protected by the First Amendment is based on the lyrics, not the music. The Sheriff's brief denies any intention to put rap music to the test, but states "it is abundantly obvious that it is only the 'lyrical' content which makes 'As Nasty As They Wanna Be' obscene." Assuming that music is not simply a sham attempt to protect obscene material, the *Miller* test should be applied to the lyrics and the music of "As Nasty As They Wanna Be" as a whole. The basic guidelines for the trier of fact must be: (a) whether "the average person, applying contemporary community standards" would find that the work, taken as a whole, appeals to the prurient interest; (b) whether the work depicts or describes, in a patently offensive way, sexual conduct specifically defined by the applicable state law; and (c) whether the work, taken as a whole, lacks serious literary, artistic, political, or scientific value. 413 U.S. at 24, 93 S. Ct. at 2615. This test is conjunctive. *Penthouse Intern., Ltd. v. McAuliffe*, 610 F.2d 1353, 1363 (5th Cir.1980). A work cannot be held obscene unless each element of the test has been evaluated independently and all three have been met. *Id.*

Appellants contend that because the central issue in this case is whether "As Nasty As They Wanna Be" meets the definition of obscenity contained in a Florida criminal statute, the thrust of this case is criminal and the Sheriff should be required to prove the work's obscenity beyond a reasonable doubt. In the alternative, appellants assert that at minimum, the importance of the First Amendment requires that the burden of proof in the district court should have been by "clear and convincing evidence," rather than by "a preponderance of the evidence." Assuming, *arguendo*, that the proper standard is the preponderance of the evidence, we conclude that the Sheriff has failed to carry his burden of proof that the material is obscene by the *Miller* standards under that less stringent standard. Thus, to reverse the declaratory judgment that the work is obscene, we need not decide which of the standards applies.

There are two problems with this case which make it unusually difficult to review. First, the Sheriff put in no evidence but the tape recording itself. The only evidence concerning the three-part *Miller* test was put in evidence by the plaintiffs. Second, the case was tried by a judge without a jury, and he relied on his own expertise as to the prurient interest community standard and artistic value prongs of the *Miller* test.

First, the Sheriff put in no evidence other than the cassette tape. He called no expert witnesses concerning contemporary community standards, prurient interest, or serious artistic value. His evidence was the tape recording itself.

The appellants called psychologist Mary Haber, music critics Gregory Baker, John Leland and Rhodes Scholar Carlton Long. Dr. Haber testified that the tape did not appeal to the average person's prurient interest.

Gregory Baker is a staff writer for *New Times Newspaper*, a weekly arts and news publication supported by advertising revenue and distributed free of charge throughout South Florida. Baker testified that he authored "hundreds" of articles about popular music over the previous six or seven years. After reviewing the origins of hip hop and rap music, Baker discussed the process through which rap music is created. He then outlined the ways in which 2 Live Crew had innovated past musical conventions within the genre and concluded that the music in "As Nasty As They Wanna Be" possesses serious musical value.

John Leland is a pop music critic for *Newsday* magazine, which has a daily circulation in New York, New York of approximately six hundred thousand copies, one of the top ten daily newspaper circulations in the country. Leland discussed in detail the evolution of hip hop and rap music, including the development of sampling technique by street disc jockeys over the previous fifteen years and the origins of rap in more established genres of music such as jazz, blues, and reggae. He emphasized that a Grammy Award for rap music was recently introduced, indicating that the recording industry recognizes rap as valid artistic achievement, and ultimately gave his expert opinion that 2 Live Crew's music in "As Nasty As They Wanna Be" does possess serious artistic value.

Of appellants' expert witnesses, Carlton Long testified most about the lyrics. Long is a Rhodes scholar with a Ph.D. in Political Science and was to begin an assistant professorship in that field at Columbia University in New York City shortly after the trial. Long testified that "As Nasty As They Wanna Be" contains three oral traditions, or musical conventions, known as call and response, doing the dozens, and boasting. Long testified that these oral traditions derive their roots from certain segments of Afro-American culture. Long described each of these conventions and cited examples of each one from "As Nasty As They Wanna Be." He concluded that the album reflects many aspects of the cultural heritage of poor, inner city [Black people] as well as the cultural experiences of 2 Live Crew. Long suggested that certain excerpts from "As Nasty As They Wanna Be" contained statements of political significance or exemplified numerous literary conventions, such as alliteration, allusion, metaphor, rhyme, and personification.

The Sheriff introduced no evidence to the contrary, except the tape.

Second, the case was tried by a judge without a jury, and he relied on his own expertise as to the community standard and artistic prongs of the *Miller* test.

The district court found that the relevant community was Broward, Dade, and Palm Beach Counties. He further stated:

> This court finds that the relevant community standard reflects a more tolerant view of obscene speech than would other communities within the state. This finding of fact is based upon this court's personal knowledge of the community. The undersigned judge has resided in Broward County since 1958. As a practicing attorney, state prosecutor, state circuit judge, and currently, a federal district judge, the undersigned has traveled and worked in Dade, Broward, and Palm Beach. As a member of the community, he has personal knowledge of this area's demographics, culture, economics, and politics. He has attended public functions and events in all three counties and is aware of the community's concerns as reported in the media and by word of mouth.
>
> In almost fourteen years as a state circuit judge, the undersigned gained personal knowledge of the nature of obscenity in the community while viewing dozens, if not hundreds of allegedly obscene films and other publications seized by law enforcement.

The plaintiffs' claim that this court cannot decide this case without expert testimony and the introduction of specific evidence on community standards is also without merit. The law does not require expert testimony in an obscenity case. The defendant introduced the "Nasty" recording into evidence. As noted by the Supreme Court in *Paris Adult Theatre I* [*v. Slaton*, 413 U.S. 49, 93 S. Ct. 2628, 37 L.Ed.2d 446 (1973)], when the material in question is not directed to a "bizarre, deviant group" not within the experience of the average person, the best evidence is the material, which "can and does speak for itself." *Paris Adult Theatre I*, 413 U.S. at 56 & n. 6, 93 S. Ct. at 2634 & n. 6.

In deciding this case, the court's decision is not based upon the undersigned judge's personal opinion as to the obscenity of the work, but is an application of the law to the facts based upon the trier of fact's personal knowledge of community standards. In other words, even if the undersigned judge would not find "As Nasty As They Wanna Be" obscene, he would be compelled to do so if the community's standards so required.

It is difficult for an appellate court to review value judgments. Although, generally, these determinations are made in the first instance by a jury, in this case the district judge served as the fact finder, which is permissible in civil cases. Because a judge served as a fact finder, however, and relied only on his own expertise, the difficulty of appellate review is enhanced. A fact finder, whether a judge or jury, is limited in discretion. In this case, it can be conceded without deciding that the judge's familiarity with contemporary community standards is sufficient to carry the case as to the first two prongs of the *Miller* test: prurient interest applying community standards and patent offensiveness as defined by Florida law. The record is insufficient, however, for this Court to assume the fact finder's artistic or literary knowledge or skills to satisfy the last prong of the *Miller* analysis, which requires determination of whether a work "lacks serious artistic, scientific, literary or political value." *Miller*, 413 U.S. at 24, 93 S. Ct. at 2615.

In *Pope v. Illinois*, the Court clarified that whether a work possesses serious value was not a question to be decided by contemporary community standards. The Court reasoned that the fundamental principles of the First Amendment prevent the value of a work from being judged solely by the amount of acceptance it has won within a given community:

Just as the ideas a work represents need not obtain majority approval to merit protection, neither, insofar as the First Amendment is concerned, does the value of the work vary from community to community based on the degree of local acceptance it has won. 481 U.S. at 500–01, 107 S. Ct. at 1921.

The Sheriff concedes that he has the burden of proof to show that the recording is obscene. Yet, he submitted no evidence to contradict the testimony that the work had artistic value. A work cannot be held obscene unless each element of the *Miller* test has been met. We reject the argument that simply by listening to this musical work, the judge could determine that it had no serious artistic value.

REVERSED.

Discussion questions

1. In the 1990s, 2 Live Crew were frequently in the news and the courts. In a later case about a different 2 Live Crew album/song, the Supreme Court of the United States decided that their parodic cover of the Roy Orbison song 'Pretty Woman," should be protected under the Fair Use defense of Copyright Law because the song transformed Orbison's song into something completely new. See *Campbell v. Acuff-Rose Music, Inc.*, 510 U.S. 569 (1994). Perform some brief background research and learn about 2 Live Crew and their front-person, Luther Campbell. Write a short narrative that describes 2 Live Crew's social, racial, and geographic identities. Described how the group could be described as an "outsider" group.
2. What brought this case to the Eleventh Circuit Court of Appeals?
3. What is the three-part test for determining whether something is obscene or not?
4. What evidence did the Sheriff put in to prove that 2 Live Crew's album was obscene?
5. What evidence did 2 Live Crew submit to show that their album was not obscene?
6. How did the trial court judge (who was overruled) justify his credentials to decide that the album was obscene?
7. How did the trial court judge construct the concepts of "average person" and "community" for determining that 2 Live Crew's album should be considered obscene?
8. How did the advocacy choices of 2 Live Crew's attorneys create the opportunity for the Eleventh Circuit to consider alternative cultural voices?

Baxter v. Bracey, 751 Fed. Appx. 869 (6th Cir. 2018)

This case concerns the qualified immunity doctrine, a court-made doctrine that limits civil liability for police officers who use force against a citizen unless they are acting unreasonably. As you read this case, critically consider (1) the way "reasonableness" surfaces in this doctrine; and (2) the way that dichotomous reasoning (analogy versus distinction) drives the court's reasoning.

Opinion

This case was not selected for publication in West's Federal Reporter.

NALBANDIAN, Circuit Judge.

A neighbor caught Alexander Baxter burglarizing a house and called the police. Soon Baxter heard sirens and saw a helicopter looking for him, so he ran to another house (one he had broken into before) and hid in the basement. But the canine unit arrived and quickly sniffed him out. After giving several warnings, one of the officers released his dog, who apprehended Baxter with a bite to the arm. Baxter says he had already surrendered when the dog was released, and so the two officers violated his constitutional right to be free from excessive force. The case is before us now on an interlocutory appeal after the district court denied the officers' claims of qualified immunity. We reverse that decision because the officers' conduct, whether constitutional, did not violate any clearly established right.

Officers Spencer Harris and Brad Bracey arrested Alexander Baxter on January 8, 2014 after he committed an aggravated burglary and fled the scene. A neighbor caught Baxter breaking into a home and called the police. He fled once he heard sirens and saw the helicopter—first hiding in a car, and then seeking refuge in the basement of a house he had previously broken into. There, Baxter hid between a chimney and a water heater while he watched and listened to the officers outside.

Harris and Bracey were part of Nashville's canine unit, which is deployed for serious crimes such as aggravated burglary. The two of them entered the house with their dog, Iwo. Bracey announced they would release the canine if Baxter did not surrender. Although Baxter heard the warnings, he stayed quiet. Harris—the dog's handler—repeated the warning. Again, Baxter remained quiet. So Harris released Iwo, who quickly found Baxter downstairs.

The two officers followed Iwo into the basement and—according to Baxter—surrounded him. Baxter claims that he raised his hands in the air when they came downstairs. But he never responded to the officers' warnings or communicated about where he was hiding. Within five to ten seconds of discovering Baxter, Harris again released Iwo—this time to apprehend him. Iwo restrained Baxter with a bite to the arm. The medical records reveal only one bite on Baxter's underarm, revealing that Iwo followed his training by apprehending Baxter with a single bite. Harris eventually commanded Iwo to release Baxter and placed him under arrest.

Baxter, proceeding *pro se*, sued Harris and Bracey under 42 U.S.C. § 1983. He asserts an excessive-force claim against Harris and a failure-to-intervene claim against Bracey. Originally, Bracey alone moved to dismiss the suit against him, arguing that qualified immunity shielded him from Baxter's somewhat amorphous claim that he failed to prevent the canine apprehension. Baxter's complaint, we held, pleaded sufficient facts to withstand a motion to dismiss. But those facts must bear out during discovery for Baxter to defeat a motion for summary judgment. And that is where we are today.

After discovery, both officers moved for summary judgment, and the district court rejected both claims. The district court held that summary judgment was inappropriate because Baxter's testimony corroborated the factual assertions in the complaint that this court previously upheld against a motion to dismiss. If those facts were enough to defeat qualified immunity in a complaint, the court reasoned, Baxter's supporting testimony should do the same. Harris and Bracey then filed this interlocutory appeal. See *Plumhoff v. Rickard*, 572 U.S. 765, 771–72, 134 S. Ct. 2012, 188 L.Ed.2d 1056 (2014).

Our inquiry here is guided by the interlocutory posture of the case. Because the district court denied summary judgment to the defendants, we must determine whether "the undisputed facts or the evidence viewed in the light most favorable to the plaintiff fail to establish a prima facie violation of clear constitutional law." *Berryman v. Rieger*, 150 F.3d 561, 563 (6th Cir. 1998). We will not weigh into credibility issues or try to resolve factual disputes. See *Estate of Carter v. City of Detroit*, 408 F.3d 305, 310 (6th Cir. 2005). Our task is much simpler. We must decide the "neat abstract issue[] of law" regarding whether Baxter's version of the facts amounts to a clear constitutional violation. See *Berryman*, 150 F.3d at 563 (quoting *Johnson v. Jones*, 515 U.S. 304, 317, 115 S. Ct. 2151, 132 L.Ed.2d 238 (1995)).

The clarity of the constitutional violation is critical. An individual suing under § 1983 must demonstrate two things: First, that the officer violated his constitutional rights. And second, that the violation was "clearly established at the time." *District of Columbia v. Wesby*, U.S., 138 S. Ct. 577, 589, 199 L.Ed.2d 453 (2018) (internal quotation marks omitted). The "clearly established" prong sets up an exacting standard in which the plaintiff must show that "every reasonable official would understand that what he is doing is unlawful." *Id.* (internal citations and quotations omitted). "It is not enough that the rule is *suggested* by then-existing precedent"—it must be "beyond debate" and "settled law." *Id.* at 589–90 (emphasis added) (quoting *Hunter v. Bryant*, 502 U.S. 224, 228, 112 S. Ct. 534, 116 L.Ed.2d 589 (1991)). The effect is that qualified immunity protects "all but the plainly incompetent or those who knowingly violate the law." *Malley v. Briggs*, 475 U.S. 335, 341, 106 S. Ct. 1092, 89 L.Ed.2d 271 (1986).

Relevant here, courts can jump straight to the second question and dispose of a claim without deciding whether the officer's conduct violated the plaintiff's constitutional rights. See *Ashcroft v. al-Kidd*, 563 U.S. 731, 735, 131 S. Ct. 2074, 179 L.Ed.2d 1149 (2011). So long as the alleged violation has not been clearly established, the officers receive qualified immunity and the suit can be dismissed. See *id.* Proceeding in this way is often appropriate in "cases in which the briefing of constitutional questions is woefully inadequate." See *Pearson v. Callahan*, 555 U.S. 223, 239, 129 S. Ct. 808, 172 L.Ed.2d 565 (2009). By resolving the issue on only the second prong, courts avoid "expending scarce judicial resources to resolve difficult and novel questions of constitutional or statutory interpretation that will have no effect on the outcome of the case." *Ashcroft*, 563 U.S. at 735, 131 S. Ct. 2074 (internal quotations and citations omitted).

That is the case here. The officers are entitled to qualified immunity because Harris's use of the canine to apprehend Baxter did not violate clearly established law. And because this court does not have the benefit of sophisticated adversarial briefing from both parties, we decline to resolve the more complex constitutional question raised by Baxter's claim. See *Pearson*, 555 U.S. at 239, 129 S. Ct. 808.

The Fourth Amendment's prohibition against unreasonable seizures protects individuals from an officer's use of excessive force while making an arrest. See *Graham v. Connor*, 490 U.S. 386, 394–95, 109 S. Ct. 1865, 104 L.Ed.2d 443 (1989). Whether the force was excessive turns on its objective reasonableness under the totality of the circumstances. *Id.* at 395–96, 109 S. Ct. 1865; *Kostrzewa v. City of Troy*, 247 F.3d 633, 639 (6th Cir. 2001). And the reasonableness of the officer's force "must be judged from the perspective of a reasonable officer on the scene, rather than with the 20/20 vision of hindsight." *Graham*, 490 U.S. at 396, 109 S. Ct. 1865.

We have demarcated the outer bounds of excessive-force cases involving canine seizures with some degree of clarity. In this circuit, for example, we have held that officers cannot "use[] an inadequately trained canine, without warning, to apprehend two suspects who were not fleeing." *Campbell v. City of Springboro*, 700 F.3d 779, 789 (6th Cir. 2012). But just as clearly, we have upheld the use of a well-trained canine to apprehend a fleeing suspect in a dark and unfamiliar location. See *Robinette v. Barnes*, 854 F.2d 909, 913–14 (6th Cir. 1988). These cases and their progeny establish guidance on the ends of the spectrum, but the middle ground between the two proves much hazier.

Baxter's case looks closer to *Robinette* than *Campbell*—but the fit is not perfect. Like the suspect in *Robinette*, Baxter fled the police after committing a serious crime and hid in an unfamiliar location. He also ignored multiple warnings that a canine would be released, choosing to remain silent as he hid. And unlike *Campbell*, the canine here was properly trained with no apparent history of bad behavior. All of these facts would lead a reasonable officer to believe that the use of a canine to apprehend Baxter did not violate the Fourth Amendment. See *Graham*, 490 U.S. at 396, 109 S. Ct. 1865; *Robinette*, 854 F.2d at 913–14.

Militating against those facts is Baxter's claim that he surrendered by raising his hands in the air before Harris released the dog. This conduct might show that he did not pose the kind of safety threat justifying a forceful arrest. See, e.g., *Ciminillo v. Streicher*, 434 F.3d 461, 467 (6th Cir. 2006). But Baxter does not point us to any case law suggesting that raising his hands, on its own, is enough to put Harris on notice that a canine apprehension was unlawful in these circumstances. That's because even with Baxter's hands raised, Harris faced a suspect hiding in an unfamiliar location after fleeing from the police who posed an unknown safety risk—all factors the *Campbell* court identified as significant to determining whether the seizure was lawful. See *Campbell*, 700 F.3d at 788–89.

Given all of this, we cannot say that Harris violated any clearly established law in using Iwo to apprehend Baxter. Even if Baxter raised his hands, the other circumstances—undisputed in the record below—weigh against a finding that "every reasonable official would understand that what [Harris did] is unlawful." *Wesby*, 138 S. Ct. at 589 (internal quotations omitted). For that reason, Harris is entitled to qualified immunity.

We reach this decision mindful of the fact that, on appeal from the prior motion to dismiss, we held that Baxter's right to be free from excessive force was clearly established under *Campbell*. But there, we looked only at the facts as pleaded in the complaint. Baxter alleged that he surrendered before the arrest, and his complaint was understandably silent about whether Iwo had proper training or the time that elapsed before Harris released the dog. The facts revealed during discovery add much-needed color to this case—as they often do. We now know that Iwo was well-trained, that Harris released him within only a few seconds after entering the basement, and that Baxter fled the scene, hid in the basement, was warned twice, and still never communicated with the officers before being apprehended. All of these facts change the analysis and move the well-pleaded claims to a place where we cannot say that "every reasonable official would understand that what he is doing is unlawful." *Wesby*, 138 S. Ct. at 589 (internal quotation marks omitted).

Finally, it follows from there that Bracey receives the same protection of qualified immunity. Police officers "can be held liable for failure to protect a person from the use of excessive force." *Turner v. Scott*, 119 F.3d 425, 429 (6th Cir. 1997). Such a claim requires proving that the officer "observed or had reason to know that excessive force would be or was being used" and "the officer had both the opportunity and the means to prevent the harm from occurring." *Id.* While there are numerous reasons to find that Baxter cannot prevail on this claim, the first is the most obvious: If it is not clearly established that Harris used excessive force in apprehending Baxter, it cannot be that Bracey observed or had reason to know that excessive force would be used.

III

For the above-stated reasons, we REVERSE the district court's order denying summary judgment.

Discussion questions

1. This case received a quite a bit of attention as the debate over the qualified immunity doctrine continues. For context, review the following sources:
    - Carlisle, M. (2021) "The Debate over Qualified Immunity Is at the Heart of Police Reform. Here's What to Know," *Time Magazine*, [online] June 3. Available from: https://time.com/6061624/what-is-qualified-immunity/.
    - Schweikert, J. (2020) "Qualified Immunity: A Legal, Practical, and Moral Failure," *The Cato Institute*, [online] September 14. Available from: www.cato.org/policy-analysis/qualified-immunity-legal-practical-moral-failure.
    - Boyd, H. and Reyes, D. (2021) "The Invisible Shield: How Qualified Immunity Prevents Victims of Police Abuse from Seeking Justice, Part 2," *Amsterdam News*, [online] April 8. Available from: https://amsterdamnews.com/news/2021/04/08/invisible-shield-how-qualified-immunity-prevents-v/.
2. After reading some of the journalistic descriptions of the case cited in question 1, identify the rhetorical choices Judge Nalbandian made in the introductory portion of the case to introduce the actors in the case. What facts did he leave out? Rewrite the facts from Mr. Baxter's perspective as a *pro se litigant*.
3. Because this was a civil lawsuit, he was not entitled to court-appointed counsel. Consider how Mr. Baxter's *pro se* status affected the briefing and advocacy in his case.
4. How would you describe the way that reasonableness, as a concept, works to broaden the doctrine of qualified immunity? In this context, does reasonableness mesh with, or conflict with, classical and Enlightenment concepts of reason (as a virtuous thing) examined in Chapter 1?

5. This case turned on a dichotomous analogy/distinction between the facts and holdings of two cases, *Robinette* and *Campbell*. The Sixth Circuit decided that the facts were more analogous to *Robinette* than *Campbell*. Is there a competing argument for the Judge's analytical choice? Flesh out that argument.

Sequoyah et al v. Tennessee Valley Authority, 620 F.2d 1159 (1980)

In this class action case, a group of Cherokee people brought suit to enjoin the flooding of lands in Monroe County, Tennessee on the basis that it would destroy sacred sites. As you read this case, consider how Westernized concepts of time, property, and religion influenced the holding of the case to the detriment of the plaintiffs.

Opinion

LIVELY, Circuit Judge.

This appeal requires the court to make a determination of the legal efficacy of a claim based on the Free Exercise Clause of the First Amendment.

I

The plaintiffs brought this class action on behalf of "all those present or future Cherokee Indians who practice the traditional Cherokee religion and adhere to Cherokee Indian tradition and culture." The principal relief sought in the complaint was an injunction to prevent completion and flooding of the Tellico Dam on the Little Tennessee River in Monroe County, Tennessee. The complaint alleged that the impoundment created by the dam will cause irreparable injury to the plaintiffs. This injury will be caused by flooding of the "sacred homeland" of the plaintiffs along the river, which will result in destruction of "sacred sites, medicine gathering sites, holy places and cemeteries, (and) will disturb the sacred balance of the land." It was further stated that the threatened actions of the defendant would cause "irreversible loss to the culture and history of the plaintiffs."

The claim of a constitutional violation based on the Free Exercise Clause was stated as follows:

> the individual named Plaintiffs will suffer injury by the infringement of their right to worship the religion of their choice in the manner of their choosing by the destruction of sites which they hold in reverence and in denial of access to

> such sites by the Defendant. This injury will also be suffered by other members of the class which these individual Plaintiffs represent.

The complaint also contained claims based upon other provisions of the First Amendment, the Fifth and Ninth Amendments, the American Indian Religious Freedom Act, 42 U.S.C. s 1996, the National Historic Preservation Act, 16 U.S.C. s 470 et seq. and various laws of the State of Tennessee.

The plaintiffs filed some 25 affidavits with the complaint in support of their motion for a preliminary injunction. The defendant filed a motion to dismiss for failure to state a claim, pursuant to Rule 12(b)(6), Fed.R.Civ.P., together with an alternative motion for summary judgment pursuant to Rule 56. This motion was accompanied by three affidavits. In a brief in support of its motion for summary judgment, the defendant asserted that the plaintiffs were estopped to make their claim and were barred by laches. In their response, the plaintiffs argued that there were genuine issues of material fact, particularly with respect to the defense of laches, and that this was not a proper case for summary judgment.

All issues were fully briefed and the district court heard extensive oral arguments. Thereafter the court filed a memorandum opinion and entered an order denying the plaintiffs' motion for injunction and granting the defendant's motion to dismiss. In its memorandum, the district court concentrated on the religious freedom arguments and quickly disposed of the other constitutional claims and those based on statutes. At the outset the district court stated, "The Court assumes that the land to be flooded is considered sacred to the Cherokee religion and that active practitioners of that religion would want to make pilgrimages to this land as a precept of their religion." The court found that the only "coercive effect" of the impoundment on the plaintiffs' religious beliefs or practices would consist of preventing access to certain land owned by the government. The district court then held, "the free exercise clause is not a license in itself to enter property, government-owned or otherwise, to which religious practitioners have no other legal right or access." The court stated specifically that it did not reach the defenses of estoppel and laches. *Sequoyah v. TVA*, 480 F. Supp. 608 (E.D.Tenn.1979).

II

Though the district court granted the motion to dismiss, it is clear from the transcript and from his memorandum that Judge Taylor considered the various affidavits which were in the record. Under Rule 12(b) when matters outside the pleadings are presented to the court, and not excluded, a motion to dismiss for failure to state a claim is treated as one for summary judgment. We treat the decision of the district court as one granting summary judgment. See *Compania De Remorque Y. Salvamento, S.A. v. Esperance, Inc.*, 187 F.2d 114 (2d Cir. 1951). In reviewing summary judgment for the defendant this court must view the entire record in the light most favorable to the plaintiffs. *Aetna Insurance*

Co. v. Loveland Gas & Electric Co., 369 F.2d 648 (6th Cir. 1966); *Bohn Aluminum & Brass Corp. v. Storm King Corp.*, 303 F.2d 425 (6th Cir. 1962).

A.

We agree with the holding of the district court that the defendant was entitled to judgment on the plaintiffs' claim of violation of their right to freedom of speech and association, to due process and equal protection of the law, and rights reserved to them by the Ninth Amendment. Accepting all the pleadings and affidavits as true, no claim for relief was stated with respect to these theories and the defendant was entitled to judgment as a matter of law. Relief under the American Indian Religious Freedom Act, the National Historic Preservation Act and laws of Tennessee is foreclosed by a provision of the Energy and Water Development Appropriation Bill, Pub. Law No. 96-69, signed by President Carter on September 25, 1979: "[N]otwithstanding provisions of 16 U.S.C., Chapter 35 (The Endangered Species Act) *or any other law*, the Corporation (TVA) is authorized and directed to complete construction, operate and maintain the Tellico Dam" (italics supplied). No clearer congressional command is imaginable. No law is to stand in the way of the completion and operation of the dam. The only basis upon which the district court or this court would be empowered to enter an order contrary to the express will of Congress is that a violation of the Constitution will result from carrying out the congressional mandate.

B.

Before analyzing the complaint and affidavits of the plaintiffs we note that the Tellico Dam has engendered controversy and litigation from the time it was first proposed. A brief description of the Little Tennessee River, the historical significance of the region and the litigation spawned by Tellico is contained in the opening paragraphs of the Supreme Court's opinion in the "snail darter" case, *TVA v. Hill*, 437 U.S. 153, 156–59, 98 S. Ct. 2279, 2282–84, 57 L.Ed.2d 117 (1978).

The record in the present case discloses that some of the plaintiffs objected to the dam and sought to prevent its construction as early as 1965. However, the documents in the record indicate that the Cherokee objections to the Tellico Dam were based primarily on a fear that their cultural heritage, rather than their religious rights, would be affected by flooding the Little Tennessee Valley. Only with the filing of the complaint in this action, on October 12, 1979 less than a month before impoundment was scheduled to begin did any Cherokee make an explicit claim based on the Free Exercise Clause.

C.

The allegations of the complaint which relate to free exercise of religion have been set forth, ante. Examination of the contents of the affidavits filed by the plaintiffs discloses the following:

(1) The plaintiff Ammoneta Sequoyah is a medicine man and a direct descendant of Sequoyah, the inventor of the Cherokee writing system. This affiant stated that he had gone to the Valley all his life and had lived in an abandoned cabin at Chota[1] for six years. His ancestor Sequoyah was born at Tuskegee, another of the Cherokee village sites in the Valley. The affiant stated that he goes to the Valley three or four times a year to get medicine which must be gathered by a medicine man "to work a cure." The Cherokees believe that all a person knows is placed in the ground with that person when he is buried. Flooding the Valley or digging up the bodies of Indians buried there will destroy "the knowledge and beliefs of (the) people who are in the ground" and destroy what they have taught. Mr. Sequoyah believes he will lose his knowledge of medicine if the Valley is flooded.

(2) Richard Crowe had been going to the lands at Tellico for more than 30 years and learned from his people that "This is where WE begun." Over the years Mr. Crowe has visited the area more than 20 times, and he took his children there when they were young. Chota is one of the sacred Cherokee places, spoken of by his family as the birthplace of the Cherokee. It was understood by the Cherokees that "this location was our connection with the Great Spirit."

(3) Lloyd Sequoyah, brother of the plaintiff Ammoneta Sequoyah, is also a medicine man. He stated in his affidavit that he had visited the Valley "on two occasions," and that the only place that he can find his medicine is where the Cherokee forefathers lived. It was his belief that "If these lands are flooded they will destroy the spiritual strength of the Cherokee people."

(4) Robert Blankenship stated, "Chota, and the Little Tennessee River ... are sacred because they are the only two tangible items left for me and other Cherokee people to worship."

(5) A number of other affidavits described the land in the Little Tennessee Valley as sacred and holy to Cherokees and stated that burial sites should not be disturbed.

(6) Several affidavits were filed by anthropologists who specialize in American Indian studies. These affidavits affirmed the importance of particular places in Cherokee tradition and religion. They also testified to the importance of living in harmony with nature and the belief that interference with natural objects, such as damming rivers, is wrong. All also testified to the importance of prophecies to traditional Cherokees, and stated that many of their prophecies rest on oral history of earlier events in the "Old Country" of North Carolina, Georgia and Tennessee.

D.

The Cherokees who are plaintiffs in this action obviously have great reverence for their ancestors and believe that the places where their ancestors lived, gathered medicines, died and were buried have cultural and religious significance. Similar feelings are shared by most people to a greater or lesser extent. However, because of their beliefs respecting the transmission of knowledge and spiritual powers to succeeding generations, particular geographic locations figure more prominently in Indian religion and culture than in those of most other people.

III

There is no requirement that a religion meet any organizational or doctrinal test in order to qualify for First Amendment protection. Orthodoxy is not an issue. The fact that Cherokees have no written creeds and no man-made houses of worship is of no importance. The Cherokees have a religion within the meaning of the Constitution and the sincerity of the adherence of individual plaintiffs to that religion is not questioned. However, in bringing this action, the plaintiffs are asserting that otherwise lawful and wholly secular activity of the government should be prohibited. Accepting every statement of fact as true, the question is whether the plaintiffs have shown a constitutionally cognizable infringement of a First Amendment right.

It is the flooding of a particular place which is claimed to deny the right freely to exercise the plaintiffs' religion. It is clear, even from the plaintiffs' affidavits, that the exact location of Chota and the other village sites was unknown to the Cherokees until TVA undertook archeological explorations with the assistance of the University of Tennessee. It appears that the plaintiffs are now claiming that the entire Valley is sacred. Yet none of the affidavits stated this explicitly. For more than 100 years prior to its acquisition by TVA the land in the Valley was owned by persons other than the plaintiffs or members of the class. There is no showing that any Cherokees other than Ammoneta Sequoyah and Richard Crowe ever went to the area for religious purposes during that time. At most, plaintiffs showed that a few Cherokees had made expeditions to the area, prompted for the most part by an understandable desire to learn more about their cultural heritage.

IV

Two recent Supreme Court cases establish a two-step analysis in which courts should engage when deciding a Free Exercise claim. First, it must be determined whether the governmental action does in fact create a burden on the exercise of the plaintiffs' religion. If a burden is found it must be balanced against the governmental interest, with the government being required to show an overriding or compelling reason for its action. See *Sherbert v. Verner*, 374 U.S. 398, 402–03, 83 S. Ct. 1790, 1792–93, 10 L.Ed.2d 965 (1963); *Wisconsin v. Yoder*, 406 U.S. 205, 214–15, 92 S. Ct. 1526, 1532–33, 32 L.Ed.2d 15 (1972). The first step in this analysis is described in *Yoder* as evaluating the "quality of the claims" alleged to be religious. 406 U.S. at 215, 92 S. Ct. at 1533.

Many of the reported decisions concerning Indian religious claims offer little help because they arose in entirely different factual contexts from that of the present case. In the one reported case which is similar to the present one, individual Navajo Indians and three Navajo "Chapters" claimed that the waters of Lake Powell encroached upon their ancestral worship site within the Rainbow Bridge National Monument in Utah. The district court granted summary judgment for the government defendants on two grounds: (1) the fact that the plaintiffs had no property interest in the Monument was held to deprive them of a cognizable First Amendment claim; (2) if the plaintiffs were found to have a cognizable claim, when the opposing interests were balanced those of the defendants were found to outweigh those of the plaintiffs. *Badoni v. Higginson*, 455 F. Supp. 641 (D.C.Utah 1977), appeal pending, No. 78-1517 (10th Cir.).

The district court in the present case based its holding on the plaintiffs' lack of any property interest in the Tellico area. 480 F. Supp. at 612. While this is a factor to be considered, we feel it should not be conclusive in view of the history of the Cherokee expulsion from Southern Appalachia followed by the "Trail of Tears" to Oklahoma and the unique nature of the plaintiffs' religion. Nevertheless, there are criteria by which the constitutional validity of a claim based on the Free Exercise Clause must be tested. In *Wisconsin v. Yoder*, *supra*, the Supreme Court found that the religious faith and the mode of life of the Amish are "inseparable and interdependent," and that "the traditional way of life of the Amish is not merely a matter of personal preference, but one of deep religious conviction, shared by an organized group, and intimately related to daily living." 406 U.S. at 215–16, 92 S. Ct. at 1533. In *Frank v. Alaska*, 604 P.2d 1068 (Alaska 1979), the Supreme Court of Alaska reversed the conviction of an Athabascan Indian who had been found guilty of violating game laws when he killed a moose for a funeral feast, or potlatch. The court found that "[t]he funeral potlatch is the most important institution in Athabascan life" and that "[f]ood is the cornerstone of the ritual." 604 P.2d at 1071. "While moose itself is not sacred, it is needed for proper observance of a sacred ritual which must take place soon after death occurs. Moose is the centerpiece of the most important ritual in Athabascan life and is the equivalent of sacred symbols in other religions." *Id.* at 1073 (footnotes deleted). In *People v. Woody*, 61 Cal.2d 716, 40 Cal.Rptr. 69, 394 P.2d 813 (1964), the hallucinogenic drug peyote was found to play a central role in the ceremony and practice of the Native American Church, an organization of American Indians. The "meeting" ceremony, involving the use of peyote, was found to comprise the cornerstone of the religion. Peyote was found to be more than a sacrament; it was itself an object of worship. "[P]rohibition of the use of peyote results in a virtual inhibition of the practice of defendants' religion. To forbid the use of peyote is to remove the theological heart of Peyotism." 40 Cal.Rptr. at 73–74, 394 P.2d at 817–18.

Examination of the plaintiffs' affidavits discloses no such claim of centrality or indispensability of the Little Tennessee Valley to Cherokee religious observances. Granting as we do that the individual plaintiffs sincerely adhere to a religion which honors ancestors and draws its spiritual strength from feelings of kinship with nature, they have fallen short of demonstrating that worship at the particular geographic location in question is inseparable from the way of life (*Yoder*), the cornerstone of their religious observance (*Frank*), or plays the central role in their religious ceremonies and practices (*Woody*). Rather, the affidavits disclose that medicines are obtainable there which may be found at higher elevations in other locations, that it is believed by some that the knowledge of previous generations will be lost if graves are disturbed or flooded and that the locations of Chota and other village sites are sacred places. These affidavits appear to demonstrate "personal preference" rather than convictions "shared by an organized group." *Yoder, supra*, 406 U.S. at 216, 92 S. Ct. at 1533. When the affidavits are "indulgently treated," *Bohn Aluminum & Brass Corp. v. Storm King Corp., supra*, 303 F.2d at 427, at most they establish a feeling by the individual affiants that the general location of the dam and impoundment has a religious significance which will be destroyed by the flooding. The claim of centrality of the Valley to the practice of the traditional Cherokee religion, as required by *Yoder*, *Woody* and *Frank*, is missing from this case. The overwhelming concern of the affiants appears to be related to the historical beginnings of the Cherokees and their cultural development. It is damage to tribal and family folklore and traditions, more than particular religious observances, which appears to be at stake. The complaint asserts an "irreversible loss to the culture and history of the plaintiffs." Though cultural history and tradition are vitally important to any group of people, these are not interests protected by the Free Exercise Clause of the First Amendment.

It is a difficult and sensitive determination. However, we have looked at "the quality of the claims," as required by *Yoder, supra*, 406 U.S. at 215, 92 S. Ct. at 1533, and conclude that plaintiffs have not alleged infringement of a constitutionally cognizable First Amendment right. In the absence of such an infringement, there is no need to balance the opposing interest of the parties or to determine whether the government's interest in proceeding with its plans for the Tellico Dam is "compelling."

V

The plaintiffs have urged this court to remand to the district court for a trial. However, at the hearing on the motions the district court particularly asked what issues would require a trial, given the affidavits filed by the parties. Counsel for the plaintiffs emphasized the need for further proof in order for the district court to pass on the defense of laches and estoppel and in balancing the competing claims, assuming a finding of infringement. Neither the district court nor this court found it necessary to reach these issues. No argument was made that further proof was required to establish the required quality of the claims. When asked at oral argument in this court, counsel for the plaintiffs was unable to state what further proof was required. It is our conclusion, for the reasons set forth, that the defendant was entitled to judgment as a matter of law. Rule 56(c), Fed.R.Civ.P. Nor is it necessary to remand because we have decided the case for reasons somewhat different from those stated by the district court. The grounds of our decision are supported by the record and the parties have fully briefed and argued these grounds. See *Paskaly v. Seale*, 506 F.2d 1209 (9th Cir. 1974).

The judgment of the district court is affirmed. No costs allowed on appeal.

Footnote:

[1] Chota was one of the nine sites of 18th-century Cherokee villages located in the Valley. Chota was perhaps the most important of these; it was both the capital of the Cherokee Nation and a "peace town" or sanctuary.

Discussion questions

1. Why was this land sacred to the Cherokee people?
2. What was the two-part test the Sixth Circuit applied to determine whether Plaintiffs could enjoin the flooding?
3. How did the trial court use property concepts to hold that the Cherokee plaintiffs did not demonstrate that they would be harmed when the land was flooded? What are/were the issues with this line of reasoning? (Note that the Sixth Circuit Court of Appeals disagreed with the trial court's line of reasoning.)
4. Identify the synthesized test, drawn from three previous cases, for determining whether the flooding would be a burden on the plaintiffs' exercise of their religion.
5. How did this test, which used traditional rhetorical techniques, greatly narrow plaintiffs' options for recovery? What are some alternative tests that could have been formulated?
6. What are the ways in which this test reinforced Westernized conception of religion and excluded non-Western approaches to spirituality and sacredness?
7. What role did a Westernized concept of time play in this opinion?

6

Interrupting the Canon

Gideon v. Wainwright, 373 U.S. 335 (1963)

Summary of Gideon v. Wainwright

In *Gideon*, the Supreme Court acknowledged that the Fourteenth Amendment requires states to ensure due process by appointing an attorney to represent criminal defendants accused of a serious crime. Prior to *Gideon*, states were not required to appoint counsel for criminal defendants unless the defendant was charged with a capital offense *or* there was some other special circumstance warranting appointment of counsel. This rule was established in *Betts v. Brady*,[1] and it led to great inconsistencies across jurisdictions, even though by the time of *Gideon*, most states had adopted some sort of system for ensuring the representation of criminal defendants, at least in felony cases. Florida, however, was one of the hold-out states that did not permit appointment of counsel absent evidence of some special circumstance.

Clarence Earl Gideon was charged with burglary of a billiard hall, and before he was tried, he asked the court to appoint an attorney to represent him. The trial court denied his request, and Gideon was ultimately convicted and sentenced to prison. From there, he sent a hand-written petition to the United States Supreme Court begging for relief. The Supreme Court granted review and posed the question, "Should this Court's holding in *Betts v. Brady* be overruled?"[2] It then appointed attorney Abe Fortas to represent the indigent Clarence Earl Gideon and answer this question.

In his initial brief, Abe Fortas employed a variety of interrupters that ultimately convinced the United States Supreme Court to overrule its decision in *Betts v. Brady*. These interrupters disrupted the canon by retreating from blind adherence to *stare decisis* through demonstrating the flaws inherent in the special circumstances test. They also obscured the syllogism by relying on studies and policy arguments as a prominent source of support rather than pure legal doctrine, and then using persuasive legal authority from other jurisdictions to argue for a change in the law. In the Petitioner Brief, the legal syllogism is challenging for the reader to identify, yet the Brief is ultimately persuasive and effective.

Excerpt from Petitioner's Brief in Gideon v. Wainwright

(All footnotes have been omitted.)

I The Fourteenth Amendment requires that counsel be appointed to represent an indigent defendant in every criminal case involving a serious offense

In *Betts v. Brady*, 316 U.S. 455, decided in 1942, this Court ruled that the 14th Amendment does not require that the state courts furnish counsel to an indigent defendant in a non-capital case unless the total facts and circumstances in the particular case show that there has been "a denial of fundamental fairness, shocking to the universal sense of justice." *Id.* at 462. In short, counsel need not be appointed unless there are "special circumstances showing that without a lawyer a defendant could not have an adequate and a fair defense." *Palmer v. Ashe*, 342 U.S. 134, 135 (1951).

For twenty years, this Court, the lower federal courts, and the courts of a number of states have been charged with the duty of administering this rule. The experience has not been a happy one. We respectfully suggest that the data, summarized in this brief, demonstrate that the quality of criminal justice and the relations between the federal and state courts, have suffered as a result of *Betts v. Brady*.

We believe that "time has set its face" against *Betts v. Brady*; that a fresh evaluation of the holding in that case is timely and appropriate; and that *Betts v. Brady* should be overruled in the present case.

In the following portions of this brief, we believe that we shall demonstrate that the "special circumstances" rule, devised to assure the 14th Amendment's requirement of due process in state criminal cases, has not achieved its basic constitutional objective: It has not assured and cannot be expected to assure that counsel will be provided where necessary in the interests of fundamental fairness in state criminal proceedings.

We shall also show, we believe, the overwhelming evidence that the rule of *Betts v. Brady* is not compatible with due respect for the separate processes of the states. It is not an appropriate adaptation of the 14th Amendment to the demands of federalism. To the contrary, it is a rule which compels continual, unseemly, and improper intervention by the federal courts in state criminal proceedings not on the basis of applying a concrete, fundamental principle but by the corrosive and irritating process of case-by-case review. *Betts v. Brady* has produced and will continue to produce a series of *ad hoc* decisions by this Court and other federal courts—exercising supervision over the conduct of trials by state courts and state judges—which are disruptive of our federal system and which create friction between the states and the federal government.

In other words, *Betts v. Brady* has not meant, and will not mean, *less* federal intervention in state criminal proceedings than would be the case if the 14th Amendment were construed to require that counsel be furnished in all state criminal prosecutions. Because of the intensely factual, subjective, and *post-facto* nature of its standards, *Betts v. Brady* means *more* federal intervention on a case by case basis, and in a much more exacerbating form.

The present case, in our opinion, raises the fundamental question as to whether *Betts v. Brady* should be overruled. Apart from the technical and procedural question resulting from the failure of petitioner to allege special circumstances and from the nature of the proceedings before the Florida Supreme Court to which we have referred above, we can claim neither extreme youth, inexperience, mental incapacity, nor illiteracy on the part of the defendant. It is true that the defendant could not possibly have fully understood the legal subtleties of the crime with which he was charged; he could not have been aware of the decisions of the Supreme Court of Florida or principles of *corpus juris* which might affect his defense. He could not have been alert to the opportunities theoretically offered by the law to cope with the problems of jury selection or the testimony of witnesses adduced by the State. It is true, too, that the judge in Gideon's case did not serve as Gideon's defense counsel—although it is obvious that he tried to conduct the trial fairly.

In Appendix B to this Brief we analyze the specific points that demonstrate that Gideon did not receive the benefits and protection which would presumably have been afforded him by counsel. We believe that these constitute a vivid demonstration of the fact that he was deprived of his due process rights under the Fourteenth Amendment: that he did not have a fair trial in the constitutional sense. But it is our opinion that these points are not peculiar to Gideon's case. We believe, *mutatis mutandis*, these points are present in every criminal prosecution. In short, we believe that the circumstances of this case are no more "special" than in other criminal cases—unless we are to draw a line between tweedledee and tweedledum. We are therefore of the opinion that the fundamental question of *Betts v. Brady* is at issue in the present case.

1. *The aid of counsel is indispensable to a fair hearing.* As we shall discuss, we believe that the real point of difference between the advocates and opponents of the "special circumstances" rule of *Betts v. Brady* relates to the requirements of federalism in the application of the Fourteenth Amendment. It is not the issue of whether counsel is or is not needed for a trial which is fair and decent. The necessity for counsel in a criminal case is too plain for argument. No individual who is not a trained or experienced lawyer can possibly know or pursue the technical, elaborate, and sophisticated measures which are necessary to assemble and appraise the facts, analyze the law, determine contentions, negotiate the plea, or marshal and present all of the factual and legal considerations which have a bearing upon his defense. Even a trained, experienced criminal lawyer cannot—and will not, if he is sensible—undertake his own defense.

In the absence of counsel an accused person cannot determine whether his arrest is lawful; whether the indictment or information is valid; what, if any, preliminary motions should be filed. He cannot accurately evaluate the implications of a plea to a lesser offense, and he is at a loss in discussions with the prosecuting attorney relating to such a plea.

The indigent, apart from all other considerations, has probably been in jail from the time of arrest because of inability to furnish bail. How can he prepare his case? And how unreal it is to suppose that a layman can conduct a *voir dire* of the petit jury, or cross-examine the prosecution's witnesses, or interpose objections to incompetent and prejudicial testimony. See Douglas, J., concurring in *Carnley v. Cochran*, 369 U.S. 506 (1962). The truth is that "The unrepresented defendant in many cases does not really know what is going on ..." Ass'n. of the Bar of the City of New York, *Report of the Magistrate's Courts Visitation Committee* 30 (undated). As this Court pointed out in *Reynolds v. Cochran*, 365 U.S. 525, 532–33 (1961), "even in the most routine-appearing proceedings the assistance of able counsel may be of inestimable value."

In the event of conviction, the unrepresented defendant is further seriously disadvantaged at the sentencing stage.

"Automatic sanctions, which predominated in earlier historical periods, have been largely replaced by judicial discretion. ... Consequently, counsel may be called upon to play a role in sentencing which requires wide knowledge and experience." Ass'n. of the Bar of the City of New York, Special Committee to Study Defender Systems, *Equal Justice for the Accused* 35–36 (1959). See also *Gadsden v. United States*, 223 F.2d 627, 630–33 (D.C. Cir. 1955); Kadish, *The Advocate and the Expert—Counsel in the Peno-Correctional Process*, 45 Minn. L. Rev. 803, 806 (1961).

Moreover, it is patent that many constitutional rights are meaningless in the absence of legal assistance. As an eminent State Supreme Court judge has stated: "Of all the rights that an accused person has, the right to be represented by counsel is by far the most pervasive, for it affects his ability to assert any other rights he may have." Schaefer, *Federalism and State Criminal Procedure*, 70 Harv. L. Rev. 1, 8 (1956).

In the past twenty years, this Court has stated a number of principles of constitutional law with respect to state criminal procedure, which have a direct and practical bearing on the conduct of trials. The law of involuntary confessions and searches and seizures as applied to the states, for example, post-dates almost in its entirety the decision in *Betts v. Brady*. Important procedural safeguards cannot be implemented effectively without the assistance of counsel. An uncounseled defendant manifestly cannot be expected, for example, to be a master of the intricacies of the law relating to searches and seizures, e.g., whether a search warrant is required, whether there is "probable cause," whether there has been a waiver, and so on. An inexperienced person cannot possibly appraise the implications of invoking the privilege against self-incrimination or determine whether a statement he wishes to make may constitute a waiver of the privilege. In brief, what is required for the effective assertion of constitutional rights and privileges is "the assistance of a learned gentleman to speak for an unlearned man" (5 The Speeches of the Right Hon. Charles James Fox in the House of Commons (London 1815) 78, quoted by Mr. Justice Clark in *Kinsella v. Unified States ex rel. Singleton*, 361 U.S. 234, 244, n. 10 [1960]).

2. *The absolute requirement of counsel in federal prosecutions confirms the need for an attorney.* The parallel development of the right to counsel in the federal courts confirms the conclusion that an unrepresented defendant cannot adequately advocate his rights. In 1938, in *Johnson v. Zerbst*, 304 U.S. 458, this Court held that counsel must be furnished in every case to a person tried in the federal courts. To quote the Court: "If the accused ... is not represented by Counsel and has not competently and intelligently waived his constitutional right, the Sixth Amendment stands as a jurisdictional bar to a valid conviction and sentence depriving him of his life or his liberty." 304 U.S. at 468.

Johnson v. Zerbst was not the unchallenged product of the ineluctable language of the Sixth Amendment. There are those who assert that the right conferred on the accused "to have the assistance of counsel for his defense" meant only "that in the Federal courts the defendant in a criminal case was entitled to be represented by counsel retained by him," and that it did not comprehend "the right of a prisoner to have counsel assigned to him by the court if, for financial or other reasons, he was unable to retain counsel." Holtzoff, *The Right of Counsel Under the Sixth Amendment*, 20 N.Y.L.Q. Rev. 1, 7–8 (1944).

That view was rejected by the Court in *Johnson v. Zerbst*. In speaking for the Court, Mr. Justice Black made it clear that the conclusion of the case rested upon "the obvious truth that the average defendant does not have the professional legal skill to protect himself when brought before a tribunal with power to take his life or liberty, wherein the prosecution is presented by experienced and learned Counsel." 304 U.S. at 462–463.

Our accusatorial system of criminal justice presupposes that the cause of the defendant as well as that of the state will be vigorously advocated.

It makes no sense to urge that the availability of counsel is required in the federal courts in order "to insure fundamental human rights of life and liberty" (*id.* at 304 U.S. 462), but that it is not fundamental if the prosecution occurs in a state courthouse. We do not think it arguable that federal judges or prosecutors are less solicitous of the accused than are their state counterparts, or that the indigent accused in state criminal proceedings are more learned in the law than their counterparts who are involved in the federal process.

3. *The trial judge cannot act as defense counsel.* The trial judge must assure himself by a meticulous and thorough investigation that the accused has not ignorantly or incompetently waived his right to counsel, *Von Moltke v. Gillies*, 332 U.S. 708, 723–24 (1948), but we do not believe that it can properly be urged that the trial judge can or should perform the functions of ascertaining and advancing the legal and factual points available to the accused. The judge comes on the scene too late in point of time; crucial events have already taken place and important decisions made by default or otherwise. The judge cannot investigate the facts; he cannot and should not engage in the probing of a defendant necessary for representation; he cannot and should not cross-examine the state's witnesses.

In a word, a man cannot act both as trial judge and as defense counsel. As Mr. Justice Sutherland stated, in speaking for the Court in *Powell v. Alabama*, 287 U.S. 45, 61 (1932):

> '[H]ow can a judge, whose functions are purely judicial, effectively discharge the obligations of counsel for the accused? He can and should see to it that in the proceedings before the court the accused shall be dealt with justly and fairly. He cannot investigate the facts, advise and direct the defense, or participate in those necessary conferences between counsel and accused which sometimes partake of the inviolable character of the confessional.'

4. *The distinction between capital and non-capital offenses does not furnish a valid basis for deciding when to appoint counsel.* In one class of criminal cases tried in the state courts—those involving capital offenses—this Court has rejected the *Betts v. Brady* rule. *Hamilton v. Alabama*, 368 U.S. 52 (1961); *Uveges v. Pennsylvania*, 335 U.S. 437, 441 (1948); *Bute v. Illinois*, 333 U.S. 640, 674 (1948). As the Court stated *in Hamilton v. Alabama, supra*: "When one pleads to a capital charge without benefit of counsel, we do not stop to determine whether prejudice resulted." 368 U.S. at 55.

We do not believe this distinction between capital and non-capital offenses furnishes an appropriate or constitutionally valid basis for determining when counsel must be appointed. The due process clause protects against deprivation of "liberty" and "property" as well as against deprivation of "life." Moreover, the necessity for legal assistance, not the nature of the sanction, should be the controlling consideration. As one commentator has observed:

> [I]n determining whether absence of counsel has denied a fair hearing, the important consideration seems less the penalties that may be imposed than the *need* for skilled representation. Any experienced defense lawyer is likely to testify that most murder cases, in which capital penalties are involved, are by no means the most difficult to try or those in which representation is most urgently required. Indictments charging such crimes as embezzlement, confidence game, or conspiracy are likely to place the defendant in a far more helpless position. The distinction that the Court has drawn lacks integrity, and so long as it persists, the law of the subject will remain in a state of unstable equilibrium. Allen, *The Supreme Court and State Criminal Justice*, 4 Wayne L. Rev. 191, 197 (1958).

This Court has specifically rejected the distinction between capital and non-capital offenses in the military court-martial cases, involving rights secured by Article III and the Fifth and Sixth Amendments. *Kinsella v. United States ex rel. Singleton*, 361 U.S. 234 (1960). In view of the importance of the court-martial cases to this particular issue, we discuss the cases at more length … *infra*.

It is true that these court-martial decisions involved the power of Congress under Art. 1, §8, "To make Rules for the Government and Regulation of the land and naval Forces" and did not involve limitations upon state power under the Fourteenth Amendment. The cases turned upon the status of the accused. But if the capital and non-capital distinction is rejected in a case involving the right to trial by jury before a constitutionally appointed judge, among other privileges, we perceive no reason why it should be considered as controlling with respect to the closely allied right to counsel.

Further, in 1961, this Court in *Ferguson v. Georgia*, 365 U.S. 570, rejected the capital–non-capital distinction in a Fourteenth Amendment case. The Court concluded in that case that the Fourteenth Amendment invalidated a Georgia statute which prohibited a defendant in a criminal case from testifying under oath in his own defense, in response to questions of counsel. The Court stated: "Our decision does not turn on the facts that the appellant was tried for a capital offense and was represented by employed counsel. The command of the Fourteenth Amendment also applies in the case of an accused tried for a non-capital offense, or represented by appointed counsel." 365 U.S. at 596. *Griffin v. Illinois*, 351 U.S. 12 (1956), a non-capital case, similarly rejected the capital–non-capital distinction with respect to the availability to indigents of transcripts for appeal purposes.

In sum, we submit that the possibility of a death sentence does not constitute a valid constitutional criterion for determining who shall have the assistance of counsel.

5. *Denial of counsel to the indigent violates both due process and equal protection.* The refusal to appoint an attorney to represent a destitute person results in discrimination against defendants based solely upon poverty. There is no doubt that a defendant in a state criminal trial has an unqualified right under the Fourteenth Amendment to be heard through counsel he has retained. *Chandler v. Fretag*, 348 U.S. 3, 9 (1954); see *In re Groban's Petition*, 352 U.S. 330, 332 (1957). We submit that if a person with funds is entitled to be heard through an attorney, the same privilege must be extended to indigents. In the case of those able financially to hire counsel, the rule is not limited to capital cases or to "special circumstances." It is absolute and complete, and a state may not restrict it. How, then, can the right be restricted in the case of the poor? We have agreed since *Powell v. Alabama*, 287 U.S. 45 (1932), that the state has a duty to appoint counsel for the indigent in at least some criminal cases in order to meet the requirements of due process. If this is so, counsel must be provided in all criminal cases in which there is a constitutional requirement to permit counsel to appear and act for those who have the funds to hire them. The indigent defendant cannot be denied an "unqualified right" solely because of poverty; to do so results in a denial of equal protection. "The need of counsel is the same, whatever the economic status of the accused." *McNeal v. Culver*, 365 U.S. 109, 118 (1961) (Douglas, J., concurring); see also Douglas, *Vagrancy and Arrest on Suspicion*, 70 Yale L.J. 1, 10–11 (1960).

This principle was articulated in *Griffin v. Illinois*, 351 U.S. 12 (1956), which held that the Fourteenth Amendment requires that "Destitute defendants must be afforded as adequate appellate review as defendants who have money enough to buy transcripts." 351 U.S. at 19. The Court said that the "constitutional guaranties of due process and equal protection both call for procedures in criminal trials which allow no invidious discriminations between persons and different groups of persons. Both equal protection and due process emphasize the central aim of our entire judicial system—all people charged with crime must, so far as the law is concerned, 'stand on an equality before the bar of justice in every American court.'" 351 U.S. at 17.

And the Court added:

"In criminal trials a State can no more discriminate on account of poverty than on account of religion, race, or color. ... There is no meaningful distinction between a rule which would deny the poor the right to defend themselves in a trial court and one which effectively denies the poor an adequate appellate review accorded to all who have money enough to pay the costs in advance. ... There can be no equal justice where the kind of trial a man gets depends on the amount of money he has." 351 U.S. at 17–19. See Willcox and Bloustein, *The Griffin Case—Poverty and the Fourteenth Amendment*, 43 Cornell L.Q. 1, 23 (1957); see also *Smith v. Bennett*, 365 U.S. 708 (1961); *Douglas v. Green*, 363 U.S. 192 (1960); *Burns v. Ohio*, 360 U.S. 252 (1959); *Eskridge v. Washington Prison Bd.*, 357 U.S. 214 (1958); cf. *Coppedge v. United States*, 369 U.S. 438 (1962).

Where counsel are not designated to assist indigent persons, whether a defense of any kind will be asserted, and the type of defense, tends to depend more upon the personality and temperament of the accused than upon guilt or innocence or any other factor. The large percentage of guilty pleas in our courts may reflect the helplessness of the arrested and their lack of counsel as well as the efficiency of the police. Certainly, the frequency of guilty pleas suggests that those who are arrested, particularly the penniless and persons who are members of minority groups, are more likely hopelessly to resign themselves to fate than aggressively to act like the defense counsel portrayed on television. In sum:

> To say that trials without counsel can be fair is to assume either that the defense which counsel might have presented would not have changed the result in the case or that in certain types of cases counsel serves no useful function. The first assumption is hindsight and unprovable. The second, if true, would convict a portion of the bar of taking money under false pretenses in all those "simple" cases where counsel accepts a retainer but apparently cannot influence the result. We cannot with justice keep the existing "fight" theory of criminal law and force the indigent defendant to fight alone. If our vaunted claim of "equal justice under law" is to be more than an idle pretense, the right to have counsel must be extended in practice to all persons accused of crime. Beaney, *The Right to Counsel in American Courts* 234–235 (1955).

II The demands of federalism do not dictate continued adherence to *Betts v. Brady*

In view of the foregoing, we believe that the real argument against the position that the 14th Amendment requires that counsel be furnished to indigent persons in all state criminal proceedings is that it "would disregard the basic and historic power of the states to prescribe their own local court procedures," i.e., the demands of federalism. *Bute v. Illinois*, 333 U.S. 640, 668 (1948). We submit two answers to this argument: *First*, we do not believe it necessary to dilute, denigrate, and diminish the quality of due process in our criminal proceedings or subtract from the equal administration of justice in deference to the few states, like Florida, which continue to defy the general opinion as to the right to counsel. *Second*, we believe that the argument is based on a premise that experience has rejected. The "special circumstances" rule increases the problems of federalism. It does not decrease them.

1. *The great majority of the states now make provision for the appointment of counsel in all felony cases, either explicitly or as a matter of practice.* In 1942, the Court concluded in *Betts v. Brady*, after canvassing the law in each state, that "in the great majority of the states, it has been the considered judgment of the people, their representatives and their courts that appointment of counsel is not a fundamental right, essential to a fair trial." *Betts v. Brady*, 316 U.S. at 471.

This factual premise of *Betts v. Brady* has evaporated during the past twenty years. "Although not every state today offers counsel to the indigent defendant in the serious, but noncapital, criminal case, the trend is unmistakably in that direction." Schaefer, *Federalism and State Criminal Procedure*, 70 Harv. L. Rev. 1, 9 (1956).

In 1961, in an appendix attached to a concurring opinion in *McNeal v. Culver*, 365 U.S. 109, 119–122, Mr. Justice Douglas listed 35 states which provide for "Appointment of counsel for indigents in all felony cases, as of course, by force of the State Constitution, statutes, court rule, or judicial decision." (*Id.* at 120). Subsequent to compilation of the appendix, Colorado made appointment of counsel obligatory in all felony cases, Colo. R. Crim. P. 44 (set out in 34 Rocky Mt. L. Rev. 1, 89 [1961]), and Michigan apparently should be added to the list, see Mich. Ct. R. 35A (Honigman's Mich. Ct. Rules Anno.).

There are thus presently thirty-seven states which expressly provide, in one form or another, for the designation of counsel in behalf of destitute defendants in all felony cases. In a majority of the states listed in Justice Douglas' appendix in *McNeal v. Culver*, *supra*, the court must inform the accused of his right to counsel and inquire whether he desires an attorney. In all thirty-seven states appointment is mandatory in all felony cases if requested by the defendant. See Appendix, "Provision for the Assignment of Counsel for Indigent Defendants in Criminal Cases," in Ass'n. of the Bar of the City of New York, Special Committee to Study Defender Systems, *Equal Justice for the Accused* (1959).

Further, a study, just completed, concludes on the basis of extensive documentation that of the remaining thirteen states, it is the general practice in eight states—Pennsylvania, Maryland, Maine, New Hampshire, Rhode Island, Vermont, Delaware, and Hawaii—to furnish legal assistance in each case where such aid is requested. Kamisar, *The Right to Counsel and the Fourteenth Amendment: A Dialogue on "The Most Pervasive Right" of an Accused*, 30 U. of Chi. L. Rev. 1 (1962).

There remain only five states—Alabama, Florida, Mississippi, North Carolina, and South Carolina—which do not make provision for appointment of counsel in behalf of indigents in all felony cases. Even in these states, however, there are cities and counties where public defenders or court appointed counsel are assigned to represent impoverished defendants at various stages in the proceeding. See Kamisar, *op. cit. supra*.

There is far less contrariety of views among the states with respect to the right to counsel than was the case with respect to the exclusion of evidence secured by an illegal search and seizure. When *Mapp v. Ohio*, 367 U.S. 643, was decided in 1961, one-half of the states still adhered to the rule that illegally seized evidence was admissible. 367 U.S. at 680 (dissenting opinion); see *Elkins v. United States*, 364 U.S. 206, 224 (1960). This Court held, however, that the 14th Amendment required that the state courts exclude unlawfully procured evidence. With respect to the plea that the decision infringed the principle of federalism, the Court said (367 U.S. at 656):

> This Court has not hesitated to enforce as strictly against the States as it does against the Federal Government the rights of free speech and of a free press, the rights to notice and to a fair, public trial, including, as it does, the right not to be convicted by use of a coerced confession ...

We recognize, of course, that resolution of an important question of constitutional law cannot and should not be made simply by taking a census of the states. But the practice among the states was emphasized in *Betts v. Brady* as a factor to be used in determining the standard of procedural fairness required by the due process clause. *Betts v. Brady*, 316 U.S. at 465. There is no doubt that there is today widespread consensus among the states that legal assistance should be furnished to indigent persons. Further, it is a principle which has the overwhelming support of the bar. The task here is essentially a modest one: to bring into line with the consensus of the states and professional opinion the few "stragglers" who persist in denying fair treatment to the accused.

2. Betts v. Brady *has created friction between the states and the Federal Courts*. Two decades of experience have borne out the forecast of Mr. Justice Black, dissenting in *Betts v. Brady*, that the "special circumstances" test would require this Court and other federal courts to exercise "vast supervisory powers" over the state courts. 316 U.S. at 475. *Betts v. Brady* has engendered conflict between the federal and state courts because of the case by case review it entails and because it does not prescribe a clearcut standard which the state courts can follow. As one commentator has noted: "[T]he very vagueness of the fair-trial test has encouraged recourse to the lower federal courts and to the Supreme Court by state convicts." Beaney, *The Right to Counsel in American Courts* 196 (1955).

A vast number of petitions have been filed in the federal courts collaterally attacking the validity of convictions for failure to assign counsel. A recent study of 35 federal habeas corpus cases in which a state prisoner successfully attacked the judgment under which he was committed led to the following conclusions:

> A most striking fact discovered from the 35 cases studied is the dominance of the issue of right to counsel as the contention most likely to succeed in federal habeas corpus. In roughly half of the cases, the state judgment fell on this ground. As only four of these cases involved a capital offense, *the largest stumbling block in the administration of state criminal law is revealed as the nonabsolute right to counsel for indigents in non-cases*. Reitz, *Federal Habeas Corpus: Postconviction Remedy for State Prisoners*, 108 U. Pa. L. Rev. 461, 483 (1960) (emphasis added).

Moreover, the "special circumstances" rule involves federal supervision over the state courts in its most noxious form. In effect, the federal courts are given a roving commission to scrutinize the proceeding in the state court to determine if it is "shocking to the universal sense of justice." It is difficult to conceive of a test more likely to promote friction between federal and state tribunals. But, as Mr. Justice Stewart has stated, "The very essence of a healthy federalism depends upon the avoidance of needless conflict between state and federal courts." *Elkins v. United States*, 364 U.S. 206, 221 (1960).

Finally, the flood of habeas corpus petitions spawned by *Betts* has led to agitation to curtail the "Great Writ." The undesirable consequences of *Betts* thus extend beyond the immediate issue of right to counsel. A decision overruling *Betts* would benefit the federalist principle by eliminating a major irritant.

3. *Experimentation by the States will not be eliminated if the special circumstances test is jettisoned.* An absolute rule that counsel must be furnished indigents accused of serious offenses will still leave open an area in which federalism will operate. The states undoubtedly will meet the demands of the rule in a variety of ways. Some states may elect to provide counsel through a governmentally financed public defender system; others through court assignment of members of the bar; still others by use of a privately financed voluntary defender system. See A'ssn. of the Bar of the City of New York, Special Committee to Study Defender Systems, *Equal Justice for the Accused* 47–53 (1959). Some states may choose to follow the system established by Congress in the District of Columbia Legal Aid Act (74 Stat. 229, D.C. Code Anno. §§ 2-2201-2210 (1961 ed.)), which provides for compensation to counsel employed by a publicly financed legal aid agency and reimbursement of expenses to volunteer or court-assigned counsel.

In other words, the states will remain at liberty to experiment and to adopt a system for the appointment of counsel consonant with community needs and resources, subject only to the requirement that the system adopted fulfill the constitutional imperative and guarantee effective legal aid to all persons accused of a serious offense who do not competently and intelligently waive such assistance. We believe that this is an instance of federalism in operation in an appropriate form: Under our system, we submit, the demands and the benefits of federalism should take the form of a diversity of *method*. Federalism properly considered does not demand or permit a negation of basic constitutional principle.

III The rule of *Betts v. Brady* has not proved to be a satisfactory standard for judicial admin istration

Two decades have shown that *Betts v. Brady* is not an operable guide.

1. The cases decided by this Court under the "special circumstances" test, to quote one commentator, "are distinguished neither by the consistency of their results nor by the cogency of their argument." Allen, *The Supreme Court, Federalism, and State Systems of Criminal Justice*, 8 De Paul L. Rev. 213, 230 (1958). The difficulty inheres in the subjective, ambiguous nature of the rule itself. Thus, the following factors have been deemed relevant in deciding whether the proceeding was "fundamentally unfair":

(i) the complexity of the statute under which the defendant is prosecuted and the nature of the offense charged;
(ii) the fact that specific objections or arguments could have been, but were not, made;
(iii) illiteracy or lack of education;
(iv) mental illness or mental retardation;
(v) youth of the accused;
(vi) a plea of guilty by a co-defendant;
(vii) the extent of the accused's prior experience with criminal proceedings;
(viii) the adequacy of guidance by the trial court;
(ix) misconduct by the trial judge or the prosecutor;
(x) the severity of the sentence.

No standards have been delineated, however, with respect to the weight or importance to be assigned each of the foregoing factors. Thus, for example, in *DeMeerleer v. Michigan*, 329 U.S. 663 (1947), the Court deemed the youth of the accused (seventeen) significant and reversed his conviction, but in *Gayes v. New York*, 332 U.S. 145 (1947), the conviction was not set aside despite the fact that the defendant was "a lad of sixteen" (*id.* at 146) when he was convicted without counsel. In *Qwicksall v. Michigan*, 339 U.S. 660 (1950), the Court felt it reasonable to presume from the accused's prior appearances in court that he knew of his right to counsel, and since he made no request for legal aid, his rights were held not infringed. But recently in *Carntey v. Cochran*, 369 U.S. 506 (1962), the Court felt that a prior criminal record magnified the importance of the assistance of counsel because of its implications in the event the accused takes the witness stand.

It is likewise difficult to reconcile *Gryger v. Burke*, 334 U.S. 728 (1948), with *Townsend v. Burke*, 334 U.S. 736 (1948), both decided on the same day. In *Gryger*, a defendant sentenced to life imprisonment, argued that the state court mistakenly assumed that the applicable statute made the penalty mandatory. In *Townsend*, the defendant contended that the court imposed a sentence under the erroneous impression that defendant's record included convictions on two charges as to which, in fact, he had been acquitted. In both cases, the defendants, who were unrepresented, claimed that if counsel had been present the mistake would have been corrected. In *Townsend*, this Court concluded that the accused was so disadvantaged by lack of counsel that the conviction could not be permitted to stand, but in *Gryger* the Court affirmed the order denying habeas corpus. It is difficult to perceive why the denial of counsel was deemed prejudicial as a constitutional matter in one case but not in the other.

2. In the present case, the trial court did not call petitioner's attention to the "special circumstances" bearing on the right to appointment of counsel. As the state court decisions discussed below show, the "special circumstances" rule has only infrequently led the state courts to appoint counsel. Some of the state decisions are startling. For example, in *Commonwealth ex rel. Simon v. Maroney*, 405 Pa. 562, 176 A. 2d 94 (1961), pet. for cert. pending, No. 41 Misc., Oct. Term, 1962, the defendant, an 18 year old boy, was sentenced in 1942 to a term of 20 to 40 years imprisonment following a conviction for rape, robbery, and assault and battery. The Pennsylvania Supreme Court recently

denied relief. It felt that denial of counsel did not produce an "ingredient of unfairness" although the court recognized that "The defendant was not wholly a normal person ... A behavior clinic study made of the defendant shortly after his arrest revealed him to be a high grade moron with an intelligence quotient of 59," equivalent to a "mental age of only nine." 405 Pa. at 565–67, 176 A. 2d at 96, 97. The defendant was "illiterate" (405 Pa. at 570, 176 A. 2d at 99), but the court felt no prejudice occurred because "There were no 'intricacies of criminal procedure,' no 'improper conduct on the part of the court or prosecuting officials,' and nothing complicated about the charges of robbery and rape." 405 Pa. at 565–66, 176 A. 2d at 96.

In *Butler v. Culver*, 111 So. 2d 35 (Fla. 1959), the court refused to set aside a conviction for second degree murder for which the defendant had been sentenced to life imprisonment, although there was a "showing in this record that approximately two months after the petitioner pleaded guilty to second degree murder [without counsel], it was formally adjudicated that he was suffering from an acute condition of insanity, described as paranoid schizophrenia." *Id.* at 37–38. The court said no contention was made on appeal that the accused was mentally incompetent at the time of trial.

In *Shauffer v. Warden*, 211 Md. 635, 126 A. 2d 573 (1956), the accused was convicted without counsel on charges of burglary. The accused contended that "he was only nineteen years of age and the average in mental capacity and was suffering from a congenital speech defect." *Ibid.* The defendant maintained that as a result of his speech defect a plea of not guilty was mistaken as a plea of guilty; that he was unable because of his speech impediment to make the trial court understand the whereabouts of certain necessary witnesses; and that he vainly attempted to "stammer out" a request for appointment of counsel. 211 Md. at 636–37, 126 A. 2d at 573–74. The conviction was upheld.

The opinion of the Alabama Court of Appeals in *Artrip v. State*, 136 So. 2d 574 (Ct. App. Ala. 1962), reads in a similar vein. The court felt the following pertinent to its conclusion that petitioner was not prejudiced by denial of his request for counsel in a prosecution for escaping from the penitentiary:

> Artrip was considered a good all round mechanic and electrician by his supervisor at the Kilby motor pool. His original brief was well typed and concisely stated a number of pertinent points. His supplemental briefs which exhibit good penmanship are also pertinent to the contentions he advances. *Id.* at 576.

Contrast with the foregoing cases the opinions of this Court in *Carnley v. Cochran*, 369 U.S. 506 (1962); *Chewning v. Cunningham*, 368 U.S. 443 (1962); and *McNeal v. Culver*, 365 U.S. 109 (1961).

3. There is an inherent incongruity in the "special circumstances" test. The rule is invoked primarily after trial in connection with an appeal or a petition for habeas corpus. A defendant, who had no counsel at trial, must file a petition, without the assistance of counsel, alleging that he was denied due process by reason of the refusal to appoint counsel. We submit that it is highly unlikely that a layman knows what constitutes

"special circumstances" within the meaning of the rule in *Betts v. Brady*, or that he has sufficient technical competence to allege these matters. If the accused lacked funds to retain counsel to defend him at trial, he will be unable to afford counsel once he is in prison. Thus, the factors which would justify invalidating the conviction may not be brought to the attention of the appellate court.

Even in the unlikely event that the accused has the assistance of counsel in preparing the documents on appeal, the prejudicial factors may not be adduced for the reason that the record does not reveal the "special circumstances." For example, the accused may be mentally retarded or mentally ill, but that fact may not be reflected in the record, although it would be a decisive factor under the rule of *Betts v. Brady*. See *McNeal v. Culver*, 365 U.S. 109 (1961); *Massey v. Moore*, 348 U.S. 105 (1954).

Denied qualified professional assistance at trial, the accused, confined in prison, tends to turn for legal advice to "jailhouse lawyers." The volume of post-conviction petitions in this and other courts and the assertion of important constitutional rights are thus left, we surmise, largely to untrained, unqualified prisoners. Cf. *Schware v. Board of Bar Examiners of the State of New Mexico*, 353 U.S. 232, 247 (1957) (Frankfurter, J., concurring). It is ironic, but we believe true, that in final analysis, whether a post-conviction petition is filed, or whether a poverty-ridden prisoner gets a hearing on his right to counsel, may turn upon the quality of the fellow-inmate—usually equally untrained—who is the jailhouse lawyer.

4. The essentially post-trial character of the "special circumstances" rule is unfair to defendants in another respect: The accused may languish in prison for years before his conviction is adjudged to have been unfair by reason of the absence of counsel. The defendant in *Moore v. Michigan*, 355 U.S. 155 (1957), was sentenced in 1938 to "solitary confinement at hard labor for life"; in December, 1957, some 19 years later, this Court ruled that he had been denied his constitutional right to legal assistance. The lapse of time between trial and reversal for want of counsel was 15 years in *DeMeerleer v. Michigan*, 329 U.S. 663 (1947), and in *United States ex rel. Stoner v. Randolph*, 165 F. Supp. 284 (E.D. Ill. 1958); 14 years in *Garton v. Tinsley*, 171 F. Supp. 387 (D. Colo. 1959); and 10 years in *Uveges v. Pennsylvania*, 335 U.S. 437 (1948).

Indeed, a defendant may serve his entire sentence protesting throughout that his conviction is invalid by reason of the denial of counsel, and the case may be mooted before the wrong can be corrected. See *Parker v. Ellis*, 362 U.S. 574 (1960), writ of certiorari dismissed as moot, where four members of this Court agreed that the defendant "was convicted of a felony in flagrant disregard of his constitutional right to assistance of counsel" after a trial characterized as a "sham." *Id.* at 577–578 (Warren, C.J., dissenting).

5. The long periods of delay associated with *Betts v. Brady* are undesirable for the state as well as for the defendant. If the conviction is invalidated it may be difficult, if not impossible, to conduct a new trial years later. Witnesses may have died; records may have been lost; memories will have faded. In short, we respectfully submit that it is to the advantage of the state, as well as to the defendant, to furnish counsel to indigent persons at all trials for serious offenses.

IV The right to counsel minimally includes appointment of an attorney to assist an indigent person at the trial of a serious offense

It is, of course, unnecessary in deciding the present case to delineate all of the metes and bounds of the right to counsel in state criminal proceedings. This case involves the right of an accused to legal assistance at the trial stage of the prosecution. Whatever the perimeter of the right, it surely comprehends the assignment of counsel at the trial on the merits.

We believe the right of indigents to legal assistance should be commensurate with that of persons who have means to employ counsel. An accused person who desires to consult an attorney should have the right to do so at any time immediately after arrest. Indeed, "there is a strong argument that the time a defendant needs counsel most is immediately after his arrest and until trial." Ass'n. of Bar of City of New York, et al, *Equal Justice for the Accused* 60 (1959). In any event, counsel should be furnished to destitute defendants at the same point in time at which an accused person with funds would be entitled under the 14th Amendment to consult an attorney.

V The practical implications with respect to persons already imprisoned do not militate against overruling *Betts v. Brady*

Finally, a word should be said about the contention that *Betts v. Brady* should not be overruled because it may result in releasing indeterminate numbers of prisoners in some states. See *Foster v. Illinois*, 332 U.S. 134, 139 (1947).

First, it must be noted that a defendant who obtains a reversal of his conviction may be retried for the offense of which he was convicted. See *Green v. United States*, 355 U.S. 184, 189 (1957); *id.* at 219 (Frankfurter, J., dissenting). Moreover, it is possible that an even more severe sentence than that originally levied may be imposed at the conclusion of the second trial. See *Robinson v. Johnston*, 50 F. Supp. 774 (N.D. Cal. 1943); *Robinson v. United States*, 324 U.S. 282 (1945) (defendant sentenced to life imprisonment successfully attacked conviction for failure to appoint counsel; following retrial, he was sentenced to death for the same offense).

Second, the claim that some offenders would go free was urged in opposition to the decisions in *Mapp v. Ohio*, 367 U.S. 643 (1961), and *Griffin v. Illinois*, 351 U.S. 12 (1956). In both cases, this Court brushed aside that consideration. The practical implications of the ruling in *Mapp* are in some respects more drastic than the ruling sought here. As a consequence of *Mapp*, illegally obtained evidence cannot be used; the prosecution may be completely disarmed. But no comparable handicap will be imposed upon the prosecution by reversal of *Betts v. Brady*. Further, the claims of the Petitioner here are stronger than those of the petitioner in *Griffin*. *Griffin* involved the rights of a *convicted person* seeking equality of treatment in connection with an appeal; as the Court pointed out in that case, there is no constitutional right to an appeal. 351 U.S. at 18. The present case, however, involves the rights of persons presumed to be innocent who are seeking meaningful protection of their right to a fair trial, a right which is safeguarded by the Constitution.

Thirty years have passed since the Court, in *Powell v. Alabama*, *supra*, spoke of the necessity for appointment of counsel by the states. The states have had adequate notice and ample time to conform their practice to the requirements of a constitutional imperative. As Mr. Justice Clark stated in *Mapp v. Ohio*, *supra*, "further delay in reaching the present result could have no effect other than to compound the difficulties" in the future. 367 U.S. at 659, n. 9.

Conclusion

In 1942, shortly after *Betts v. Brady* was announced, the present Dean of the Harvard Law School, Erwin N. Griswold, and Benjamin Cohen, Esquire, expressed their protest against that decision in words which, we feel, have been underscored by the passage of time:

"[A]t a critical period in world history, *Betts v. Brady* dangerously tilts the scales against the safeguarding of one of the most precious rights of man. For in a free world no man should be condemned to penal servitude for years without having the right to counsel to defend him. The right of counsel, for the poor as well as the rich, is an indispensable safeguard of freedom and justice under law." (N.Y. Times, Aug. 2, 1942, §IV, p 6, col. 5, quoted in *Butt v. Illinois*, 333 U.S. 640, 677, n. 1 (1948) (Douglas, J., dissenting)).

For the reasons stated, *Betts v. Brady* should be overruled, and the judgment of the Court below should be reversed.

Traditional legal rhetoric in Gideon v. Wainwright

The Petitioner Brief operates within the traditional legal rhetoric framework, but it does so in unexpected ways. Before moving on to the interrupters, it is important to identify the boundaries of what is being interrupted.

Discussion questions

1. Identify and articulate the legal syllogism(s) throughout the Petitioner Brief.
2. Explain how the author deconstructs *stare decisis*.
3. Identify the values emphasized by the author.
4. How would the values identified in your response to the previous question appeal to the audience?
5. How does the author establish credibility with the audience?
6. Which feature of traditional legal rhetoric is featured most prominently in the Petitioner Brief: *logos*, *pathos*, or *ethos*?

Interrupters in Gideon v. Wainwright

Empathy as an interrupter

Section I of the Brief begins by providing a concise background of the special circumstances test as established in *Betts v. Brady* and then gains a foothold by empathizing with the Court about the challenges the special circumstances test has created since its inception. The Brief laments that

> [f]or twenty years, this Court, the lower federal courts, and the courts of a number of states have been charged with the duty of administering this rule. The experience has not been a happy one. We respectfully suggest that the data, summarized in this brief, demonstrate that the quality of criminal justice and the relations between the federal and state courts, have suffered as a result of *Betts v. Brady*.

The use of empathy at the beginning creates an intimate relationship between the Court and Gideon's counsel by suggesting to the Court that both advocate and Court are on the same team, working together toward a common cause, together seeking a solution to a difficult problem. Importantly, the shortcomings of the special circumstances test are not framed as a failure of the Court. Of course, Gideon's attorney could have taken the route of blaming the Court for crafting an impossible test when it decided *Betts v. Brady*. But such an approach would have certainly put the Court on the defensive from the beginning.

As explained in Chapter 2, individuals who react in a defensive manner are less likely to change their minds and are more likely to entrench themselves in the status quo of their existing position. Empathy works as an interrupter because it lowers the defenses of the audience. Once their defenses are lowered, the decisionmakers can think more rationally about the problem they are tasked with solving. Empathy makes it safe to admit a past decision was mistaken, and it paves a path toward a better future. In other words, it gives the decisionmaker an out that is palatable and nonjudgmental.

Discussion questions

1. What other examples of empathy can you identify in the Brief?
2. Read the *Gideon* Opinion at 372 U.S. 335 (1963). Do you think the Court was receptive to the appeal to empathy in the Brief?
3. How do race and gender factor into your response to Question 2?
4. In what ways is the appeal to empathy constrained by traditional legal rhetoric?
5. How is the legal syllogism undermined by the appeal to empathy?

Invisibilization as an interrupter

Section I of the *Gideon* Brief employs invisibilization by relegating Gideon's facts to an appendix. Somewhat shockingly, the Brief reads:

> [i]n Appendix B to this Brief we analyze the specific points that demonstrate that Gideon did not receive the benefits and protection which would presumably have been afforded him by counsel. We believe that these constitute a vivid demonstration of the fact that he was deprived of his due process rights under the Fourteenth Amendment: that he did not have a fair trial in the constitutional sense. But it is our opinion that these points are not peculiar to Gideon's case. We believe, *mutatis mutandis*, these points are present in every criminal prosecution. In short, we believe that the circumstances of this case are no more "special" than in other criminal cases—unless we are to draw a line between tweedledee and tweedledum. We are therefore of the opinion that the fundamental question of *Betts v. Brady* is at issue in the present case.

Basic first year legal writing advice is to personalize the client, tell a compelling story, hook the reader, and make the client sympathetic because judges tend to rule in favor of people with whom they can identify, or at least empathize. Yet, despite asserting that Gideon's case provides a "vivid demonstration" of the failure of the special circumstances test to ensure due process, Gideon's attorney chose to relegate his personal story to an appendix.

To be fair, Gideon was not a particularly likable character. Gideon had an extensive criminal history and had spent most of his adult life in and out of jail. Florida's attorney general even argued that *because* of his criminal history, Gideon was well positioned to understand the goings-on of the courtroom and to defend himself. Because of who he was, Gideon's story likely would have alienated the Justices and triggered any manner of bias, whether implicit or explicit, that might have caused the Court to rule against him.[3]

As explained in Chapter 2, invisibilization works as an interrupter to prevent inherent biases from triggering prejudiced responses. Although courts like to believe they are making rational decisions, free from the influence of their biases and personal proclivities, it is simply not possible for human beings to remove all bias from their decisionmaking. Invisibilization works as an interrupter here because it pivots the audience away from a potentially negative bias toward a more positive one.

Abe Fortas aptly predicted that the Justices were likely to be biased against Gideon, or at a minimum that they would not empathize with him or his circumstances. Thus, instead of trying to force a false connection or paint Gideon in a positive light belied by the reality of who he was, Gideon's attorney simply removed him from consideration entirely. He replaced Gideon with the reified idea of fundamental fairness and justice by arguing that "*mutatis mutandis*, these points are present in every criminal prosecution." In the context of traditional legal rhetoric, a reified idea is a principle or policy that takes on a material character within the legal argument.[4] By making the case about fairness and justice more generally, instead of about Gideon, Fortas interrupted the inherent biases likely to be held against a man with multiple convictions and replaced them with positive principles fundamental to the Court's identity.

Discussion questions

1. Do you think the outcome of *Gideon v. Wainwright* would have been the same if Gideon had been featured prominently in the opinion? Explain your answer.
2. How does invisibilizing Gideon advance the locked-in inertia of traditional legal rhetoric?
3. Do you think it was a risky decision to invisibilize Gideon? Explain your answer.
4. Aside from the reified idea "fundamental fairness and justice," can you identify other reified ideas used in the brief as a stand-in for Gideon?
5. Do you think the State or the Court is invisibilized in the brief? If so, what reified idea or ideas are used as a stand in?

Boldness as an interrupter

Section I of the Brief boldly asserts that Gideon does not suffer from any special circumstances that would warrant appointment of counsel. The Brief unapologetically proclaims that

> [a]part from the technical and procedural question resulting from the failure of petitioner to allege special circumstances and from the nature of the proceedings before the Florida Supreme Court to which we have referred above, we can claim neither extreme youth, inexperience, mental incapacity, nor illiteracy on the part of the defendant.

In other words, Gideon's attorney candidly admitted the case was decided correctly under the existing *Betts v. Brady* standard. Under traditional legal rhetoric, *stare decisis* and the syllogism would have demanded the Court rule against Gideon under the circumstances. Utilizing the principles of traditional Aristotelian rhetoric, the legal syllogism should have looked something like Table 6.1.

The classic syllogism obviously dictated that Gideon was not entitled to appointment of an attorney. Although the classic syllogism informs that the law is neutral and that the correct application of the law inevitably leads to

Table 6.1: Legal syllogism for traditional rhetoric, part I

Major premise	States are not required to appoint counsel to represent criminal defendants unless there is a special circumstance warranting appointment.
Minor premise	Gideon does not suffer from any special circumstance.
Conclusion	Therefore, Gideon was not entitled to appointment of counsel.

correct and just results, Gideon's attorney was able to convince the Supreme Court that, at least in this case, the syllogism was wrong by replacing the major premise with the more abstract principles embodied by the Fourteenth Amendment. The bold declaration created an interruption sufficient to stop the inertia of the *Betts v. Brady* standard and change the law.

As explained in Chapter 2, boldness as an interrupter alerts the audience that something is amiss with the law. It forces a pause that allows the advocate time to deconstruct what is wrong with the law and to also propose a new framework to replace the former standard.

Had Gideon's attorney beat around the bush, the Court might not have so readily understood the extent of the injustice, although the Court's framing of the question presented seemed to indicate that the Court was at least primed to reconsider its previous holding in *Betts v. Brady*. The audacity with which the Brief asserts that Gideon did not suffer any special circumstances demonstrated the absurdity of carrying the special circumstances test to its logical conclusion. The Brief forced the Court to pause and reconsider its decision in *Betts v. Brady* and replace the special circumstances test with a higher authority, unconditional application of due process on the states by virtue of the Fourteenth Amendment.

Discussion questions

1. What other examples of boldness can you identify in the Brief?
2. Explain how the boldness you have identified dismantles the legal syllogism.
3. How do race and gender factor into the effectiveness of boldness as an interrupter?
4. How does the brief deploy boldness unoffensively to this audience?
5. If the audience had a different race and gender composition, would boldness be as effective? Explain your answer.

Flattery as an interrupter

Throughout the Brief, Gideon's attorney deploys flattery to appeal to the egos of the justices. At Section I(1), the Brief argues that

> [t]he necessity for counsel in a criminal case is too plain for argument. No individual who is not a trained or experienced lawyer can possibly know or pursue the technical, elaborate, and sophisticated measures which are necessary to assemble and appraise the facts, analyze the law, determine contentions, negotiate the plea, or marshal and present all of the factual and legal considerations which have a bearing upon his defense. Even a trained, experienced criminal lawyer cannot—and will not, if he is sensible—undertake his own defense.

Essentially, what Fortas is saying is that to deny counsel to an indigent defendant would be the same as admitting the indigent defendant is capable of self-representation. And if that is true, then it means that there is really nothing so special about being a lawyer. Toward the end of Section I, the Brief clarifies this point, quoting Beaney, *The Right to Counsel in American Courts* 234–235 (1955):

> [t]o say that trials without counsel can be fair is to assume either that the defense which counsel might have presented would not have changed the result in the case or that in certain types of cases counsel serves no useful function. The first assumption is hindsight and unprovable. The second, if true, would convict a portion of the bar of taking money under false pretenses in all those "simple" cases where counsel accepts a retainer but apparently cannot influence the result. We cannot with justice keep the existing "fight" theory of criminal law and force the indigent defendant to fight alone. If our vaunted claim of "equal justice under law" is to be more than an idle pretense, the right to have counsel must be extended in practice to all persons accused of crime.

This line of reasoning drives at the veracity of the major premise, which on this issue would be as seen in Table 6.2.

The classic syllogism obviously dictated that Gideon is capable of representing himself. By deploying the tool of flattery, Gideon's attorney was able to appeal to the egos of the Justices in such a way that they were inclined to reconsider the assumptions underlying the major premise that supported the ruling in *Betts v. Brady*. Once it was pointed out that not even

Table 6.2: Legal syllogism for traditional rhetoric, part II

Major premise	Criminal defendants are capable of representing themselves unless they suffer from some special circumstance.
Minor premise	Gideon does not suffer from any special circumstance.
Conclusion	Therefore, Gideon is capable of representing himself.

trained lawyers are truly capable of representing themselves, they quickly understood how the *Betts v. Brady* rule undermined the legal profession as a whole. After all, what would be the value of ever hiring an attorney if even the least sophisticated of criminal defendants is capable of self-representation? Here, flattery created an interruption sufficient to stop the inertia of the *Betts v. Brady* standard, leading to a drastic change in the law.

As explained in Chapter 2, flattery works as an interrupter because it makes the decisionmaker the center of attention and demonstrates how a favorable decision would preserve or promote their position. In this example, flattery undermined the major premise, but in other circumstances it could undermine the minor premise or the conclusion. Ultimately, flattery is a successful interrupter because it inserts the decisionmaker into the dynamic of the syllogism. Human beings tend to act in ways that protect and preserve their own self-interests, and flattery makes it easier for the decisionmaker to extrapolate the consequences of the legal standard as applied in their own lives.

Discussion questions

1. What other examples of flattery can you identify in the Brief?
2. What part of the syllogism is undermined by the flattery you have identified?
3. How does flattery lock in traditional legal rhetoric? Explain your answer.
4. How does the Court's composition as an all-White male body affect the effectiveness of flattery as a strategy?
5. In what ways does flattery help the Court dismantle *stare decisis*?

Loving v. Virginia, 188 U.S. 1 (1967)

Summary of Loving v. Virginia, *188 U.S. 1 (1967)*

In *Loving*, the U.S. Supreme Court ratified the right of interracial couples to marry in all 50 states of the Union. Prior to *Loving*, states were permitted to enact and enforce anti-miscegenation laws that prohibited interracial marriages. Virginia was one such state.

Mildred Jeter, a Black woman, and Richard Perry Loving, a White man, fell in love and decided to marry each other. As residents of Virginia, their marriage was not permitted. So, on June 2, 1958, they traveled to Washington, D.C., where they were permitted to lawfully marry one another. When they returned to Virginia, however, they were arrested and charged with attempting to evade the Virginia ban on interracial marriages. Their arrest was traumatic, with law enforcement raiding their home in the middle of the night and taking them to jail. They pled guilty to the charges and were sentenced to one year in jail, but the court suspended their sentences on the condition that they leave the state of Virginia and not return for 25 years.

Life in Washington, D.C., was not pleasant for the native Virginians, and they soon began to sneak back to Virginia to visit family. But their travels were risky, and Mildred often traveled hiding in the trunk of the car so that she would not be discovered if law enforcement decided to pull them over. So, in 1963, Mildred wrote a letter to U.S. Attorney General Robert F. Kennedy seeking his intervention so that she and Richard could return to their home in Virginia. He put them in touch with the American Civil Liberties Union, which ultimately agreed to take their case. In October of 1964, their attorneys filed a class action in the United States District Court for the Eastern District of Virginia requesting that Virginia be enjoined from enforcing the Lovings' convictions while they were litigating the appeal of those convictions in state court. A few months later, in February 1965, the federal court issued an interlocutory order permitting the Lovings to return to Virginia to live, "safe from further arrest and prosecution."[5]

The Lovings' case made it to the Supreme Court after languishing for years in the Virginia state court system. In November 1963, they filed a Motion to Vacate Judgment and Set Aside Sentence that was denied by Judge Bazile, the judge who originally sentenced them. In his Opinion, he reasoned that "Almighty God created the races [W]hite, black, yellow, malay and red, and he placed them on separate continents. And but for the interference with his arrangement there would be no cause for such marriages. The fact that he separated the races shows that he did not intend for the races to mix."[6] This rationale is consistent with traditional legal rhetoric's foundations as the project of elite, White, straight, Christian men.

After Judge Bazile's decision, the Lovings appealed to the Supreme Court of Appeals of Virginia, which affirmed their convictions but set aside their sentences as being overly broad, and remanded the case for further sentencing. A few weeks later, the Supreme Court of Appeals of Virginia stayed the execution of its judgment to permit the Lovings to file a "petition for appeal" to the Supreme Court of the United States to review the decision.

In declaring Virginia's anti-miscegenation law unconstitutional, the United States Supreme Court:

> reject[ed] the notion that the mere "equal application" of a statute containing racial classifications is enough to remove the classifications from the Fourteenth Amendment's proscription of all invidious racial discriminations, [and it refused to] accept the State's contention that these statutes should be upheld if there is any possible basis for concluding that they serve a rational purpose.[7]

It went on to hold that "[t]here can be no question but that Virginia's miscegenation statutes rest solely upon distinctions drawn according to race" and "[t]here is patently no legitimate overriding purpose independent of invidious racial discrimination which justifies this classification."[8] This decision was rendered nearly ten years after the Lovings married.

In the Petitioner brief, attorneys Bernard Cohen and Philip Hirschkop employed a variety of interrupters that ultimately convinced the United States Supreme Court to declare Virginia's anti-miscegenation law unconstitutional.

Excerpt from Petitioner's Brief, Loving v. Virginia

(All footnotes have been omitted.)

I The validity of the entire Virginia statutory scheme prohibiting interracial marriage is at issue in this case

The "evasion statute," Section 20-58, under which appellants were convicted supplements Virginia's basic prohibition of Negro–white marriages celebrated within Virginia (Va. Code § 20-54); it deals with Virginia residents who leave the State with the intention of returning in order to marry in a State permitting Negro–white marriages and who then return and cohabit in Virginia as man and wife. By the terms of the evasion statute, a marriage of such a couple "shall be governed by the same law as if it had been solemnized in this State." Accordingly, such couples are (i) subject to the same criminal punishment as Negroes and whites who marry in Virginia, namely, the penalty imposed by Va. Code § 20-59 of imprisonment for not less than one nor more than five years, and (ii) their marriages are considered void under Virginia law. Va. Code § 20-57; *Naim v. Naim*, 197 Va. 80, 87 S.E. 2d 749 (1955). (In an annulment action, marriage held void where the Virginia couple had gone to North Carolina to evade the Virginia law.) Furthermore, the terms "white person" and "colored person" in the evasion statute are comprehensible, if at all, only by use of the definitions in other provisions of Virginia's anti-miscegenation laws. (Va. Code § 20-54 defines "white person" and § 1-14 defines "colored person.")

Because appellants' miscegenetic marriage is void under Virginia law, various outrageous civil effects can result: one spouse may be prevented from inheriting from his or her mate by other heirs who prove the forbidden interracial nature of the marriage (see, e.g., *In re Shun Takahashi's Estate*, 113 Mont. 400, 129 P. 2d 217 (1942)); participants in such marriages can lose their marital rights under intestacy and similar statutes, *Stevens v. United States*, 146 F.2d 120 (10th Cir. 1944), and the benefits of Social Security (see 42 U.S.C. § 416(h)(1)), of joint income tax returns, and of workmen's compensation—all of which are contingent upon a marital relationship. *Toler v. Oakwood Smokeless Coal Corp.*, 173 Va. 425, 4 S.E. 2d 364 (1939). A husband may desert his mate and their children without the usual legal consequences and apparently free of any obligation of support. See generally GREENBERG, RACE RELATIONS AND AMERICAN LAW 348 (1959). The Lovings' three children may be illegitimate, *Greenhow v. James' Executor*, 80 Va. 636 (1885), even though a Virginia statute legitimatizes the issue of void marriages, and they may lose inheritance rights in their parents' estates.

Even if there were no evasion statute (or if some technical ground could be found to invalidate only the evasion statute and leave the rest of Virginia's anti-miscegenation scheme in effect), appellants' situation would not be significantly changed. Under Virginia law, their marriage is void for both criminal and civil law purposes because Virginia follows the established conflict of laws principle that the state of the domicile of the parties at the time of their marriage will refuse to recognize its validity if the marriage is offensive to such State's public policy. *Kinney v. Commonwealth*, 71 Va. 858 (1878); *Greenhow v. James' Executor*, 80 Va. 636 (1885); See generally RESTATEMENT, CONFLICT OF LAWS §§ 133–134 (1934); RESTATEMENT (SECOND) CONFLICT OF LAWS § 132 (Ten. Draft No. 4–1957); Taintor, *Marriage in the Conflict of Laws*, 9 VAND.L. REV. 607, 627–29 (1956). Thus the same civil effects of the marriage would result and also appellants would be subject to criminal prosecution for illegal cohabitation, *Kinney v. Commonwealth, supra*, § 18.1–193 (VA. CODE ANN. 1950, Vol. 4, p. 253), or fornication, *McPherson v. Commonwealth*, 69 Va. 939 (1877), § 18.1-188 (VA. CODE ANN. 1950, Vol. 4, p. 253), or perhaps both.

The reality of Virginia's statutory scheme prohibiting miscegenation is clear. Both the evasion statute (§ 20-58) and the basic prohibition of miscegenetic marriages (§ 20-54) serve and are necessary to effect the same unjustifiable purpose: to prohibit and penalize interracial marriages involving persons who after their marriage reside as man and wife in Virginia. We doubt that the basic prohibition would be invoked against a couple married in Virginia if they did not cohabit there as man and wife. Of course the evasion statute requires cohabitation as an essential element of its proscribed crime. Nevertheless, any technical distinction between the statutes is academic. The constitutionality of the evasion statute, as applied to appellants in light of Virginia's clear public policy against miscegenation and the relevant conflict of laws principle, cannot be determined separately from a determination of the constitutionality of Virginia's civil and criminal bans on interracial marriages celebrated in Virginia. There is no constitutional or other legal argument of substance which would justify allowing Virginia to deny the validity of an interracial marriage, under its civil or criminal law, if such marriage were celebrated in Virginia while prohibiting Virginia from penalizing the marriage if the marriage of Virginia residents took place outside of Virginia.

Accordingly, a holding that the evasion statute is invalid, on some limited ground, without reaching the basic question of the validity of Virginia's bans on miscegenetic marriages, would seem disingenuous and incorrect under the circumstances. Of even more importance, such a holding would not do justice to appellants. Their marital life has been in continuous legal jeopardy for over eight and one-half years, and their marriage, under settled Virginia law, with or without the evasion statute, is void. Therefore, they would be subject to further prosecution for the same acts that have caused their prior convictions, namely, the interracial nature of their marriage together with their cohabitation as man and wife in Virginia.

II The history of the Virginia anti-miscegenation laws shows they are relics of slavery and expressions of racism

To understand that the Virginia anti-miscegenation laws at issue here are both relics of slavery and expressions of modern day racism which brand Negroes as an inferior race, it is necessary to consider their history.

As Professor Wadlington has recently noted, it is surprising that Virginia which prides itself on the story of how one of her early white sons married an Indian princess today maintains one of the strictest statutory bans on racial intermarriage. Virginia has enacted a great deal of anti-miscegenation legislation beginning in the seventeenth century and spanning a period of nearly three centuries to 1932 when the last enactment on this subject was passed.

Early history

The first Negroes arrived in the colony of Virginia in 1619. Their numbers increased slowly. White indentured servants served as the principal source of manpower in the early colonial period before plantation owners recognized the value of the Negro slave. See generally BRUCE, ECONOMIC HISTORY OF VIRGINIA IN THE SEVENTEENTH CENTURY, Vol. I, Chap. IX (Macmillan & Co. 1896). As late as 1673, white servants still outnumbered Negroes by four to one. REUTER, THE AMERICAN RACE PROBLEM: A STUDY OF THE NEGRO 136 (New York: Thomas Y. Crowell Company, revised ed. 1938) (Hereafter cited as "Reuter"). Generally, indentured white servants came from the lowest social strata in England or elsewhere and the Virginia colonists considered them originally on the same level as the Indian slave or servant and the Negro. A principal difference among persons of the servant class was their tenure of service; the white servant usually served out a seven-year contract while the Negro or Indian might be enslaved for life. As a result of their common status, this class intermixed to a considerable extent both within and outside the banns of marriage. Reuter, 134–138.

Some of the earliest actions of the colonial government involving miscegenation reflected religious prejudice against Christian-heathen intermixing. See Bruce, *supra*, Vol. II, pp. 109–110 and Wadlington, 1191. However, with the establishment of Negro slavery, economic reasons for restricting miscegenation became dominant. Slave-owners wanted protection from the loss of their slave property through intermarriage with a free white Christian by laws that all offspring of slaves with whites, whether free or indentured servants, would be deemed slaves.

By the 1660s, illegitimate births from relationships among Negro slaves and white masters presented problems primarily relating to the status of the children. A 1662 Act provided that any child of an "Englishman" and a "negro woman" should be slave or free according to the condition of the mother. 2 Laws of Va. 170 (Hening 1823). This kind of legislation, according to some historians, led to intentional slave breeding by slave-owners.

At the time of the 1662 Act, there was nothing to prevent interracial marriages of whites and Negroes. The colonial society and the church viewed any such marriages in a disparaging manner and in some cases mobs may have acted to apply extralegal punishment to the couples. Reuter, 137.

Apparently social pressure was insufficient to prevent such marriages, for in April of 1691, the Virginia Assembly passed the first law proscribing Negro–white marriages as part of "An Act for Suppressing Outlying Slaves." 3 Laws of Va. 86 (Hening 1823). One stated purpose of this Act was to prevent "that abominable mixture and spurious issue which hereafter may arise" from interracial unions, demonstrating that racial prejudice as well as economic reasons led to the early miscegenation laws. The free white person marrying a Negro was to be banished from Virginia forever. (Considering the practical banishment of the Lovings in 1959, Virginia's policy has not changed much since 1691.) This same Act provided that any English white woman who had a bastard by a Negro should pay the church wardens fifteen pounds or, in default of payment, she would be indentured for a term of five years. The child in each instance would be bound out by the church wardens until he or she reached thirty years of age.

In 1705, the Assembly eliminated the banishment penalty for miscegenation and instead imposed a six-month prison sentence, without bail, and a fine. Ministers marrying such persons were also penalized and, to this day, Virginia punishes a minister who performs such a marriage by a fine, one-half of which goes to the informer. VA. CODE ANN. § 20-60 (1960).

By the end of Virginia's colonial period, Negroes with few exceptions were enslaved. Negro children by a white father were free or bond according to the condition of the Negro mother. White women, free or bond, were severely penalized for bearing a child from a miscegenetic union and such child was bound out in prescribed periods of servitude by the parish vestrymen. Finally, the legislature had constructed a law punishing the free white partner of a miscegenetic marriage by both imprisonment and fine.

No change of significance occurred until the Code of 1849 in which it was provided that any marriage between a white person and a Negro was absolutely void without further legal process. VA. CODE ch. 109 § 1, Vol. I at 471 (1849) (now § 20-57).

After the Civil War no essential changes were made in Virginia's anti-miscegenation laws until the enactment of the Racial Integrity Act of 1924. However, the first evasion statute, the predecessor of Section 20-58 under which the Lovings were convicted, was passed in 1878 to deal with interracial couples leaving the State to marry in a jurisdiction which allowed their marriages and then returning to live in Virginia even though the Virginia courts had treated such marriages as void without a statute. In the same year, for the first time, the penalty imposed on a party to a miscegenetic marriage was made clearly applicable to the Negro spouse. Also, the penalty was enlarged to not less than two nor more than five years in the penitentiary. Va. Acts of Assembly 1877–1878, ch. VII, § 8 at 302 (now § 20-59).

Despite the existence of deterrent legislation, interracial sexual relationships continued and increased after the Civil War. Reuter, 141. The rising tide of mulatto offspring and the passing of many of them as whites motivated a tightening of the definition of Negro and enactment of stronger anti-miscegenation legislation. In the slave days, there had been essentially economic motivations for denying Negro slaves the legal right to marry. In fact, as previously indicated, no criminal penalties were imposed on the Negro partner of a miscegenetic marriage until 1878. With the end of slavery, unfortunately, new motivations arose which were purely racist and based on the theory that Negroes and other non-whites are members of inferior races.

Racial Integrity Act of 1924

After World War I, the United States experienced a period of intolerance and racial animosity expressed in the spread of all forms of hate groups and super-patriotic orders with dogmas of "yellow peril," "mongrelization of the white race" and "un-Americanism." In fact, at the time of passage of the Racial Integrity Act of 1924, racists predicted the destruction of the white race if Negro–white miscegenation and the tide of immigrants arriving in the United States each year were not suppressed. Earnest Sevier Cox, in his book entitled WHITE AMERICA (Richmond: White America Society, 1923), posed this alleged threat to America and suggested federally supported colonization and uniform legislation barring the mixing of the races in any form.

White racial superiority, a carry-over in the South from slavery days, formerly had rested primarily on observations by 19th century scientists and questionable Biblical texts. The authority which the new and popular science of eugenics provided for this concept was eagerly received in Virginia. Originally eugenics had dealt with the breeding of animals and the disclosure of their heredity traits. Race-conscious Americans seized upon immature conclusions of eugenicists and subjected them to an overdose of racial pride embodied in the concept of "Anglo-Saxonism." New Englanders and Southerners alike talked about "mongrelization of the white race" and "race suicide." Racial prejudice increased; "Anglo-Saxon clubs of America" sprang up throughout Virginia and sponsored legislation designed to halt the mixing of the races in Virginia.

On February 7, 1924, on petition from these organizations, and in response to the racist sentiment of the time, a number of State senators initiated the bill which ultimately became the Racial Integrity Act of 1924, and was originally entitled *"A Bill to Preserve the Integrity of the White Race."* Members of both houses of the General Assembly displayed a great interest in the bill. The House of Delegates invited John Powell, a renowned Virginia pianist and local racist, to speak before it on the dangers of "racial amalgamation." According to the *Richmond Times Dispatch* of February 18, 1924, the delegates selected Powell because of his knowledge of "ethnological problems and conditions in various parts of the world and his wide acquaintance among European authorities and statesmen." Powell was very much involved in the national eugenics movement and had, himself, organized many of the Virginia Anglo-Saxon clubs which petitioned the Assembly to take action to preserve the white race. Powell stressed to a "well-filled gallery" the need to preserve the white race from contamination with non-white blood and observed that when a white race absorbed the Negro through amalgamation its civilization disintegrated. Powell was assisted in his efforts by Dr. W.A. Plecker, the State Registrar of Vital Statistics, who supplied "vital statistics" to show confusion in Virginia concerning racial origins and the necessity for a stronger anti-miscegenation law to preserve racial integrity. *Richmond Times Dispatch*, February 13, 1924, p. 1. In response to Powell's address and the statistics of Dr. Plecker, the House introduced a bill of its own only three days after Powell's address.

Thereafter, apparently without significant debate or controversy between the Senate and the House of Delegates, the Act, technically entitled "An Act to Preserve Racial Integrity" (Va. Acts of Assembly, 1924, ch. 371), passed the Senate on February 27, 1924, and the House on March 8, 1924, and was approved by the Governor on March 20, 1924.

It in part repeated earlier prohibitions on miscegenation but also effected "a sweeping change in the scope of the law ... by keying the miscegenation provisions to a new and very narrow definition of a 'white person.'" Wadlington, 1200. Under this new definition, a white person was forbidden to marry anyone other than another white person defined to be one "who has no trace whatsoever of any blood other than Caucasian ..." (now § 20-54). For the first time, Virginia prohibited the marriage of whites with Mongoloids and other non-Negro races as well as Negroes. Earnest Sevier Cox, in his book, THE SOUTH'S PART IN MONGRELIZING THE NATION (Richmond: White America Society, 1926), called the Virginia law "probably the most perfected expression of the white racial ideal since the institution of caste in India some four thousand years ago." At p. 98.

Other new provisions of the 1924 legislation which remain in force today remind one of the laws of Nazi Germany: The State Registrar of Vital Statistics was empowered to prepare a form so that persons could certify to their "racial composition" to local registrars who could issue duplicate certificates of racial composition, one for the person registering and one for the State Registrar (now § 20-50). The knowing or willful falsification of a registration certificate as to color or race was made a felony punishable by one year in the penitentiary. A marriage license was not to be issued unless the issuing official had "reasonable assurance" that the statements of the parties as to color were correct, and the Act assigned the burden of proof, if a question should arise, to the persons applying for the license (now § 20-53).

All statutes relating to racial intermarriage which were in effect in 1924 were made applicable to marriages prohibited by the new provisions. Thus the 1924 act carried forward the provision making Negro–white marriages void, the civil and criminal applicability of the evasion provision [Section 20-58], and the criminal penalties applicable to the parties to an interracial marriage and to the minister performing the ceremony.

III Anti-miscegenation laws cause immeasurable social harm

There is still another history to be told; it lurks beneath the surface of the "written" history we have examined. This is the story of what these laws have done to our entire people. Unhappily this is the familiar chronicle of race relations in our nation. Here briefly is some intimation of what the miscegenation laws—born out of oppression and hatred—contribute to our legacy.

The high degree of racial mixture that exists in the United States—estimates of the ratio of Negro Americans with at least one known white forebear run as high as 72 to 83 per cent, PETTIGREW, A PROFILE OF THE NEGRO AMERICAN 68 (1964)—has occurred predominantly in the South under illicit conditions fostered by the miscegenation laws. Of more relevance, this racial mixing was almost entirely in the context of illicit exploitative sexual intercourse; white male of Negro female. MYRDAL, AN AMERICAN DILEMMA, Chapter 5 especially at pp. 1204–1207 (1962) (Hereafter cited as "Myrdal"); CASH, THE MIND OF THE SOUTH 87–88 (1941).

This history of illicit sex relationships conditions, psychologically and sociologically, the entire pattern of American race relations. Nor can its importance be overemphasized since "[t]o the ordinary white American the caste line between white and Negro is *based upon*, and *defended by*, the anti-amalgamation doctrine," and "[moreover this] ... doctrine, *more than anything else*, gives the Negro problem its uniqueness among other problems of lower status groups, not only in terms of the intensity of feeling but more fundamentally in the character of the problem." Myrdal, 54 (emphasis added). This socio-psychological taproot of American racial prejudice is nowhere more vividly described than in Lillian Smith's great work, KILLERS OF THE DREAM, in the chapter entitled "Three Ghost Stories" (1961 ed.), and in W.J. Cash's, THE MIND OF THE SOUTH (1941).

Considering such accounts, it is difficult to avoid Myrdal's conclusion that

> [t]he fixation on the purity of white womanhood, and also part of the intensity of emotion surrounding the whole sphere of segregation and discrimination, are to be understood as the backwashes of the sore conscience on the part of white men for their own or their compeers' relations with, or desires for, Negro women. Myrdal, 591.

The Negro participant in this abnormal sex relationship did not escape psychologically unscathed. Although isolating psychogenic factors is difficult, there can be no doubt of the profound adverse effect racial discrimination has had on the individual personality traits of the Negro. See Pettigrew, *supra* at Chapter I, "The Role and Its Burdens" (1964); cf., *Brown v. Board of Education*, 347 U.S. 483 (1954). It is a frightful thing, to use one example, if Miss Smith is right when she claims "... there is a burning blasting scorn of white men growing in the minds ... of nearly every woman of the colored race." Smith, *supra* at 109. Any social construct which can engender such group hatred and personal antagonism is wrong.

Admitting the futility of attempts to expunge the sins of the past, Virginia's anti-miscegenation laws (and those of sixteen Southern and border States) stand as a present day incarnation of an ancient evil. As such, these laws do not simply bar interracial marriage, they perpetuate and foster illicit exploitative sex relationships. Moreover, these laws are explicitly designed to that end. To fail to understand such invidious purpose is to doom the reasonable man to an unrequited search for logic, viz:

> the relative license of white men to have illicit intercourse with Negro women does not extend to formal marriage. The relevant difference between these two types of relations is that the latter, but not the former, does give social status to the Negro woman and does take status away from the white man. These status concerns ... are functions of the caste apparatus which, in popular theory, is itself explained as a means of preventing intermarriage, *the whole theory* [thus] *becoming largely a logical circle*. Myrdal, 590. (Emphasis added)

The relevance of such purpose to our scope of inquiry here—the present day impact of these laws—seems clear. Cutting through the psychological overlay and rationalizations, Myrdal explains that:

> The great majority of non-liberal white Southerners utilize the dread of "intermarriage" ... to justify discriminations which have quite other and wider goals than the purity of the white race ... what white people really want is to keep the Negroes in a lower status. Myrdal, 590–91.

And enlarging on the same theme he adds:

> The persistent preoccupation with sex and marriage in the rationalization of social segregation and discrimination against Negroes is ... an irrational escape on the part of the whites from voicing an open demand for difference in social status between the two groups for its own sake. *Ibid.*

In short, the basis of harm that makes this Court's warrant equal to the ultimate evil of these laws is that they constitute an infliction of indignity upon every person cast among others as not good enough to marry a "white person."

Paradoxical as it may seem that this most blatant ascription of inferior status is the last to be condemned by this Court, it is fitting that the opportunity to make the condemnation universal presents itself. The miscegenation laws, understood as the paradigm of "all of these thousand and one precepts, etiquettes, taboos, and disabilities inflicted upon the Negro [having the] common purpose: to express the subordinate status of the Negro people and the exalted position of the whites," Myrdal, 66, and functioning chiefly as the State's official symbol of a caste system, must be dealt with accordingly.

IV The legislative history of the Fourteenth Amendment does not exempt anti-miscegenation laws from its application

The only substantive argument advanced by the Commonwealth of Virginia in its Statement opposing the noting of jurisdiction by this Court was that the legislative history of the Fourteenth Amendment conclusively establishes that it was not intended to apply to miscegenation laws. Eclectic statements from the debates on the bill which became the Civil Rights Act of 1866 are used to support this thesis, which was also advanced in the School Segregation Cases, and a law review article, Pittman, *The Fourteenth Amendment: Its Intended Effect on Anti-Miscegenation Laws*, 43 N.C.L. REV. 92 (1964). (A more recent article in support of the same thesis, which was not cited by the Commonwealth, is Avins, *Anti-Miscegenation Laws and the Fourteenth Amendment: The Original Intent*, 52 VA.L. REV. 1224 (1966).)

A close examination of such statements indicates that many legislators who felt the Civil Rights Act of 1866 was not intended to reach miscegenation laws based their views on the now discredited equal application theory (later enunciated as a judicial construction of the equal protection clause in *Pace v. Alabama*, 106 U.S. 583 (1883)). For example, the Commonwealth quotes Senator Trumbull as follows (at p. 8 of its Statement):

> How does this interfere with the law of Indiana preventing marriages between whites and blacks? Are not both races treated alike by the law of Indiana? Does not the law make it just as much a crime for a white man to marry a black woman as for a black woman to marry a white man, and *vice versa*? *I presume there is no discrimination in this respect, and therefore your law forbidding marriages between whites and blacks operates alike on both races*. This bill does not interfere with it. If the negro is denied the right to marry a white person, the white person is equally denied the right to marry the negro. I see no discrimination against either in this respect that does not apply to both. (Emphasis added)

But Senator Trumbull's presumption has proven incorrect; equal application of inequalities based on race is unconstitutional. *McLaughlin v. Florida*, 379 U.S. 184, 188 (1964).

If such legislative history—whatever its real meaning assuming one could read the minds of the legislators from the historical record—were determinative of the scope of the Fourteenth Amendment, then it might not have been applicable to school segregation, jury service and other forms of segregation. See, e.g., *Brown v. Board of Education*, 347 U.S. 483 (1954); *Strauder v. West Virginia*, 100 U.S. 303 (1880); *Norris v. Alabama*, 294 U.S. 587 (1935); Bickel, *The Original Understanding and the Segregation Decision*, 69 HARV.L. REV. 1, 64–65 (1956).

A correct appraisal of the legislative history of the broad guarantees of the Fourteenth Amendment for purposes of constitutional adjudication is that they were open-ended and meant to be expounded in light of changing times and circumstances. See Bickel, *supra*, at 64 ("But the relevant point is that the Radical leadership succeeded in obtaining a provision whose effect was left to future determination."); Kelly, *Clio and the Court: An Illicit Love Affair*, 1965 SUP. CT. REV. 119, 145 (Evidence from the debates indicates that Bingham and others "hoped that the prohibitions on racial discrimination would have an open-ended character, i.e., would grow through judicial interpretation and congressional legislation with the progress of time"); Wechsler, *Toward Neutral Principles of Constitutional Law*, 73 HARV.L. REV. 1, 32 (1959) ("... the words [of the equal protection clause] are general and leave room for expanding content as time passes and conditions change"); *Burton v. Wilmington Parking Authority*, 365 U.S. 715, 722 (1961) ("Because the virtue of the right to equal protection of the laws could lie only in the breadth of its application, its constitutional assurance was reserved in terms whose imprecision was necessary if the right were to be enjoyed in the variety of individual–state relations which the Amendment was designed to embrace").

In short, the applicability in 1967 of the equal protection and due process clauses to miscegenation laws cannot be ascertained by a resort to doubtful legislative history but must be determined by this Court, utilizing all appropriate means of constitutional adjudication and bearing in mind Chief Justice Hughes' admonition:

> If ... the great clauses of the Constitution must be confined to the interpretation which the framers, with the conditions and outlook of their time, would have placed upon them, the statement carries its own refutation. It was to guard against such a narrow conception that Chief Justice Marshall uttered the memorable warning—"we must never forget that it is *a constitution* we are expounding" (*McCulloch v. Maryland*, 4 Wheat. 316, 407) ... *Home Bldg. & Loan Ass'n v. Blaisdell*, 290 U.S. 398, 442–43 (1934).

V The Virginia anti-miscegenation laws are racially discriminatory and deny appellants equal protection of the laws

There can be no doubt that the conviction of the Lovings was because Mrs. Loving is a Negro. But for this fact, and that Richard Loving is a "white person" under Va. Code § 20-54, no crime would have been committed. Except for the difference of color, the state never raised any objection to the marriage. If both had been white or both had been other than white, their marriage would be valid.

In *Brown v. Board of Education*, 347 U.S. 483 (1954), this Court struck down segregation in public schools as a violation of equal protection. Whether *Brown* means that (i) the Fourteenth Amendment prohibits the intentional disadvantaging of Negroes as Negroes by any form of legalized segregation (Black, *The Lawfulness of the Segregation Decisions*, 69 YALE L.J. 421 (1960)) or, (ii) there can be no rational basis for a statutory classification which stamps Negroes as inferior (Applebaum, *Miscegenation Statutes: A Constitutional and Social Problem*, 53 GEO.L.J. 49, 86 (1965)) as the Virginia anti-miscegenation laws do or, (iii) a state statute cannot constitutionally deny Negroes the freedom to associate with whites (Wechsler, *Toward Neutral Principles of Constitutional Law*, 73 HARV.L. REV. 1, 34 (1959)), we agree with Professor Bickel that the principle of the *Brown* case should control the constitutionality of miscegenation laws. BICKEL, THE LEAST DANGEROUS BRANCH 71 (1962).

In fact, miscegenation laws seem more clearly unconstitutional than school segregation since (i) the right of two consenting, competent adults to marry each other seems even more fundamental than the right of students to attend an integrated public school, (ii) there clearly is no equal alternative and (iii) both parties to an interracial marriage wish to associate or join together as man and wife, while in *Brown*, arguably, the white students, or some of them, did not wish to associate with the Negro students.

When a Negro is denied the right, solely because he is a Negro, to marry a white woman who wishes to marry him, the law discriminates against him and denies him as well as the woman equal protection of the laws. While miscegenation laws have been upheld in the past by use of the "equal application" theory of *Pace v. Alabama*, that these laws do not discriminate because both whites and Negroes are prohibited from intermarrying (see, e.g., *Jackson v. City and County of Denver*, 109 Colo. 196, 124 P. 2d 240 (1942)), this theory "... represents a limited view of the Equal Protection clause which has not withstood analysis in the subsequent decisions of this Court." *McLaughlin v. Florida*, 379 U.S. 184, 188 (1964).

Statutory distinctions based on race alone have been struck down in many cases involving rights much less substantial than the right to marry. See, e.g., *Hamm v. Virginia State Board of Elections*, 230 F. Supp. 156 (E.D. Va.), *aff'd per curiam*, 379 U.S. 19 (1964) (designation of race in voting and property records); *Anderson v. Martin*, 375 U.S. 399 (1964) (designation of race on nomination papers and ballots); *Watson v. City of Memphis*, 373 U.S. 526 (1963) (segregation in public parks and playgrounds); *Oyama v. California*, 332 U.S. 633 (1948) (racial restriction involving alienation of land); *Takahashi v. Fish & Game Commission*, 334 U.S. 410 (1948) (racial restriction on commercial fishing licenses); *Yick Wo v. Hopkins*, 118 U.S. 356 (1886) (racial restriction on licensing of laundries). And this Court has enunciated as the law of the land that:

> Distinctions between citizens solely because of their ancestry are by their very nature odious to a free people whose institutions are founded upon the doctrine of equality. For that reason, legislative classification or discrimination based on race alone has often been held to be a denial of equal protection. *Hirabayashi v. United States*, 320 U.S. 81, 100 (1943).

In fact, "classification based on race alone is inherently discriminatory." *Dorsey v. State Athletic Comm.*, 168 F. Supp. 149, 151 (E.D. La. 1958), *aff'd per curiam*, 359 U.S. 533 (1959).

In *McLaughlin v. Florida, supra*, this Court held that there must be "some overriding statutory purpose requiring the proscription of the specified conduct when engaged in by the white person and a Negro, but not otherwise," 379 U.S. at 192, and also stated, in effect, that the burden of demonstrating this overriding purpose is on the State because:

> the central purpose of the Fourteenth Amendment was to eliminate racial discrimination emanating from official sources in the States. This strong policy renders racial classifications "constitutionally suspect" ... and "in most circumstances irrelevant" to any constitutionally acceptable legislative purpose. 379 U.S. at 192.

At least two members of this Court have recognized that there can be no such "overriding statutory purpose" to justify a miscegenation law:

> I cannot conceive of a valid legislative purpose under our Constitution for a state law which makes the color of a person's skin the test of whether his conduct is a criminal offense. (Mr. Justice Stewart, joined by Mr. Justice Douglas, concurring in *McLaughlin*, 379 U.S. at 198)

The Supreme Court of Appeals of Virginia upheld the miscegenation laws in this case (R. 25) by reliance on its earlier decision in *Naim v. Naim*, 197 Va. 80, 87 S.E. 2d 749 (1955). In *Naim*, the purposes of these laws were set forth as follows:

> We are unable to read in the Fourteenth Amendment to the Constitution, or in any other provision of that great document, any words or any intendment which prohibit the State from enacting legislation to preserve the racial integrity of its citizens, or which denies the power of the State to regulate the marriage relation so that it shall not have a mongrel breed of citizens. We find there no requirement that the State shall not legislate to prevent the obliteration of racial pride, but must permit the corruption of blood even though it weaken or destroy the quality of its citizenship. 87 S.E. 2d at 756.

Of course the maintenance of racial purity or integrity is a meretricious basis for these laws for there is no evidence to support the existence of so-called "pure" races. MONTAGU, MAN'S MOST DANGEROUS MYTH: THE FALLACY OF RACE (4th ed. 1964); see authorities discussed in Weinberger, *A Reappraisal of the Constitutionality of Miscegenation Statutes*, 42 CORNELL L.Q. 208, 217 (1957). The idea of a pure race is a subterfuge to cloak ignorance of the phenomenon of racial variation.

Even if racial purity were a constitutionally acceptable purpose, the Virginia laws are not reasonably calculated to effect this purpose. The only race kept "pure" is the Caucasian. This is because the Virginia laws are not designed to preserve the purity of races but, as the original name of Virginia's 1924 Racial Integrity Act indicates and its legislative history affirms, to preserve only the integrity of one group: members of the so-called "White" or "Anglo-Saxon Race." A person of Chinese ancestry, for example, is not included within the definition of "colored persons" [Va. Code § 1-14], or "white persons" [Va. Code § 20-54]. Thus the marriage of a Chinese and a "white person" would be unlawful under Va. Code § 20-54, *Naim v. Naim*, 197 Va. 80, 87 S.E. 2d 749 (1955). On the other hand, a marriage between a Chinese and a "colored person" would be neither unlawful nor subject to prosecution. Certainly this is not equal protection. In fact, Virginia's concept of "race," based on statutory definitions which are a combination of legal fiction and genetic nonsense, is a social rather than a scientific concept, designed to preserve the social status of Virginia's politically dominant group.

The other articulated legislative purpose is the prevention of "corruption of the blood" from racial intermixing which would "weaken or destroy the quality of its [Virginia's] citizenship." To assume this is a valid legislative purpose—as the highest Virginia court did—which justifies miscegenation laws is not enough to meet the State's burden with respect to laws which on their face discriminate on the basis of race or color. Virginia has not presented, and we submit cannot present, reputable scientific evidence to prove that a person of mixed blood is somehow "inferior" in quality to one of racial purity, assuming *arguendo* that a person of racial purity such as a pure Caucasian exists. Most serious students of anthropology do not even consider this question a present problem for research, agreeing that the races of the world are essentially equal in native ability and capacity for civilization and that group differences are for the most part cultural and environmental, not hereditary. See, e.g., THE RACE QUESTION AND MODERN SCIENCE: THE STATEMENT ON THE NATURE OF RACE AND RACE DIFFERENCES, Article 7 (UNESCO, 1952).

As for the progeny of racial intermixing, there is not a single anthropologist teaching at a major university in the United States who subscribes to the theory that Negro–white matings cause biologically deleterious results. See letter to editor from members of Department of Anthropology, Columbia University, *N.Y. Times*, December 15, 1964. On the contrary, some conclude that, because of a certain hybrid vigor, interracial marriage may be desirable and the offspring superior, citing the Hawaiian population, among others, to support this view. See SHAPIRO, RACE MIXTURE (UNESCO, 1965), and the authorities discussed in Cummins & Kane, *Miscegenation, The Constitution and Science*, 38 DICTA 24, 47–49 (1961).

We will not postulate unarticulated legislative purpose. In the final analysis, these laws are unjustifiable relics of slavery—initially passed to foster that peculiar and distasteful institution, and re-enacted in their present form as part of the surge of racial antagonism and intolerance of the 1920's. They deny Negroes and other nonwhites equal protection of the law and stamp them as inferior citizens.

VI The Virginia anti-miscegenation laws violate the due process clause of the Fourteenth Amendment

Marriage is perhaps the most important and most personal of all human relationships. We think it clear that the "liberty" which is protected by the due process clause of the Fourteenth Amendment includes the right to marry. *Meyer v. Nebraska*, 262 U.S. 390, 399 (1922) (dictum). Justice Traynor so held in his opinion in *Perez v. Sharp*, 32 Cal. 2d 711, 198 P. 2d 17 (1948) (*sub nom. Perez v. Lippold*), which invalidated California's anti-miscegenation statute. In *Skinner v. Oklahoma*, 316 U.S. 535, 541 (1942), this Court described marriage as "one of the basic civil rights of man." See generally Applebaum, *Miscegenation Statutes: A Constitutional and Social Problem*, 53 Geo. L.J. 49, 67–68 (1964).

The recent holding in *Griswold v. Connecticut*, 381 U.S. 479 (1965), that the privacy of the marital relationship is a constitutionally protected freedom—whether under the rubric of a right of privacy or under the concept of ordered liberty embodied in the due process clause, *Palko v. Connecticut*, 302 U.S. 319 (1937)—signifies that the right to marry is itself protected from arbitrary governmental interference by the basic guarantees of our Constitution. Furthermore, the right to marry, regardless of race or color, may appropriately be deemed part of a broader constitutional freedom of association as enunciated in *Griswold* by Mr. Justice Douglas and previously recognized to some extent in *NAACP v. Alabama*, 357 U.S. 449 (1958), and *NAACP v. Button*, 371 U.S. 415, 430–31 (1963).

Of course the right to marry is not an absolute right and a State may restrict it in certain circumstances, for example, by imposing reasonable age and health limitations and prohibiting incestuous or polygamous marriages. The question, however, as in the equal protection area, is whether the anti-miscegenation statute has a legitimate legislative purpose and whether the manner of regulation bears a reasonable relationship to such purpose. See, e.g., *Nebbia v. New York*, 291 U.S. 502, 525 (1934); *Bolling v. Sharpe*, 347 U.S. 497, 499–500 (1954) ("Segregation in public education is not reasonably related to any proper governmental objective, and thus it imposes on Negro children of the District of Columbia a burden that constitutes an arbitrary deprivation of their liberty in violation of due process."); *Buchanan v. Warley*, 245 U.S. 60 (1917).

The Virginia anti-miscegenation laws have no legitimate governmental objective. Their enforcement deprives appellants of personal liberty—their right to marry—without due process of law just as it also denies them equal protection of the laws.

Conclusion

For the foregoing reasons, Sections 20-58 and 20-59 of the Virginia Code should be held unconstitutional, and this Court should make clear that neither Virginia nor any other State can constitutionally prohibit or penalize interracial marriages.

The elaborate legal structure of segregation has been virtually obliterated with the exception of the miscegenation laws. White racists can still point to these laws to support their appeal to the ultimate superstition fostering racial prejudice—the myth that Negroes are innately inferior to whites. There are no laws more symbolic of the Negro's relegation to second-class citizenship. Whether or not this Court has been wise to avoid this issue in the past, the time has come to strike down these laws; they are legalized racial prejudice, unsupported by reason or morals, and should not exist in a good society.

Traditional legal rhetoric in Loving v. Virginia

The Petitioner Brief operates within the traditional legal rhetoric framework, but it does so in unexpected ways. Before moving on to the interrupters, it is important to identify the boundaries of what is being interrupted.

Discussion questions

1. Identify and articulate the legal syllogism(s) throughout the Petitioner Brief.
2. Explain how the author deconstructs *stare decisis*.
3. Identify the values emphasized by the author.

4. How would the values identified in your response to the previous question appeal to the audience?
5. How does the author establish credibility with the audience?
6. Which feature of traditional legal rhetoric is featured most prominently in the Petitioner Brief: *logos*, *pathos*, or *ethos*?

Interrupters in Loving v. Virginia

Boldness as an interrupter

Like the *Gideon* Brief, the *Loving* Brief deploys boldness as an interrupter by unequivocally labeling Virginia's anti-miscegenation laws as racist. The heading for Section II declares "[t]he history of the Virginia anti-miscegenation laws shows they are relics of slavery and expressions of racism." At the end of that same section, the Brief unapologetically compares the Virginia legislation to the laws of Nazi Germany when it asserts that "[o]ther new provisions of the 1924 legislation which remain in force today remind one of the laws of Nazi Germany." In the conclusion, the Brief proclaims "[w]hite racists can still point to these laws to support their appeal to the ultimate superstition fostering racial prejudice–the myth that Negroes are innately inferior to [W]hites."

Notably, the *Loving* Brief relies heavily on *pathos*, or the appeal to emotion. The historical analysis demonstrates the discord between Virginia's anti-miscegenation laws and evolving societal norms. In this Brief, boldness as an interrupter fulfills its duty to alert the audience that something is amiss with the law, but it did not explicitly deconstruct the premise that racism is wrong because, by 1967, that notion was relatively well settled, at least within the mainstream liberal consensus that had emerged in 1967. During the height of the 1960s Civil Rights movement, the Supreme Court did not want to be perceived as endorsing or perpetuating laws that explicitly discriminated on the basis of race. By boldly identifying Virginia's statutory scheme as explicitly racist, the Brief signals to the Supreme Court that it must strike down the law to distance itself from the monster of racism.

Discussion questions

1. What other examples of boldness can you identify in the Brief?
2. Explain how the boldness you have identified dismantles the legal syllogism.
3. How do race and gender factor into the effectiveness of boldness as an interrupter?
4. How does the brief deploy boldness unoffensively to this audience?
5. If the audience had a different race and gender composition, would boldness be as effective? Explain your answer.

Shame as an interrupter

The *Loving* Brief deftly employs interdisciplinary and historical analysis to reveal the shame associated with the country's racist legacy of slavery. As explained in Chapter 2, shame works as an interrupter because it provokes a negative emotion in the decisionmaker, causing the decisionmaker to pivot or adjust course.

In Section II, the Brief recounts that "[r]ace-conscious Americans seized upon immature conclusions of eugenicists and subjected them to an overdose of racial pride embodied in the concept of 'Anglo-Saxonism'. New Englanders and Southerners alike talked about 'mongrelization of the [W]hite race' and 'race suicide.'"[9] It also emphasizes that:

> Judge Bazile in his opinion below gave the following religious justification for miscegenation laws which requires no comment: Almighty God created the races [W]hite, black, yellow, malay and red, and he placed them on separate continents. And but for the interference with his arrangement there would be no cause for such marriages. The fact that he separated the races shows that he did not intend for the races to mix. (R. 16)

And in the conclusion, the Brief deploys what can only be characterized as a challenge to the Supreme Court to stop avoiding the issue of anti-miscegenation laws and address it head on:

> White racists can still point to these laws to support their appeal to the ultimate superstition fostering racial prejudice—the myth that Negroes are innately inferior to [W]hites. There are no laws more symbolic of the Negro's relegation to second-class citizenship. Whether or not this Court has been wise to avoid this issue in the past, the time has come to strike down these laws; they are legalized racial prejudice, unsupported by reason or morals, and should not exist in a good society.

The explicit shame of slavery and racism is something the Court would certainly want to distance itself from. The shame interrupter, therefore, accomplishes its purpose of creating a pause sufficient to encourage the Court to strike down the racist statutory scheme.

Discussion questions

1. How else is shame demonstrated in the Brief?
2. What risks are associated with using shame as an interrupter?
3. Do you think that shame was an effective tool in this case? Explain your answer.

4. What race and gender considerations influenced your answer to Question 3? Explain your answer.
5. Do you think shame would have been as effective if the Supreme Court was reviewing a federal law instead of a state law? Explain your answer.

Exasperation as an interrupter

In the first section, the Brief utilizes exasperation to demonstrate the sheer absurdity of Virginia's statutory scheme. It sets forth:

> Because appellants' miscegenetic marriage is void under Virginia law, various outrageous civil effects can result: one spouse may be prevented from inheriting from his or her mate by other heirs who prove the forbidden interracial nature of the marriage (see, e.g., *In re Shun Takahashi's Estate*, 113 Mont. 400, 129 P. 2d 217 (1942)); participants in such marriages can lose their marital rights under intestacy and similar statutes, *Stevens v. United States*, 146 F.2d 120 (10th Cir. 1944), and the benefits of Social Security (see 42 U.S.C. § 416(h)(1)), of joint income tax returns, and of workmen's compensation—all of which are contingent upon a marital relationship. *Toler v. Oakwood Smokeless Coal Corp.*, 173 Va. 425, 4 S.E. 2d 364 (1939). A husband may desert his mate and their children without the usual legal consequences and apparently free of any obligation of support. See generally GREENBERG, RACE RELATIONS AND AMERICAN LAW 348 (1959). The Lovings' three children may be illegitimate, *Greenhow v. James' Executor*, 80 Va. 636 (1885), even though a Virginia statute legitimatizes the issue of void marriages, and they may lose inheritance rights in their parents' estates.

Use of the word "outrageous" in the first sentence is powerful and prompts the reader to feel the same outrage expressed by the author. Later, in Section III, the Brief recounts the social harm that has been perpetuated by racism and the legacy of slavery, stating:

> There is still another history to be told; it lurks beneath the surface of the "written" history we have examined. This is the story of what these laws have done to our entire people. Unhappily this is the familiar chronicle of race relations in our nation. Here briefly is some intimation of what the miscegenation laws—born out of oppression and hatred—contribute to our legacy.

The Brief also argues that "[t]he idea of a pure race is a subterfuge to cloak ignorance of the phenomenon of racial variation." The State of Virginia attempted to justify its racist laws by urging that maintaining the "purity of the races" was a compelling state interest. This argument is flawed, however, as the Brief points out, because "there is no evidence to support the existence of so-called 'pure' races. MONTAGU, MAN'S MOST DANGEROUS MYTH: THE FALLACY OF RACE (4th ed. 1964); see authorities discussed in Weinberger, A Reappraisal of the Constitutionality of Miscegenation Statutes, 42 CORNELL L.Q. 208, 217 (1957)."

As explained in Chapter 2, exasperation works as an interrupter because it provokes an emotional response that demands the decisionmaker change the status quo. It places the Court in a position to understand that silence is complicity and a ratification of blatant racism. The overall tone of the Brief as it rebuts the State of Virginia's arguments is one of exasperation that the State continues to advance false myths that have repeatedly been debunked. Because the State will obviously not "do the right thing," it is imperative that the Court issue a clear opinion about the unconstitutionality of Virginia's statutory scheme.

Discussion questions

1. What are other ways the Brief demonstrates exasperation?
2. What risks does the author take when deploying such a strong emotional appeal?
3. Do you think the fact that a federal court is reviewing a state court decision impacts the effectiveness of exasperation? Explain your answer.
4. Do you think exasperation was an effective tool considering the race and gender composition of the audience?
5. Do you think exasperation was effective in dismantling any part of locked-in system established by elite, White, straight, Christian men? Explain your answer.

Conclusion

While interrupters work to pause the inertia of *stare decisis*, they still operate within the traditional legal rhetoric framework. When boldness interrupts the syllogism, the new argument must still be cast as a syllogism in order to replace the old logic. Similarly, when boldness interrupts *pathos*, it is successful because it identifies a competing, stronger value or emotion. Interrupters are limited by all the same limitations endemic to Western rhetoric identified in Chapters 1 and 2 of this book, even if they can accomplish some incremental progress. And, as demonstrated in the 2022 *Dobbs* decision,[10] precedent that is built upon interrupters like those examined in this chapter are vulnerable to being overruled as inconsistent with *logos* and the Framers' original intent.

Thus, to achieve transformative equity and equality, we must also look to multicultural reasoning and analytic paradigms, as set forth in Chapters 3 and 4 of this book.

Notes

1 316 U.S. 455 (1942), overruled by *Gideon v. Wainwright*, 372 U.S. 335 (1963).
2 Brief for Petitioner, *Gideon v. Wainwright*, 372 U.S. 335 (1963) (No. 155).
3 Megale, 2013, pp 234–43.
4 Megale, 2013, p 240.
5 *Loving v. Virginia*, 388 U.S. 1 (1967) (No. 395), Brief for Petitioner.
6 *Loving v. Virginia*, 388 U.S. 1 (1967) (No. 395), Brief for Petitioner.
7 *Loving v. Virginia*, 388 U.S. 1, 8 (1967).
8 *Loving v. Virginia*, 388 U.S. 1, 11 (1967).
9 *Loving v. Virginia*, Appellant's Brief, 1967 WL 113927 (U.S.), 21 (U.S., 2004).
10 142 S. Ct. 2228.

7

Disrupting the Canon: Multicultural Rhetorical Strategies in Action

Rethinking how we "do" law

Chapter 4 provides comprehensive explanations and tabular summaries of Indigenous, African and Asian Diasporic, and Latine reasoning and analytic paradigms. The next step is thinking through integration of these strategies into how we "do" law, practice law and advocacy, in drafting various legal genres (pleadings, memos, briefs, judicial opinions) with an eye toward changing our practice to "make space" for the knowledge and experiences of minoritized persons.

The universe in which invocations for justice function is vibrant, innovative, and capacious enough to hold the rhetorical traditions of multiple groups, whereas the universe in which law functions is flat, two-dimensional, and calibrated to White cultural hegemony (Figures 7.1 and 7.2). As such, it can hold no space for cultural traditions that assert themselves as equal. It will remain unchanged to the extent that in its current form it can only accept these traditions, as it has accepted its people, through assimilation into what is ideologically "American." Recall the words of George Washington quoted by Michigan Congressman Grant M. Hudson as he advocated for the Immigration Act of 1924 (as recounted in Chapter 3), "Citizens by birth or choice, of common country, that country has a right to concentrate your affection … with slight shades of difference, you have the same religion, manners, habits, and political principals."[1]

In order to put the multicultural rhetorical traditions to work in the service of justice, we must shift our focus to how we draft legal genres. By assessing the parts of the most common legal genres taught to law students and drafted by attorneys, we can best determine where these traditions can serve as interventions to disrupt—break apart, destroy, disorder—Western rhetorical devices, reasoning, and analytic forms.

Figure 7.1: Multicultural rhetoric chart

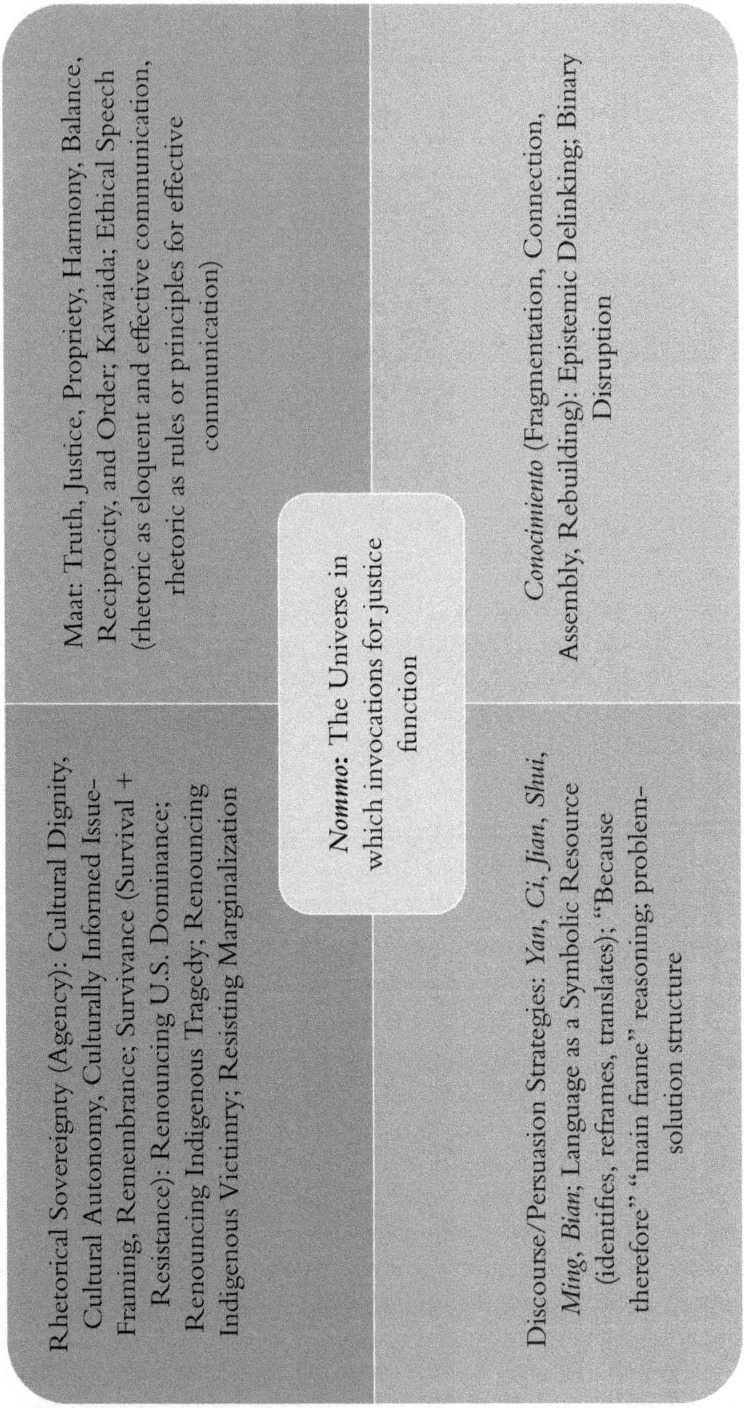

Figure 7.2: Traditional rhetoric chart

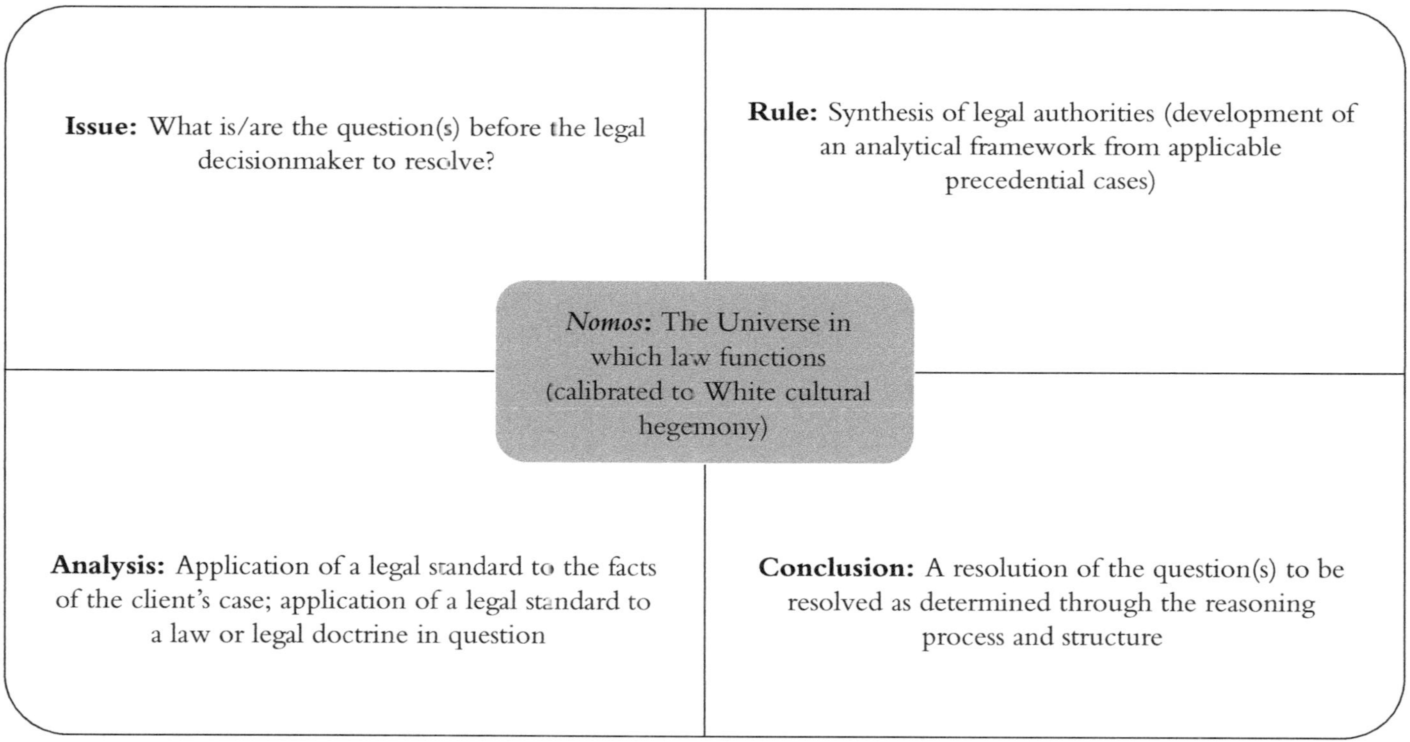

Multicultural rhetoric in action

What follows are "maps" of various genres, by type and with a description of each of its parts, along with a list of multicultural rhetorical strategies that can be used in each part. After each map is an exercise that provides the opportunity for you to put multicultural rhetoric in action. As demonstrated in Chapter 3, Indigenous, African and Asian Diasporic, and Latine rhetorical strategies can be used in a variety of ways—from centering minoritized experiences in a Statement of Facts to widening the scope of the analytic framework and therefore the "facts" relevant to the analysis. The lists are by no means exhaustive, but they are sources to prime the pump of your creativity as you learn and experiment with legal drafting. The strategies are widely applicable, even though they originate from specific cultural traditions.

Multicultural rhetorical strategies in various legal genres

The Complaint

Complaint excerpt: Brian Flores v. The National Football League; New York Football Giants, Inc.; Miami Dolphins, Ltd.; Denver Broncos; and John Doe Teams 1 through 29, Class Action Complaint—Trial Jury Demanded, February 1, 2022

(All footnotes have been omitted.)

On February 1, 2022, the first day of the celebration of Black History Month, Brian Flores, Senior Defensive Coach for the Pittsburgh Steelers, filed this Complaint against the NFL, alleging racial discrimination in its hiring and retention practices for Black head coaches, coordinators, and general managers.

> "Sorry—I fucked this up. I double checked and misread the text. I think they are naming Brian Daboll. I'm sorry about that. BB."—Bill Belichick informing Plaintiff Brian Flores, three days before his interview with the New York Giants that Brian Daboll had already been selected for the job.
>
> "Morals cannot be legislated, but behavior can be regulated. The law cannot make an employer love me, but it can keep him from refusing to hire me because of the color of my skin."—Dr. Martin Luther King, Jr.

Preliminary statement

1. As this Class Action Complaint is filed on the first day of Black History Month, we honor the brave leaders that fought so hard to help break down racial barriers of

Table 7.1: A rhetorical comparison grid for The Complaint

Complaint	Multicultural rhetorical strategies
Title: What is the type of the complaint (ex. complaint, first amended complaint, amended complaint—jury trial requested and so on)	African Diasporic rhetoric • Rhetoric as the rules or principles for eloquent and effective communication
Nature of the action: Context in which the action is brought; a "big picture" summary of the key components of the case	Indigenous rhetoric • Survivance African Diasporic rhetoric • Rhetoric as eloquent and effective communication o Kawaida • Maat (truth; propriety) Asian Diasporic rhetoric • Discourse of persuasion/persuasion strategies (*ming*) Latine rhetoric • Epistemic delinking • Binary disruption
Jurisdiction and venue: The authority by which the court can adjudicate a particular cause of action; the authority of a court in a particular location to adjudicate a particular cause of action	African Diasporic rhetoric • Rhetoric as the rules or principles for eloquent and effective communication
Parties: The naming and brief explanation of the parties to the lawsuit	Indigenous rhetoric • Survivance African Diasporic rhetoric • Maat (propriety, harmony, balance) Latine rhetoric • Binary disruption
Facts: The facts that give rise to the cause(s) of action	Indigenous rhetoric • Rhetorical sovereignty • Survivance African Diasporic rhetoric • Kawaida (agency and liberation) • Rhetoric as eloquent and effective speech • Maat (truth, propriety, harmony, balance) Asian Diasporic rhetoric • Discourse of persuasion/persuasion strategies (*ci*, *jian*) • Language as a symbolic resource Latine rhetoric • Epistemic delinking • Binary disruption

(continued)

Table 7.1: A rhetorical comparison grid for The Complaint (continued)

Complaint	Multicultural rhetorical strategies
Causes of action (aka claims for relief)**:** Articulation of the law(s) broken or rights violated recited as a series of 'counts' (ex. Count I: Civil Conspiracy)	Indigenous rhetoric • Rhetorical sovereignty • Survivance African Diasporic rhetoric • Kawaida (agency and liberation; expansive transformation) • Rhetoric as the rules or principles for eloquent and effective communication • Maat (justice) Asian Diasporic rhetoric • Discourse of persuasion/persuasion strategies (*ci*, *jian*, *ming*) Latine rhetoric • *Conocimiento* • Epistemic delinking • Binary disruption
Prayer for Relief: Brief statements/averments of the remedies sought from the legal decisionmaker	Indigenous rhetoric • Rhetorical sovereignty • Survivance African Diasporic rhetoric • Kawaida (agency and liberation; expansive transformation) • Rhetoric as the rules or principles for eloquent and effective communication • Maat (justice) Asian Diasporic rhetoric • Discourse of persuasion/persuasion strategies (*ci*, *jian*, *ming*) Latine rhetoric • *Conocimiento* • Epistemic delinking • Binary disruption
Jury demand (if applicable)**:** Request for a jury to be empaneled in the case	African Diasporic rhetoric • Rhetoric as the rules or principles for eloquent and effective communication

injustice. Martin Luther King Jr., Harriet Tubman, Rosa Parks, Frederick Douglass, Jackie Robinson and Mamie Till, to name only a few.

2. Unfortunately, however, there is so much more to be done. While racial barriers have been eroded in many areas, Defendant the National Football League ("NFL" or the "League") lives in a time of the past. As described throughout this Class Action Complaint, the NFL remains rife with racism, particularly when it comes to the hiring and retention of Black Head Coaches, Coordinators and General Managers. Over the years, the NFL and its 32-member organizations (the "Teams") have been given every

chance to do the right thing. Rules have been implemented, promises made—but nothing has changed. In fact, the racial discrimination has only been made worse by the NFL's disingenuous commitment to social equity.

3. As such, in the face of the risks associated with combating racism and injustice, and in particular standing up to organizations as powerful as the NFL and its Teams, Mr. Flores has determined that the only way to effectuate real change is through the Courts, where the NFL's conduct can be judged by a jury of Mr. Flores' peers. A judgment that is long overdue.
4. In certain critical ways, the NFL is racially segregated and is managed much like a plantation. Its 32 owners—none of whom are Black—profit substantially from the labor of NFL players, 70% of whom are Black. The owners watch the games from atop NFL stadiums in their luxury boxes, while their majority-Black workforce put their bodies on the line every Sunday, taking vicious hits and suffering debilitating injuries to their bodies and their brains while the NFL and its owners reap billions of dollars.
5. Many players desire to coach for their post-playing careers. Others desire to work their way into management-level positions at one of the NFL's 32 Teams. Unfortunately, for Black individuals, that is easier said than done.
   - Only 1 of the NFL's 32 teams (3%) employs a Black Head Coach;
   - Only 4 of the NFL's 32 teams (12%) employ a Black Offensive Coordinator;
   - Only 11 of the NFL's 32 teams (34%) employ a Black Defensive Coordinator;
   - Only 8 of the NFL's 32 teams (25%) employ a Black Special Teams Coordinator;
   - Only 3 of the NFL's 32 teams (9%) employ a Black Quarterback Coach; and
   - Only 6 of the NFL's 32 teams (19%) employ a Black General Manager.
6. These numbers come from a pool of players that is approximately 70% Black. This is not by chance. Rather, the statistics above and those described throughout this Complaint are the result of race discrimination.
7. The NFL has effectively conceded this point. Troy Vincent, the NFL Executive Vice President of Football Operations, recently stated with regard to Black Head Coaches:

'There is a double standard, and we've seen that … And you talk about the appetite for what's acceptable. Let's just go back to … Coach Dungy was let go in Tampa Bay after a winning season … Coach Wilks, just a few years prior, was let go after one year … Coach Caldwell was fired after a winning season in Detroit … It is part of the larger challenges that we have. But when you just look over time, it's over-indexing for men of color. These men have been fired after a winning season. How do you explain that? There is a double standard. I don't think that that is something that we should shy away from. But that is all part of some of the things that we need to fix in the system. We want to hold everyone to why does one, let's say, get the benefit of the doubt to be able to build or take bumps and bruises in this process of getting a franchise turned around when others are not afforded that latitude?

[W]e've seen that in history at the [professional] level.'

8. Similarly, Jonathan Beane, the NFL's Senior Vice President and Chief Diversity & Inclusion Officer, stated:

   > Any criticism we get for lack of representation at the GM and head coach positions, we deserve. We see that we're not where we want to be. We have to do much better. We're focusing on all roles at the league, and all these roles are key roles ... But certainly at the top of the house, general manager and head coach, that's the responsibility of the NFL to make sure that we are representing our current fan base and we're representing those that are in the league today. And if you look at it right now, we're grossly underrepresented.

9. Perhaps worst of all, in connection with its distribution of settlement monies to retirees who suffer from traumatic brain injury, the NFL insisted on applying so-called "race-norms." Put simply, the NFL took the position that white people simply have better baseline cognitive function than Black people. This is the very definition of racism—the assumption that someone is not as smart as another person because of the color of his or her skin. It also perhaps explains why the NFL and its Teams are so loath to hire Black Head Coaches, Coordinators and General Managers ("GMs"), just as for years the League discriminated against Black quarterbacks.
10. These are literal admissions of liability and fault on the part of the NFL and its owners, and yet no meaningful remedial action has been taken to remedy this recognized discrimination.
11. Even when Black candidates get hired for Head Coaching positions, a rarity, they are discriminated against in connection with the terms and conditions of their employment and compensation and terminated even as far less successful white Head Coaches are retained. Moreover, Black Head Coaches are far less likely than white Head Coaches to receive second chances even as white Head Coaches are routinely hired by Teams even after they fail elsewhere.
12. It has been nearly 20 years since the NFL implemented the Rooney Rule, purportedly to try to combat the utter lack of Black Head Coaches in the NFL. As first implemented, the Rooney Rule required NFL Teams to interview at least one Black person in connection with any Head Coach vacancy. The Rooney Rule has since been expanded to cover General Manager and other front office positions, as well as Assistant Head Coach and Coordinator positions. Moreover, as it relates to Head Coach positions, teams are now required to interview two minority coaching candidates, at least one of whom must be interviewed in person.
13. The Rooney Rule may have been well intentioned, although it is hard to attribute benevolence to the NFL given the complete lack of action that it has taken post–Rooney Rule to remedy discrimination that it admits exists. However, well intentioned or not, what is clear is that the Rooney Rule is not working. It is not working because the numbers of Black Head Coaches, Coordinators and Quarterback Coaches are not even close to being reflective of the number of Black athletes on the field. The Rooney Rule is also not working because management is not doing

the interviews in good-faith, and it therefore creates a stigma that interviews of Black candidates are only being done to comply with the Rooney Rule rather than in recognition of the talents that the Black candidates possess.

14. In January 2022, Mr. Flores, who spent three years as the Head Coach of Defendant Miami Dolphins, Ltd. (the "Dolphins" or "Miami"), found himself without a job. He was fired by the Dolphins after leading the team to its first back-to-back winning seasons since 2003. The purported basis for his termination was alleged poor collaboration. In reality, the writing had been on the wall since Mr. Flores' first season as Head Coach of the Dolphins, when he refused his owner's directive to "tank" for the first pick in the draft. Indeed, during the 2019 season, Miami's owner, Stephen Ross, told Mr. Flores that he would pay him $100,000 for every loss, and the team's General Manager, Chris Grier, told Mr. Flores that "Steve" was "mad" that Mr. Flores' success in winning games that year was "compromising [the team's] draft position."
15. After the end of the 2019 season, Mr. Ross began to pressure Mr. Flores to recruit a prominent quarterback in violation of League tampering rules. Mr. Flores repeatedly refused to comply with these improper directives. Undeterred, in the winter of 2020, Mr. Ross invited Mr. Flores onto a yacht for lunch. Shortly after he arrived, Mr. Ross told Mr. Flores that the prominent quarterback was "conveniently" arriving at the marina. Obviously, Mr. Ross had attempted to "set up" a purportedly impromptu meeting between Mr. Flores and the prominent quarterback. Mr. Flores refused the meeting and left the yacht immediately. After the incident, Mr. Flores was treated with disdain and held out as someone who was noncompliant and difficult to work with.
16. From that point forward, Mr. Flores was ostracized and ultimately he was fired. He was subsequently defamed throughout the media and the League as he was labeled by the Dolphins brass as someone who was difficult to work with. This is reflective of an all too familiar "angry black man" stigma that is often casted upon Black men who are strong in their morals and convictions while white men are coined as passionate for those very same attributes.
17. Thus, last week, Defendant New York Football Giants, Inc. (the "Giants" or "New York Giants") had an opportunity to move a step in the right direction, if even only one. The Giants had the chance to hire Mr. Flores, an eminently qualified Black man, to be the first Black Head Coach in the Giants' nearly 100-year history.
18. Instead, the New York Giants made the decision to hire Brian Daboll—and disclosed that decision to third parties—during a time when the Giants were scheduled to still interview Mr. Flores and when Mr. Flores was deceptively led to believe he actually had a chance at this job.
19. Thus, on Wednesday, January 26, 2022, Mr. Flores was forced to sit through a dinner with Joe Schoen, the Giant's new General Manager, knowing that the Giants had already selected Mr. Daboll. Much worse, on Thursday, January 27, 2022, Mr. Flores had to give an extensive interview for a job that he already knew he would not get—an interview that was held for no reason other than for the Giants to demonstrate

falsely to the League Commissioner Roger Goodell and the public at large that it was in compliance with the Rooney Rule.

20. The Giants would likely have gotten away with this most insidious form of discrimination if New England Patriots Coach Bill Belichick had not mistakenly disclosed it to Mr. Flores in the below text messages.
21. Incredibly, this was not Mr. Flores' first sham interview that was held only in an effort to comply with the Rooney Rule. Indeed, in 2019 Mr. Flores was scheduled to interview with the Denver Broncos. However, the Broncos' then–General Manager, John Elway, President and Chief Executive Officer Joe Ellis and others, showed up an hour late to the interview. They looked completely disheveled, and it was obvious that they had drinking heavily the night before. It was clear from the substance of the interview that Mr. Flores was interviewed only because of the Rooney Rule, and that the Broncos never had any intention to consider him as a legitimate candidate for the job. Shortly thereafter, Vic Fangio, a white man, was hired to be the Head Coach of the Broncos.
22. Having discovered what the Giants and the rest of the NFL had hoped to keep in the dark, Mr. Flores now brings this Class Action Complaint to shine a light on the racial injustices that take place inside the NFL and to effectuate real change for the future.
23. Among the other relief sought, Mr. Flores seeks the following injunctive relief:
    i. Increase the influence of Black individuals in hiring and termination decisions for General Manager, Head Coach and Offensive and Defensive Coordinator positions;
        a. Ensure diversity of ownership by creating and funding a committee dedicated to sourcing Black investors to take majority ownership stakes in NFL Teams;
        b. Ensure diversity of decision-making by permitting select Black players and coaches to participate in the interviewing process for General Manager, Head Coach and Offensive and Defensive Coordinator positions;
    ii. Increase the objectivity of hiring and termination decisions for General Manager, Head Coach and Offensive and Defensive Coordinator positions;
        a. Require NFL Teams to reduce to writing the rationale for hiring and termination decisions, including a full explanation of the basis for any subjective influences (e.g., trust, personality, interview performance, etc.);
        b. Require NFL Teams to consider side-by-side comparisons of objective criteria, such as past performance, experience and objective qualifications;
    iii. Increase the number of Black Offensive and Defensive Coordinators;
        a. Create and fund a training program for lower-level Black coaches who demonstrate an aptitude for coaching and an interest in advancing to a Coordinator position;
    iv. Incentivize the hiring and retention of Black General Managers, Head Coaches and Offensive and Defensive Coordinators through monetary, draft and/or other compensation such as additional salary cap space; and

v. Complete transparency with respect to pay for all General Managers, Head Coaches and Offensive and Defensive Coordinators.

24. Defendants' conduct has violated Section 1981 of the Civil Rights Act of 1866 ("Section 1981"), the New Jersey Law Against Discrimination ("NJLAD"), the New York State Human Rights Law, N.Y. Exec. Law §§ 290 et seq. ("NYSHRL") and the New York City Human Rights Law, N.Y.C. Admin. Code §§ 8–101 et seq. ("NYCHRL").

Administrative procedures

25. Plaintiff will file a Charge of Discrimination with the Equal Employment Opportunity Commission, an administrative pre-requisite to filing an action under Title VII of the Civil Rights Act of 1964 ("Title VII") and will amend this action to include claims under Title VII at the appropriate time.
26. Pursuant to NYCHRL § 8-502, Plaintiff will serve a copy of this Complaint upon the New York City Commission on Human Rights and the New York City Law Department, Office of the Corporation Counsel within 10 days of its filing, thereby satisfying the notice requirements of this action.
27. Plaintiff has complied with any and all other prerequisites to filing this action.

Jurisdiction and venue

28. The Court has jurisdiction over this matter pursuant to 28 U.S.C. §§ 1331 and 1343 as this action involves federal questions regarding the deprivation of Plaintiff's rights under § 1981. The Court has supplemental jurisdiction over Plaintiff's related state and local law claims pursuant to 28 U.S.C. § 1367(a)
29. Venue is proper in this district pursuant to 28 U.S.C. § 1391(b) because a substantial part of the events or omissions giving rise to this action, including certain of the unlawful employment practices alleged herein, occurred in this district.

Parties

30. Plaintiff Brian Flores is a Black man and the former Head Coach of the Miami Dolphins. Mr. Flores was not only denied the Head Coach position of the New York Giants but was humiliated in the process as the New York Giants subjected him to a sham interview in an attempt to appear to provide a Black candidate with a legitimate chance at obtaining the job.
31. Defendant the National Football League is a trade association made up of 32 professional football teams and with a principal place of business located at 345 Park Avenue, New York, NY 10154.
32. Defendant New York Football Giants, Inc. is a corporation that owns and operates the New York Giants professional football team. New York Football Giants, Inc. is headquartered at 1925 Giants Drive, East Rutherford, NJ 07073.

33. Defendant Miami Dolphins, Ltd. is a corporation that owns and operates the Miami Dolphins professional football team. Miami Dolphins, Ltd. is headquartered at 346 Don Shula Drive, Miami Gardens, FL 33056.
34. Defendant Denver Broncos, former corporate name PDB Sports, Ltd., is a corporation that owns and operates the Denver Broncos professional football team. The Denver Broncos are headquartered at 13655 Broncos Parkway, Englewood, Colorado 80112.
35. Defendants John Doe Teams 1 through 29 are intended to identify NFL teams who have engaged in discriminatory conduct towards the Members of the Proposed Class, including potentially the Arizona Cardinals, Atlanta Falcons, Baltimore Ravens, Buffalo Bills, Carolina Panthers, Chicago Bears, Cincinnati Bengals, Cleveland Browns, Dallas Cowboys, Detroit Lions, Green Bay Packers, Houston Texans, Indianapolis Colts, Jacksonville Jaguars, Kansas City Chiefs, Las Vegas Raiders, Los Angeles Chargers, Los Angeles Rams, Minnesota Vikings, New England Patriots, New Orleans Saints, New York Jets, Philadelphia Eagles, Pittsburgh Steelers, San Francisco 49ers, Seattle Seahawks, Tampa Bay Buccaneers, Tennessee Titans and/or the Washington Football Team.

Factual allegations

1. History of race discrimination in the NFL

36. The NFL has a tortured and unacceptable history with race relations that requires immediate focus in the first instance. The League remains mired in a culture that lacks inclusivity and where a barrier to entry still exists today for Black professionals in leadership.
37. The first iteration of the NFL began in 1920, and it was rife with racism.
38. From 1920 through 1926, a total of only nine Black players were permitted into the League. At that time, the only reason Black players were permitted at all was because the then-existing teams had difficulty filling out their rosters in the League's early days.
39. Heading into the 1927 season, all five of the remaining Black players at the time left the League and, from 1927 to 1933, only a handful of Black players were permitted to participate. Indeed, during that time frame there was no more than one Black player in the League per year.
40. In 1933, the League had only two Black players, but they left at the end of the year, leaving the NFL with none. At this point, the NFL was reportedly financially viable and no longer needed Black players to fill vacant positions.
41. This led to one of the most despicable moments in the history of professional sports in the United States: it is widely accepted that the NFL used the absence of Black players as an opportunity to impose a "gentleman's agreement" to ban Black players entirely.
42. This initiative was led by the Washington Football Team's owner George Preston Marshall. The League's other founding owners—including but not limited to, Tim

Mara of the New York Giants—appear to have colluded and cooperated in this widespread racial ban.

43. It was not until 1946 that Black players re-entered professional football.
44. However, the reentry of Black players into the League was not the result of introspection and a commitment to equality. Rather, when the Cleveland Rams moved to Los Angeles, the publicly funded playing venue, the Los Angeles Coliseum, forced the Rams to integrate at least one Black player in order to comply with the Supreme Court's decision in *Plessy v. Ferguson* that banned segregation in places of public accommodation.
45. In fact, it was reported that during a meeting between local officials, community activists and the Rams' General Manager Charles F. Walsh, Mr. Walsh admitted to the unwritten racist "gentlemen's agreement" of barring Black players.
46. As it would happen, the Rams ultimately signed two Black players for the 1946 season, but two more years would go by before any other team would sign a Black player.
47. As of 1950, fewer than half of the NFL's ten teams had signed a Black player and it was not until more than a decade later that the Washington Football Team signed its first Black player.
48. In 1959, 13 years later after the start of integration, only 12 percent of the League's players were Black.
49. Even as integration slowly progressed, the stain of racism persisted. Teams reportedly put unwritten quotas on how many Black players could be signed, and often teams would stack Black players at the same position so that they would be eliminated as a matter of competition and roster cuts. It was also reported that Black players received less compensation than their white counterparts.
50. The NFL only engaged in genuine full scale racial integration when it became economically necessary due to outrage and protests from writers and fans, the emergence of the rival and more racially progressive leagues (such as the All-America Football Conference ("AAFC") and American Football League ("AFL")) and the success of numerous minority athletes in college football.
51. Of course, integration was hardly the end of Black struggle in the NFL—untold forms of discrimination still followed Black players from team-to-team, city-to-city, stadium-to-stadium and hotel-to-hotel. In fact, though the NFL had integrated 23 years earlier, when Washington's owner, Mr. Marshall, died in 1969, he abhorrently stipulated that his estate be used to establish the Redskins Foundation, on the condition that it was barred from spending money for "any purpose which supports or employs the principle of racial integration in any form."
52. The NFL has profited immensely from the racial integration of its players. Initially considered a second-tier sport, the NFL has thrived as an integrated League over the last 75 years.
53. While the NFL was forced to racially integrate its players to generate these immense profits, it was not forced to do so in other areas—so it did not.
54. It took approximately 20 years for the League to hire its first black official (Burl Toler).

55. It is widely known by even casual NFL fans that it took until at least the 1980s—approximately 40 years after integration—for teams to genuinely accept Black players at the quarterback position (i.e. Warren Moon and Randall Cunningham).
56. It took 43 years for the first Black Head Coach to be hired (Art Shell).
57. It took 54 years for an NFL team to hire a Black General Manager (Ozzie Newsome).
58. Now, 76 years following integration, there has never been a Black Commissioner and there has never been a Black majority owner of an NFL team.
59. For a League and its team owners who have profited immensely off the talent of Black players, the NFL has never fully acknowledged its history of racism or taken appropriate steps to address its racial disparities. As a Black sportswriter once wrote:

> [P]ersons, corporations or business almost always forget the people or incidents that made them big ... [the NFL] took all the aid the colored American could give and then as soon as it became "big league," promptly put a bar up against the very backbone of its existence.

60. Case in point: Mr. Marshall, in many ways the personification of the NFL's deep-seated institutional racism, is enshrined in the NFL Hall of Fame—and his contributions are lauded by the Hall of Fame's website, with only a passing reference to the fact that he "endured his share of criticism for not integrating his team until being forced to do so in 1962." That is, the NFL does not even acknowledge, much less condemn, Mr. Marshall's role in the League's history with racism. Rather, it only notes that he received criticism from others.

2. The NFL's ongoing problems with race

61. History shows that the NFL is synonymous with ownership resistance to anti-racist protest—and that continues to the present day.

a. Discrimination against Colin Kaepernick

62. As has been well documented, during the 2016 NFL season, Colin Kaepernick protested societal racial injustice by kneeling during the national anthem.
63. Following the 2016–17 season—a season in which over the course of 11 games started he had 16 touchdowns against only four interceptions, 468 rushing yards and a passer rating of 90.7—no NFL team would offer him a job, even as a backup.
64. To even a casual observer it was clear that Mr. Kaepernick was more than qualified for a roster spot in the NFL.
65. Seahawks Head Coach Pete Carroll explained the Seahawks' rationale for not bringing him in: "He's a starter in this league. And we have a starter. But he's a starter in this league, and I can't imagine that someone won't give him a chance to play."

66. The New York Giants gave Mr. Kaepernick no consideration and suggested that it was because the team feared backlash from the fans if it signed Mr. Kaepernick—a statement that journalists understandably labeled "dangerous."
67. In an August 2017 article titled, "Colin Kaepernick is Not Supposed to Be Unemployed," the statistics website FiveThirtyEight stated, "It's obvious Kaepernick is being frozen out for his political opinions," that "[n]o above-average quarterback has been unemployed."
68. Mr. Kaepernick's protests received a variety of reactions—both positive and negative—with then-President Donald J. Trump siding against him and calling on the nearly all-white NFL owners to "fire" players who protest during the national anthem. President Trump referred a player who protested (clearly referring to Mr. Kaepernick) as "that Son of a Bitch."
69. In an October 2017 meeting among owners, players and League executives to address racial injustice protests by players, NFL owners effectively endorsed President Trump's opinion that a player who protests racial injustice is a "Son of a Bitch" and a stated an unwillingness to act contrary to Trump's directives.
70. As time went on, still no team would sign Mr. Kaepernick for any role, starter or backup, despite the fact that he clearly deserved such a role based on merit, skill and experience. While some owners gave lip service to solidarity with Black players, NFL owners still collectively refused to employ Mr. Kaepernick following his racial justice protests.
71. During these years, many teams—Including the New York Giants—could have used his services as a clear roster upgrade. But he remained blackballed.
72. Against the backdrop of the League's history, this conduct remains an appalling example of the League's continued problems with race.

b. Acquiescence to discrimination by Head Coach John Gruden

73. John Gruden, the 30-year NFL insider and three-time Head Coach, is the embodiment of the NFL's acquiescence to racism.
74. In October 2021, it was disclosed that between 2011 and 2018, Mr. Gruden exchanged a slew of emails containing racist, misogynistic and homophobic slurs to Washington Football Team's then–General Manager Bruce Allen.
75. Mr. Gruden remarked that DeMaurice Smith, the NFL Players' Association Executive Director, had "lips the size of Michelin tires."
76. Mr. Gruden also stated that players who protested the national anthem to protest racial inequality should be "fired."
77. Mr. Smith responded to reports of these emails saying, "Racism like this comes from the fact that I'm at the same table as they are and they don't think someone who looks like me belongs."
78. As stated, Mr. Gruden's emails also contained a slew of additional offensive conduct. The emails referred to Mr. Goodell as a "faggot" and a "clueless anti football pussy," and said Mr. Goodell should not have pressured the Rams to draft "queers" (referring

to the drafting of Michael Sam, the first openly gay player drafted by an NFL team in 2014), something which the Rams coach has denied. Mr. Gruden also called then United States Vice President Joe Biden a "nervous clueless pussy."

79. Mr. Gruden and Mr. Allen also exchanged emails with other members of the Washington Football Team staff with photos of topless women, including two team cheerleaders.
80. In one email from 2015 that includes several football insiders including Mr. Allen, Gruden asked Mr. Allen to tell Bryan Glazer (part of the family which owns the Tampa Bay Buccaneers) to perform oral sex on him.
81. Mr. Gruden also mocked Caitlyn Jenner, a transgender former Olympic athlete.
82. It simply cannot be a surprise to NFL executives, insiders and team owners—who have collectively spent the last three decades in the proximity of Mr. Gruden—that this is who Mr. Gruden is and that these are the beliefs he harbors.
83. Nonetheless, Mr. Gruden remained an inner-circle candidate for virtually every Head Coach position over the 10-year period that followed his departure from the Tampa Bay Buccaneers in 2008.
84. Ultimately, in 2018, Mr. Gruden received the largest contract in history for an NFL Head Coach, when the Las Vegas Raiders signed him to a 10-year, $100 million deal.
85. The Raiders' hiring of Mr. Gruden occurred in close succession with the Raiders' firing of General Manager Reggie McKenzie, one of the few Black General Managers in the League.
86. Under Mr. McKenzie, the Raiders had the highest percentage of Black players at 82.3%, and he won the NFL Executive of the Year Award in 2016 after compiling a 12–4 record.
87. Only two years later, Mr. McKenzie was fired and replaced by Mike Mayock, a white candidate. Under all-white leadership (Owner, General Manager and Head Coach), the percentage of Black players on the Raiders decreased every year that followed. By 2021, the percentage of Black players on the Raiders roster dropped to 67.2%.
88. Though Mr. Gruden is no longer employed by the Raiders, it has been reported that the NFL was well aware of Mr. Gruden's offensive emails for several months and took no action.
89. When the news of Mr. Gruden's racist emails finally surfaced, rather than an unequivocal rebuke and a for-cause termination, the Raiders allowed him to graciously resign and claim that it was due to his desire not to be a distraction.
90. Mr. Gruden even had the gall to blame the NFL and Mr. Goodell, claiming that they were responsible—not him for his own actions—for his termination.

c. The NFL's concussion settlement discriminated against Black players

91. In 2011, retired NFL players began filing personal injury actions in courts around the country seeking damages or relief in the form of medical monitoring. Some of these actions were filed on behalf of a class, some for small groups of former players and others for individuals (collectively, the "Concussion Lawsuits").

92. As alleged in the Concussion Lawsuits, the NFL for decades was aware of the evidence and the risks associated with repetitive traumatic brain injuries, but nevertheless "ignored, minimized, disputed, and actively suppressed broader awareness of the link between subconcussive and concussive injuries in football and the chronic neuro-cognitive damage, illnesses, and decline suffered by former players."
93. The NFL was also alleged to have "failed to warn [players] and/or impose safety regulations governing this health and safety problem" and "produced industry-funded, biased, and falsified research that claimed that concussive and sub-concussive head impacts in football do not present serious, life-altering risks."
94. The Concussion Lawsuits identified a number of retired NFL players who were diagnosed with traumatic brain injury ("TBI") following their playing career, and sought money damages for injury and death, as well as medical treatment for retired players diagnosed with TBI.
95. Ultimately, the claims were consolidated and settled in 2014. Under the settlement agreement, a former player who has a "Qualifying Diagnosis" is eligible for monetary benefits. A diagnosis is "Qualifying" primarily—but not exclusively—if rendered by physicians approved by the NFL or in conjunction with the NFL's Baseline Assessment Program ("BAP"). The BAP is intended both to identify symptoms of eligible conditions and to collect data for comparison to later testing, to establish any subsequent decline in a retired player's cognitive functioning.
96. Claims for monetary awards are first reviewed by a Claims Administrator. In the first instance, any appeals of the Claims Administrator's determinations are heard by an Appeals Advisory Panel. Any appeals from the Appeals Advisory Panel are brought to the court that entered the settlement agreement.
97. According to a lawsuit filed by former Black NFL players Kevin Henry and Najeh Davenport, as well as media reports, the NFL began regularly insisting that physicians use "race-norms" in determining whether a retiree had suffered cognitive impairment (the "Race-Norming Lawsuit"). When Black retirees were deemed to be cognitively impaired, the NFL regularly appealed such determinations if race-norming was not used.
98. As alleged in the Race-Norming Lawsuit, "the National Football League … [has] been avoiding paying head-injury claims under the Settlement Agreement based on a formula for identifying qualifying diagnoses that explicitly and deliberately discriminates on the basis of race. When being evaluated for the Qualifying Diagnoses of Neurocognitive Impairment, Black former players are automatically assumed (through a statistical manipulation called 'race-norming') to have started with worse cognitive functioning than white former players. As a result, if a Black former player and a white former player receive the exact same raw scores on a battery of tests designed to measure their current cognitive functioning, the Black player is presumed to have suffered less impairment, and he is therefore less likely to qualify for compensation."
99. Put another way, the NFL insisted that white people simply have better cognitive function than Black people. Thus, if a Black person was found to be cognitively

impaired, the NFL would often not accept that diagnosis unless the physician gave adequate consideration to the possibility that Black people simply do not function cognitively as well as white people. This is the very definition of racism—the assumption that someone is not as smart as another person because of the color of his or her skin.

d. The NFL's attempt to pander during widespread, societal racial protests

100. In June 2020, following protests over George Floyd's murder and other instances of racially charged violence, Roger Goodell publicly apologized for the League's previous response to player protests saying, "we were wrong for not listening to NFL players earlier."
101. Goodell further "encourage[d] all to speak out and peacefully protest" and said, "[w]ithout black players, there would be no National Football League and the protests around the country are emblematic of the centuries of silence, inequality and oppression of black players, coaches, fans and staff."
102. Despite the blatant collusion against him, Mr. Goodell declared in a publicly released video that "Black Lives Matter" and announced that the NFL desired to work with Mr. Kaepernick in the creation and distribution of a $250 million foundation for social justice initiative.
103. These remarks and actions—emblematic of the phrase "too little too late"—were largely ridiculed by the public as hypocritical and an obvious attempt to pander to growing public sentiment against racial injustice. Racial discrimination requires real and meaningful attention—not mere soundbites when it is in the League's financial interest.

e. Lack of Black coaches and the failure of the Rooney rule

104. Troy Vincent, a Black, Hall of Fame former cornerback, and current NFL Executive Vice President of Football Operations, recently stated with regard to the treatment of Black Head Coaches in the NFL:

> 'There is a double standard, and we've seen that ... And you talk about the appetite for what's acceptable. Let's just go back to ... Coach Dungy was let go in Tampa Bay after a winning season ... Coach Wilks, just a few years prior, was let go after one year ... Coach Caldwell was fired after a winning season in Detroit ... It is part of the larger challenges that we have. But when you just look over time, it's over-indexing for men of color. These men have been fired after a winning season. How do you explain that? There is a double standard. I don't think that that is something that we should shy away from. But that is all part of some of the things that we need to fix in the system. We want to hold everyone to why does one, let's say, get the benefit of the doubt to be

> able to build or take bumps and bruises in this process of getting a franchise turned around when others are not afforded that latitude? [W]e've seen that in history at the [professional] level.'

105. Mr. Vincent's common-sense analysis of the NFL's predicament with respect to the lack of Black Head Coaches hits the nail on the head: "There is a double standard." This double standard has led to a consistent dearth of Black Head Coaches despite an abundance of highly qualified candidates. For Black Head Coaches who are hired, retention of the job is routinely more difficult than for white counterparts.
106. Historically, Head Coach positions were closed to Black candidates until Art Shell broke this color barrier in 1989. Still, Mr. Shell was only one of five Black Head coaches between then and 2003. As one sportswriter noted, "In 2003, NFL franchise owners had to be prodded to seriously consider Black candidates to coach their teams. They were willing to sign Black players [to] make them money while risking their health. They were reluctant to let them lead their teams after they were done playing." This was a reference to what is commonly known as the "Rooney Rule."
107. By way of brief background, in 2002, Johnnie L. Cochran Jr., civil rights attorney Cyrus Mehri and labor economist Dr. Janice Madden together produced a detailed report on the NFL's head-coaching hiring practices entitled "Black Coaches in the National Football League: Superior Performance, Inferior Opportunities." The report analyzed the NFL's hiring and firing practices over the previous 15 seasons, and the statistics showed evidence of discrimination, including that Black Head Coach candidates were less likely to be hired and that Black head coaches were more likely to be fired.
108. Due to the public sentiment gathering to address this problem, on October 31, 2002, the NFL appointed a "Committee on Workplace Diversity," headed by Pittsburgh Steelers' President Dan Rooney, to study the issue further. On December 20, 2002, this committee issued its recommendations, including that NFL teams make a commitment to interview minority candidates for every Head Coach job opening (with limited exceptions). In December 2002, the owners approved this recommendation.
109. Since its passage, the Rooney Rule has been amended several times in an effort to strengthen its impact on diversity and inclusion, or to at least appear to do that. It now applies to General Manager and other front office positions, as well as Assistant Head Coach and Coordinator positions. Moreover, teams are now required to interview two minority Head Coach candidates, and at least one in person. However, the Rooney Rule has failed to yield any meaningful change to an institution so fully steeped in discriminatory practices.
110. In the 20 years since the Rooney Rule was passed, only 15 Head Coaching positions have been filled by Black Candidates. During that time, there have been approximately 129 Head Coaching vacancies. Thus only 11% of Head Coach positions have been filled by Black candidates—in a league where 70% of players

are Black. With few exceptions, the Black candidates who have obtained Head Coach positions have been on a "short leash" and lasted for extremely short periods, while white candidates have much lengthier opportunities to prove their worth. In addition, upon information and belief, in general Black coaches at all levels are paid less than similarly qualified white coaches.

111. Indeed, not a single one of the 10 Black Head Coaches hired since 2012 still holds his Head Coach job today. In contrast, approximately 25% of white Head Coaches hired during the same time frame remain employed as a Head Coach. Moreover, since 2012, Black Head Coaches have been fired in an average of 2.5 years, whereas (accounting for Head Coaches that are expected to return next year) white Head Coaches have averaged nearly 3.5 years on the job. Put another way, white Head Coaches are afforded an entire additional year to establish themselves relative to Black Head Coaches.

112. Moreover, since 1978, only 16 winning teams have fired their head coach (3%). Even though Black men only held a small fraction of the Head Coach positions during that time, an astounding 25% (four of the 16) of the Head Coaches fired after a winning season were Black. This statistic is even more remarkable given that there have only ever been 17 Black Head Coaches who have coached a full season, and four of them (23.5%) were fired after a winning season. In contrast, only 6.9% of white coaches were fired after a winning season (12 out of 174). Thus, Black Head Coaches are 3.5 times more likely to be fired even when successful.

113. Moreover, unsuccessful white Head Coaches routinely get second and third chances in critical positions, including as a Head Coach or Offensive or Defensive Coordinator. Indeed, according to a 2021 NFL Diversity and Inclusion report, since 1963, 116 white individuals have been hired as a Head Coach or Coordinator after an initial Head Coach opportunity, whereas only 21 individuals of color have received the same second chances. The same report noted that only one person of color has received three Head Coaching opportunities, whereas 15 white men have received three Head Coaching opportunities (two of the 15 received four opportunities).

114. Thus, while the Rooney Rule was and remains well-intentioned, its effectiveness requires NFL teams to take it seriously, and not treat it as a formality that must be endured simply to formalize the pre-determined hiring of a white coach. Moreover, it requires that teams provide Black Head Coaches a fair and legitimate chance—a chance commensurate with the circumstances and comparable to the chances given to white Head Coaches—to thrive.

115. But that has not happened. As a result, following the recent terminations of Mr. Flores and David Culley, former Head Coach of the Houston Texans, there is currently only one Black Head Coach out of 32 NFL teams. The following photo[2] array speaks for itself.

116. At the time the Rooney Rule was instituted, almost twenty years ago, there were three Black Head Coaches. There is now only one. That marks a complete lack of improvement, and in fact, a move backwards in the wrong direction.

117. As was recently well-put by sportswriter Jemele Hill,

> [M]ost NFL owners have been white men, and they have seldom been willing to let African Americans or Latinos call plays—either on the field or from the sidelines. This is no different from when franchises presumed that black players weren't smart enough to play quarterback and lacked leadership skills to command men. The league's paltry record of hiring minority head coaches comes from the same mind-set. And its primary effort to address the problem has been a failure, because a policy can't compensate for ignorance … If the NFL wants to create an equitable system for minority head coaches, the owners can't rely on a rule to create institutional change.

118. Ms. Hill continued, "NFL owners must recognize that their lazy stereotypes of black male leadership have created this embarrassing problem. In time, we'll see whether they have the courage to fix it." As has been evidenced by The New York Giants' Head Coach search and treatment of Mr. Flores—the NFL and its teams clearly do not.

Discussion questions

1. Which multicultural rhetorical strategies, if any, are present in the Flores Complaint? Be specific and name the cultural tradition and the strategy.
2. In what part(s) of this genre is it being used?
3. How/for what purpose is it being used in each part? Name the strategy and how the author uses it in each part, where relevant.
4. Is the drafter's use of the strategy effective? Be specific, why or why not?
5. Given what you now know about multicultural rhetorical strategies, describe how this Complaint is effective in a way that one drafted using traditional rhetoric might not be.

The Memo

Memos are generally not thought about as documents of persuasion; however, all memos are written in a context that is not objective and in which external forces affect audience and information delivery. They are included here because not all multicultural rhetorical strategies have the goal of "persuasion," but rather inclusive problem-solving for the good of the community and in the service of justice.

Table 7.2: A rhetorical comparison grid for The Memo

Memo	Multicultural rhetorical strategies
Issue(s)/question(s) presented: Communicates to the reader the area or areas of law that the case involves; the particular legal question that the memo seeks to answer; and the facts of the client's case that are important to resolving that question	Indigenous rhetoric • Rhetorical sovereignty (culturally informed issue-framing) • Survivance African Diasporic rhetoric • Kawaida (agency and liberation; expansive transformation) • Rhetoric as the rules or principles for eloquent and effective communication • Maat (truth, propriety, harmony, balance, reciprocity, and order) Asian Diasporic rhetoric • Discourse of persuasion/persuasion strategies (*jian, ming*) • Language as a symbolic resource • "Because therefore" "frame-main" reasoning (legal question(s)/problem at issue) • Problem-solution structure (initiation component) Latine rhetoric • *Conocimiento* • Epistemic delinking
Short answer: States the legal standard for evaluating the facts; briefly describes how the facts of the client's case meet or do not meet the legal standard	Indigenous rhetoric • Rhetorical sovereignty (culturally informed issue-framing) • Survivance African Diasporic rhetoric • Kawaida (agency and liberation; expansive transformation) • Rhetoric as eloquent and effective communication • Maat (truth, propriety, harmony, balance, reciprocity, and order) Asian Diasporic rhetoric • Discourse of persuasion/persuasion strategies (*jian, ming*) • Language as a symbolic resource • "Because therefore" "frame-main" reasoning (reasons and assertions) • Problem-solution structure (initiation act, articulation of the current problem) Latine rhetoric • *Conocimiento* • Epistemic delinking
Statement of Facts: Communicates the salient facts of the client's case to the reader	Indigenous rhetoric • Rhetorical sovereignty • Survivance

Table 7.2: A rhetorical comparison grid for The Memo (continued)

Memo	Multicultural rhetorical strategies
	African Diasporic rhetoric • Kawaida (agency and liberation) • Rhetoric as eloquent and effective speech • Maat (truth, propriety, harmony, balance) Asian Diasporic rhetoric • Discourse of persuasion/persuasion strategies (*ci, jian*) • Language as a symbolic resource Latine rhetoric • Epistemic delinking • Binary disruption
Discussion: Communicates the standard(s) for resolving the question(s) that the case involves; applies that standard to the facts of the client's case, law, or legal doctrine	Indigenous rhetoric • Rhetorical sovereignty • Survivance African Diasporic rhetoric • Kawaida • Rhetoric as eloquent and effective communication • Rhetoric as the rules or principles for eloquent and effective communication • Maat Asian Diasporic rhetoric • Discourse of persuasion/persuasion strategies (*ci, jian, ming, bian*) • Language as a symbolic resource • "Because therefore" "frame-main" reasoning • Problem-solution structure Latine rhetoric • *Conocimiento* • Epistemic delinking • Binary disruption
Conclusion: Predicts the most likely outcome for the client's case given the reasoning in the Discussion section; sometimes contains a checklist of "next steps" to take	Indigenous rhetoric • Rhetorical sovereignty • Survivance African Diasporic rhetoric • Kawaida (agency and liberation; expansive transformation) • Rhetoric as the rules or principles for eloquent and effective communication • Maat (justice) Asian Diasporic rhetoric • Discourse of persuasion/persuasion strategies (*ci, jian, ming*) Latine rhetoric • *Conocimiento* • Epistemic delinking • Binary disruption

Removal of Japanese Aliens and Citizens from Hawaii to the United States, Memorandum Opinion for the Attorney General of the United States, by Oscar C. Cox, Deputy Attorney Assistant Solicitor General, May 16, 1942

(All footnotes have been omitted.)

The referenced memorandum was issued three months after Executive Order 9066, 7 Fed. Reg. 1407 (Feb. 19, 1942), which authorized the Secretary of War:

> to prescribe military areas in such places and of such extent as he or the appropriate Military Commander may determine, from which any or all persons may be excluded, and with respect to which, the right of any person to enter, remain in, or leave shall be subject to whatever restrictions the Secretary of War or the appropriate Military Commander may impose in his discretion.

It is not clear from our files what precipitated this opinion request from the Attorney General, or to whom the opinion may have been forwarded. The opinion does not appear to have been directed to a particular executive or military order, although it preceded by days a string of Civilian Restrictive Orders (8 Fed. Reg. 982–88), requiring the removal of "persons of Japanese ancestry" to various internment camps in the western United States. Another relocation/internment order—Civilian Exclusion Order No. 34, 7 Fed. Reg. 3967 (May 3, 1942), requiring the removal of persons of Japanese ancestry from Alameda County, California, and issued just two weeks prior—was upheld against constitutional challenge by the Supreme Court in *Korematsu v. United States*, 323 U.S. 214 (1944).

At the time of this opinion, military authorities had already set up internment camps on the Hawaiian Islands, including in particular Sand Island, through which internees were then transferred to internment camps on the continent. In 1988, Congress formally recognized that "a grave injustice was done to both citizens and permanent resident aliens of Japanese ancestry by the evacuation, relocation, and internment of civilians during World War II,"[3] and ordered restitution for Japanese American citizens and resident aliens who had been confined under one of the relocation/internment orders.[4]

Japanese who are aliens can be brought to the continental United States from Hawaii and interned under the provisions of 50 U.S.C. § 21. This statute, however, is probably not applicable to the Japanese who are American citizens.

Although not free from doubt, an argument can be made for removing Japanese who are American citizens from Hawaii to a restricted zone in the United States on grounds of military necessity.

In view of the changed conditions of modern warfare, the Supreme Court would likely follow the views of the dissenting justices in *Ex parte Milligan* [71 U.S. 2 (1866)], sustaining a declaration of martial law in places outside the zone of active military operations upon a showing of military necessity for such action. From the nature and purpose of martial law, it would seem to be properly applicable to particular areas rather than to particular persons.

May 16, 1942

Memorandum opinion for the Attorney General

1. Attached [see note 3 in this chapter] is a legal memorandum on the subject.
2. As a practical matter, I understand that the Army feels the problem can be satisfactorily handled by removing the Japanese citizens from Hawaii and treating them the same way as those evacuated from the West Coast.
3. If this is so, it is not necessary to pass on the legal questions which you put. I should think therefore, that the War Department ought not now to be told the theory of removing and interning the Japanese. It is a conclusion not without doubt and it might be extended or abused. Like unto the Supreme Court, I think the decision ought to be saved for the specific case in which it is necessary.

* * * * *

You have asked me to consider whether (1) Japanese moved from Hawaii to the United States could be placed in a delimited zone in which martial law could be declared; (2) martial law could be declared with respect to a group of Japanese.

I

Those Japanese who are aliens can be brought to the continental United States and interned under the provisions of 50 U.S.C. § 21 (1940). This statute, however, is probably not applicable to the Japanese who are citizens.

II

Although not free from doubt, an argument can be made for removing Japanese who are American citizens from Hawaii to a restricted zone in the United States.

* * * * *

This is total war. It is quite unlike any prior war. Fifth column activities, espionage, and sabotage have been and are being employed on an unprecedented scale. What the Nazis did in Norway, Holland, Belgium, and France—to mention but a few places—through citizens of those places as well as through German nationals is now well known. The

Japanese have used similar techniques. Axis agents—American citizens as well as non-citizens—participated in making the Japanese attack on Pearl Harbor so successful to the Japanese.

As a result of the Japanese attack, Hawaii has been put under martial law. Military necessity dictated that move—a move well justified under the legal authorities. *Ex parte Milligan*, 71 U.S. (4 Wall.) 2 (1866); *United States v. Diekelman*, 92 U.S. 520, 526 (1875). Hawaii is still within the Pacific theatre of war and subject to attack again. Continuance of martial law in Hawaii is doubtless justified. If military necessity dictates it—as it well may—those Japanese who were interned in Hawaii or those whose presence is dangerous can be removed. To hold otherwise would be deciding upon the impractical. Hawaii is virtually an armed fortress. All of the energies of the armed forces there should doubtless be concentrated on resisting or striking the enemy. If, because of the military needs, the forces cannot be spared to guard or watch the Japanese in Hawaii, they can be removed.

The strongest legal ground upon which to make the removal would be under an order of the military commander in Hawaii to a restricted area—a military area or military zone—designated by the Secretary of War under Public Law 77-503, 56 Stat. 173 (1942), *codified at* 18 U.S.C. § 97a (Supp. II 1942).

If this is done, it would not be necessary to declare martial law with respect to these Japanese as a group. A declaration of martial law as to a group is of doubtful legal validity except possibly under unusual circumstances. The circumstances here involved might be such. But I would be inclined not to rely on this method of handling the problem.

III

The existing case law indicates some doubt on the power to remove and intern the Japanese citizens in the United States. But the conditions of modern warfare are different from those of prior wars. Because of this the courts might well follow a different course than that indicated by the earlier decisions. *Ex parte Ventura*, 44 F. Supp. 520 (W.D. Wash. 1942).

If the majority opinion in *Ex parte Milligan* should be followed today, a declaration of martial law outside the zone of active military operations at a place where the courts are functioning would probably not be approved by the Supreme Court. It is believed, however, that, in view of the changed conditions of warfare, the Supreme Court, in a proper case, would follow the views of the dissenting justices in the *Milligan* case sustaining a declaration of martial law in places outside the zone of active military operations upon a showing of military necessity for such action. Martial law, however, is ordinarily made applicable to districts or areas and when established applies to all persons within the district or area so long as they remain therein. There appear to be no precedents sustaining a declaration of martial law with respect only to a particular group of persons as suggested in your question numbered 2. From the nature and purpose of martial law, it would seem to be properly applicable to particular areas rather than to particular persons.

The establishment of martial law in a delimited zone for the sole purpose of confining therein a particular citizen or group of citizens would also raise questions of policy and public morals. If this can be done with respect to the Japanese here involved, it might be done at any time with respect to any citizen. Thus, it would approach the practices of the German and Italian governments, so bitterly denounced in this country, of establishing citizen concentration camps in which citizens may be confined without due process of law.

There is considerable authority for the position that military necessity for the establishment of martial law is a political question into which the courts will not inquire. There is, however, authority on the other side of this question, and in the comparatively recent case of *Sterling v. Constantin*, 287 U.S. 378 (1932), the Court inquired into this question and determined that military necessity did not exist. That case may be distinguishable since it involved a question of conflict between state and federal jurisdiction. There is sufficient language to indicate, however, that the Court would have the right to and would inquire into the necessity for declaring martial law if the occasion arose. A declaration of martial law in a delimited zone for the sole purpose of confining therein objectionable citizens might not be a good case in which to have this question directly passed upon by the Court.

The desired result might be obtained by a suspension of the privilege of the writ of habeas corpus as to the Japanese citizens involved. There is precedent for the suspension of the privilege of the writ as to particular persons. See 6 *A Compilation of the Messages and Papers of the Presidents (1789–1908)* 19 (James D. Richardson ed., 1909). This, however, raises the same question of policy and public morals above discussed. If the privilege of the writ can be suspended as to Japanese citizens, it can likewise be suspended as to other citizens at any time. Also, if the suspension should be made by the President, it would reopen the age-old question of whether the President has the authority to suspend or whether that right lies in the Congress alone. I think the President has the power, but whether the controversy over this subject should be again precipitated at this time is a question which should be carefully considered.

IV

1 If it is at all practical to do so, the safest legal procedure would be to hold the Japanese who are American citizens in Hawaii.

2 The next best legal procedure would be, under the martial law prevailing in Hawaii or under an order pursuant to Public Law 77-503, to intern them in Hawaii and then give them the option to come to the United States if they sign up as members of the work corps of the War Relocation Authority under an agreement to serve for the duration of the war.

3 It would also be proper to evacuate the Japanese citizens from Hawaii under Executive Order 9066 and Public Law 77-503 and then treat them the same as the Japanese evacuated from the West Coast.

4 If it is not necessary for these Japanese to be kept in strict confinement it may be that, in view of the large industrial plants along the East Coast and in many cities extending westward to the Mississippi, military areas might be declared along the entire East Coast and extending inward some distance, thus requiring the Japanese,

under Public Law 77-503, to reside in the Middlewest, where they would probably have less opportunity to engage in activities dangerous to the national safety.

5 It is possible that the Japanese citizens legally could be removed from Hawaii and interned in the United States.

Discussion questions

1. In what ways does traditional legal rhetoric dictate the facts and law relevant to resolving the question presented/issue in the memo? Be specific in naming the role of White cultural hegemony in shaping the analytic framework and scope of relevant facts.
2. Is the drafter's use of traditional legal rhetoric effective? If so, for what purpose?
3. Does the drafter's use of traditional legal rhetoric lead to a just result? Explain your answer.
4. Pick a section or sections of this memo to rewrite using relevant cultural rhetorical strategies. For this part of the exercise, you may need to consult additional sources to better contextualize the dispute (such as law review articles, scholarly articles from non-legal disciplines, books from legal and non-legal disciplines, additional case law, legislative histories, and so on).
5. In what way do the strategies you employ change the facts and law relevant to resolving the question presented/issue in the memo? Be specific and name the cultural tradition and the strategy.

The Trial Brief

Rogers v. Virginia State Registrar, Plaintiff's Memorandum in support of Motion for Temporary Restraining Order or Preliminary Injunction, United States District Court, Eastern District of Virginia, September 5, 2019

(All footnotes have been omitted.)

This case concerns the requirement that parties seeking to be married in the state of Virginia declare their race when applying for a marriage license. Two of the Plaintiffs, Sophie Rogers and Brandyn Churchill, requested a temporary restraining order, as the date for their wedding had already been set. They, along with the other four plaintiffs, objected to this requirement as a holdover of the Racial Integrity Act of 1924 and the anti-miscegenation law litigated in *Loving v. Virginia*, 388 U.S. 1 (1967).

Table 7.3: A rhetorical comparison grid for The Trial Brief

Trial Brief	Multicultural rhetorical strategies
Notice of Motion or Cover Sheet: Gives notice of the filing of the motion (Notice of Motion) and of the response to the motion (Cover Sheet)	African Diasporic rhetoric • Rhetoric as the rules or principles for eloquent and effective communication
Certificate of Service: Certifies that a copy of the brief has been filed with the appropriate court and sent to the parties to the lawsuit	African Diasporic rhetoric • Rhetoric as the rules or principles for eloquent and effective communication
Table of Contents: Provides the reader with an overview of the arguments contained in the brief as communicated through persuasively written subject headings (point headings)	Indigenous rhetoric • Rhetorical sovereignty • Survivance African Diasporic rhetoric • Kawaida (agency and liberation; expansive transformation) • Rhetoric as eloquent and effective communication • Maat Asian Diasporic rhetoric • Discourse of persuasion/persuasion strategies (*jian, ming*) • Language as a symbolic resource • "Because therefore" "frame-main" reasoning (reasons and assertions) • Problem-solution structure (initiation act, articulation of the current problem) Latine rhetoric • *Conocimiento* • Epistemic delinking • Binary disruption
Table of Authorities: Communicates the type and weight of authority that the brief writer uses to support the arguments in the brief	Indigenous rhetoric • Rhetorical sovereignty • Survivance African Diasporic rhetoric • Kawaida (agency and liberation; expansive transformation) • Rhetoric as eloquent and effective communication • Maat Asian Diasporic rhetoric • Discourse of persuasion/persuasion strategies (*jian, ming*)

(continued)

Table 7.3: A rhetorical comparison grid for The Trial Brief (continued)

Trial Brief	Multicultural rhetorical strategies
	Latine rhetoric • *Conocimiento* • Epistemic delinking • Binary disruption
Legal Standard/Motion Standard of Review: The legal criteria by which a court can grant or deny various types of motions brought before or during a trial (motion for summary judgment, motion to suppress, motion to dismiss, motion *in limine*, and so on)	Indigenous rhetoric • Rhetorical sovereignty • Survivance African Diasporic rhetoric • Kawaida (expansive transformation) • Rhetoric as eloquent and effective communication • Rhetoric as the rules or principles for eloquent and effective communication • Maat (truth, propriety, harmony, balance) Asian Diasporic rhetoric • Discourse of persuasion/persuasion strategies (*ci*, *jian*, *ming*) Latine rhetoric • *Conocimiento* • Epistemic delinking
Introduction: Introduces the reader to the theory of the case (the theme or main idea of the brief) through a summary of the attorney's best arguments in the brief	Indigenous rhetoric • Survivance African Diasporic rhetoric • Rhetoric as eloquent and effective communication • Kawaida • Maat (truth, propriety) Asian Diasporic rhetoric • Discourse of persuasion/persuasion strategies (*ming*) Latine rhetoric • Epistemic delinking • Binary disruption
Statement of Facts: Communicates the salient facts of the client's case in a manner most favorable to the client	Indigenous rhetoric • Rhetorical sovereignty • Survivance African Diasporic rhetoric • Kawaida (agency and liberation) • Rhetoric as eloquent and effective speech • Maat (truth, propriety, harmony, balance)

Table 7.3: A rhetorical comparison grid for The Trial Brief (continued)

Trial Brief	Multicultural rhetorical strategies
	Asian Diasporic rhetoric • Discourse of persuasion/persuasion strategies (*ci, jian*) • Language as a symbolic resource Latine rhetoric • Epistemic delinking • Binary disruption
Argument: Communicates the analysis of the client's case through a careful explanation of the standards used to resolve the dispute and an application of that standard to the facts of the case, law, or legal doctrine	Indigenous rhetoric • Rhetorical sovereignty • Survivance African Diasporic rhetoric • Kawaida • Rhetoric as eloquent and effective communication • Rhetoric as the rules or principles for eloquent and effective communication • Maat Asian Diasporic rhetoric • Discourse of persuasion/persuasion strategies (*ci, jian, ming, bian*) • Language as a symbolic resource • "Because therefore" "frame-main" reasoning • Problem-solution structure Latine rhetoric • *Conocimiento* • Epistemic delinking • Binary disruption
Conclusion/Prayer for Relief: Formal request for the preferred outcome of the case made to the legal decisionmaker	Indigenous rhetoric • Rhetorical sovereignty • Survivance African Diasporic rhetoric • Kawaida (agency and liberation; expansive transformation) • Rhetoric as the rules or principles for eloquent and effective communication • Maat (justice) Asian Diasporic rhetoric • Discourse of persuasion/persuasion strategies (*ci, jian, ming*) Latine rhetoric • *Conocimiento* • Epistemic delinking • Binary disruption

***

Plaintiffs Sophie Rogers and Brandyn Churchill have moved this court for a temporary restraining order ("TRO") or a preliminary injunction. For the following reasons this motion should be granted.

Procedural note

While each of the six plaintiffs wish to get married in Virginia, it is only Ms. Rogers and Mr. Churchill whose wedding is already set—for October 19, 2019, in Fincastle, Virginia. Because the other plaintiffs are not facing such a short deadline, they do not have occasion to request temporary or preliminary relief and thus are not moving parties on this motion. Ms. Rogers and Mr. Churchill having only recently joined this legal effort, the undersigned counsel has proceeded as promptly as possible to complete the work required for the proper presentation of the case and this motion, in time to give fair notice thereof to the defendants should they determine to defend the case. While, in an abundance of caution, counsel has styled this motion as one for a TRO or a preliminary injunction, as a practical matter it seems properly considered as a motion for preliminary injunction, as four weeks' notice is being given to defendants of the date at which the motion is being set for a hearing. The motion is thus being briefed as one for an injunction rather than an *ex parte* TRO.

For ease of reference, in this motion Ms. Rogers and Mr. Churchill will be referred to as "plaintiffs."

Introduction

This lawsuit challenges what may be the last vestige of *de jure* Jim Crow in Virginia: the requirement, set forth in Va. Code Ann. § 32.1-267(A) that parties wishing to marry identify themselves by race as a condition of obtaining a marriage license in Virginia. Virginia joins seven other states in imposing this requirement on those wishing to marry. To avoid this offensive and impermissible burden, plaintiffs ask this court to order that their marriage license application be processed without their having to affix racial labels to themselves, so that they might get married as planned within a few weeks following the scheduled hearing on this motion.

Standard for issuing a Preliminary Injunction

"A plaintiff seeking a preliminary injunction must establish that he is likely to succeed on the merits, that he is likely to suffer irreparable harm in the absence of preliminary relief, that the balance of equities tips in his favor, and that an injunction is in the public interest." *Winter v. Natural Resources Defense Council, Inc.*, 555 U.S. 7, 20 (2008). Each of these factors weighs in the plaintiffs' favor in each of their constitutional claims.

I. Likelihood of success on the merits

Plaintiffs have brought several constitutional challenges to the requirement that they label themselves racially in order to exercise their right to marry. Their likelihood of success on each is substantial.

A. The right to marry is fundamental and can be infringed only for compelling reasons

"The right to marry is fundamental as a matter of history and tradition." *Obergefell v. Hodges*, 135 S. Ct. 2584, 2602 (2015); *Zablocki v. Redhail*, 434 U.S. 374 (1978) ("decisions of this Court confirm that the right to marry is of fundamental importance for all individuals"). See *Griswold v. Connecticut*, 381 U.S. 479 (1965) (right to marry is part of the fundamental right of privacy implicit in the Fourteenth Amendment's Due Process Clause). As the Supreme Court observed unanimously in a decision serving as an appropriate backdrop to the instant case: "The freedom to marry has long been recognized as one of the vital personal rights essential to the orderly pursuit of happiness by free men." *Loving v. Va.*, 388 U.S. 1, 12 (1967).

Statutes that impinge upon fundamental rights are subject to critical examination by the courts and must be justified by compelling state interests. See, *Obergefell*, 135 S. Ct. at 2616 (Roberts, C.J., dissenting) (right to marry is "so rooted in the traditions and conscience of our people as to be ranked as fundamental, and therefore cannot be deprived without compelling justification"); *Zablocki*, 434 U.S. at 383 ("the right to marry is of fundamental importance, and since the classification at issue here significantly interferes with the exercise of that right, we believe that 'critical examination' of the state interests advanced in support of the classification is required").

B. Plaintiffs have presented a compelling case establishing the discriminatory history and functional disutility of the race question on the marriage application, and its resulting unconstitutionality

The complaint, supported by nineteen exhibits as well as declarations from three historians, two prominent human geneticists, and a former director of the United States Census Bureau, lays out in detail the sorry history of Va. Code Ann. § 32.1-267(A), as well as its functional disutility. Given the expansive presentation of demonstrably supported facts in the complaint, rather than revisiting them in the instant memorandum, counsel respectfully refers the court and the defense to the complaint, the supporting documentary evidence, and the declarations under penalty of perjury made by plaintiffs' experts. Plaintiffs respectfully submit that this body of evidence well justifies the introductory paragraph of the complaint:

> In this lawsuit for declaratory and injunctive relief, plaintiffs ask this court to declare unconstitutional and enjoin defendants' enforcement of Va. Code Ann.

> § 32.1-267(A), requiring that persons seeking a license to marry, under threat of prosecution for perjury, label themselves according to "race," using unscientific, highly controversial, misleading, useless, and tainted categories reflecting Virginia's historical repression of non-white persons. Virginia is one of eight states that impose this requirement by statute. In Virginia, the requirement reflects a regulatory scheme embodied in the Virginia Racial Integrity Act of 1924, originally called "An Act to Preserve the Integrity of the White Race." The requirement to identify by "race" uses terms grounded in ignorance and bigotry, not in science. The statutory scheme is implemented by the clerks of the circuit courts of Virginia as they see fit, using inappropriate categories duly made available by the Virginia Department of Health and Human Resources, and other, more offensive, categories as well. Fifty-two years after the Supreme Court struck down laws preventing the marriage of white and non-white persons, the Commonwealth of Virginia continues to require its residents, including plaintiffs, affirmatively to label themselves, against their will, according to categories rooted in a malignant statutory scheme working to the detriment of non-white persons.

In the face of the history and practical operation of the statute in question, its interference with the right to marry cannot survive the heightened scrutiny that a challenge like this requires. The statute breathes the very racial bias giving rise to *Loving v. Virginia*. It should be struck down as possibly the last remaining *de jure* vestige of that shameful legislative preoccupation. It is in equal measures astounding and appalling to have to contend with state action in 2019 requiring, or permitting, individuals to label themselves as "Octoroon," "Quadroon," "Mulatto," "Aryan," or "White American" as a condition of exercising their right to marry. See Exh. 2 to the complaint.

Nor can the statute be defended on grounds not associated with its unseemly origins. As is clear from the verified averments in the complaint and the various exhibits thereto, particularly exhibits 1, 2, and 12–19, as well as from the Declaration of Kenneth Prewitt, former Director of the United States Census Bureau, from any practical standpoint the requirement to assign oneself a race fails to generate information that might be—or has been—put to use. Simply a comparison of the divergent racial categories designated by numerous Northern Virginia jurisdictions (Exhibits 1, 17, and 18), the 230 racial classifications designated by Rockbridge County (Exhibit 2), and a comparison of all the above with the "black, white and other" statistics published by the Commonwealth's Division of Vital Statistics (Exhibit 19), yields the ready conclusion that nothing of consequence is emerging from Virginia's racial inquiry on its marriage license applications. The declarations of two prominent human geneticists (Marcus Feldman and Sarah Tishkoff) reach the same conclusion from a scientific standpoint, although it is not apparent that such in-depth scrutiny need even be made here, where there is no pretense of scientific use of the collected data. And for good reason, as the federal Office of Management and Budget—the font of current racial classification in the United States—cautioned, for a second time, in 1997, that its own racial categories "should not be interpreted as being scientific or anthropological in nature," having "no scientific basis for legitimacy." Compl. 63–64. This is presumably why Virginia is in the small minority of states with statutory requirements of this sort—a total of eight—and why the National Conference of Commissioners on Uniform State Laws did not include such an inquiry in its Model (formerly Uniform) Marriage and Divorce Act.

The view that racial classifications and separation were necessary governmental objectives did not die easily in Virginia. As late as 1955, Virginia's Supreme Court reaffirmed that laws banning marriage between blacks and whites were required in order that the Commonwealth not end up with "a mongrel breed of citizens." Comp. ¶26.) And it took the United States Supreme Court to repudiate, in 1967, a ruling affirmed by the Virginia Supreme Court to the effect that "Almighty God created the races white, black, yellow, malay and red, and placed them on separate continents. ... The fact that he separated the races shows that he did not intend for them to mix." (Quoted in *Loving v. Virginia*, *supra*, 388 U.S. at 3 (reversing 206 Va. 924 (1966)).

The racial classifications here at issue drag us back to this bygone era. They exemplify the racist underpinning of laws requiring racial identification relative to all walks of life, including but hardly limited to marriage, whether in the form of § 32.1-267(A) or its predecessors and cognates in the days of Jim Crow. Section 32.1-267 cannot be separated from its unconstitutional origins, nor can it be shown to serve any useful purpose sufficient to justify its maintenance in 2013. We do not need the state requesting and receiving the identification of races of "Octoroons," "Quadroons," "Mulattoes," "Aryans," or "White Americans" in 2019. Given the demise of Virginia's miscegenation laws, the statute here at issue cannot be justified.

1. The requirement of mandatory racial identification denies plaintiffs substantive due process of law

Virginia requires persons who wish to marry to label themselves by racial categories that are redolent of racism and serve no articulable—to say nothing of compelling—governmental purpose. Given especially the long-established fundamental right to marry, this requirement is flatly unconstitutional. *Obergefell, Zablocki, Griswold, supra* at 3. "The freedom to marry has long been recognized as one of the vital personal rights essential to the orderly pursuit of happiness by free men." *Loving*, 388 U.S. at 12 (famously addressing the unconstitutionality of prohibitions effectuated by means of racial identification). Under settled law, plaintiffs have a strong likelihood of succeeding on the merits of their substantive due process claim brought under the Fourteenth Amendment.

2. The requirement of mandatory racial identification violates plaintiffs' right to freedom of speech

The First Amendment protects an individual's "right to speak freely and the right to refrain from speaking at all." *Wooley v. Maynard*, 430 U.S. 705, 714 (1977). The government may not compel individuals to partake in affirmative acts that constitute speech utterances. See *Agency for Int'l Dev. v. All. for Open Soc'y Int'l, Inc.*, 570 U.S. 205, 209–10, 221 (2013); *Wooley v. Maynard*, 430 U.S. 705, 715–16 (1977); *West Virginia State Bd. of Educ. v. Barnette*, 319 U.S. 624, 640–42 (1943). Government regulations that compel speech are subject to heightened scrutiny. *Wooley*, 430 U.S. at 716–17.

Va. Code Ann. § 32.1-267 is a compelled speech statute. It requires individuals affirmatively to label themselves racially as a pre-requisite for exercising their constitutionally protected right to marry. This compulsion is constitutionally impermissible both because of its malignant origins and past uses, and because the categories, including (beyond the absurd ones provided by the Rockbridge Circuit Court), "mixed" and "other," can and do provide no data on the basis of which policy makers, social scientists or medical researchers can rely for any useful purpose. See, the declarations of Kenneth Prewitt, Marcus Feldman and Sarah Tishkoff submitted herewith. The child of Chinese and Bolivian parents can end up—and probably would end up—in the same catch-all category as the child of Nigerian and Eskimo parents. And since anyone can claim to be "mixed" or "other," persons who might qualify as "Aryan" or "White Americans" pursuant to such Rockbridge County's categories could join as well. What useful policies can arise out of such "data"?

According to the State Registrar, the Vital Records Division provides only the number of Virginia marriages to the National Center for Health Statistics, not any racial data. It appears that no study has been conducted by the Virginia Department of Health regarding the racial data collected from Virginia marriage records. Nor has this racial data been the subject of data sharing requests directed to the Division by third parties. There is no evidence of racial information presented on marriage license applications being used to offer any benefits or protections to any marriage applicant or any other person or group, or otherwise to serve any useful governmental function, to say nothing of a compelling one. The requirement of stating one's race on a marriage application emerges as no more than a retrograde repetition of the provisions of Virginia's 1924 Racial Integrity Act.

Beyond the general proscription on compelling speech absent a compelling government need for same, the state is barred from compelling the dissemination of information that is factually disputed, controversial, or a matter of opinion. See, *Zauderer v. Office of Disciplinary Counsel of Supreme Court of Ohio*, 471 U.S. 626, 651 (1985); *Kimberly-Clark Corp. v. D.C.*, 286 F. Supp. 3d 128, 143 (D.D.C. 2017). The state simply "may not compel affirmance of a belief with which the speaker disagrees." *Harley v. Irish-American Gay, Lesbian & Bisexual Group of Boston, Inc.*, 515 U.S. 557, 573 (1995).

In the matter at hand, apart from the multiplicity of racial definitions purporting to effectuate Va. Code Ann. § 32.1-267(A), authorities from every sphere have noted the uncertain, capricious and unreliable nature of the racial divisions nevertheless employed. Thus:

* With regard to the 1790 restriction of naturalization to "white persons," a restriction charitably characterized as being "most uncertain, ambiguous, and difficult both of

construction and application. ... There have been a number of decisions in which the question has been treated, and the conclusions arrived at in them are as unsatisfactory as they are varying." *Ex Parte Shahid*, 205 F. 812, 813 (E.D.S.C. 1913) (Syrian not white, notwithstanding that "such a construction would exclude persons coming from the very cradle of the Jewish and Christian religions as professed by the nations of Europe whose descendants form the great bulk of citizens of the United States." *Id.* at 816).

* " '[T]he innumerable varieties of mankind run into one another by insensible degrees,' and to arrange them in sharply bounded divisions is an undertaking of such uncertainty that common agreement is practically impossible." *United States v. Thind*, 261 U.S. 204, 211 (1923). See, in this connection, the photographs of Angelica Dass portraying the shades and hues of humanity blending into one another (Exhibit 10), and the photographs of the Biggs Twins, fraternal twins, one black and one white. Complaint ¶43 and Exhibit 11.
* The Office of Management and Budget ("OMB"), whose Directive No. 15 is the template of conventional racial classification in the United States, cautioned at the outset that "These classifications should not be interpreted as being scientific or anthropological in nature, nor should they be viewed as determinants of eligibility for participation in any Federal program." Complaint ¶¶ 53–55, Exhibit 13.
* The National Academy of Sciences elaborated on the problems with Dir. No. 15:

> [T]he current classification ... lacks a consistent logic. Some of the categories are racial, some are geographic, some are cultural. ... The categories now represent a combination of historical, legal, and sociological factors, but that is not explicitly acknowledged. Much of the difficulty in the creation of a consistent, rational classification system lies in the fluid nature of what race and ethnicity are. Race and ethnicity are inherently complex concepts, with multiple sources of definition. There is no scientific basis for the legitimacy of race or ethnicity as taxonomic categories.

* OMB did nothing to fix the identified problems, but it did subsequently restate its caution: "The categories represent a social-political construct designed for collecting data on the race and ethnicity of broad population groups in this country, and are not anthropologically or scientifically based." Exhibit 15 at 3.

It is thus no surprise that Virginia finds itself among a handful of states with statutory mandates for racial identification on marriage license applications, and that the authors of the Model Marriage & Divorce Act included no such provision. See complaint at ¶50.

Given that even the propounders and defenders, or effectuators, of conventional racial classification are in accord that the scheme is inexact, not scientifically based, and fluid—increasingly so as social norms change and increasing numbers of younger persons are partnering with persons from "other" groups—and without regard to the riot of classifications that is available solely in Virginia, it is even more constitutionally suspect for the state to require racial identification according to pre-existing, unstable and sometimes absurd categories, thereby compelling dissemination of information that is factually disputed, controversial, or a matter of opinion. Plaintiffs enjoy a substantial likelihood of prevailing on their First Amendment claim.

3. Code of Va. Ann. § 32.1-267(A) violates plaintiffs' right to privacy

By statute, all the data to be provided on a marriage license application, including the racial identification, is deemed material. An applicant swears to the responses and may be prosecuted for perjury, as a felony, for providing false information, and if convicted be adjudged "forever incapable of holding any office of honor, profit or trust under the Constitution of Virginia, or of serving as a juror." Va. Code Ann. § 18.2-434. As a result, persons who, for private reasons, may not wish to reveal their racial or ethnic heritage and provide an inaccurate answer are at risk of being convicted of a felony if found out. Doubtless, the situation is not dire, as it was when, in 1937, Walter Plecker wrote as follows to the Botetourt County Circuit Court clerk after having been advised by an "informant" of a wedding between one Mohler and one Branham:

> This family of Mohlers ... belongs to the class of respectable white people. ... These Branhams ... are unquestionably mixed bloods, negroid in every appearance, speech and behavior. ... [T]hese mixed breeds ... go around to other counties where they are not known and in their [marriage license] applications swear that they are white. These people are usually well known in their own counties and their clerks will not issue licenses for them to marry white people. ... We are sending a copy of this letter to the Commonwealth's Attorney.

Exhibit 6. Regardless of the unlikelihood of criminal prosecution as a practical matter, issues of personal pride, family heritage, and the need for candor with one's spouse-to-be are matters properly left to the discretion of the person at issue, and not forced upon such person by the state. The state has no business requiring an individual to make revelations about his or her ancestry as a condition of getting married. To do so is an unwarranted invasion of privacy. The First Amendment affords protection to an individual's identity, and the United States Supreme Court has routinely struck down laws that require exposing aspects of one's identity as a pre-requisite for engaging in speech. See *Watchtower Bible & Tract Soc'y of New York v. Vill. of Stratton*, 536 U.S. 150, 165–8 (2002); *Buckley v. Am. Constitutional Law Found., Inc.*, 525 U.S. 182, 199–200 (1999); *McIntyre v. Ohio Elections Comm'n*, 514 U.S. 334, 347, 353 (1995).

On each of their constitutional claims, then, plaintiffs are likely to prevail on the merits.

II Ms. Rogers and Mr. Churchill will suffer irreparable harm absent preliminary relief

Ms. Rogers and Mr. Churchill are getting married on October 19, 2019, two weeks following the hearing date for the instant motion. This date was set long before they became aware of what was at issue relative to their marriage license application and determined to join this lawsuit. They will be getting married whether or not they receive the requested relief. The question at bar is whether this court should support Virginia's right to condition their getting married on abiding by the state's requirement that they label themselves, against their will, according to racial terms with a malign past and a useless present as regards marriage license applications.

For all the reasons set forth above, Ms. Rogers and Mr. Churchill have a constitutional right not to label themselves racially against their will, even pursuant to their local circuit court's absurd itemization of 230 available racial identities. They have a substantive due process right not to have their constitutionally protected right to marry burdened by subscribing to Virginia's scheme that smacks of the era of Jim Crow even as it confers no benefit on anyone. They have a First Amendment right not to be compelled to engage in unwanted speech, and particularly when no compelling purpose can be stated for the compulsion, and the speech at issue is a matter of doubt, conjecture and opinion. And they can invoke a right to keep private details of their personal ancestry that the state has no business demanding them to publicize as a condition of getting married.

It has repeatedly been recognized by the federal courts at all levels that violation of constitutional rights constitutes irreparable harm as a matter of law. *Elrod v. Burns*, 427 U.S. 347, 373–374 (1976); *Ross v. Meese*, 818 F.2d 1132, 1135 (4 Cir.1987); *Deerfield Medical Center v. City of Deerfield Beach*, 661 F.2d 328, 338 (5th Cir.1981); *Milwaukee County Pavers Assn. v. Fiedler*, 707 F. Supp. 1016, 1031–1032 (W.D. Wis.1989); *Albro v. County of Onondaga, New York*, 627 F. Supp. 1280, 1287 (ND N.Y.1986); *Walters v. Thompson*, 615 F. Supp. 330, 341 (N.D. Ill 1985); *Cohen v. Coahoma Cty., Miss.*, 805 F. Supp. 398, 406 (N.D. Miss. 1992). Wright & Miller summarize the law in their treatise: "When an alleged deprivation of a constitutional right is involved, such as the right to free speech or freedom of religion, most courts hold that no further showing of irreparable injury is necessary." 11A Wright & Miller, *Federal Practice and Procedure* 11A (3d ed.). It is clear, then, that plaintiffs Rogers and Churchill will suffer irreparable harm if they do not receive the preliminary relief for which they here apply.

III The balance of equities favors the plaintiffs

Ms. Rogers' and Mr. Churchill's substantial interest in receiving the relief they request is clear from the complaint. What, then, is the harm that befalls the Commonwealth if these two can marry without having labeled themselves with unscientific names of malignant origin which as a practical matter cannot be shown to serve any useful purpose?

No interest of the Commonwealth is harmed if the requested relief is forthcoming. The current racial classification system provides no meaningful or useful data to the state, nor has the state used this to any useful purpose. As exemplified by the racial categories embraced by the circuits at issue in this case, there is no uniformity among Virginia's judicial circuits for racial terminology. Beyond that, the catch-all "other" or "mixed" categories, in particular, provide meaningless data that is useless for genetic, medical, or scientific purposes. See, declarations of Prewitt, Tishkoff and Feldman.

The preliminary relief here at issue, while a great boon to the plaintiffs, thus yields no cognizable harm to the Commonwealth. Much to the contrary, "a state is in no way harmed by issuance of a preliminary injunction which prevents the state from enforcing restrictions likely to be found unconstitutional. If anything, the system is improved by such injunction." *Centro Tepeyac v. Montgomery County*, 722 F.3d 184, 191 (4th Cir. 2013). The equities of the matter lie clearly with Ms. Rogers and Mr. Churchill.

IV Preliminary relief is in the public interest

Courts have repeatedly recognized that "upholding constitutional rights surely serves the public interest." *Giovani Carandola, Ltd. v. Bason*, 303 F.3d 507, 521 (4th Cir. 2002); see also *Chabad of Southern Ohio v. City of Cincinnati*, 363 F.3d 427, 436 (6th Cir. 2004) ("[T]he public interest is served by preventing the violation of constitutional rights."); *Christian Legal Society v. Walker*, 453, F.3d 853, 859 (7th Cir. 2006) ("[I]njunctions protecting First Amendment freedoms are always in the public interest."). These strictures apply here word for word, and support the relief plaintiffs request.

Conclusion

For these reasons, the court should issue a temporary restraining order or preliminary injunction enjoining the defendants from enforcing the provision Va. Code Ann. § 32.1-267(A) as to them, thereby permitting them to obtain a timely marriage license without having to label themselves by race.

Discussion questions

1. In what ways do the arguments in this brief demonstrate the "lock-in" phenomenon (the law as self-validation) discussed in Chapter 2, with respect to the function of *United States v. Bhagat Singh Thind* (discussed in Chapter 5)?
2. In what ways do the arguments in this brief demonstrate the "lock-in" phenomenon (the law as self-validation) discussed in Chapter 2, with respect to the function of

the Racial Integrity Act of 1924 and the anti-miscegenation law litigated in *Loving v. Virginia* (discussed in Chapters 1 and 6)? In what ways does the Racial Integrity Act of 1924 function as major premise in the syllogism?
3. What assumptions about racial categories do the plaintiffs seek to uncover in their brief? Are they effective at doing so within the constraints of traditional legal rhetoric? Explain your answer.
4. Do the causes of action through which the plaintiffs are forced to argue their dispute (Substantive Due Process, Freedom of Speech, and so on) aid them in uncovering the racist underpinnings of Va. Code Ann. § 32.1-267(A)? Be specific in your answer. In what ways do the causes of action aid their efforts? In what ways do the causes of action hinder their efforts?
5. In what ways could the plaintiffs' advocates have used any of the multicultural rhetorical strategies to reveal how the law perpetuates White cultural hegemony in regulating marriage? Be specific and name the cultural tradition, the strategy, and the part(s) of the genre where they would be best utilized.
6. Pick a section or sections of this brief to rewrite using relevant cultural rhetorical strategies. For this part of the exercise, you may need to consult additional sources to better contextualize the dispute (such as law review articles, scholarly articles from non-legal disciplines, books from legal and non-legal disciplines, additional case law, legislative histories, and so on), including looking up the sources referenced in the brief.

The Appellate Brief

Juliana v. United States of America, Appellants' Reply Brief, On Appeal from the United States District Court for the District of Oregon to the United States Court of Appeals, Ninth Circuit, March 8, 2019

This case was brought by a group of young adults (minors) against the United States Government and its officials for policies and practices that support fossil fuel-based energy to the detriment of the environment. The plaintiffs sought to redress harms to themselves and future generations as a result of damage to the environment pursuant to the Fifth Amendment substantive Due Process rights granted to them by the United States Constitution.

(All footnotes have been omitted.)

Introduction

As explained in our opening brief, Plaintiffs have not satisfied the three prerequisites for Article III standing, nor have they brought a cognizable case or controversy. And Plaintiffs

Table 7.4: A rhetorical comparison grid for The Appellate Brief

Appellate Brief	Multicultural rhetorical strategies
Cover Page: Identifies for the reader the court where the case originated, the name of the reviewing court (where the case will be heard), the case caption, docket number, type of document filed, and the name(s) of counsel of record. Content varies dependent on the jurisdiction of the reviewing court	<u>African Diasporic rhetoric</u> • Rhetoric as the rules or principles for eloquent and effective communication
Table of Contents: Provides the reader with an overview of the arguments contained in the brief as communicated through persuasively written subject headings (point headings)	<u>Indigenous rhetoric</u> • Rhetorical sovereignty • Survivance <u>African Diasporic rhetoric</u> • Kawaida (agency and liberation; expansive transformation) • Rhetoric as eloquent and effective communication • Maat <u>Asian Diasporic rhetoric</u> • Discourse of persuasion/persuasion strategies (*jian, ming*) • Language as a symbolic resource • "Because therefore" "frame-main" reasoning (reasons and assertions) • Problem-solution structure (initiation act, articulation of the current problem) <u>Latine rhetoric</u> • *Conocimiento* • Epistemic delinking • Binary disruption
Table of Authorities: Communicates the type and weight of authority that the brief writer uses to support the arguments in the brief	<u>Indigenous rhetoric</u> • Rhetorical sovereignty • Survivance <u>African Diasporic rhetoric</u> • Kawaida (agency and liberation; expansive transformation) • Rhetoric as eloquent and effective communication • Maat <u>Asian Diasporic rhetoric</u> • Discourse of persuasion/persuasion strategies (*jian, ming*)

Table 7.4: A rhetorical comparison grid for The Appellate Brief (continued)

Appellate Brief	Multicultural rhetorical strategies
	Latine rhetoric • *Conocimiento* • Epistemic delinking • Binary disruption
Statement of the Case: Communicates the judicial history of the case to the reader	Indigenous rhetoric • Rhetorical sovereignty • Survivance African Diasporic rhetoric • Rhetoric as the rules or principles for eloquent and effective communication • Maat (truth, propriety) Asian Diasporic rhetoric • Discourse of persuasion/persuasion strategies (*ming*) Latine rhetoric • Epistemic delinking • Binary disruption
Summary of the Argument: Introduces the reader to the theory of the case (the theme or main idea of the brief) through a summary of the attorney's best arguments in the brief	Indigenous rhetoric • Survivance African Diasporic rhetoric • Rhetoric as eloquent and effective communication • Kawaida • Maat (truth, propriety) Asian Diasporic rhetoric • Discourse of persuasion/persuasion strategies (*ming*) Latine rhetoric • Epistemic delinking • Binary disruption
Questions Presented/Statement of the Issues: States the issue(s) on appeal from the client's perspective; states the matter before the court (a characterization of what the lower court did or did not do correctly, or the particular legal question that you wish the court to resolve); states the governing law (locates the court as to the governing authority); and states the facts that are necessary for the court to review and adjudicate the legal question before it and/or the alleged error	Indigenous rhetoric • Rhetorical sovereignty (culturally informed issue-framing) • Survivance African Diasporic rhetoric • Kawaida (agency and liberation; expansive transformation) • Rhetoric as the rules or principles for eloquent and effective communication • Maat (truth, propriety, harmony, balance, reciprocity, and order)

(continued)

Table 7.4: A rhetorical comparison grid for The Appellate Brief (continued)

Appellate Brief	Multicultural rhetorical strategies
	Asian Diasporic rhetoric • Discourse of persuasion/persuasion strategies (*jian, ming*) • Language as a symbolic resource • "Because therefore" "frame-main" reasoning (legal question(s)/problem at issue) • Problem-solution structure (initiation component) Latine rhetoric • *Conocimiento* • Epistemic delinking • Binary disruption
Statement of Jurisdiction: States the basis for the court's jurisdiction of the case. Avoids a *sua sponte* dismissal for lack of jurisdiction	African Diasporic rhetoric • Rhetoric as the rules or principles for eloquent and effective communication
Statement of Facts: Communicates the salient facts of the client's case in a manner most favorable to the client	Indigenous rhetoric • Rhetorical sovereignty • Survivance African Diasporic rhetoric • Kawaida (agency and liberation) • Rhetoric as eloquent and effective speech • Maat (truth, propriety, harmony, balance) Asian Diasporic rhetoric • Discourse of persuasion/persuasion strategies (*ci, jian*) • Language as a symbolic resource Latine rhetoric • Epistemic delinking • Binary disruption
Standard of Review: Identifies the level of deference an appellate court (including a court of last resort) will give to a lower court ruling; dependent on whether the question to resolve is one of fact, law, or a mixed question of law and fact	Indigenous rhetoric • Rhetorical sovereignty • Survivance African Diasporic rhetoric • Kawaida (expansive transformation) • Rhetoric as eloquent and effective communication • Rhetoric as the rules or principles for eloquent and effective communication • Maat (truth, propriety, harmony, balance)

Table 7.4: A rhetorical comparison grid for The Appellate Brief (continued)

Appellate Brief	Multicultural rhetorical strategies
	Asian Diasporic rhetoric • Discourse of persuasion/persuasion strategies (*ci, jian, ming*) Latine rhetoric • *Conocimiento* • Epistemic delinking
Argument: Communicates the analysis of the client's case through a careful explanation of the standards used to resolve the dispute and an application of that standard to the facts of the case, law, or legal doctrine	Indigenous rhetoric • Rhetorical sovereignty • Survivance African Diasporic rhetoric • Kawaida • Rhetoric as eloquent and effective communication • Rhetoric as the rules or principles for eloquent and effective communication • Maat Asian Diasporic rhetoric • Discourse of persuasion/persuasion strategies (*ci, jian, ming, bian*) • Language as a symbolic resource • "Because therefore" "frame-main" reasoning • Problem-solution structure Latine rhetoric • *Conocimiento* • Epistemic delinking • Binary disruption
Conclusion/Prayer for Relief: Formal request for the preferred outcome of the case made to the legal decisionmaker	Indigenous rhetoric • Rhetorical sovereignty • Survivance African Diasporic rhetoric • Kawaida (agency and liberation; expansive transformation) • Rhetoric as the rules or principles for eloquent and effective communication • Maat (justice) Asian Diasporic rhetoric • Discourse of persuasion/persuasion strategies (*ci, jian, ming*) Latine rhetoric • *Conocimiento* • Epistemic delinking • Binary disruption

(continued)

Table 7.4: A rhetorical comparison grid for The Appellate Brief (continued)

Appellate Brief	Multicultural rhetorical strategies
Certificate of Service: Certifies that a copy of the brief has been filed with the appropriate court and that a copy has been sent to the parties	African Diasporic rhetoric • Rhetoric as the rules or principles for eloquent and effective communication
Certificate of Compliance: Certifies to the court that counsel has complied with all of the rules governing the content and format requirements for brief submissions in that jurisdiction	African Diasporic rhetoric • Rhetoric as the rules or principles for eloquent and effective communication

have failed to bring their claims challenging agency action and inaction pursuant to the Administrative Procedure Act and other statutes by which Congress has authorized—and channeled—judicial review. If anything, Plaintiffs' answering brief makes the threshold defects of this action clearer. No federal court has ever permitted an action that seeks to review decades of agency action (and alleged inaction) by a dozen federal agencies and executive offices—all in pursuit of a policy goal ("decarbonization") currently under debate by the representative branches. Indeed, the proposed remedial scope of this action dwarfs the prior high-water mark for judicial reach in institutional reform cases, making the judicial administration of entire school districts and prison systems appear modest by comparison.

Finally, none of Plaintiffs' claims succeeds on the merits. Plaintiffs identify no historical basis for a fundamental right to a stable climate system or any other constitutional right related to the environment. They invite this Court to expand the narrow state-created danger doctrine far beyond any previous application. Plaintiffs' public trust theory also fails on multiple grounds: the doctrine has no basis in federal law, is displaced by statute, and does not apply to management of the atmosphere.

Appellate jurisdiction

Plaintiffs argue that the Court should reconsider its decision to permit this appeal pursuant to 28 U.S.C. § 1292(b), but there is no reason to do so. The Court correctly granted the government's petition for permission to appeal because the appeal involves "controlling question[s] of law as to which there is substantial ground for difference of opinion," and it "may materially advance the ultimate termination of the litigation." *Id.*

First, this appeal involves several controlling questions of law: (1) whether Plaintiffs' claims are justiciable under Article III; (2) whether the types of agency actions challenged by Plaintiffs may be reviewed only within the framework of the Administrative Procedure Act (and other statutes authorizing judicial review); and (3) whether Plaintiffs have stated claims on which relief can be granted. The government's arguments on all of these questions are purely legal, and no factual development is necessary. Both this

Court and the Supreme Court have already acknowledged that these questions present a "substantial ground for difference of opinion." 2 E.R. 173–74.

Second, resolution of this appeal doubtless "may materially advance the ultimate termination of the litigation." If the Court rules in the government's favor on any of the threshold issues, then the litigation will end. That fact alone meets the standard. As to the merits, a resolution in the government's favor will also terminate the litigation because the merits of all of Plaintiffs' claims are now before the Court. Opening Brief 42–47. The government moved to dismiss Plaintiffs' entire "action," *id.* at 42–43, and then moved for summary judgment on "each of the four claims" in the operative complaint, *id.* at 44. Plaintiffs argue that the government confuses "counts" and "claims," Answering Brief 5–6, but the government's phrasing tracked the operative complaint, which does not mention "counts" and which asserts four—and only four—"Claim[s] for Relief," 3 E.R. 452, 453, 454, 455. In any event, Plaintiffs incorrectly contend that some claims remain unexamined. Answering Brief 7. In fact, the district court addressed each one and decided to move forward on only some of them. Opening Brief 42–46.

Third and finally, even if this Court had accepted certification on only one controlling question decided by the district court, it may "address any issue fairly included within the certified order[s]." *Rivera v. NIBCO, Inc.*, 364 F.3d 1057, 1063 (9th Cir. 2004) (internal quotation marks omitted). Thus, Plaintiffs could have argued the merits of any remaining claims in their answering brief. Opening Brief 45. Because they failed to do so, any potential arguments about those claims are now forfeited.

Argument

I. The district court lacked jurisdiction over this action

A. Plaintiffs lack Article III standing

Before turning to the three prongs of standing, we address Plaintiffs' argument that "[e]very issue of Plaintiffs' standing raised by Defendants requires an evidentiary analysis." Answering Brief 10. Plaintiffs are wrong: the government's standing arguments are entirely legal and do not turn on disputed issues of material fact. Neither Plaintiffs nor the district court have identified any such issues that are relevant to the government's arguments. Our brief accepts the relevant facts as alleged by Plaintiffs and then argues from that baseline as a matter of law.

Plaintiffs assert that a "district court's determination that the evidence presented by the parties raises genuine factual disputes is not reviewable on interlocutory appeal." Answering Brief 10 (quoting *Mendocino Environmental Center v. Mendocino County*, 192 F.3d 1283, 1291 (9th Cir. 1999)). But *Mendocino* addresses the interlocutory appeal of the denial of a motion for qualified immunity, which balances interests particular to that context, and not a Section 1292(b) appeal. In the Section 1292(b) context, courts routinely review the propriety of the denial of a motion for summary judgment. See, e.g., *Hill v. Xerox Business Services, LLC*, 868 F.3d 758, 760 (9th Cir. 2017).

1. Plaintiffs cannot identify any injury to a concrete and particularized legally protected interest because their grievance is universally shared and generalized

As explained in our opening brief, Plaintiffs' claimed interests are universally shared and generalized and thus insufficient to establish standing. Opening Brief 13–17. That is, Plaintiffs cannot make the required showing of injury to a concrete and particularized legally protected interest that is distinct from the rest of the public.

Plaintiffs assert that the government's "generalized grievance theory ... is unsupported by precedent." Answering Brief 12. But the cases cited in our opening brief are clear that generalized grievances cannot be used to establish standing. Opening Brief 13 (citing *Lujan v. Defenders of Wildlife*, 504 U.S. 555, 575 (1992); *Lexmark International, Inc. v. Static Control Components, Inc.*, 572 U.S. 118, 125, 127 n.3 (2014)). Even the district court here recognized the "generalized grievance rule," 1 E.R. 82, but it seriously erred in applying it, Opening Brief 15–16.

Plaintiffs also argue that their injuries and interests are not generalized because they have identified "a broad range of personal injuries caused by human induced climate change." Answering Brief 10 (quoting E.R. 30). But alleging "personal injuries" does not solve Plaintiffs' standing problem. Climate change, as Plaintiffs conceive it, is a *universal* problem, and addressing it is a *universal* interest. From this standpoint, almost any individual on the planet could identify a climate-change related harm that he or she allegedly will suffer. Article III standing serves to ensure that universal problems concerning "the public interest" are addressed to and by the representative branches, not by Article III courts.

Moreover, the difference between climate change and the "widely shared" problems cited by Plaintiffs, Answering Brief 12–13, is plain. Alleged injuries from climate change are not like the injury shared by purchasers of "domestic ocean cargo shipping services on west coast Hawaii routes," *Novak v. United States*, 795 F.3d 1012, 1016 (9th Cir. 2015), or by those caught up in alleged warrantless searches of internet traffic and telecommunications, *Jewel v. NSA*, 673 F.3d 902, 909 (9th Cir. 2011), or by those alleging spiritual harm from the inscription "In God We Trust," *Newdow v. Lefevre*, 598 F.3d 638, 642 (9th Cir. 2010). Plaintiffs' alleged harms are the rare truly universal harm, making them the archetype of a generalized grievance that only the representative branches can legitimately address.

Plaintiffs attempt to avoid the universality problem by asserting that their "claims do not rest on 'global universal harm' " but rather on the harms described in their declarations. Answering Brief 13 (quoting Opening Brief 15). But those harms are simply examples of harms that could be alleged by anyone in the country or the world. Plaintiffs cannot simply disavow the universality of the problems they identify and the public interest in addressing them through the representative branches. When an interest is generalized and public, it implicates the separation-of-powers concerns that motivate Article III standing requirements, regardless of what a plaintiff says. See *Defenders of Wildlife*, 504 U.S. at 559–60. In any event, Plaintiffs do not (and cannot) claim that their action is actually challenging anything that is narrower than *global* climate change.

Plaintiffs assert that the government "*conceded*" injury-in-fact below both at a hearing and in its pretrial memorandum. Answering Brief 12. But a party cannot concede the jurisdictional requirement of standing. In any event, Plaintiffs misstate the record. At the hearing, the government attorney first acknowledged the district court's opinion concluding that Plaintiffs had alleged sufficient injuries at the pleading stage and then noted that Plaintiffs had submitted declarations in support of those allegations. 1 S.E.R. 6–7. The attorney never conceded that the alleged injuries were sufficient to establish Article III standing. Nor does the government's pretrial memo make such a concession. It dismisses some claimed injuries as not cognizable at all because Plaintiffs did not directly experience them or because they are based on speculative fears. The memo recognizes that other claimed injuries are potentially cognizable under Article III—that is, they could *theoretically* be used to establish standing—but it argues Plaintiffs had not met their burden here. 5 S.E.R. 925.

Plaintiffs are also wrong that merely alleging a constitutional violation is enough to demonstrate the required injury for standing. Answering Brief 14. The case cited by Plaintiffs stands only for the proposition that actual "[i]mpairments" (i.e., injuries) "to a constitutional right" are enough for standing. *Council of Insurance Agents & Brokers v. Molasky-Arman*, 522 F.3d 925, 931 (9th Cir. 2008). There, the Court plainly identified an actual injury—"discriminatory administrative burdens placed on [the plaintiff] because of her nonresident status"—and did not rely on the allegation of a constitutional violation alone. *Id.* And the Supreme Court has repeatedly held that a court's standing inquiry is in no way lessened by a plaintiff's assertion that government action is unconstitutional. Rather, a court must be "especially rigorous when reaching the merits of the dispute would force [it] to decide whether an action taken by one of the other two branches of the Federal Government was unconstitutional." *Clapper v. Amnesty International USA*, 568 U.S. 398, 408 (2013) (quoting *Raines v. Byrd*, 521 U.S. 811, 819–20 (1997)).

2. Plaintiffs have not established that their injuries are caused by Defendants' actions

According to Plaintiffs, the "chain of causation is simple." Answering Brief 15. And that chain is simple because Plaintiffs just state their conclusion without any attempt to parse responsibility: "Defendants have substantially caused and contributed to climate change." *Id.*

But as we have explained, Plaintiffs cannot show causation by simply asserting that the U.S. government caused climate change. See Opening Brief 17–19 (discussing the private and international dimensions of the issue). Here, neither Plaintiffs nor the district court have attempted to determine the respective responsibilities of producers of greenhouse-gas emitting fuels; the direct consumers of those fuels (such as the power plants that burn some of them); and the consumers who use the gasoline, the electricity, and the products that result (i.e., all of us).

Moreover, this Court has rejected a plaintiff's attempt to bypass the requirement to show that the government caused alleged climate change injuries simply by asserting that the government could have curbed emissions. E.g., Answering Brief 16 (complaining of "federally authorized emissions"); *id.* (asserting that the government has "control over the fossil-fuel based energy system"). Where standing rests on alleged climate change injuries, "simply saying that the Agencies have failed to curb emission of greenhouse gases, which contribute (in some undefined way and to some undefined degree) to their injuries, relies on an attenuated chain of conjecture insufficient to support standing." *Washington Environmental Council v. Bellon*, 732 F.3d 1131, 1143 (9th Cir. 2013) (internal quotation marks omitted). Plaintiffs attempt to distinguish *Bellon* on the ground that the level of greenhouse gas emissions there was small. Answering Brief 21. But Plaintiffs actually weaken their causation argument by "aggregating" decades of federal action and inaction. See Opening Brief 20–21. Such aggregation makes it impossible to trace an actual connection between any identifiable agency action and Plaintiffs' claimed harm; hence their resort to the assertion that all United States greenhouse gas emissions must be the government's fault.

Plaintiffs cite a constitutional provision and a variety of statutory provisions in support of their claim that the government "controls" or "authorizes" greenhouse gas emissions. Answering Brief 18 n.11. But these provisions do not connect the dots. As for the Constitution, Plaintiffs cite Article I, Section 3, Clause 2, which addresses the election of Senators and seems wholly irrelevant. They cite hundreds of sections of the U.S. Code, relating to a wide range of topics (e.g., federal lands, deepwater ports, permits to fill waters of the United States, and energy conservation). They cite the Clean Air Act as well, but they never pause to explain how the Act regulates air pollution. Aggregating a large portion of the U.S. Code, as well as a handful of regulations, does not demonstrate the required causation.

Nor is it sufficient to claim that the government "promot[ed] a fossil fuel based energy system." Answering Brief 16. That claim does not do the work required by *Bellon*. First, even if the government does in fact "promote" the use of fossil fuels, Plaintiffs err in jumping to the conclusion that the government is therefore responsible for all emissions resulting from such use, i.e., all "CO_2 emissions during 1850–2012 from the United States," Answering Brief 16, rather than the millions of third parties not before the Court who actually use and consume fossil fuels and thereby produce those emissions.

Second, while Plaintiffs cite hundreds of record pages purportedly "detailing nine components of Defendants' national fossil fuel-based energy system," Answering Brief 17, 19, nowhere in those pages is there an actual causation analysis. Instead, there is a collection of various federal policies and actions relating to energy use and development. The components describe massive segments of the U.S. economy and various federal actions relating to them, e.g., "[e]nergy planning and policies," "power plants and refineries," and "road, rail, freight, and air transportation." *Id.* at 18 n.10. Plaintiffs need not trace the molecules of CO_2 to have standing. *Id.* at 22. But they cannot simply point to large swaths of the economy and assert, based on a string-cite of hundreds of sections of the U.S. Code, that the government should have controlled the emissions therefrom. Moreover, they cannot show that the contributions of all U.S. sources of emissions, separated out from the contributions of all other nations on the globe, cause any identifiable harm to any given Plaintiff here.

Plaintiffs also assert that the actions of third parties are "produced by 'determinative or coercive effect' of Defendants as part of their creation and control of the national energy system." Answering Brief 18 (quoting *Bennett v. Spear*, 520 U.S. 154, 169 (1997)). But they do not then identify any (allegedly) determinative or coercive actions by Defendants. In *Bennett*, the determinative and coercive effect was the result of a specific government opinion that functioned as a permit for another government agency; the agency receiving the opinion either had to follow it or to disregard it and potentially face civil and criminal penalties. 520 U.S. at 170. Plaintiffs identify nothing like this in the government's actions "promoting a fossil fuel based energy system." Answering Brief 16.

Plaintiffs also fault the government for not addressing the evidence linking climate change to their alleged injuries. *Id.* at 19–20. But the government has not contested this part of the causal chain at any stage in this proceeding. Plaintiffs are responding to an argument the government has not made.

Finally, a district court recently rejected a similar causation argument in a lawsuit brought by other young plaintiffs who likewise claim that the government's climate change-related action and inaction violated due process and a federal public trust doctrine. The court held that these plaintiffs had not satisfied the causation requirement of Article III standing, explaining that they "simply ignore that Defendant agencies and officers *do not produce* greenhouse gases, but act to regulate those third parties that do: innumerable businesses and private industries." *Clean Air Council v. United States*, No. 2:17-cv-04977-PD, 2019 WL 687873, at *7 (E.D. Pa. Feb. 19, 2019).

3. The district court cannot redress Plaintiffs' alleged injuries

Plaintiffs argue that our brief engages in "hyperbolic speculation" about the relief they seek in order to claim that it is beyond the authority of the federal courts to award. Answering Brief 4. But our brief simply walks through both the relief sought in Plaintiffs' complaint and the relief proposed by the district court. Opening Brief 3–5, 22–23 (discussing, inter alia, 1 E.R. 88–90). This is not speculation: it is what Plaintiffs are seeking and what the district court offered in response to the government's redressability argument.

Moreover, Plaintiffs' brief confirms that Plaintiffs seek an order requiring the *wholesale decarbonization of the United States economy*. Although Plaintiffs are willing to let the government propose "a remedial plan" of the government's "own devising," Answering Brief 26, that plan must "undo that [fossil fuel energy] system and create a clean, decarbonized system," and the district court can command the government's "existing authorities" to achieve that system, *id.* at 26 & n.17. Thus, the complaint asks for decarbonization, the district court has relied on Plaintiffs' demand for decarbonization as a remedy, and Plaintiffs' brief reiterates that decarbonization is required. But ordering decarbonization of the United States economy—which is shorthand for totally reordering (and upending) the economic life of the Nation, all without voting under our democratic system—is beyond the authority of a district court, and so it is not a remedy available to Plaintiffs and thus fails to demonstrate redressability. Opening Brief 23.

Relying in large part on *Brown v. Board of Education*, 347 U.S. 483 (1954), Plaintiffs argue that at least their "psychological and emotional injuries" could be redressed "if the courts affirm their fundamental rights" and give them, apart from any other relief, "a judicial declaration of the unlawfulness of governmental climate destruction." Answering Brief 24. Plaintiffs' attempt to equate their circumstances with those of the schoolchildren challenging overt racial segregation as a violation of the express terms of the Equal Protection Clause in *Brown* is deeply misguided. Although *Brown* recognized the severe psychological and emotional harms inflicted by unconstitutional racial segregation, it did not suggest that the mere prospect that asserted "psychological and emotional injuries will lessen," Answering Brief 24, could create Article III standing.

Plaintiffs also suggest that enjoining Defendants "from discriminatorily discounting the economic value of young people's lives" would redress their equal protection claim. *Id.* at 25. Because Plaintiffs did not advance this argument in response to the government's motion for summary judgment, 2 E.R. 315–82, it is forfeited, *Smith v. Marsh*, 194 F.3d 1045, 1052 (9th Cir. 1999). In any event, the argument for standing lacks merit; it is just an assertion that the universal effects on which the claims rest will continue into the future.

Plaintiffs cite desegregation and institutional reform cases to argue that their requested decarbonization "relief is firmly within the competence of the judiciary." Answering Brief 26. The high-water mark for the federal courts' traditional equitable authority has come in these cases, where the Supreme Court found such authority sufficiently broad to address the discrete constitutional claims at issue there. See, e.g., *Swann v. Charlotte-Mecklenburg Board of Education*, 402 U.S. 1, 16 (1971). But even the systemic relief there paled in comparison to Plaintiffs' requested relief. The plaintiffs in those cases sought injunctions against particular school districts for particular constitutional violations distinctly experienced by particular individuals. Or the plaintiffs sought injunctions to address the conditions in a particular prison system at a particular time. The courts then directed injunctions at the institutions and required particular actions to remedy the violations. Plaintiffs here challenge decades of climate change-related policies, allegedly affecting the population at large. They ask the district court to take control of that entire range of government policy-making in order to achieve U.S. decarbonization. This relief is irreconcilable with Article III. Plaintiffs have failed to demonstrate redressability.

* * *

In sum, Plaintiffs have not established that they suffered injury-in-fact, that Defendants caused the injury, or that the injury can be redressed. They lack Article III standing.

B. Plaintiffs' action is not otherwise a case or controversy cognizable under Article III

As we have explained, see Opening Brief 24–27, Plaintiffs' action is not a case or controversy "of the sort traditionally amenable to, and resolved by, the judicial process," *Vermont Agency of Natural Resources v. United States ex rel. Stevens*, 529 U.S. 765, 774 (2000) (internal quotation marks omitted). Plaintiffs ask the district court to review and assess the entirety of Congress's and the Executive Branch's programs and regulatory decisions relating to climate change over decades, and then to pass on the comprehensive constitutionality of all of those policies, programs, and alleged inaction in the aggregate. See Answering Brief 17, 22; 3 E.R. 571–86. No federal court has ever purported to use the "judicial power" to perform such a sweeping policy review.

In response to this argument, Plaintiffs claim that "Defendants' theory that the judiciary is without power to assess the constitutionality of large and pervasive government policies and systems would have been the downfall of cases addressing desegregation, prison reform, interracial and same-sex marriage, and the rights of women to serve on juries and have access to contraception, among other rights." Answering Brief 30. But all of these cases addressed particular places and times, as discussed in the previous section. None sought review of decades of actions by multiple agencies made pursuant to a host of unspecified statutes, and none sought a remedy remotely approaching the scale of nationwide decarbonization.

A quick look at the climate change issues and actions pending before Congress and the Executive Branch confirms that Plaintiffs have petitioned the wrong branch. Some in Congress seek a "Green New Deal." H.R.J. Res. 109, 116th Cong., 1st Sess. (2019). Others prefer a carbon tax. H.R. 7173, 115th Cong., 2d Sess. (2018). Still others support neither. In the meantime, EPA is considering actions under the Clean Air Act, including a potential replacement for the Clean Power Plan. See 83 Fed. Reg. 44,746 (Aug. 31, 2018). On the international front, the President has indicated that the United States will withdraw from the 2015 Paris Climate Accord. In derogation of these normal workings of democracy, Plaintiffs seek to put a single district court, at the behest of a handful of litigants, in charge of directing American energy and environmental policy.

Plaintiffs also claim that holding that their action is not cognizable under Article III would "upend the judiciary's core role as a check and balance in our Nation's system of separated powers, particularly in enforcing constitutional rights." Answering Brief 29. It would not, for "the Constitution's central mechanism of separation of powers depends largely upon common understanding of what activities are appropriate to legislatures, to executives, and to courts." *Defenders of Wildlife*, 504 U.S. at 559–60. "If a dispute is not a proper case or controversy, the courts have no business deciding it." *DaimlerChrysler Corp. v. Cuno*, 547 U.S. 332, 341 (2006). As the district court in *Clean Air Council* explained, there "is a difference ... between determining the constitutionality of particular Executive action and regulating all statutory, regulatory, budgetary, personnel, and administrative Executive actions that relate to the environment. The former is certainly within the province of the Judiciary. The latter would make the Executive a subsidiary of the Judiciary." 2019 WL 687873, at *11. This action is categorically not an Article III case or controversy, and so the district court lacked jurisdiction to entertain it.

II Plaintiffs were required to proceed under the APA but concededly did not

As explained in our opening brief, the district court should have dismissed this action for a separate threshold reason: Plaintiffs were required to proceed under the APA [Administrative Procedures Act] but did not do so. The *types* of agency actions targeted by Plaintiffs are all subject to review under the APA, including through special statutory review provisions, and Plaintiffs have not argued otherwise.

Plaintiffs first create a straw man, claiming that we are arguing that the federal courts never have equitable authority to address constitutional claims. Answering Brief 33. Not so. We have been clear that federal courts "have equitable authority in some circumstances 'to enjoin unlawful executive action.'" Opening Brief 30 (quoting *Armstrong v. Exceptional Child Center, Inc.*, 135 S. Ct. 1378, 1385 (2015)). The question here is whether an equitable cause of action is available for claims that Plaintiffs could have brought pursuant to either the APA or other statutory causes of action, where Plaintiffs have chosen not to do so.

Armstrong answers *no*. It makes clear that an equitable cause of action, even if (unlike here) one might otherwise potentially lie, is "subject to express and implied statutory limitations." 135 S. Ct. at 1385. "Where Congress has created a remedial scheme for the enforcement of a particular federal right," courts rightly "have, in suits against federal officers, refused to supplement that scheme with one created by the judiciary." *Seminole Tribe of Florida v. Florida*, 517 U.S. 44, 74 (1996). Here, the APA (together with similar statutes authorizing judicial review of agency action) provides the statutory limitation: under the APA, one cannot directly challenge decades of agency action aggregated by Plaintiffs but instead may only challenge "circumscribed, discrete agency actions." *Norton v. SUWA*, 542 U.S. 55, 62 (2004).

Plaintiffs' motion for a preliminary injunction pending appeal provides a concrete example of the pitfalls of letting Plaintiffs proceed outside the metes and bounds of either the APA or similar statutes. That motion asked the Court for, among other relief, an injunction by March 19, 2019 to block a particular lease sale by the Bureau of Ocean Energy Management (part of the Department of the Interior) in the Gulf of Mexico. DktEntry 21-1, at 5. That lease sale, however, is only the first part of a "four-stage process" that was established by the Outer Continental Shelf Lands Act (OCSLA) and that the agency must undertake "before allowing development of an offshore well, with each stage more specific than the last and more attentive to the potential benefits and costs of a particular drilling project." *Center for Sustainable Economy v. Jewell*, 779 F.3d 588, 594 (D.C. Cir. 2015). Instead of bringing their constitutional claims pursuant to the channelized judicial review mechanism established by OCSLA, see 43 U.S.C. § 1349(b)(1), Plaintiffs plow ahead as if that provision did not exist. This problem goes far beyond this particular sale, because Plaintiffs are seeking review of an untold number of unspecified agency actions aggregated over decades.

Plaintiffs argue that *Armstrong* is inapplicable because it concerned statutory rights rather constitutional claims. Answering Brief 34 n.21. That misses the point: *Armstrong* addressed the "power of federal courts to enjoin unlawful action," and its holding—that this authority can be limited by statute—was not limited to statutory claims. 135 S. Ct. at 1385. Indeed, *Armstrong* addressed whether one could sue to bar state action preempted by federal law *under the Supremacy Clause*. *Id.* at 1382–83. That is why the Court discussed the "ability to sue to enjoin *unconstitutional* actions by state and federal officials." *Id.* at 1384 (emphasis added).

Plaintiffs also argue that the Due Process Clause itself provides the required cause of action. Answering Brief 34–35. No authority supports the notion that a sweeping cause of action against the Executive Branch writ large could be implied by a court under that Clause. But in addition, that argument misses the point: even if that were so, Congress in the APA and other statutes providing for review of agency action has channeled those claims into a particular framework that Plaintiffs may not choose to ignore.

The cases cited by Plaintiffs do not stand for the proposition that constitutional challenges to agency action may be brought without regard to the APA or similar statutes. In *Franklin v. Massachusetts*, 505 U.S. 788 (1992), the Supreme Court considered the viability of the plaintiffs' constitutional claims outside of the APA *only after* the Court determined that the APA review was unavailable because of a lack of final agency action and because presidential action was unreviewable under the statute. *Id.* at 801. As for *Webster v. Doe*, 486 U.S. 592 (1988), the plaintiff in that case asserted that he was "entitled, *under the APA*, to judicial consideration" of his constitutional claims. *Id.* at 602 (emphasis added). And, after rejecting the government's argument that those claims were "unreviewable under the APA," the Court permitted those claims to proceed. *Id.* at 603. The decision thus endorses review of constitutional challenges under the APA. Neither *Franklin* nor *Webster* held that a plaintiff may unilaterally ignore the APA (or similar statutes like OCSLA) for claims of the sort at issue here.

Plaintiffs also err in equating the APA's waiver of sovereign immunity with whether a cause of action is available. As we have acknowledged, this Court has held that the APA waives sovereign immunity for claims seeking non-monetary relief against the government regardless of whether the claims are brought pursuant to the APA or an alternative mechanism like the courts' general equitable authority. See Opening Brief 33 (discussing *Navajo Nation v. Department of Interior*, 876 F.3d 1144, 1167–73 (9th Cir. 2017), and *Presbyterian Church (USA) v. United States*, 870 F.2d 518, 525 & n.9 (9th Cir. 1989)). But this Court has never held that a plaintiff possesses a cause of action outside of the APA simply because the APA's waiver of sovereign immunity might apply to such a cause of action. And Plaintiffs are wrong that the two issues must be equated. Answering Brief 34.

Finally, Plaintiffs argue that requiring them to bring their constitutional claims pursuant to the APA would violate their rights to procedural due process. Answering Brief 37–40. As an initial matter, Plaintiffs are wrong that proceeding pursuant to the APA would bar judicial review entirely. The language they quote from *Davis v. Passman*, 442 U.S. 228, 242 (1979), addresses whether a statute may bar judicial review of a claim of a constitutional violation entirely, not whether a statute may channel that review. Moreover, Plaintiffs point to no decision holding that the APA's judicial review provisions are constitutionally deficient, either as a general matter, or as applied to plaintiffs who bring constitutional claims.

Plaintiffs are free to challenge particular agency actions or inactions before the agencies and the courts, to petition the agencies for rulemakings or for the repeal of certain rules (and to later seek judicial review of the agencies' responses vel non), or to pursue any of a number of various options provided by Congress in the APA and similar statutes to vindicate their alleged constitutional rights in the context of discrete agency actions and in a concrete factual setting. In such a setting, Plaintiffs could argue that the particular action they are challenging is unconstitutional because it is part of an (allegedly) unconstitutional "fossil fuel energy system."

Consequently, to vindicate their aggregation/systemic constitutional theory, Plaintiffs would not need to challenge "thousands of agency actions." Answering Brief 38. Plaintiffs instead could target particular actions and argue their theory in those cases. There is simply no basis to conclude that Plaintiffs have a procedural due process right to bring *one omnibus action* making a litany of vague assertions against more than fifty years of unspecified and unconnected actions (or inactions), policies, and practices, by a dozen executives agencies and offices.

Finally, even if the Court were to resort to the factors set forth in *Matthews v. Eldridge*, 424 U.S. 319 (1976), which for the reasons stated above is not appropriate, those factors only underscore that no due process violation has occurred here. There is no fundamental right at stake, see *infra* pp. 23–25, and Plaintiffs can make their constitutional arguments if they were to seek review of a particular agency action.

III Plaintiffs' constitutional claims fail on the merits

A. There is no fundamental right to a "stable climate system"

Plaintiffs' purported right to a "climate system capable of sustaining human life" has no basis whatsoever in this Nation's history or tradition and is therefore not a fundamental right. See *Washington v. Glucksberg*, 521 U.S. 702, 720 (1997). The right to climate conditions that Plaintiffs deem "capable of sustaining human life" is wholly unrelated to any of the fundamental rights that the Supreme Court has previously recognized, which protect quintessentially "personal decisions," i.e., "intimate and personal choices ... central to personal dignity and autonomy." *Planned Parenthood of Southeastern Pennsylvania v. Casey*, 505 U.S. 833, 851 (1992). Nor is it possible to derive a right to particular climate conditions from any of those fundamental rights. No federal court, other than the district court here, has ever recognized any fundamental right that relates to the climate or the environment. See Opening Brief 37–38.

Moreover, Plaintiffs do not come close to identifying "concrete examples involving fundamental rights found to be deeply rooted in our legal tradition," as is necessary to support recognition of a new fundamental right. *Glucksberg*, 521 U.S. at 722. The snippets that Plaintiffs quote from John Locke ("laws human must be made according to the general laws of Nature," Answering Brief 46); Thomas Jefferson (the earth belongs "in usufruct to the living," *id.*); James Madison ("[d]eprived of [the atmosphere], they all equally perish," *id.* at 48); and the 1893 Fur Seal Arbitration, *id.* at 48, are neither examples nor concrete. Indeed, the selected statements are so devoid of context that they barely have meaning. Likewise, the notion that individual Framers derived a "transcendent feeling of nationhood" from the country's "nature, soil and plants," *id.* at 47, indicates only that they appreciated the natural world; it provides no basis for Plaintiffs' "climate right." The Framers appreciated many things; their appreciation does not convert those things into fundamental rights protected by the Due Process Clause of the Fifth Amendment. Moreover, the unremarkable precept that the government cannot privatize "light, air, and water," *id.* at 45, does no work here, as Plaintiffs have not alleged that the government's alleged mismanagement of the atmosphere constitutes privatization.

Plaintiffs may be frustrated by what they perceive as the government's "mismanagement" of fossil fuels, but they have not identified a violation of a constitutional right: "the Constitution does not provide judicial remedies for every social and economic ill." *Lindsey v. Normet*, 405 U.S. 56, 74 (1972). Indeed, numerous federal courts have already rejected arguments similar to the ones Plaintiffs raise here. See Opening Brief 37–38 (collecting cases). Most recently, a district court rejected a similar due process argument brought by other youth plaintiffs and explained that the "*Juliana* Court certainly contravened or ignored longstanding authority" when it recognized a fundamental right to a livable climate. *Clean Air Council*, 2019 WL 687873, at *8. This Court should do the same.

B. Plaintiffs' state-created danger claims fail

The state-created danger doctrine is a narrow exception to the rule that the Constitution does not impose on the government an affirmative duty to protect individuals from harm. Applying the doctrine to these circumstances would allow that exception to swallow the rule, and Plaintiffs have failed to identify any case that applied the doctrine on even remotely similar facts.

This matter is readily distinguishable from all other state-created danger cases that this Court has found viable, which generally include (1) immediate harms to an individual's personal security or bodily integrity; (2) specific government actions or actors that put an individual at immediate and obvious risk; and (3) government actions that endangered particular individuals, as distinguished from the public at large. Opening Brief 39–42; see also *Pauluk v. Savage*, 836 F.3d 1117, 1129 (9th Cir. 2016) (Murguia, J., concurring in part and dissenting in part) (collecting cases).

Plaintiffs' interpretation of the state-created danger exception would extend it far beyond all reasonable bounds. Plaintiffs assert that they "need only establish 'the state engaged in affirmative conduct'" that "creates, exposes, or increases a risk of harm Plaintiffs would not have faced to the same degree" had the government not acted. Answering Brief 51. But if that were enough, the government would violate the Fifth Amendment every time it took a regulatory action—ranging from increasing the speed limit to decreasing food safety standards—as long as it knew that the action could increase the risk of harm to some segment of the population. This approach is completely unprecedented.

The majority opinion in *Pauluk v. Savage* does not help Plaintiffs. There, a state employee died after continued exposure to toxic mold in his workplace. 836 F.3d at 1119–20. The employee's supervisors had transferred him to the mold-infested building over his objection, and they later refused to transfer him to another building even after he presented proof that the mold was affecting his health. *Id.* at 1125. This Court held that Pauluk's family had stated a claim under the state-created danger doctrine because a reasonable jury could find that his supervisors "acted with deliberate indifference toward the danger posed by toxic mold … to [his] health" when they decided to transfer him to a building that they knew was infested. *Id.*

Plaintiffs rely on *Pauluk* for the proposition that they need not identify "immediate, direct, physical, and personal" harms to state a viable due process claim under the exception, Answering Brief 51–52, but they are mistaken. *Pauluk* includes the same essential features as earlier cases: (1) Pauluk suffered direct harm to his "life, liberty, or property"; (2) specific government actors (his supervisors) put him at immediate physical risk when they sent him to the mold-infested building; (3) and the supervisors knew that Pauluk in particular was harmed by the exposure because he presented proof that it was damaging his health. 836 F.3d at 1119–20, 1124–25. Plaintiffs' claims of harm from decades of government action and inaction regarding, for example, "nine components of Defendants' national fossil fuel-based energy system," Answering Brief 17, have none of those features. Opening Brief 39–42.

Plaintiffs' also rely on *Farmer v. Brennan*, 511 U.S. 825, 843 (1994), cited in Answering Brief 53. There, a prisoner asserted that the government had acted with deliberate indifference when it failed to protect her from an attack by a fellow prisoner. 511 U.S. at 830. The prisoner relied not on the Due Process Clause but rather on the Eighth Amendment, which requires the government to "take reasonable measures to guarantee the safety of the inmates." *Id.* at 832. The Court rejected her claim, but it clarified that a prison official may not evade liability for deliberate indifference by showing that "he did not know that the complainant was especially likely to be assaulted by the specific prisoner who eventually committed the assault." *Id.* at 843.

Farmer is readily distinguishable because Plaintiffs are not incarcerated and do not rely on the Eighth Amendment. It is well-established, moreover, that particularization is required. See, e.g., *Kennedy v. City of Ridgefield*, 439 F.3d 1055, 1063 (9th Cir. 2006) (holding that the affirmative act must have exposed the plaintiff to "an actual, particularized danger"); *Ketchum v. Alameda County*, 811 F.2d 1243, 1247 (9th Cir. 1987) (requiring evidence that the government "has affirmatively placed the plaintiff" in danger). Such particularization is altogether lacking here, where Plaintiffs have identified only generalized harms resulting from a global phenomenon allegedly caused by decades of agency actions and inaction. See Opening Brief 41–42.

C. All of Plaintiffs' constitutional theories are before this Court in this appeal, and none has merit

Plaintiffs insist that not all of their constitutional claims are before the Court in this appeal. Answering Brief 7. But because the government moved to dismiss and for summary judgment on all of Plaintiffs' claims, Plaintiffs are wrong. Opening Brief 42–45; *supra* pp. 2–3. Because Plaintiffs offer no argument on why their other claims provide an alternative ground for affirmance, we do not address them again here. See Opening Brief 45–47 (explaining why the claims are meritless).

* * *

Therefore, all of Plaintiffs' constitutional claims fail on the merits.

IV No federal public trust doctrine creates a right to particular climate conditions

The government's opening brief identified three independent reasons why Plaintiffs' public trust theory fails, Opening Brief 47–57, and Plaintiffs' answering brief rebuts none of those reasons.

A. No federal public trust doctrine binds the federal government

Plaintiffs identify no case holding that the federal government is subject to some sort of judicially enforceable public trust doctrine, and their claim that "courts have routinely found public trust obligations to attach to federal property," Answering Brief 55, misstates the legal landscape. The Supreme Court and numerous federal appellate courts have treated public trust doctrine as a matter of *state* law with no federal basis. The Court's clear statements in *PPL Montana, LLC v. Montana*, 565 U.S. 576, 603–04 (2012) that the contours of any public trust doctrine "do not depend upon the Constitution" and that any such doctrine "remains a matter of state law" are definitive and are consistent with other precedents. See *Alec L. ex rel. Loorz v. McCarthy*, 561 Fed. Appx. 7, 8 (D.C. Cir. 2014) (collecting cases); Opening Brief 48–51. That should be the end of the matter.

Likewise, the fact that the government has previously called itself a "trustee," Answering Brief 55–56, does not mean that it is bound by any extra-constitutional and extra-statutory public trust doctrine. The federal government holds "resources … in trust for its citizens in one sense," because Congress tasks it with "utiliz[ing] the assets that come into its hands as sovereign in the way that it decides is best for the future of the Nation." *Alabama v. Texas*, 347 U.S. 272, 277 (1954) (Reed, J. concurring). The federal government does not, however, manage those assets "in the sense that a private trustee holds for a *cestui que* trust"—i.e., for a trust beneficiary. *Id.*

B. Any federal public trust doctrine is displaced by statute

Even if a public trust doctrine at one time had some basis in federal law, it has since been displaced by the Clean Air Act and other statutes that grant federal agencies authority to manage fossil fuel development, such as the Mining and Minerals Policy Act of 1970, 30 U.S.C. § 21a. Plaintiffs contend that their public trust claims cannot be displaced for two reasons, Answering Brief 57–58, but neither has merit.

First, Plaintiffs assert that because the district court held that their public trust claims rest "directly on the Due Process Clause of the Fifth Amendment," *id.* at 57, the claims cannot be displaced by statute. As we have explained, however, Plaintiffs never argued that their public trust claims rested on the Fifth Amendment, and the district court erred when it rewrote their complaint to say that they had. Opening Brief 51–52. The court's efforts fall flat in any event: just as there is no support for a right to a "livable climate," there is no support for the Fifth Amendment-based federal public trust right envisioned by Plaintiffs. See *id.* at 35–38, 52. Plaintiffs also acknowledge that the public trust right they envision would impose affirmative "fiduciary obligations." Answering Brief 54. But Plaintiffs and the district court ignore that the Due Process Clause imposes a *negative limit* on the federal government's ability to act and "cannot fairly be extended to impose an *affirmative obligation* on the [government]." *DeShaney*, 489 U.S. at 195 (emphasis added).

Second, Plaintiffs' assertion that *American Electric Power Co. v. Connecticut (AEP)*, 564 U.S. 410 (2011), cannot apply to their claims because they do not seek abatement of emissions from specific power plants, Answering Brief 57–58, misreads that case. *AEP*'s displacement holding was not, as Plaintiffs contend, limited to "cause[s] of action directly against private party emissions." *Id.* at 58. Instead, *AEP* held that it remains for federal agencies—not federal courts—to decide whether and to what extent to reduce carbon dioxide emissions, no matter their source. 564 U.S. at 428. Here, Plaintiffs urge the judiciary to make that policy determination in the first instance and thereby ignore Congress's intent to make expert federal agencies the "primary regulator [s] of greenhouse gas emissions." *Id.*; see also *Alec L. v. Jackson*, 863 F. Supp. 2d 11, 16 (D.D.C. 2012) (applying same logic), *aff'd*, 561 Fed. Appx. 7. That path is patently inconsistent with *AEP*.

Finally, the fact that Plaintiffs seek a remedy different from the one sought in *AEP*, Answering Brief 58, makes no difference: "The Supreme Court has instructed that the type of remedy asserted is not relevant to the applicability of the doctrine of displacement." *Native Village of Kivalina v. ExxonMobil Corp.*, 696 F.3d 849, 857 (9th Cir. 2012) (collecting cases). That is, "if a cause of action is displaced, displacement is extended to all remedies." *Id.*

C. The "climate system" is not part of a public trust

Plaintiffs have consistently argued that the government has a trust duty to "manage the atmosphere," 3 E.R. 613, ¶ 309, because the harms that they identify result from "increased atmospheric concentrations of greenhouse gas," Answering Brief 15. As we have explained, the atmosphere is not within a protected trust, and Plaintiffs have identified no support for the notion that it is. Opening Brief 55–56. The fact that the government manages "airspace" for example, Answering Brief 60, means only that it controls air *traffic*, not the composition of the air itself. See 49 U.S.C. § 40103 (discussing "navigable airspace").

Plaintiffs have also changed the trust *res* that the government assertedly must protect from not only the atmosphere, but also to the "hydrosphere," "lithosphere," "cryosphere," and "biosphere." Answering Brief 41 n.27. The refocusing does not help Plaintiffs; indeed, it renders their assertion even more implausible. If the atmosphere is not within a protected trust, then the rest of the climate system is not either. Plaintiffs' effort to argue otherwise, by linking the climate system to the resources historically discussed in public trust cases, merely underscores the absurdity of their theory. Plaintiffs argue that the system is within a protected trust because it includes the hydrosphere; which includes the "territorial sea"; which is an aquatic asset; which renders it similar to the tidelands, submerged lands, and waterways traditionally held to be within a state's trust. *Id.* at 59. That territorial waters are affected by atmospheric changes does not mean that the entire system is within a federally protected trust. Plaintiffs' flimsy chain of reasoning provides no grounding for their theory.

Conclusion

For the foregoing reasons, the orders of the district court should be reversed, and this matter should be remanded with instructions to dismiss the complaint.

Discussion questions

1. Whose experiences and stories are included in this brief? Whose are missing? Why does it matter? Explain your answer.
2. How does traditional legal rhetoric operate in this brief to obfuscate, and render neutral, the role of settler colonialism in climate change?
3. How does traditional legal rhetoric operate in this brief to silence the impact of climate change on minoritized communities?
4. Which multicultural rhetorical strategies would be useful in helping the advocates to identify the origins of climate change, its harm to future generations, and the federal government in precipitating that harm? Be specific and name the cultural tradition and the strategy.
5. Pick a section or sections of this brief to rewrite using relevant cultural rhetorical strategies. For this part of the exercise, you may need to consult additional sources to better contextualize the dispute (such as law review articles, scholarly articles

from non-legal disciplines, books from legal and non-legal disciplines, additional case law, legislative histories, and so on).

6. As you rewrite this section, consider how advocacy against the plaintiff's stated position might still result in community harmony and revelations about the role of traditional rhetoric in perpetuating community harms.

The Judicial Opinion

Inupiat Community of the Artic Slope, a federally-recognized tribe; Ukpeagvik Inupiat Corporation, a native village corporation v. The United States of America, 548 F. Supp. 182 (United States District Court, District of Alaska), October 1, 1982

This case concerns the rights of the Inupiat people to self-determination and to maintain their way of life on their ancestral lands, as against the interests of the state of Alaska and the federal government.

(All footnotes have been omitted.)

Opinion

In this case the Inupiat people of Alaska's north slope seek to quiet title in large portions of the Beaufort and Chukchi Seas beyond the three mile limit. The plaintiffs include the Inupiat Community of the Arctic Slope, a federally recognized tribe, suing on its own behalf and on behalf of its members, the Ukpeagvik Inupiat Corporation, a village corporation organized pursuant to the Alaska Native Claims Settlement Act suing on its own behalf and on behalf of its members, and two native allotees. The defendants include numerous oil companies, the United States, its Secretary of the Interior and its Director of Land Management, and the State of Alaska, its Governor and its Commissioner of Natural Resources.

This is not the first time that these parties have met in a courtroom. This suit is but the latest in a line of legal actions through which the Inupiat Eskimo have sought control over the region in which they have long resided. In an earlier proceeding the Inupiat sought recovery in damages for trespass on native lands in the time period prior to the enactment of the Alaska Native Claims Settlement Act (ANCSA), 43 U.S.C. ss 1601–1628, *United States v. Atlantic Richfield Co.*, 435 F. Supp. 1009 (D. Alaska 1977), aff'd, 612 F.2d 1132 (9th Cir.), cert. denied, 449 U.S. 888, 101 S. Ct. 243, 66 L.Ed.2d 113 (1980); see also *Edwardsen v. Morton*, 369 F. Supp. 1359 (D.D.C.1973). Later the Inupiat filed proceedings in the Court of Claims alleging that the United States had breached a trust responsibility in not protecting the Arctic slope from development and that

Table 7.5: A rhetorical comparison grid for The Judicial Opinion

Judicial Opinion (Trial Court Judge/Proposed Orders)	Multicultural rhetorical strategies
Summary of the Case and Ruling: A summary of the case before the court, what the court is being asked to decide, and a brief statement of and explanation for its ruling on the matter	<u>Indigenous rhetoric</u> • Survivance <u>African Diasporic rhetoric</u> • Rhetoric as eloquent and effective communication • Kawaida • Maat (truth, propriety) <u>Asian Diasporic rhetoric</u> • Discourse of persuasion/persuasion strategies (*ming*) <u>Latine rhetoric</u> • Epistemic delinking • Binary disruption
Factual Background: The facts of the case as summarized, paraphrased, and quoted from pleadings, answers to interrogatories, depositions, and other documents in the record. This section contains background facts, as well as legally relevant facts	<u>Indigenous rhetoric</u> • Rhetorical sovereignty • Survivance <u>African Diasporic rhetoric</u> • Kawaida (agency and liberation) • Rhetoric as eloquent and effective speech • Maat (truth, propriety, harmony, balance) <u>Asian Diasporic rhetoric</u> • Discourse of persuasion/persuasion strategies (*ci*, *jian*) • Language as a symbolic resource <u>Latine rhetoric</u> • Epistemic delinking • Binary disruption
Procedural History: The legal path the case took to arrive in the present court	<u>Indigenous rhetoric</u> • Rhetorical sovereignty • Survivance <u>African Diasporic rhetoric</u> • Rhetoric as the rules or principles for eloquent and effective communication • Maat (truth, propriety) <u>Asian Diasporic rhetoric</u> • Discourse of persuasion/persuasion strategies (*ming*) <u>Latine rhetoric</u> • Epistemic delinking • Binary disruption

(continued)

Table 7.5: A rhetorical comparison grid for The Judicial Opinion (continued)

Judicial Opinion (Trial Court Judge/Proposed Orders)	**Multicultural rhetorical strategies**
Legal Standard/Motion Standard of Review: The legal criteria by which a court can grant or deny various types of motions brought before or during a trial (motion for summary judgment, motion to suppress, motion to dismiss, motion *in limine*, and so on)	Indigenous rhetoric • Rhetorical sovereignty • Survivance African Diasporic rhetoric • Kawaida (expansive transformation) • Rhetoric as eloquent and effective communication • Rhetoric as the rules of principles for eloquent and effective communication • Maat (truth, propriety, harmony, balance) Asian Diasporic rhetoric • Discourse of persuasion/persuasion strategies (*ci*, *jian*, *ming*) Latine rhetoric • *Conocimiento* • Epistemic delinking
Issue: The question or questions that the court is tasked with resolving. In distilling the question for its review, the court is free to take the question as presented by the parties in their briefs or otherwise, or create a question or questions based on the same	Indigenous rhetoric • Rhetorical sovereignty (culturally informed issue-framing) • Survivance African Diasporic rhetoric • Kawaida (agency and liberation; expansive transformation) • Rhetoric as the rules or principles for eloquent and effective communication • Maat (truth, propriety, harmony, balance, reciprocity, and order) Asian Diasporic rhetoric • Discourse of persuasion/persuasion strategies (*jian*, *ming*) • Language as a symbolic resource • "Because therefore" "frame-main" reasoning (legal question(s)/problem at issue) • Problem-solution structure (initiation component) Latine rhetoric • *Conocimiento* • Epistemic delinking

Table 7.5: A rhetorical comparison grid for The Judicial Opinion (continued)

Judicial Opinion (Trial Court Judge/Proposed Orders)	Multicultural rhetorical strategies
Analysis: The court builds an analytic framework from the appropriate and available sources for arguments (primarily case law as precedent) that articulates the legal criteria for resolving each issue before it. It then applies that framework to the relevant facts as stated in the Factual Background for each legal issue to arrive at conclusions for each	<u>Indigenous rhetoric</u> • Rhetorical sovereignty • Survivance <u>African Diasporic rhetoric</u> • Kawaida • Rhetoric as eloquent and effective communication • Rhetoric as the rules or principles for eloquent and effective communication • Maat <u>Asian Diasporic rhetoric</u> • Discourse of persuasion/persuasion strategies (*ci, jian, ming, bian*) • Language as a symbolic resource • "Because therefore" "frame-main" reasoning • Problem-solution structure <u>Latine rhetoric</u> • *Conocimiento* • Epistemic delinking • Binary disruption
Conclusion: An overall conclusion to the Issue(s) before the court	<u>Indigenous rhetoric</u> • Rhetorical sovereignty • Survivance <u>African Diasporic rhetoric</u> • Kawaida (agency and liberation; expansive transformation) • Rhetoric as the rules or principles for eloquent and effective communication • Maat (justice) <u>Asian Diasporic rhetoric</u> • Discourse of persuasion/persuasion strategies (*ci, jian, ming*) <u>Latine rhetoric</u> • *Conocimiento* • Epistemic delinking • Binary disruption

extinguishment of their trespass claims by ANCSA was an unconstitutional taking. That claim was also rejected. *Inupiat Community of the Arctic Slope v. United States*, 680 F.2d 122 (Ct.Cl.1982).

More recently, the Inupiat sought to enjoin on environmental grounds the 1979 Beaufort Sea lease-sale. They claimed that the sale and its consequent environmental damage to their traditional fishing and whaling areas would violate a federal trust responsibility owed to them and would violate numerous federal statutes as well. Although the district court granted the injunction, it was overturned by the court of appeals which found that the federal government had acted in conformity with the applicable law. *North Slope Borough v. Andrus*, 486 F. Supp. 332 (D.D.C.1980), rev'd. 642 F.2d 589 (D.C.Cir.1980). In May of 1981, the Inupiat moved to intervene in an action currently pending before the United States Supreme Court acting under its original jurisdiction. *United States v. Alaska*, No. 84 Orig. (U.S.1980). That action concerns a dispute over the exact location of the three mile limit in the Beaufort Sea. By their complaint in intervention, the Inupiat have requested that the United States Supreme Court hear essentially the same title and sovereignty claims which they assert here.

In this present proceeding, the Inupiat again challenge the lease-sale made in the Beaufort Sea in 1979. They assert that they possess sovereign rights and unextinguished aboriginal title to the area lying from three to sixty-five miles off-shore in the Beaufort and Chukchi Seas of the Arctic Ocean. In support of the contention, the Inupiat claim exclusive use and occupancy of the superjacent sea ice from time before human memory. This claim, according to the Inupiat, establishes rights to the surface of the sea, the water column beneath it, the seabed, and the minerals lying beneath the seabed within the geographic boundaries of their claim. In addition to injunctive relief, the Inupiat seek damages and a declaration of their title to and control over the area.

This litigation does not involve property rights arising out of federal statute or by reason of any treaty to which the United States is a party. The Inupiat claims rest on immemorial use and occupancy alone. To support their allegations they have filed in this court numerous documents including affidavits, government records and scholarly works attempting to document their traditional use of the sea ice as living space.

All defendants have answered the Inupiat claims and have moved for judgment on the pleadings reserving for later issues of limitation, standing and capacity. At this time I address only the motion for judgment on the pleadings which shall be considered as a motion for summary judgment since additional documents have been filed and considered. Fed.R.Civ.P. 12(c).

In support of their motions the defendants argue, among other things, that the result of this case is controlled by a line of Supreme Court cases beginning with *United States v. California*, 332 U.S. 19, 67 S. Ct. 1658, 91 L.Ed. 1889 (1947) in which the Court first recognized the paramount rights of the United States in ocean waters lying seaward of the ordinary low water mark. In opposition, the Inupiat undertake to distinguish these authorities by arguing that the previous cases deal only with the competing rights of the federal government and the states and have little to do with the rights of American natives such as themselves. I disagree. To accept the interpretation now urged by the

Inupiat would be to ignore the underlying principle upon which the Supreme Court has placed reliance, that federal supremacy over the adjacent seas is an essential element of national sovereignty. I therefore conclude that claims of sovereign power over the oceans whether made by one of the several states in the Union or by the Inupiat or by any other native tribe is inconsistent with national sovereignty and must fail. *United States v. Maine*, 420 U.S. 515, 95 S. Ct. 1155, 43 L.Ed.2d 363 (1975); *United States v. Texas*, 339 U.S. 707, 70 S. Ct. 918, 94 L.Ed. 1221 (1950); *United States v. Louisiana*, 339 U.S. 699, 70 S. Ct. 914, 94 L.Ed. 1216 (1950); *United States v. California*, 332 U.S. 19, 67 S. Ct. 1658, 91 L.Ed. 1889 (1947).

The controlling issue of whether the state or the federal government had the right to lease mineral resources of the ocean seabed was addressed by the Supreme Court for the first time in *United States v. California*, 332 U.S. 19, 67 S. Ct. 1658, 91 L.Ed. 1889. In reaching its decision the Court reasoned that "protection and control of (the three mile belt) has been and is a function of national external sovereignty." *Id.* at 34, 67 S. Ct. at 1666. This was necessarily so, the Court concluded, since [A]s peace and world commerce are the paramount responsibilities of the nation, rather than an individual state, so, if wars come, they must be fought by the nation. The state is not equipped in our constitutional system with the powers or facilities for exercising the responsibilities which would be concomitant with the dominion which it seeks. … [N]ational interests, responsibilities and therefore national rights are paramount in waters lying to the seaward in the three-mile belt. 332 U.S. at 35–36, 67 S. Ct. at 1666–1667. If a state is not equipped with the powers and facilities necessary to undertake the responsibilities concomitant with dominion over the seas, certainly the Inupiat are less so.

In *United States v. Louisiana*, 339 U.S. at 699, 70 S. Ct. at 914, 94 L.Ed. 1216, the Supreme Court extended the holding of California beyond the three-mile limit and applied it to the outer continental shelf. Once again, the Court reiterated that the marginal sea is a national, not a state concern. National interests, national responsibilities, national concerns are involved. The problems of commerce, national defense, relations with other powers, war and peace focus there. National rights must therefore be paramount in that area. 339 U.S. at 704, 70 S. Ct. at 916. In extending federal control as far as 27 miles off-shore, the Court said:

> If, as we held in California's case, the three-mile belt is in the domain of the Nation rather than that of the separate States, it follows a fortiori that the ocean beyond that limit also is. The ocean seaward of the marginal belt is perhaps even more directly related to the national defense, the conduct of foreign affairs, and world commerce than is the marginal sea. Certainly, it is not less so. 339 U.S. at 705, 70 S. Ct. at 917.

In the companion case of *United States v. Texas*, 339 U.S. at 707, 70 S. Ct. at 918, 94 L.Ed. 1221, the Court rejected state claims of sovereignty and ownership over the seabed extending some ten miles offshore and dating from the period when Texas was an independent republic. In doing so, the Court said:

> [O]nce low-water mark is passed the international domain is reached. Property rights must then be so subordinated to political rights as in substance to coalesce and unite in the national sovereign. Today the controversy is over oil. Tomorrow it may be over some other substance or mineral or perhaps the bed of the ocean itself. If the property, whatever it may be, lies seaward of low-water mark, its use, disposition, management, and control involve national interests and national responsibilities. That is the source of national rights in it. 339 U.S. at 719, 70 S. Ct. at 924.

The Court has recently reaffirmed these principles in the face of a strong challenge from the 13 eastern seaboard states. *United States v. Maine*, 420 U.S. 515, 95 S. Ct. 1155, 43 L.Ed.2d 363 (1975). These states base their claim to the entire continental shelf on a demonstration of interest and sovereignty dating from earliest colonial times. While they argued that their claims were not foreclosed by the previous line of cases beginning with California, they also argued that that line of cases was incorrect and should be overruled. The Court firmly rejected both contentions and described the California line of cases as having held that, as a matter of "purely legal principle ... the Constitution ... allocated to the federal government jurisdiction over foreign commerce, foreign affairs and national defense" and that "it necessarily follows, as a matter of constitutional law, that as attributes of these external sovereign powers the federal government has paramount rights in the marginal sea." *United States v. Maine*, 420 U.S. at 522–23, 95 S. Ct. at 1159–60.

If, as a matter of constitutional law, the federal government must be possessed of paramount rights in offshore waters, it makes no difference whether the competing domestic claimant is a state or a tribe of American natives. All are subordinate to the federal government, and neither can, under the Constitution, claim rights which are at odds with those which are of necessity entrusted to the one external sovereign recognized by the Constitution. *United States v. Wheeler*, 435 U.S. 313, 323, 326, 98 S. Ct. 1079, 1086, 1087, 55 L.Ed.2d 303 (1978). (Indian tribes are "dependent ... within our territorial jurisdiction" and have no "freedom to determine external relations.")

Moreover, the federal government has consistently exercised exclusive jurisdiction and control over the adjacent waters and the seabed on the continental shelf. In the exercise of this jurisdiction, Congress has on occasion enacted statutory provisions permitting certain rights of subsistence for natives. See e.g., Fishery Conservation and Management Act of 1976, 16 U.S.C. ss 1801–1882 (Indian treaty fishing rights given special recognition). Marine Mammal Protection Act, 16 U.S.C. s 1371(b) (Explicit exemption for native subsistence whaling). The necessary implication is that Congress intended to permit use by Alaska natives of subsistence rights only to the extent authorized. Hence, federal recognition of any sovereign power or property right arising out of subsistence activities would be both inconsistent and illogical. Other federal legislation also reflects the complete and exclusive power of the federal government in the adjacent waters and in the seabed on the continental shelf. See e.g., Outer

Continental Shelf Lands Act, 43 U.S.C. ss 1331–43 (1953); Submerged Lands Act, 43 U.S.C. ss 1301–15 (1953).

I conclude as well that the Inupiat people could not have acquired rights to the sea surface, water column and bed in the disputed area prior to 1867 when the United States purchased the area from Russia for, as the Supreme Court noted in *United States v. California*, as late as 1876 the concept of territorial sovereignty over adjacent seas remained doubtful under international law. 332 U.S. at 31–33, 67 S. Ct. at 1664–65. Nor could the Inupiat have acquired those rights after 1867 because once a tribe of American natives is brought within the jurisdiction of the federal government, it loses all elements of external sovereignty including the capacity to acquire sovereignty over or ownership of unclaimed lands. *Montana v. United States*, 450 U.S. 544, 101 S. Ct. 1245, 67 L.Ed.2d 493, rehearing denied, 452 U.S. 911, 101 S. Ct. 3042, 69 L.Ed.2d 414 (1981); *United States v. Wheeler*, 435 U.S. 313, 323, 326, 98 S. Ct. 1079, 1086, 1087, 55 L.Ed.2d 303 (1978); *Cherokee Nation v. Georgia*, 30 U.S. (5 Pet.) 1, 17, 8 L.Ed. 25 (1832); *Johnson v. McIntosh*, 21 U.S. (8 Wheat) 543, 572–73, 5 L.Ed. 681 (1923).

Much of the Inupiat's claim to the Beaufort and Chukchi Seas off-shore areas is based on notions of tribal sovereignty. The Inupiat constantly reiterate that they have never been conquered, have never voluntarily submitted to the jurisdiction of the United States, and have at every opportunity resisted federal and state regulation of their hunting, fishing, whaling, and sealing rights. In effect, the Inupiat claim that they have all the rights of self-determination and sovereignty of an independent nation. These assertions sweep far too broadly.

Tribes of American natives, especially those living on reservations, do possess some powers of self-determination and sovereignty over their territory. *White Mountain Apache Tribe v. Bracker*, 448 U.S. 136, 142, 100 S. Ct. 2578, 2583, 65 L.Ed.2d 665 (1980). These powers are especially strong when they relate to the internal sovereignty of the tribe and its rights to self-government and management of the affairs of its members. *McClanahan v. Arizona State Tax Commission*, 411 U.S. 164, 173, 93 S. Ct. 1257, 1262, 36 L.Ed.2d 129 (1973); *United States v. Kagama*, 118 U.S. 375, 381–82, 6 S. Ct. 1109, 1112–13, 30 L.Ed. 228 (1886). The external sovereignty of the tribes, however, is sharply limited by their dependent status. *Oliphant v. Suquamish Indian Tribe*, 435 U.S. 191, 208–09, 98 S. Ct. 1011, 1020–21, 55 L.Ed.2d 209 (1978). In areas where the security of the United States as a nation and its dealings with foreign countries are a major concern, the intrinsic authority of the tribes is revoked by implication. *Id.* at 209–10, 98 S. Ct. at 1021–22. The Supreme Court has repeatedly noted the dominant interests of the national sovereign in the outer continental shelf. *United States v. Maine*, 420 U.S. 515, 521, 95 S. Ct. 1155, 1158, 43 L.Ed.2d 363 (1975); *United States v. Texas*, 339 U.S. 707, 719, 70 S. Ct. 918, 924, 94 L.Ed. 1221 (1950). Any exercise of external sovereignty by the Inupiat in the area of the outer continental shelf would be inconsistent with their status as members of the United States and hostile to the interests of the nation as a whole.

The Inupiat also plead their title and sovereignty claims in terms which assert the violation of a trust relationship which they contend exists between themselves and the federal government. Complaint P 35. This claim also fails. Unless Indian money or property is involved, a trust relationship can only arise from a legislative enactment, a treaty, or executive order. *North Slope Borough v. Andrus*, 642 F.2d 589, 612 (D.C.Cir.1980); *Navajo Tribe of Indians v. United States*, 624 F.2d 981, 988 (Ct.Cl.1980). ("[I]f no tribal money or property is involved and the question is, for instance, whether the United States has a general fiduciary obligation to educate Indians, then existence of the special relationship for that purpose depends upon the proper interpretation of the terms of some document (e.g. statute, treaty, executive order).") *No Oilport! v. Carter*, 520 F. Supp. 334, 373 (W.D.Wash.1981). ("A generalized trust responsibility does not exist in the abstract, but rather only arises from a statute, treaty, or executive order.") *Cape Fox Corporation v. United States*, 456 F. Supp. 784 (D. Alaska 1978). No such language has been brought to the attention of this court. Since I have found that the Inupiat have no property rights in the area claimed and no treaty, statute or executive order has been offered to support the claim of a trust relationship, I conclude that the Inupiat's claim of trust relationship is without foundation.

Moreover, I find that this claim is collaterally estopped by the court's finding in *North Slope Borough v. Andrus*, 642 F.2d at 611–12, because the claim that the plaintiffs make here is essentially identical to the one asserted there, and the plaintiffs, while not the same, are so closely aligned as to be "virtual representatives" of each other. *United States v. Rayonier, Inc.*, 627 F.2d 996, 1003 (9th Cir. 1980) (and cases cited therein.)

Finally, I conclude that the Inupiat's religious claim is also without foundation. It meets neither of the two elements of the test set by *Wisconsin v. Yoder*, 406 U.S. 205, 92 S. Ct. 1526, 32 L.Ed.2d 15 (1972). First, the action of the federal government in initially leasing in the Beaufort and Chukchi Seas beyond the three mile limit does not create a serious obstacle to the exercise of the plaintiff's religion. While the Inupiat allege that the government's actions threaten to deny them access to sacred sites, those they identify are located on land, well outside the area at issue in this suit. They offer no explanation of the religious significance of even those sites, see *Sequoyah v. TVA*, 620 F.2d 1159, 1163 (6th Cir.), cert. denied, 449 U.S. 953, 101 S. Ct. 357, 66 L.Ed.2d 216 (1980), and they offer no explanation of how the defendants' activities may interfere with their free exercise of religion. See *Badoni v. Higginson*, 638 F.2d 172, 180 (10th Cir. 1980), cert. denied, 452 U.S. 954, 101 S. Ct. 3099, 69 L.Ed.2d 965 (1981). They also allege possible disruption of appeasement ceremonies, again without definition.

In essence, the Inupiats claim that their religious beliefs are inextricably intertwined with their hunting and gathering life-style, and since all exploratory activities negatively affect some portion of their subsistence area, all such activity should be interdicted on free-exercise grounds. Carried to its ultimate, their contention would result in the creation of a vast religious sanctuary over the Arctic seas beyond the state's territorial waters. A claim to such a large area based on such non-specific grounds cannot provide the sort of "serious obstacle" contemplated by *Yoder*. Cf. *Sequoyah v. TVA*, 620 F.2d at 1164–65.

The Inupiats' claim also fails to meet the second requirement of *Yoder*. The government's interest in pursuing the development of the area outweighs the alleged interference with the plaintiffs' religious beliefs. The federal government has a significant economic stake in the development of energy resources within its borders. *Conservation Law Foundation, et al v. Andrus, et al*, 617 F.2d 296, 298 (1st Cir. 1980); *North Slope Borough v. Andrus*, 642 F.2d 589, 591, 593 (D.C.Cir.1980). Perhaps more importantly, the United States has treaty obligations to keep the high seas freely available for international passage and fishing. Convention on the Continental Shelf, done, Apr. 29, 1958, 15 U.S.T. 471, T.I.A.S. No. 5578, Article 3; Convention on the High Seas, *done*, Apr. 29, 1958, 13 U.S.T. 2312, T.I.A.S. No. 5200, Articles 1 & 2. Against these specific needs and obligations, I find that the generalized claims of the Inupiat are not adequate to strike the balance in their favor. Cf. *Badoni v. Higginson*, 638 F.2d at 177–79. (Impoundment behind dam flooded several Navajo gods and denied access to specific sacred prayer place. Government also gave tourists access to prayer spot with resulting desecrations. Summary dismissal of Indian claims affirmed because government's decision to build dam and fill impoundment vital to multistate water-storage and power generation project.)

Finally, I observe that the relief sought by the Inupiat creates serious Establishment Clause problems. The Supreme Court has held repeatedly that the First Amendment may not be asserted to deprive the public of its normal use of an area. E.g., *Shuttlesworth v. Birmingham*, 394 U.S. 147, 152, 89 S. Ct. 935, 939, 22 L.Ed.2d 162 (1969); *Food Employees Local 590 v. Logan Valley Plaza, Inc.*, 391 U.S. 308, 320, 88 S. Ct. 1601, 1609, 20 L.Ed.2d 603 (1968); *Cox v. Louisiana*, 379 U.S. 536, 554–55, 85 S. Ct. 453, 464–65, 13 L.Ed.2d 471 (1965), *Niemotko v. Maryland*, 340 U.S. 268, 271, 71 S. Ct. 325, 327, 95 L.Ed. 267 (1951). I deal in this suit with the high seas, an area which is public to the world under American law. Convention on the Continental Shelf, *supra*; Convention on the High Seas, *supra*. I therefore hold with other courts that a free-exercise claim cannot be pushed to the point of awarding exclusive rights to a public area. *Badoni v. Higginson*, 638 F.2d at 178–79; *Hopi Indian Tribe v. Block*, No. 81–0481, 81 I.L.R. 3073 (D.D.C. June 12, 1981) *Hopi Indian Tribe v. Block*, No. 81–0481, 81 I.L.R. 3073 (D.D.C. June 12, 1981).

For the several reasons stated above, I conclude that the defendants are entitled to judgment against all claims made by the plaintiffs.

Discussion questions

1. In what ways is this judicial opinion an exercise in rhetorical imperialism? Explain your answer.
2. In what ways does traditional legal rhetoric dictate the facts and law relevant to resolving the issues as identified? Be specific in naming the role of White cultural hegemony in shaping the analytical framework and scope of relevant facts.
3. Is the drafter's use of traditional legal rhetoric effective? If so, for what purpose?

4. Does the drafter's use of traditional legal rhetoric lead to a just result? Explain your answer.
5. Pick a section or sections of this judicial opinion to rewrite using relevant cultural rhetorical strategies. For this part of the exercise, you may need to consult additional sources to better contextualize the dispute (such as law review articles, scholarly articles from non-legal disciplines, books from legal and non-legal disciplines, additional case law, legislative histories, and so on).
6. In what way do the strategies you employ change the facts and law relevant to resolving the issues as identified in the opinion? Be specific and name the cultural tradition and the strategy.

Notes

1 Hudson, 1924.

2 Editor's note: the image referred to has been removed for copyright reasons. The image depicts the faces of 27 NFL coaches employed at the time of the complaint, with only one of the coaches pictured being a person of color.

3 Pub. L. No. 100–383, § 2(a), 102 Stat. 903, 903 (codified at 50 U.S.C. App. § 1989a(a)).

4 Pub. L. No. 100–383, § 105, 102 Stat. at 905–08 (codified at 50 U.S.C. App. § 1989b-4).

References

AALS (2023) Annual Meeting Program, [online]. Available from: https://memberaccess.aals.org/eweb/DynamicPage.aspx?WebKey=7544EA9B-2DA0-4075-9BE6-B740D7096C63&RegPath=EventRegFees&REg_evt_key=27fdc744-306c-4d3e-966e-6513558c713e&Site=AALS [Accessed March 6, 2023].

Abrahamson, S.S. (1984) "The LSAT for the 21st century," *Journal of Legal Education*, 34(3): 407–11.

Act to Protect Students from Critical Race Theory HB 1012 2022 (South Dakota), [online]. Available from: https://mylrc.sdlegislature.gov/api/Documents/Bill/226040.pdf?Year=2022 [Accessed February 1, 2023].

Act Providing for Requirements Related to Racism or Sexism Trainings At, and Diversity and Inclusion Efforts By, Governmental Agencies and Entities, School Districts, and Public Postsecondary Educational Institutions HB 802 2021 (Iowa), [online]. Available from: www.legis.iowa.gov/docs/publications/LGI/89/HF802.pdf [Accessed February 1, 2023].

Act Relating to Public Education and Declaring an Emergency HB 18 2021 (Kentucky), [online]. Available from: https://apps.legislature.ky.gov/record/22rs/hb18.html [Accessed February 1, 2023].

Act Relating to the Social Studies Curriculum in Public Schools HB 3979 2021 (Texas), [online]. Available from: https://legiscan.com/TX/text/HB3979/id/2399214 [Accessed February 1, 2023].

Adams, A. (1776) "Letter from Abigail Adams to John Adams, 31 March–5 April 1776," Massachusetts Historical Society, [online]. Available from: www.masshist.org/digitaladams/archive/doc?id=L17760331aa [Accessed November 26, 2022].

Aikin, S.F. (2008) "Three Objections to the Epistemic Theory of Argument Rebutted," *Argumentation and Advocacy*, 44(3): 130–42.

Alcoff, L. (1991) "The Problem of Speaking for Others," *Cultural Critique*, 20: 5–32.

Alkebulan, A.A. (2003) "The Spiritual Essence of African American Rhetoric," in R.L. Jackson II and E.B. Richardson (eds) *Understanding African American Rhetoric: Classical Origins to Contemporary Innovations*, Abingdon: Routledge, pp 23–42.

Alonso, C.J. (1998) *The Burden of Modernity: The Rhetoric of Cultural Discourse in Spanish America*, Oxford: Oxford University Press.

Amabebe, E.M. (2020) "Beyond 'Valid and Reliable': The LSAT, ABA Standard 503, and the Future of Law School Admissions," *New York University Law Review*, 95(6): 1860–903.

American Bar Association (2020) "Lawyers by Race and Ethnicity," American Bar Association, [online]. Available from: www.americanbar.org/groups/young_lawyers/projects/men-of-color/lawyer-demographics/ [Accessed May 4, 2022].

American Bar Association (2021) "ABA Profile of the Legal Profession," American Bar Association, [online]. Available from: www.americanbar.org/news/reporter_resources/profile-of-profession/ [Accessed May 4, 2022].

American Bar Association (2022–23) "Program of Legal Education: Curriculum—Standard 303(c)," ABA Standards and Rules of Procedure for Approval of Law Schools 2022–2023, American Bar Association, [online]. Available from www.americanbar.org/content/dam/aba/administrative/legal_education_and_admissions_to_the_bar/standards/2022-2023/22-23-standard-ch3.pdf [Accessed November 28, 2022].

Amsterdam, A.G. and Bruner, J. (2000) *Minding the Law*, Cambridge, MA: Harvard University Press.

Anzaldúa, G. (1987) *Borderlands/La Frontera: The New Mestiza* , San Francisco: Aunt Lute Books.

Aristotle (nd) Politics, transl. B. Jowett, MIT Classics Online, [online]. Available from: http://classics.mit.edu/Aristotle/politics.html [Accessed May 4, 2022].

Aristotle (nd) Posterior Analytics, transl. G.R.G. Mure, MIT Classics Online, [online]. Available from: http://classics.mit.edu/Aristotle/posterior.1.i.html [Accessed March 1, 2023].

Armstrong, S.V. and Terrell, T.P. (2009) *Thinking Like a Writer: A Lawyer's Guide to Effective Writing and Editing* (3rd edn.), New York: Practising Law Institute.

Arroyo, V. (2018) "Yuji Ichioka and Early Moments in the Asian American Movement," 1968 in American Memory: A Course Site for AMST 101: Myth and History in American Memory, [online] April 20. Available from: https://perma.cc/4U77-FVSL [Accessed November 26, 2022].

Asante, G.A. (2019) "#RhetoricSoWhite and US Centered: Reflections on challenges and Opportunities," *Quarterly Journal of Speech*, 105(4): 484–8.

Asante, M.K. (1998) *The Afrocentric Idea*, Philadelphia, PA: Temple University Press.

Asante, M.K. (2003) *Afrocentricity: The Theory of Social Change*, Gilbert, AZ: African American Images.

Auerbach, J.S. (1976) *Unequal Justice: Lawyers and Social Change in Modern America*, Oxford: Oxford University Press.

Baca, D. (2008) *Mestiz@ Scripts, Digital Migrations, and the Territories of Writing*, London: Palgrave Macmillan.

Baca, D. and Villanueva, V. (eds) (2010) *Rhetorics of the Americas: 3114* BCE *to 2012* CE, New York: Palgrave Macmillan.

Baldwin, J. (1963 [1993]) *The Fire Next Time* (Kindle edn.), New York: Vintage International.

Balkin, J.M. (2011) *Constitutional Redemption: Political Faith in an Unjust World*, Cambridge, MA: Harvard University Press.

Bell, D. (1993) *Faces at the Bottom of the Well: The Permanence of Racism*, New York: Basic Books.

Bell, D. (1994) "Racism: A Prophecy for the Year 2000," *Rutgers University Law Review*, 42(1): 93–108.

Berenguer, E., Jewel, L., and McMurtry-Chubb, T. (2020a) "Antebellum Law is the Precedent for Today's White-on-Black Violence," Race and the Law Prof Blog, [online] June 13. Available from: https://lawprofessors.typepad.com/racelawprof/2020/06/antebellum-law-is-the-precedent-for-todays-white-on-black-violence-by-professors-elizabeth-berenguer.html [Accessed June 25, 2022].

Berenguer, E., Jewel, L., and McMurtry-Chubb, T. (2020b) "Gut Renovations: Critical and Comparative Rhetoric to Remodel How the Law Addresses Privilege and Power," *Harvard Latinx Law Review*, 23(1): 205–32.

Bethune, J. (1831) "A map of that part of Georgia occupied by the Cherokee Indians, taken from an actual survey made during the present year 1831, in pursuance of an act of the general assembly of the state: this interesting tract of country contains four millions three hundred & sixty six thousand five hundred & fifty four acres, many rich gold mines & many delightful situations & though in some parts mountainous, some of the richest land belonging to the state," Library of Congress, [online]. Available from: www.loc.gov/item/2004633028/ [Accessed July 3, 2022].

Betts v. Brady, 316 U.S. 455 (1942).

Bill for an Act Prohibiting the Teaching of Critical Race Theory in Public Schools HB 1508 2021 (North Dakota), [online]. Available from: https://sos.nd.gov/files/uploaded_documents/1508.pdf [Accessed February 1, 2023].

Bill to Amend the Laws of South Carolina to Prohibit Instruction in Critical Race Theory and Related Instruction HB 4325 2021 (South Carolina), [online]. Available from: www.scstatehouse.gov/sess124_2021-2022/bills/4325.htm [Accessed February 1, 2023].

Bourdieu, P. (1987) "The Force of Law: Toward a Sociology of the Juridical Field," *Hasting Law Journal*, 38(5): 814–53.

Bowker, G.C. and Star, S.L. (2000) *Sorting Things Out: Classification and Its Consequences*, Cambridge, MA: MIT Press.

Boyer v. Garrett, 88 F. Supp. 353 (D. Md. 1949), aff'd, 183 F.2d 582 (4th Cir. 1950)

Brown v. Board of Education of Topeka, Shawnee County, Kan., 347 U.S. 483 (1954).

Bruce, W.C. (1922) *John Randolph of Roanoke 1773–1833*, New York: Putnam.

Buck v. Bell, 274 U.S. 200 (1927).

Burke v. Kleiman, 277 Ill. App. 519 (Ill. App. Ct. 1934).

California Land Act 1851 (California), [online]. Available from: https://digitalcommons.csumb.edu/hornbeck_usa_2_d/7/ [Accessed February 1, 2023].

Carden v. Bland, 199 Tenn. 665 (1956).

Chanbonpin, K.D. (2015), 'Between Black and White: The Coloring of Asian Americans," *Washington University Global Studies Law Review*, 14(4): 637–64.

Chang, E. (2021) "Barring Entry to the Legal Profession: How the Law Condones Willful Blindness to the Bar Exam's Racially Disparate Impacts," *Minnesota Law Review*, 106(2): 1019–70.

Chemerinsky, E. (2012) "The Court and the Fourth Amendment," *National Law Journal*, 34(36): 50.

Chen, G. (2011) "Moving Beyond the Dichotomy of Communication Studies: Boundary Wisdom as the Key," in G. Chen (ed) *De-Westernizing Communication Research: Altering Questions and Changing Frameworks*, Abingdon: Routledge, pp 157–71.

Chen, L. (2005) "Persuasion in Chinese Culture: A Glimpse of the Ancient Practice in Contrast to the West," *Intercultural Communication Studies*, 14(1): 28–40.

Cherokee Nation v. Georgia, 30 U.S. 1 (1831).

Cisneros, J.D. (2014) *The Border Crossed Us: Rhetorics of Borders, Citizenship, and Latina/o Identity*, Tuscaloosa, AL: University of Alabama Press.

Citizens for Renewing America (2021) *Combatting Critical Race Theory in Your Community: An A to Z Guide on How to Stop Critical Race Theory and Reclaim Your Local School Board*, Washington, DC: CRA.

Clark, R.H., Cobb, T.R.R., and Irwin, D. (1861) "1860 Code, Historical Georgia Digests and Codes," University of Georgia Digital Commons, [online]. Available from: https://digitalcommons.law.uga.edu/ga_code/18 [Accessed May 4, 2022].

Cobb, T.R.R. (1858) *An Inquiry into the Law of Negro Slavery in the United States of America to Which Is Prefixed, an Historical Sketch of Slavery*, Philadelphia, PA: T. & J.W. Johnson.

Cole, D. (2011) "Writing Removal and Resistance: Native American Rhetoric in the Composition Classroom," *Composition & Communication*, 63(1): 122–44.

Condit, C.M. and Lucaites, J.L. (1993) *Crafting Equality: America's Anglo-African Word*, Chicago: University of Chicago Press.

Couture, B. and Wojahn, P. (eds) (2016) *Drawing Boundaries: The Rhetoric of Lines Across America*, Logan: Utah State University Press.

Cover, R.M. (1983) "The Supreme Court, 1982 Term, Foreword: *Nomos* and Narrative," *Harvard Law Review*, 97(1): 4–68.

Curcio, A.A. (2002) "Better Bar: Why and How the Existing Bar Exam Should Change," *Nebraska Law Review*, 81(1): 363–423.

Dawkins, R. (2016) *The God Delusion*, London: Black Swan.

DeChaine, D.R. (ed) (2012) *Border Rhetorics: Citizenship and Identity on the US–Mexico* Frontier, Tuscaloosa, AL: University Alabama Press.

Delgado, R. (1995) *The Rodrigo Chronicles: Conversations About America and Race*, New York: NYU Press.

Delgado, R. and Stefancic, J. (2007) "Why Do We Ask The Same Questions? The Triple Helix Dilemma Revisited," *Law Library Journal*, 99(2): 307–28.

Derrida, J. and Moore, F.C.T. (1974) "White Mythology: Metaphor in the Text of Philosophy," *New Literary History*, 6(1): 5–74.

DeRuy, E. (2016) "Judge's Football Team Loses, Juvenile Sentences Go Up," The Atlantic, [online] September 7. Available from: www.theatlantic.com/-education-/archive/2016/09/judges-issue-longer-sentences-when-their-college-football-team-loses/498980/ [Accessed June 26, 2022].

Diamond, A. (2020) "The 1924 Law That Slammed the Door on Immigrants and the Politicians Who Pushed It Back Open," Smithsonian Magazine, [online] May 19. Available from: www.smithsonianmag.com/history/1924-law-slammed-door-immigrants-and-politicians-who-pushed-it-back-open-180974910/ [Accessed June 28, 2022].

Dignity and Nondiscrimination in Public Education Act HB 377 2021 (Idaho), [online]. Available from: https://legislature.idaho.gov/wp-content/uploads/sessioninfo/2021/legislation/H0377.pdf [Accessed February 1, 2023].

Divisive Concepts Act HB 312 2022 (Alabama), [online]. Available from: https://legiscan.com/AL/text/HB312/id/2551327 [Accessed February 1, 2023].

Divisive Concepts Act HB 544 2021 (New Hampshire), [online]. Available from: www.gencourt.state.nh.us/legislation/2021/HB0544.html [Accessed February 1, 2023].

Divisive Concepts Act HB 580 2021 (Tennessee), [online]. Available from: https://publications.tnsosfiles.com/acts/112/pub/pc0818.pdf [Accessed February 1, 2023].

Divisive Concepts Act HB 888 2022 (Georgia), [online]. Available from: www.legis.ga.gov/legislation/61099 [Accessed February 1, 2023].

Divisive Concepts Act HB 1775 2021 (Oklahoma), [online]. Available from: https://legiscan.com/OK/bill/HB1775/2022 [Accessed February 1, 2023].

Dobbs v. Jackson Women's Health Org., 142 S. Ct. 2228 (2022).

Douglas, D.M. (2021) "St. George Tucker (1752–1827)," Encyclopedia of Virginia, [online] December 22. Available from: https://encyclopediavirginia.org/entries/tucker-st-george-1752-1827/ [Accessed May 4, 2022].

Dred Scott v. Sandford, 60 U.S. 393 (1856).

Du Bois, W.E.B. (1903 [1987]) *The Souls of Black Folk*, New York: Library of America.

Eggert, G.G. (1985) "The Impact of the Fugitive Slave Law on Harrisburg: A Case Study," *Pennsylvania Magazine of History and Biography*, 109(4): 537–69.

Enríquez-Loya, A. and Leon, K. (2017) "Chicanx/Latinx Rhetorics as Methodology for Writing Program Design at HSIs," *Composition Studies*, 45(2): 212–15.

Eren, O. and Mocan, N. (2018) "Emotional Judges and Unlucky Juveniles," *American Economic Journal: Applied Economics*, 10(3): 171–205.

Farber, D.A. and Sherry, S. (1997) *Beyond All Reason: The Radical Assault on Truth in American Law*, Oxford: Oxford University Press.

Fehrman, D.M. (2022) "ABA's New Anti-Bias Curriculum Rule Is Insufficient," Law 360 [online], March 11. Available from: www.law360.com/articles/1471033/aba-s-new-anti-bias-curriculum-rule-is-insufficient [Accessed November 27, 2022].

Finkelman, P. (1999) "Thomas R.R. Cobb and the Law of Negro Slavery," *Roger Williams Law Review*, 5(1): 75–115.

Fischer, D.H. (1989) *Albion's Seed: Four British Folkways in America*, Oxford: Oxford University Press.

Forbes v. Warren, 184 Miss. 526 So. 325 (1939).

Fowler, L. (2015) "Arapaho and Cheyenne Perspectives: From the 1851 Treaty to the Sand Creek Massacre," *American Indian Quarterly*, 39(4): 364–90.

Fugitive Slave Act 1850 (U.S. Congress), [online]. Available from: www.loc.gov/resource/rbpe.33700200/?st=text [Accessed February 2, 2023].

Ga. 1867 Penal Code § 4627 (2011) Internet Archive, [online] November 11. Available from: https://archive.org/details/codeofstateofgeo1867clar/-page/912/mode/2up [Accessed June 26, 2022].

Ga. Code Ann. § 17-4-60 (2018) *repealed by* HB 0479 (2021).

Gallup (2023) "LGBT Identification in U.S. Ticks Up to 7.1%," Gallup, [online]. Available from: https://news.gallup.com/poll/389792/lgbt-identification-ticks-up.aspx [Accessed March 14, 2023].

Garcia, C. (2017) "In Defense of Latinx," *Composition Studies*, 45(2): 210–11.

Gardner, J.A. (2007) *Legal Argument: The Structure and Language of Effective Advocacy* (2nd edn.), Durham, NC: Carolina Academic Press.

Gehrke, P.J. (1998) "Teaching Argumentation Existentially: Argumentation Pedagogy and Theories of Rhetoric as Epistemic," *Argument and Advocacy*, 35(2): 76–86.

Gideon v. Wainwright, 372 U.S. 335 (1963).

Gleason, B.P. (2009) "The Mounted Band and Field Musicians of the U.S. 7th Cavalry During the Time of the Plains Indian Wars," *Historic Brass Society Journal*, 21: 69–91.

Glesner Fines, B. (1997) "Competition and the Curve," *UMKC Law Review*, 65(4): 879–916.

Gordon, D.B. (2006) *Black Identity: Rhetoric, Ideology, and Nineteenth-Century Black Nationalism*, Carbondale, IL: Southern Illinois University Press.

Greenwald, A.G. and Krieger, L.H. (2006) "Implicit Bias: Scientific Foundations," *California Law Review*, 94(4): 945–67.

Gresson, A.D. (1995) *The Recovery of Race in America*, Minneapolis: University of Minnesota Press.

Guinier, L., Fine, M., and Balin, J. (1997) *Becoming Gentlemen: Women, Law School, and Institutional Change*, Boston, MA: Beacon Press.

Hall, E.T. (1977) *Beyond Culture*, New York: Anchor Books.

Hansberry v. Lee, 311 U.S. 32 (1940).

Heimann, B. (1964) *Facets of Indian Thought*, Crows Nest, NSW: Allen & Unwin.

Hine, D.C. (1992) "The Black Studies Movement: Afrocentric-Traditionalist-Feminist Paradigms for the Next Stage," *The Black Scholar*, 22(3): 11–18.

hooks, b. (2004) *We Real Cool: Black Men and Masculinity*, Abingdon: Routledge.

Horton, J.O. and Horton, L.E. (1993) "A Federal Assault: African Americans and the Impact of the Fugitive Slave Law of 1850," *Chicago Kent Law Review*, 68(3): 1179–97.

Horwitz, M.J. (1992) *The Transformation of American Law 1870–1960 The Crisis of Legal Orthodoxy*, Oxford: Oxford University Press.

Hudgins v. Wright, 11 Va. 134 (1806).

Hudson, G.M. (1924) Testimony of Congressman Grant M. Hudson, 65 Congr. Rec. 5641, April 5, [online]. Available from: www.govinfo.gov/content/pkg/GPO-CRECB-1924-pt6-v65/pdf/GPO-CRECB-1924-pt6-v65-5.pdf [Accessed February 5, 2023].

Illinois v. Caballes, 543 U.S. 405 (2005).

Indian Civilization Fund Act 1819 (U.S. Congress).

Indian Removal Act 1830 (U.S. Congress), [online]. Available from: https://memory.loc.gov/cgi-bin/ampage?collId=llsl&fileName=004/llsl004.db&recNum=458 [Accessed February 2, 2023].

Innis, L.B. (2010) "A Critical Legal Rhetoric Approach to In Re African-American Slave Descendants Litigation," *Saint John's Journal of Legal Commentary*, 24(4): 649–96.

Isaac, B. (2004) *The Invention of Racism in Classical Antiquity*, Princeton, NJ: Princeton University Press.

Jack Miller Center (n.d.) "The Fourteenth Amendment: History, Ratification, and Reaction," Jack Miller Center for Teaching America's Founding Principles and History, [online]. Available from: https://jackmillercenter.org/fourteenth-amendment/ [Accessed November 26, 2022].

Jackson, R.L., II (2003) "Afrocentricity as Metatheory: A Dialogic Exploration of its Principles," in R.L. Jackson II and E.B. Richardson (eds) *Understanding African American Rhetoric: Classical Origins to Contemporary Innovations*, Abingdon: Routledge, pp 115–32.

Jackson, R.L. II and Richardson, E.B. (eds) (2003) *Understanding African American Rhetoric: Classical Origins to Contemporary Innovations*, New York: Routledge.

Jacobellis v. State of Ohio, 378 U.S. 184 (1964).

Jamison v. McClendon, No. Order Granting Qualified Immunity, 3:16-CV-595-CWR-LRA, 2020 WL 4497723 (S.D. Miss. Aug. 4, 2020).

Jewel, L. (2013) "Tales of a Fourth Tier Nothing: A Response to Brian Tamanaha's *Failing Law Schools*," *Journal of the Legal Profession*, 38(1): 125–59.

Jewel, L. (2016) "Old-School Rhetoric and New-School Cognitive Science: The Enduring Power of Logocentric Categories," *Legal Communication & Rhetoric: Journal of the Association of Legal Writing Directors*, 13: 39–77.

Jewel, L. (2017) "Neurorhetoric, Race, and the Law: Toxic Neural Pathways and Healing Alternatives," *Maryland Law Review*, 76(3): 663–95.

Jewel, L. (2018) "The Biology of Inequality," *Denver Law Review*, 95(3): 609–70.

Jewel, L. (2019) "Does the Reasonable Man Have Obsessive Compulsive Disorder?" *Wake Forest Law Review*, 54(4): 1049–88.

Jewel, L. (2022) "Comparative Legal Rhetoric," *Kentucky Law Journal*, 110(1): 107–72.

Jodoin, J. (2019) "Pro-Slavery and the Classics in Antebellum America, 1840–60: Thomas Cobb, Louisa McCord, George Frederick Holmes, George Fitzhugh, and James Henry Hammond Under Scrutiny," PhD thesis, Edinburgh Research Archive, [online] March. Available from: https://era.ed.ac.uk/bitstream/handle/1842/35731/Jodoin2019.pdf [Accessed May 4, 2022].

Johnson v. M'Intosh, 21 U.S. 543 (1823).

Johnson, S.L. (1984) "Cross-Racial Identification Errors in Criminal Cases," *Cornell Law Review*, 69(5): 934–87.

Jolls, C., Sunstein, C., and Thaler, R. (1988) "A Behavioral Approach to Law and Economics," *Stanford Law Review*, 50(5): 1471–550.

Kachru, Y. (1997) "Cultural Meaning and Contrastive Rhetoric in English Education," *World Englishes*, 16(3): 337–50.

Kahneman, D. (2013) *Thinking, Fast and Slow*, New York: Farrar, Straus and Giroux.

Kahneman, D., Slovic, P., and Tversky, A. (eds) (1982) *Judgment Under Uncertainty: Heuristics and Biases*, Cambridge: Cambridge University Press.

Kalonji, T. (2014) "The Nguzo Saba and Maat, a Path for Self-Reconstruction and Recoveredness: Exploring a Kawaida Paradigm for Healing Addiction in the Black Community," *Journal of Pan African Studies*, 7(4): 195–210.

Kang, J. and Lane, K. (2010) "Seeing Through Colorblindness: Implicit Bias and the Law," *UCLA Law Review*, 58(2): 465–520.

Karenga, M. (2003) "Nommo, Kawaida, and Communicative Practice: Bringing Good into the World," in R.L. Jackson II and E.B. Richardson (eds) *Understanding African American Rhetoric: Classical Origins to Contemporary Innovations*, Abingdon: Routledge, pp 3–22.

Keene, S. (2015) "Victim or Thug? Examining the Relevance of Stories in Cases Involving Shootings of Unarmed Black Males," *Howard Law Journal*, 58(3): 845–56.

Keene, S. (2017) "Stories that Swim Upstream: Uncovering the Influence of Stereotypes and Stock Stories in Fourth Amendment Reasonable Suspicion Analysis," *Maryland Law Review*, 76(3): 747–69.

Kendi, I.X. (2017) *Stamped from the Beginning: The Definitive History of Racist Ideas in America* (Kindle edn.), New York: Nation Books.

Kennedy, D. (2004) *Legal Education and the Reproduction of Hierarchy: A Polemic Against the System*, New York: NYU Press.

Kennedy, M.L. (ed) (1998) *Theorizing Composition: A Critical Sourcebook of Theory and Scholarship in Contemporary Composition Studies*, Westport, CT: Greenwood.

Kim, E.H. (1990) "A Critique of Strangers from a Different Shore," *Amerasia*, 16(2): 101–11.

King, L., Gubele, R. and Anderson, J.R. (eds) (2015) *Survivance, Sovereignty, and Story: Teaching American Indian Rhetorics*, Boulder: University Press of Colorado.

Kirk, R. (1957 [2002]) *The American Cause*, Wilmington, DE: Intercollegiate Studies Institute.

Kirkpatrick, A. and Xu, Z. (2012) *Chinese Rhetoric and Writing: An Introduction for Language Teachers*, Fort Collins, CO: WAC Clearinghouse.

Klein, C.A. (1996) "Treaties of Conquest: Property Rights, Indian Treaties, and the Treaty of Guadalupe Hidalgo," *New Mexico Law Review*, 26(2): 201–55.

Korematsu v. United States, 323 U.S. 214 (1944).

Kubota, R. (1997) "A Reevaluation of the Uniqueness of Japanese Written Discourse: Implications for Contrastive Rhetoric," *Written Communication*, 14(4): 460–80.

Lakoff, G. and Johnson, M (1999) *Philosophy in the Flesh: The Embodied Mind and its Challenge to Western Thought*, New York: Basic Books.

Leonetti, C. (2021) "The Innocence Checklist," *American Criminal Law Review*, 58(1): 97–153.

Lloyd, H. (2016) "Cognitive Emotion and the Law," *Law & Psychology Review*, 41: 53–106.

Loftus, E.F. and Pickrell, J.E. (1995) "The Formation of False Memories," *Psychiatric Annals*, 25(12): 720–5.

Loving v. Virginia, 388 U.S. 1 (1967).

Lu, M. and Horner, B. (2008) "Foreword," in L. Mao and M. Young (eds) *Representations: Doing Asian American Rhetoric*, Logan, UT: Utah State University Press, pp vii–xiii.

Lucaites J.L. and Condit, C.M. (2003) *Crafting Equality*, Chicago: University of Chicago Press.

Lucaites J.L., Condit, C.M., and Caudill, S. (eds) (1999) *Contemporary Rhetorical Theory: A Reader*, New York: Guilford Press.

Lyons, S.R. (2000) "Rhetorical Sovereignty: What Do American Indians Want from Writing?," *College Composition & Communication*, 51(3): 447–68.

Manhattan Institute (2021) "Woke Schooling: A Toolkit for Concerned Parents," issue brief, [online] June 17. Available from: www.manhattan-institute.org/woke-schooling-toolkit-for-concerned-parents [Accessed February 2, 2023].

Mann, B.A. (2016) *Spirits of Blood, Spirits of Breath: The Twinned Cosmos of Indigenous America*, Oxford: Oxford University Press.

Mao, L. (2006) *Reading Chinese Fortune Cookie: The Making of Chinese American Rhetoric*, Logan, UT: Utah State University Press.

Mao, L. (2014) "Beyond Bias, Binary, and Border: Mapping out the Future of Comparative Rhetoric," in L. Mao (ed) *Comparative Rhetoric: The Art of Traversing Rhetorical Times, Places, and Spaces*, Abingdon: Routledge, pp 1–17.

Mao, L. and Young, M. (eds) (2008) *Representations: Doing Asian American Rhetoric*, Logan, UT: Utah State University Press.

Mao, L., Wang, B., Lyon, A., Jarratt, S.C., Swearingen, C.J., Romano, S., Simonson, P., Mailloux, S., and Lu, X. (2015) "Manifesting a Future for Comparative Rhetoric," *Rhetoric Review*, 34(3): 239–74.

McBoyle v. U.S., 283 U.S. 25 (1931).

McCabe v. Atchison, T. & S.F. Ry. Co., 186 F. 966 (8th Cir. 1911), aff'd sub nom. *McCabe v. Atchison, T. & S.F.R. Co.*, 235 U.S. 151 (1914)

McGee, M.C. (1980) "The 'Ideograph': A Link Between Rhetoric and Ideology," *Quarterly Journal of Speech*, 66(1): 1–16.

McMurtry-Chubb, T.A. (2017) "On Writing Wrongs: Legal Writing Professors of Color and the Curious Case of 405(c)," *Journal of Legal Education*, 66(3): 575–84.

McMurtry-Chubb, T.A. (2018) "The Rhetoric of Race, Redemption, and Will Contests: Inheritance as Reparations in John Grisham's *Sycamore Row*," *University of Memphis Law Review*, 48(3): 889–958.

McMurtry-Chubb, T.A. (2019) "Still Writing at the Master's Table: Decolonizing Rhetoric in Legal Writing for a 'Woke' Legal Academy," *The Scholar: Saint Mary's Law Review on Race and Social Justice*, 21(2): 255–92.

McNeil, G.R. (1983) *Groundwork: Charles Hamilton Houston and the Struggle for Civil Rights*, Philadelphia: University of Pennsylvania Press.

McPhail, M.L. (1993) *The Rhetoric of Racism*, Lanham, MD: University Press of America.

McPhail, M.L. (2002) *The Rhetoric of Racism Revisited: Reparations or Separation?*, Lanham, MD: Rowman & Littlefield.

Megale, E. (2013) "Gideon's Legacy: Taking Pedagogical Inspiration from the Briefs that Made History," *Barry Law Review*, 18(2): 227–72.

Megale, E. (2014) "A Call for Change: A Contextual-Configurative Analysis of Florida's 'Stand Your Ground' Laws," *University of Miami Law Review*, 68(4): 1051–98.

Mertz, E. (2007) *The Language of Law School: Learning to "Think Like A Lawyer,"* Oxford: Oxford University Press.

Michael H. v. Gerald D., 491 U.S. 110 (1989).

Mignolo, W.D. (2005) *The Idea of Latin America*, Malden, MA: Blackwell.

Mills, C.W. (1999) *The Racial Contract*, Ithaca, NY: Cornell University Press.

Miranda v. Arizona, 384 U.S. 436 (1966).

Monroe, J. (1818) State of the Nation Address, [online] November 16. Available from: www.presidentialrhetoric.com/historicspeeches/monroe/stateoftheunion.1818.html [Accessed February 5, 2023].

Muller, C.A. (2015) "Wŏnhyo's Approach to Harmonization of the Mahayana Doctrines (*Hwajaeng*)," *Acta Koreana*, 18(1): 9–44.

Mutua, A.D. (1999) "Shifting Bottoms and Rotating Centers: Reflections on LatCrit III and the Black/White Paradigm," *University of Miami Law Review*, 53(4): 1177–218.

Mutua, A.D. (2006) "The Rise, Development and Future Directions of Critical Race Theory and Related Scholarship," *Denver University Law Review*, 84(2): 329–94.

Mutua, A.D. (2010) "Valuing Difference, Exercising Care in Oz: The Shaggy Man's Welcome," *Southern California Interdisciplinary Law Journal*, 20(1): 215–48.

Na'puti, T.R. (2019) "Speaking of Indigeneity: Navigating Genealogies Against Erasure and #RhetoricSoWhite," *Quarterly Journal of Speech*, 105(4): 495–501.

National Association of Law Placement (2023), "Report on Diversity in U.S. Law Firms," National Association of Law Placement, [online]. Available from: www.nalp.org/uploads/Research/2022NALPReportonDiversity_Final.pdf [Accessed March 1, 2023).

Nationality Act 1790 (U.S. Congress).

Ngũgĩ wa Thiong'o (1986) *Decolonizing the Mind: The Politics of Language in African Literature*, Nairobi: East African Educational Publishers.
O'Regan, D. (2017) "Eying the Body: The Impact of Classical Rules for Demeanor, Credibility, Bias, and the Need to Blind Legal Decision Makers," *Pace Law Review*, 37(2): 379–454.
Oliver, R.T. (1959) "The Confucian Rhetorical Tradition in Korea During the Yi Dynasty (1392–1910)," *Quarterly Journal of Speech*, 45(4): 363–73.
Oyez (nda) "Ruth Bader Ginsburg," Oyez, [online]. Available from: www.oyez.org/justices/ruth_bader_ginsburg [Accessed November 26, 2022].
Oyez (ndb) "Thurgood Marshall," Oyez, [online]. Available from: www.oyez.org/justices/thurgood_marshall [Accessed November 27, 2022].
Pernell v. Florida Board of Governors of the State University System, No. Order Granting in Part and Denying in Part Motions for Preliminary Injunction, 4:22cv304-MW/MAF (N.D. Fla. November 17, 2022).
Pew Research Center (2021) "Faith on the Hill: The Religious Composition of the 117th Congress," Pew Research Center, [online] January 4. Available from: www.pewresearch.org/religion/2021/01/04/faith-on-the-hill-2021/ [Accessed November 26, 2022].
Pearce, R.H. (1988) *Savagism and Civilization: A Study of the Indian and the American Mind*, Berkeley: University of California Press.
Pham, V.N. (2019) "The Threat of #RhetoricNotSoWhite," *Quarterly Journal of Speech*, 105(4): 489–94.
Plato (n.d.) Republic, transl. B. Jowett, MIT Classics Online, [online]. Available from: http://classics.mit.edu/Plato/republic.html [Accessed May 4, 2022].
Plessy v. Ferguson, 163 U.S. 537 (1896).
Popper, K (2002) *The Open Society and Its Enemies*, Abingdon: Routledge.
Powell, M. (2002) "Rhetorics of Survivance: How American Indians *Use* Writing," *College Composition and Communication*, 53(3): 396–434.
PREP (PragerU Resources for Educators and Parents) (2022) *Parent Action Guide*, Sherman Oak, CA: PragerU, [online]. Available from: https://assets.ctfassets.net/qnesrjodfi80/18WDTi8qlqc5FZMBMchXQy/d63107b3afeb4c3015c397d4b6f5d40d/PREP_2022ParentActionGuide_FINAL__1_.pdf [Accessed February 5, 2023].
President's Advisory 1776 Commission (2021) *The 1776 Report*, [online], January. Available from: https://trumpwhitehouse.archives.gov/wp-content/uploads/2021/01/The-Presidents-Advisory-1776-Commission-Final-Report.pdf [Accessed February 5, 2023].
Prohibited Funding for Divisive Concepts Act SB 2113 2022 (Mississippi).
Prohibition on Critical Race Theory and Antiracism Atty. Gen. Op. 1 2021 (Montana).
Prohibition on Teaching Declared Unlawful and Discriminatory HB 787 2022 (Virginia).

Project Implicit (n.d.) [online]. Available from: https://implicit.harvard.edu/implicit/ [Accessed May 4, 2022].

Quintanilla, V.D., Erman, S.C., and Frisby, M.B. (2020) "Safeguard or Barrier: An Empirical Examination of Bar Exam Cut Scores," *Journal of Legal Education*, 70(1): 125–61.

Racial Integrity Act 19245 (Virginia).

Reed, D.A. (1924) "America of the Melting Pot Comes to End; Effects of New Immigration Legislation Described by Senate Sponsor of Bill—Chief Aim, He States, Is to Preserve Racial Type as It Exists Here Today," New York Times, [online] April 27. Available from: www.nytimes.com/1924/04/27/archives/america-of-the-melting-pot-comes-to-end-effects-of-new-immigration.html [Accessed June 28, 2022].

Reynolds, D. (2019) "Meet the 10 Gay, Lesbian, and Bisexual Members of the 116th Congress," Advocate, [online], January 3. Available from: www.advocate.com/politicians/2019/1/03/meet-10-gay-lesbian-and-bisexual-members-116th-congress#media-gallery-media-1 [Accessed November 26, 2022].

Richardson, L. (2017) "Implicit Racial Bias and Racial Anxiety: Implications for Stops and Frisks," *Ohio State Journal of Criminal Law*, 15(1): 73–88.

Robbins, R.A., Johansen, S., and Chestek, K (2012) *Your Client's Story: Persuasive Legal Writing* (2nd edn.), Frederick, MD: Aspen Publishing.

Robbins-Tiscione, K.K. (2009) *Rhetoric for Legal Writers: The Theory and Practice of Analysis and Persuasion*, St. Paul, MN: West Academic Publishing.

Roe v. Wade, 410 U.S. 113 (1973).

Roithmayr, D. (2014) *Reproducing Racism: How Everyday Choices Lock in White Advantage*, New York: NYU Press.

Rose, T. (1994) *Black Noise: Rap Music and Black Culture in Contemporary America*, Middletown, CT: Wesleyan University Press.

Ross, T. (1996) *Just Stories: How the Law Embodies Racism and Bias*, Boston, MA: Beacon Press.

Ruiz, I.D. (2016) *Reclaiming Composition for Chicano/as and Other Ethnic Minorities: A Critical History and Pedagogy*, New York: Palgrave Macmillan.

Ruiz, I.D. and Sánchez, R. (eds) (2016) *Decolonizing Rhetoric and Composition Studies: New Latinx Keywords for Theory and Pedagogy*, New York: Palgrave Macmillan.

Said, E.W. (1979) *Orientalism*, New York: Vintage.

Samson, A. (ed) (2017) *The Behavioral Economics Guide*, [online] August 21. Available from: www.behavioraleconomics.com/be-guide/the-behavioral-economics-guide-2017/ [Accessed July 5, 2022].

Scalia A. and Garner B.A. (2008) *Making Your Case: The Art of Persuading Judges*, St. Paul, MN: West Group.

Schlag, P. and Skover, D. (1986) *Tactics of Legal Reasoning*, Durham, NC: Carolina Academic Press.

Schulten, S. (2018) *A History of America in 100 Maps*, Chicago: University of Chicago Press.

Scott, A.J. (2020) "Human Rights Hero: The African American Social Engineer," American Bar Association, [online] January 6. Available from: www.americanbar.org/groups/crsj/publications/human_rights_magazine_home/black-to-the-future-part-ii/human-rights-hero--the-african-american-social-engineer/ [Accessed May 5, 2022].

Scott, R.L (1999) "On Viewing Rhetoric as Epistemic," in J.L. Lucaites, C.M. Condit, and S. Caudill (eds) *Contemporary Rhetorical Theory: A Reader*, New York: Guilford, pp 131–9.

Senate Resolution on Critical Race Theory in Public Education S.R. 901 2021 (Utah).

Shepherd, G.B. (2003) "No African-American Lawyers Allowed: The Inefficient Racism of the ABA's Accreditation of Law Schools," *Journal of Legal Education*, 53(1): 103–56.

Silverstein, J. and Hannah-Jones, N. (July 14, 2019) '1619 Project' *New York Times Magazine*, [online]. Available from: www.nytimes.com/interactive/2019/08/14/magazine/1619-america-slavery.html?action=click&contentCollection=Magazine&region=TopBar&module=HomePage-Title&pgtype=Multimedia [Accessed March 14, 2023].

Simpson, A. (2014) *Mohawk Interruptus: Political Life Across the Borders of Settler States*, Durham, NC: Duke University Press.

Smith, M.R. (2002) *Advanced Legal Writing: Theories and Strategies in Persuasive Writing*, New York: Aspen Publishers.

Sowards, S.K. (2019) "#RhetoricSoEnglishOnly: Decolonizing Rhetorical Studies Through Multilingualism," *Quarterly Journal of Speech*, 105(4): 477–83.

Spivak, G.C. (1988) "Can the Subaltern Speak?" in C. Nelson and L Grossberg (eds) *Marxism and Interpretation of Culture*, Urbana: University of Illinois Press, pp 271–314.

Stanchi, K.M. (1998) "Resistance Is Futile: How Legal Writing Pedagogy Contributes to the Law's Marginalization of Outsider Voices," *Dickinson Law Review*, 103(1): 7–57.

Stanchi, K.M., Berger, L., and Crawford, B. (eds) (2016) *Feminist Judgments: Rewritten Opinions of the United States Supreme Court*, Cambridge: Cambridge University Press.

State v. Sum, 17 Wash. App. 2d 1009, review granted, 198 Wash. 2d 1025 P.3d 395 (2021), and rev'd, *State v. Sum*, 199 Wash. 2d 627 (2022).

State v. Sum, 199 Wash. 2d 627 (2022).

State v. Sum, No. 53924-1-II 2021 WL 1382608 (Wash. Ct. App. Apr. 13, 2021).

Statista (2021) "Total Population in the United States by Gender from 2010 to 2027," Statista, [online] September 10. Available from: https://www.statista.com/statistics/737923/us-population-by-gender/ [Accessed May 4, 2022].

Stevens, A. (2020) "Savannah Judge Appointed to Preside over Arbery Cases," Atlanta Journal-Constitution, [online] May 18. Available from: www.ajc.com/news/crime--law/savannah-judge-appointed-preside-over-arbery-cases/HeUxam4vDTNSnkNz25Lh5O/ [Accessed November 26, 2022].

Stevens, A. (2022) "What We Know About Criminal Charges in the Ahmaud Arbery Shooting," Atlanta Journal-Constitution, [online] February 22. Available from: www.ajc.com/news/crime--law/what-know-far-about-the-ahmaud-arbery-shooting/LXyZ46dMFBansWIm3CfzxM/ [Accessed November 26, 2022].

Stevens, R. (1983) *Law School: Legal Education in America from the 1850s to the 1980s*, Chapel Hill: University of North Carolina Press.

Stop W.O.K.E. Act HB 7 2022 (Florida).

Stout, C. and Wilburn, T. (nd) "CRT Map: Efforts to restrict teaching racism and bias have multiplied across the U.S.," Chalkbeat, [online]. Available from: www.chalkbeat.org/22525983/map-critical-race-theory-legislation-teaching-racism [Accessed March 8, 2023].

Sullivan, W.M., Colby, A., Wegner, J.W., Bond, L., and Shulman, L.S. (2007) *Educating Lawyers: Preparation for the Profession of Law*, Stanford, CA: Carnegie Foundation for the Advancement of Teaching's Report.

Sung-Gi, J. (2010) "Towards a Rhetoric of Communication, with Special Reference to the History of Korean Rhetoric," *Rhetorica: A Journal of the History of Rhetoric*, 28(3): 313–29.

Swain, S. (2009) "Supreme Court Chief Justice Roberts," C-SPAN, Interview, [online] June 19. Available from: www.c-span.org/video/?286078-1/-supreme-court-chief-justice-roberts [Accessed June 26, 2022].

Takaki, R. (1989) *Strangers from a Different Shore: A History of Asian Americans*, New York: Little, Brown.

Takaki, R. (2008) *A Different Mirror: A History of Multicultural America*, New York: Little, Brown.

Terrell, T.P. (2012) "The Art of Legal Reasoning and the Angst of Judging: Of Balls, Strikes, and Moments of Truth," *Northwestern Journal of Law & Social Policy*, 8(1): 35–88.

Terry v. Ohio, 392 U.S. 1 (1968).

Thaler, R. and Sunstein, C. (2009) *Nudge: Improving Decisions About Health, Wealth and Happiness*, New York: Penguin.

Thornton, R. (1984) "Cherokee Population Losses During the Trail of Tears: A New Perspective and a New Estimate," *Ethnohistory*, 31(4): 289–300.

Tirkkonen-Condit, S. (1985) *Argumentative Text Structure and Translation*, Jyväskylä: University of Jyväskylä.

Tomasi, M. (2004) "Studies of Western Rhetoric in Modern Japan: The Years Between Shimamura Hōgestsu's *Shin bijigaku* (1902) and the End of the Taishō Era," *Japan Review*, 16: 161–90.

Trouillot, M.R. (2003) *Global Transformations: Anthropology and the Modern World*, Basingstoke: Palgrave Macmillan.

Trump v. Hawaii, 138 S. Ct. 2392 (2018).

Tushnet, M. (1981) *The American Law of Slavery 1810–1860: Considerations of Humanity and Interest*, Princeton, NJ: Princeton University Press.

Tyler v. Harmon, 158 La. 439 (1925).

Ulali (2005) *All My Relations*, from *A Thousand Roads*, original soundtrack by Lisa Gerard to the film *Smoke Signals*, dir. C. Eyre, [online]. Available from: www.youtube.com/watch?v=EjThZUI3URc&ab_channel=JeremyLanssiers [Accessed February 5, 2023].

Unger, R.M. (1974) *Knowledge and Politics*, New York: Free Press.

United States Courts (nd) "About Federal Courts," United States Courts, [online]. Available from: www.uscourts.gov/about-federal-courts [Accessed July 5, 2022].

United States v. Johnson, 123 Fed. Appx. 240 (2005) Oral Argument, [online]. Available from: https://youtu.be/c8ksvG_X4Z4 [Accessed March 14, 2023].

United States Senate (nda) "African American Senators," United States Senate, [online]. Available from: www.senate.gov/pagelayout/history/h_multi_sections_and_teasers/Photo_Exhibit_African_American_Senators.htm [Accessed November 26, 2022]

United States Senate (ndb) "American Indian Senators," United States Senate, [online]. Available from: www.senate.gov/senators/american-indian-senators.htm [Accessed November 26, 2022]

United States Senate (ndc) "Women Senators," United States Senate, [online]. Available from: www.senate.gov/artandhistory/history/common/briefing/women_senators.htm [Accessed November 26, 2022].

University at Buffalo School of Law (n.d.) 'ABA Standard 303: Curriculum (c)," University of Buffalo School of Law, [online]. Available from: www.law.buffalo.edu/beyond/aba303c.html [Accessed February 5, 2023].

Utah v. Strieff, 579 U.S. 232, 252-4 (2016).

van Dijk, T.A. (1987) *Communicating Racism: Ethnic Prejudice in Thought and Talk*, Newbury Park, CA: Sage.

Villanueva, V. (2016) "Metonymic Borders and Our Sense of Nation," in B. Couture and P. Wojahn (eds) *Drawing Boundaries: The Rhetoric of Lines Across America*, Logan, UT: Utah State University Press, pp 29–42.

Wallace, M. (1978) *Black Macho and the Myth of the Superwoman*, New York: Dial Press.

Wang B. (2014) "Comparative Rhetoric, Postcolonial Studies, and Transnational Feminisms: A Geopolitical Approach," in L. Mao (ed) *Comparative Rhetoric: The Art of Traversing Rhetorical Times, Places, and Spaces*, Abingdon: Routledge, pp 18–34.

Wang, G. (2011) "Orientalism, Occidentalism and Communication Research," in G. Wang (ed) *De-Westernizing Communication Research: Altering Questions and Changing Frameworks*, Abingdon: Routledge, pp 58–76.

Wanzer-Serrano, D. (2019) "Rhetoric's Rac(e/ist) Problems," *Quarterly Journal of Speech*, 105(4): 465–76.

Washington v. San Kim Sum, 2022 WL 2071560 (Wash. June 9, 2022).

Weatherspoon, F. (2010) "The Status of African American Males in the Legal Profession: A Pipeline of Institutional Roadblocks and Barriers," *Mississippi Law Journal*, 80(1): 259–98.

Westen, D. (2007) *The Political Brain: The Role of Emotion in Deciding the Fate of the Nation*, New York: Public Affairs.

White, J.B. (2011) "An Old-Fashioned View of the Nature of Law," *Theoretical Inquiries in Law*, 12(1): 381–402.

Wikipedia (n.d.) "Race and Ethnicity in the United States," Wikipedia, [online]. Available from: https://en.wikipedia.org/wiki/Race_and_ethnicity_in_the_United_States [Accessed May 4, 2022].

Wiley, K. (2020), 'Special Prosecutor Appointed in Ahmaud Arbery Murder Case: Cobb County Prosecutor Appointed After Family Demands Change, Attorney Says," Associated Press, [online] May 11. Available from: www.news4jax.com/news/georgia/2020/05/11/ahmaud-arbery-family-attorney-special-prosecutor-to-take-over-case/ [Accessed November 26, 2022].

Williams, H.D. (1989) "Gambling Away the Inheritance: The Cherokee Nation and Georgia's Gold and Land Lotteries of 1832–33," *Georgia Historical Quarterly*, 73(3): 519–39.

Williams, P.J. (1991) *The Alchemy of Race and Rights*, Cambridge, MA: Harvard University Press.

Woodson, K. (2021) "Entrenched Racial Hierarchy: Educational Inequality from the Cradle to the LSAT," *Mitchell Hamline Law Review*, 47(4): 224–57.

Worcester v. Georgia, 31 U.S. 515 (1832).

Index

References to figures appear in *italic* type; those in **bold** type refer to tables.